11/12/09

Wanda,

Welcome to the
Bluffton Board!

Jms Juder

DANCING
WITH THE
KOBZAR

Studies in
Anabaptist and Mennonite History
No. 38

D1524451

To Kerry, Jackson, and Cassidy Bush
and
to the memory of Jack Caldwell

Studies in
Anabaptist and Mennonite
History

Edited by Cornelius J. Dyck, Leonard Gross, Beulah Stauffer Hostetler, Albert N. Keim, Walter Klaassen, John S. Oyer, Steve Reschly, and Editor-in-Chief Theron F. Schlabach.

Volumes 1-35 published by Herald Press, Scottdale, Pennsylvania, and Waterloo, Ontario, in cooperation with Mennonite Historical Society. Volumes 36 and 37 published by Pandora Press, Kitchener, Ontario, and Volume 38 by Pandora Press U.S., Telford, Pennsylvania, with both volumes copublished by Herald Press, in cooperation with Mennonite Historical Society. The Society is primarily responsible for the content of the studies, Herald Press and/or Pandora Press Canada, Pandora Press U.S., or other publishers for their publication.

1. Two Centuries of American Mennonite Literature, 1727-1928*
   By Harold S. Bender
2. The Hutterian Brethren, 1528-1931
   By John Horsch, 1931
3. Centennial History of the Mennonites in Illinois*
   By Harry F. Weber, 1931
4. For Conscience' Sake*
   By Sanford Calvin Yoder, 1940
5. Ohio Mennonite Sunday Schools*
   By John Umble, 1941
6. Conrad Grebel, Founder of the Swiss Brethren*
   By Harold S. Bender, 1950
7. Mennonite Piety Through the Centuries*
   By Robert Friedmann, 1949
8. Bernese Anabaptists and Their American Descendants*
   By Delbert L. Gratz, 1953
9. Anabaptism in Flanders, 1530-1650*
   By A. L. E. Verheyden, 1961
10. The Mennonites in Indiana and Michigan*
    By J. C. Wenger, 1961
11. Anabaptist Baptism: A Representative Study*
    By Rollin Stely Armour, 1966
12. Lost Fatherland: The Story of Mennonite Emigration from Soviet Russia, 1921-1927
    By John B. Toews, 1967
13. Mennonites of the Ohio and Eastern Conference*
    By Grant M. Stoltzfus, 1969
14. The Mennonite Church in India, 1897-1962
    By John A. Lapp, 1972
15. The Theology of Anabaptism: An Interpretation*
    By Robert Friedmann, 1973

16. Anabaptism and Asceticism*
   By Kenneth R. Davis, 1974
17. South Central Frontiers*
   By Paul Erb, 1974
18. The Great Trek of the Russian Mennonites to Central Asia, 1880-1884*
   By Fred R.Belk, 1976
19. Mysticism and the Early South German-Austrian Anabaptist Movement, 1525-1531*
   By Werner O. Packull, 1976
20. Conscience in Crisis: Mennonites and Other Peace Churches in America, 1739-1789
   By Richard K. MacMaster with Samuel L. Horst and Rubert F. Ulle, 1979
21. Gospel Versus Gospel: Mission and the Mennonite Church, 1863-1944*
   By Theron F. Schlabach, 1979
22. Strangers Become Neighbors: Mennonites and Indigenous Relations in the Paraguayan
   Chaco; *available from Pandora Press Canada*
   By Calvin Redekop, 1980
23. The Golden Years of the Hutterites, 1565-1578
   By Leonard Gross, 1980; rev. ed. Pandora Press Canada, 1998
24. Mennonites in Illinois*
   By Willard H. Smith, 1983
25. Petr Chelcicky: A Radical Separatist in Hussite Bohemia
   By Murray L. Wagner, 1983
26. Maintaining the Right Fellowship: A Narrative Account of Life in the Oldest Mennonite
   Community in North America*
   By John L. Ruth, 1984
27. The Life and Thought of Michael Sattler
   By C. Arnold Snyder, 1984
28. American Mennonites and Protestant Movements: A Community Paradigm
   By Beulah Stauffer Hostetler, 1987
29. Andreas Fischer and the Sabbatarian Anabaptists: An Early Reformation Episode in
   East Central Europe
   By Daniel Liechty, 1988
30. Apart and Together: Mennonites in Oregon and Neighboring States, 1876-1976
   By Hope Kauffman Lind, 1990
31. Tradition and Transition: Amish Mennonites and Old Order Amish, 1800-1900
   By Paton Yoder, 1991
32. John Smyth's Congregation: English Separatism, Mennonite Influence, and the Elect
   Nation
   By James Robert Coggins, 1991
33. The Lord's Supper in Anabaptism: A Study in the Theology of Balthasar Hubmaier,
   Pilgram Marpeck, and Dirk Philips
   By John D. Rempel, 1993
34. American Mennonites and the Great War, 1914-1918
   By Gerlof D. Homan, 1994
35. Keeping Salvation Ethical: Mennonite and Amish Atonement Theology in the Late
   Nineteenth Century
   By J. Denny Weaver, 1997
36. Andreas Ehrenpreis and Hutterite Faith and Practice
   By Wes Harrison, 1997
37. Mennonite and Nazi? Attitudes among Mennonite Colonists in Latin America, 1933-1945
   By John D. Thiesen
38. Dancing with the Kobzar: Bluffton College and Mennonite Higher Education, 1899-1999
   By Perry Bush
   *A quick-print edition of the books marked with an asterisk is available by
   arrangement with Herald Press from Wipf and Stock Publishers in Eugene,
   Oregon; tel.: 541-485-5745; fax: 541-465-9694; email: WSPub@academicbooks.com.*

DANCING
WITH THE
KOBZAR

**Bluffton College
and Mennonite Higher Education,
1899-1999**

Perry Bush

Foreword by Lee Snyder

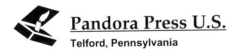 <u>Pandora Press U.S.</u>
Telford, Pennsylvania

co-published with
Herald Press
Scottdale, Pennsylvania

and
Faith & Life Press
Newton, Kansas

Pandora Press U.S. orders, information, reprint permissions:
pandoraus@netreach.net
1-215-723-9125
126 Klingerman Road, Telford PA 18969
www.PandoraPressUS.com

Copublished with Herald Press, Scottdale, PA and Waterloo, ON;
and with Faith & Life Press, North Newton, KS
Printed in the United States by Mennonite Press
Library of Congress Catalog Number: 99-086312
ISBN: 0-9665021-3-2 (pbk.); 0-9665021-8-3 (hard)
Book design by Pandora Press U.S.
and Denise Siemens
Cover design by
Denise Siemens and Jim Friesen, Mennonite Press

Library of Congress Cataloguing-in-Publication Data
Bush, Perry.
    Dancing with the Kobzar : Bluffton College and Mennonite higher
education, 1899-1999 / Perry Bush ; foreword by Lee Snyder.
    p. cm. -- (Studies in Anabaptist and Mennonite history ; no. 38)
    Includes bibliographical references and index.
    ISBN 0-9665021-3-2 (pbk. : alk. paper) -- ISBN 0-9665021-8-3 (hard : alk.
paper)
    1. Bluffton College (Bluffton, Ohio)--History. 2. Mennonites--
Education (Higher)--United States. I. Title. II. Series.

LD456.B62 B87 2000
378.771'42--dc21

99-086312

10 09 08 07 06 05 04 03 02 01 00   10 9 8 7 6 5 4 3 2 1

Contents

Foreword by Lee Snyder 09
Series Editor's Preface 11
Preface and Acknowledgements 13
Introduction: Anabaptism, Progressivism, and Little Riley Creek 17

1 Central Mennonite College and the
  Trials of Noah Hirschy, 1900-1908 • 25

2 "United Progressive Mennonites," 1909-1929 • 59

3 "One Can Hardly Imagine Bluffton College without
  Some Unrest," 1930-1938 • 97

4 Prexy Ramseyer's College, 1939-1959 • 124

5 Freedom and Order, 1960-1972 • 160

6 Bluffton College Photo Essay • 193

7 "The Mood Is Sober . . .
  But Still There Is Hope," 1973-1989 • 215

8 The Dance of the Kobzar, 1990-1999 • 246

List of Abbreviations 262
Notes 263
Select Bibliography 306
The Index 309
The Author 320

Foreword

History is still about stories. It is about people and events and ideas that have shaped the past. It is about forces both discernible and obscure that influence the present and guide the future. The twenty-five-year anniversary edition of Bluffton College's first history assessed "early experiments in Mennonite education." This new history, commemorating BC's centennial, extends that earlier effort. Seventy-five years later we continue to consider and appreciate the Bluffton College experiment. The hundred-year anniversary also provides an occasion to celebrate persons who have shaped a distinct vision of a Bluffton College able to enrich the broader stream of Mennonite higher education.

A part of BC's singular story is reflected in the selection of Perry Bush as author of this centennial history. I first met Dr. Bush— "Perry," as his colleagues and many of his students know him—at a 1994 Goshen College conference on "Anabaptist Vision(s) in the Twentieth Century: Ideas and Outcomes." The conference was designed to highlight and critique formative forces, institutions, ideas, and persons that shaped Mennonites during the Harold S. Bender era. Perry delivered a paper on "Mennonite Visions and the New Evangelicals." A young scholar, Perry was launching a college teaching career—as a Californian who had come just shortly before to BC from outside the Anabaptist mainstream. Perry's passion for his subject, flair for storytelling, and commitment to rigorous scholarship and thoughtful historical analysis were evident.

A subsequent encounter with Perry was equally memorable. I had just arrived in 1996 as new president at Bluffton College, a possibility I had not remotely imagined when first meeting Perry. Part of my orientation was to attend the traditional college talent night, organized annually to welcome new students. Perr was emcee. He forever endeared himself to those apprehensive freshmen by his enthusiastic welcome, self-effacing humor, and unselfconscious demonstration of the "Beaver yell." He exhibited in that raucous setting many of the qualities that make him ideally suited to write the Bluffton story. These include keen appreciation for BC history and traditions, curiosity about what makes BC the institution it is, love of students and of his discipline. Then there is that delightful ability to laugh and put things into perspective—even to the extent of turning uninitiated students into Beaver yellers.

The completion of a small college's first century is an auspicious occasion for reflection. Considering the past provides perhaps the most reliable glimpse we have into the future. Even as a relative newcomer to Bluffton College, I knew the choice of writer for the BC history would be critical and difficult. There was a story here that needed to be told. With an emerging reputation for impeccable scholarship, a vivid and accessible style, and an outsider's distance combined with deep commitment to Anabaptist faith, Perry seemed ideally suited to piece together the narrative and to examine the patterns in the unfolding drama.

At this juncture in BC's life and its relationship with the church, it was important to select a historian who could tell the story critically, honestly—and with appreciation for the lives and commitments which make BC history instructive. Professor Bush's brisk prose style along with careful documentation of sources offers a timely achievement that will shape our understanding of the promise and possibility of a small Mennonite school in northwest Ohio.

And it will answer the question, How did Bluffton College come to be the thriving college it is in the Mennonite church yet remain unlike all other Mennonite colleges? How did this college come to be "more than Mennonite," as President Elmer Neufeld put it when he observed, "Bluffton should not be seen as somehow less than Mennonite for its diversity, but rather more than Mennonite, with a stronger Christian peace church witness growing out of this experience" (see p. 256)? That is the story Perry Bush set out to tell.

I commend this history to alumni, faculty, staff, and BC friends who love this place. I commend it also to fellow educators who know well the challenges faced by small liberal arts colleges desiring strong denominational ties. A story both sobering and inspiring, it stirs reflection while documenting one institution's first century as an experiment in Mennonite higher education.

—*Lee Snyder, President*
  Bluffton College

Series Editor's Preface

The editors of Studies in Anabaptist and Mennonite History welcome the opportunity to help Bluffton College celebrate its centennial with Perry Bush's well-researched, sprightly story. Few features of twentieth-century American Mennonite history are more puzzling or profound than the growth, character, and influence of church-related institutions. In this, Mennonites fit a broader modern pattern, for a vast increase in the number and the complexity and the power of institutions is a major part of modern history.

Since institutions are really clusters of people, Bush's book is full of human foibles. Its pages deliver arresting tales of personal stories and aspirations. They tell of the difficulties and joys certain Mennonites have found as they have tried to form and work at common ideals. Naturally, being humans with active minds and wills, those Mennonites often found themselves in conflict. Indeed conflict helps make this book the engaging tale it is. But Bluffton College could grow and function well only when its people also cooperated and acted as a community. For that, they needed common vision. Bush is especially masterful at capturing the moods and spirit of the BC community and at pointing to Blufftonites' common vision(s).

At the same time, Bush offers evidence and insights that apply more widely than to BC. His book is American Mennonite history—and American religious history. There are many points at which this is true: constant interaction of a historic peace church with American Fundamentalism and American Evangelicalism, for instance; and providing a case study in America's pattern of church-related higher education. Three themes are especially notable. They are large themes; too large, perhaps, for definitive answers in one book. But with them, Bush raises and speaks to important historical questions.

One theme is the special nature of Bluffton as a Mennonite college and more broadly a church-related one. Bluffton is and has been a Mennonite institution, but its market has been primarily other than Mennonite. That pattern is interesting, both for Bluffton's story and for examining how church institutions function. How does an institution's governing ideology interact with market forces? More broadly, do the church's hopes and its will for its institutions make much difference? Or are religious institutions about as likely as other modern institutions to depart from their stated purposes to follow other logics: those of the market, of institutional self-preservation, and of the nature of modern institutional structure itself? If the questions sound pessimistic, Bluffton's example may not.

A second theme is much reference to how Bluffton College and its people behaved in times of war. The pervasive, often insidious influences of modern nationalism is a central concern in all twentieth-century history, and how pacifists have responded and coped is a central issue in peace church histories. This book offers ample illustrations of that theme.

A third very engaging theme, a favorite for Bush, is that Bluffton College has worked from a certain "progressive" version of an "Anabaptist vision" of activist peacemaking. That motif surely raises questions. Amid all the other lights of which Bush writes—including immigrant Mennonite traditionalism, boosterism, youth culture, American campus culture, patriotism, conservative and liberal political or social pressures, American Evangelicalism, and more—how much were Blufftonites really able to see and follow that vision? And what really were the sources of the vision? How much did the vision truly arise from Anabaptist and Mennonite understandings of the faith and what else may have shaped it? Is its "Anabaptism" more than a slogan? Thoughtful people are asking such questions of other versions of Anabaptist vision, and this version raises them as well. Bush provides some evidence.

Such are some key historical issues. At times the issues emerge indirectly. More directly, Bush offers a moving tale of vigorous people with interesting aspirations. It is a tale lively with ideas, arts, faith, pranks, athletics, financial struggles, promotions, peacemaking, patriotic fevers, self-giving service. It is a tale of humans operating at their best—and sometimes less. It is full of moods, hurts, and triumphs. The editors of the Studies in Anabaptist and Mennonite History series commend this volume as one that tells a dynamic story and in so doing addresses significant historical themes.

—*Theron Schlabach, Editor-in-Chief*
  Studies in Anabaptist and Mennonite History

Preface and Acknowledgements

This book is a centennial history of Bluffton College and a product of this larger community of learning and faith. Many have aided the project in ways both explicit and less tangible. They have read and critiqued chapters, they have steered me to archival sources, they have given generously of their time in oral interviews, and they have offered off-the-cuff suggestions in informal conversations that have turned out to be quite valuable. Whether or not all those to whom I'm indebted are explicitly named below, I hope they recognize their influence in these pages.

I have written this book with two primary audiences in mind: the college's many friends and alumni, on the one hand, and scholars of Mennonite history and peoplehood, on the other. I have tried to maintain a delicate balance between addressing a community of scholars interested in key historical questions, and college friends and alumni who in addition to scholarly agenda may be interested in the story of an institution they remember and love. Although the book will serve as Bluffton's centennial history, I also intend it as a work of historical analysis in its own right. Even as I have learned much from the Bluffton academic community, this book offers a particular historical interpretation that ultimately is mine alone.

For nearly a hundred years Bluffton College (BC) has carefully guarded a motto proclaiming that "the truth makes free." Bluffton has prized tolerance, diversity, and freedom of thought. In researching and writing this book, I have benefited immeasurably from the freedom this inheritance has provided. Never did the college president, trustees, dean, or anyone connected with the college close sources, censor my words, or try overtly to shape the development of my analysis. I have taken some of the many suggestions that my friends and colleagues have offered and have rejected or modified others. Any errors of fact or interpretation remaining here are my responsibility.

Nonetheless, in the course of this project I have accrued many debts and want at least to work at settling accounts here. I must begin by thanking the many in the college administration who have been so central to the project. President Lee Snyder and Academic Dean John Kampen offered release time from my teaching responsibilities, provided funding for the vast reservoir of student research help, and kept up with the project through periodic lunch meetings. More important, they never allowed me to forget their personal warmth and support, even when the project seemed overwhelming.

In like manner, I received much help from BC's fine director of communications, Cheryl Zehr Walker, and of publicity, Lois Wetherill. Art Shelly and Steve Rodabaugh helped with computer troubles. Joanne Niswander, a college volunteer *par excellence*, took a huge load off my shoulders by assembling the superb photographs that illustrate the text.

For eighteen months of intense work on this project, I leaned heavily on BC library and archival resources. My thanks to Dr. Joanne Passet and the staff of Musselman Library, especially archivist Paul Weaver and Ann Hilty of the Mennonite Historical Library.

I owe a special debt to Howard Krehbiel, who became much more to me than a retired math professor turned part-time archivist. Howard enjoyed history and loved Bluffton College. For months on end, as I poured through boxes of papers in the office adjacent to his, he became a confidante and fellow conspirator in my research. He delighted in this project and recharged me with his infectious enthusiasm, all while struggling valiantly with cancer. I so wish he had lived long enough for me to put a copy of this book in his hands and to once again warm to his immense grin.

Several colleagues read and offered valuable comments on parts of the manuscript: Delbert Gratz, Robert Kreider, Loren Johns. Ron Lora, Von Hardesty, J. Denny Weaver, and Gerald Biesecker-Mast read all or nearly all of it. In so doing they became insightful conversation partners who deeply enriched the development of this analysis. Michael A. King of Pandora Press U.S. and Theron Schlabach of Goshen College furnished patient and invaluable editorial oversight to the text. Denise Siemens of Mennonite Press helped much with book design and printing issues.

From the beginning of research to completion of the finished manuscript, this project took about eighteen months. This compressed production schedule would have been impossible without the tireless help of a small army of student research assistants, who spent long hours at the photocopy machine, produced hundreds of pages of notes based on obscure documents, and scurried off determinedly after additional sources. I thank Lacie Buckenmeyer, Rachael Chapman, Bob Daugherty, Kallen DeOliveira, Tamara Foster, Crystal Havens, Sarah Langhals, Lesa Lewis, Kylee Pacholski, Lenore Shumate, and Marla Thompson.

Finally, I need to express something of my own heartfelt appreciation to four individuals who contributed little on a scholarly level to this project but whose assistance proved perhaps even more instrumental in its completion. This book is dedicated to Kerry, Jackson, and Cassidy Bush. They knew something of the load of their dad's book—and through all their charm and awesome energies did their level best to lift it. As always, Elysia Caldwell Bush bore the burden with me, in ways only she can fully measure or know.

Dancing with the Kobzar is also dedicated to the memory of a close and cherished friend who fought his own heroic battle with cancer during the past year. Jack Caldwell was not an alumnus nor a close neighbor of Bluffton College. He spent his adult life in the San Joaquin Valley California. He might never have heard of this place had I not, years ago, fallen in love with and married his daughter and then, much later, been fortunate enough to secure a teaching position here. But he had a special grace, an immense personal warmth and enough of a sparkling sense of humor that Coach Burcky surely would have anointed him an honorary Beaver anyway. We were always going to watch the Cal Bears in the Rose Bowl together, or hook a big bass. This book will somehow have to suffice instead of those times and many others.

—*Perry Bush*
Bluffton, Ohio
August 1999

Introduction:
Anabaptism, Progressivism, and Little Riley Creek

Little Riley Creek is a gently rippling stream that drains a small corner of Allen County in northwest Ohio. Because it lies some thirty miles north of the Ohio Continental Divide, its waters flow north, joining the Blanchard, Auglaize, and then the Maumee rivers before pouring into the flat blue sheet of Lake Erie.

The creek lies in a limestone bed, cut six feet deep through what ecologists call a soil of "shoals silt loam," alluvium from upland soils deposited and rearranged during periodic floods. A variety of trees have taken root in this soil near the water's edge, mostly bottomland hardwoods like black walnut, honey locust, red maple, box elder, and elms. Before pioneer settlers cleared the forest alongside the creek and clouded its water with agricultural runoff, it probably ran clear and steady, lucid enough perhaps to shelter trout. Today its aquatic life is mostly limited to crawfish and minnows, but the stream also feeds and waters larger mammals such as mink, muskrat, fox, and deer. At one point the creek probably also harbored fair colonies of beaver.[1]

• • •

For a hundred years now a college has risen, grown, and flourished along the banks of Little Riley Creek. This study offers an historical analysis of that college. Because of the particular nature of the institution's own journey, its history must take nearly as many twists and turns as the Riley itself. Though the institution ultimately took

17

its name not from the waterway but from the town of Bluffton that grew at the fork of the Riley, the creek and the college still came to share similarities. Like the stream, the institution has experienced its own eras of drought and flood that stunted or accelerated its growth. For a hundred years graduates have emerged from the college's own waters, having been immersed in the rich tradition of the liberal arts, then gone out to serve their community and society in remarkably useful ways.

The college history shares another similarity with Little Riley Creek. Its own way, like the stream's, was marked by periodic opportunities to swing its main current into different and beckoning channels. At least two such alternative courses were available. One has been recently detailed by scholars such as George Marsden and James Burtchaell, who have detailed what is now generally referred to as "the secularization of the academy." They document that a wide number of American colleges and universities, both public and private, began as Christian institutions with firm denominational ties, but that most no longer remain so. The examples they offer are legion, ranging from elite national universities like Harvard and Yale to African-American institutions such as Virginia Union to small denominational colleges like St. Olaf.[2]

The secularization stream flowed easily. Even church-related colleges have almost always been founded by the innovators and academics, people who received their training in secular university settings and through the process became enamored with progressive academic culture. Eager to attract students, grow in prestige and wealth, and in other ways make their institutions prosper, they were quick to shed any trappings of "sectarianism" and instead stress common moral qualities that all interested participants could sign onto. Once matters like presidential and trustee selection, faculty tenure decisions, and student recruitment followed the same line of thinking, the game was up. Many such colleges quickly achieved the success they sought, whether measured by academic reputation, endowment, enrollment, or physical plant growth. The price they paid, however, was the disintegration of the tie with their founding churches.

There was a second course available to schools like Bluffton that promised equal helpings of the above "success," but at a different price: the transformation of their own Christian characters. Instead of secularization, we might term this process "evangelicalization." It became an increasingly popular course for small Christian colleges, particularly in the years after World War II, with the appearance of a newly resurgent group of ex-fundamentalists. Calling themselves "Neo" or "New" Evangelicals and eager to shed the bigotry, intolerance, and sectarian sensibilities of their fundamentalist colleagues, they set out to engage the mainstream of American society with a message that was both positive and revivalistic.[3]

The excitement of the laity in the pews spread like a tidal wave through the placid waters of American Protestantism. The ranks of these new evangelicals exploded in numbers, and the new enthusiasts poured both their bodies and their money into a host of church activities and agencies, including colleges. Combined with the general expansion of American higher education in the postwar years, the conditions were right for the rise of a seemingly new and identifiable entity on the higher educational landscape: the evangelical college. During the last three decades, a central consortium of such schools, the Coalition for Christian Colleges and Universities, has grown from upwards of ten to ninety members.[4]

Such institutions are diverse but, argues Burtchaell, have a number of features in common. Among these are a certain evangelical style, characterized by conservative ethics, politics, and theology, a congregational polity, biblical preaching, and a suspicion of outside culture. They also share a potent and alluring evangelical student subculture that does much to account for their sustained enrollment growth. Recasting one's institution into such evangelical hues—a path arguably chosen by schools like Azusa Pacific, Dordt, and Messiah College—thus offered struggling Christian colleges a convincing formula for success. Compared with the alternative course of secularization, such a course probably satisfied denominational traditionalists in that it rendered their college demonstrably—though generically—"Christian." Yet it may have also left them scratching their heads at a college thus stripped of nearly all denominational distinctives.[5]

What makes the story of Bluffton College so interesting—and accounts for a central thesis of this book—is that, while the college flirted with both options, it never fully adopted either. Instead, like Riley Creek, it bent this way and that way, ultimately establishing its own current that could flow forward between these two poles. It was able to do so, I will argue, because of its own creative utilization of a progressive Anabaptist approach to Mennonite higher education.

Certainly, Bluffton College was pulled powerfully towards both options. Its most important early leaders—zealous academics such as Noah Hirschy, Samuel Mosiman, Noah Byers, and C. Henry

Smith—were progressives in every sense of that term in its historical context of early twentieth-century America. Captivated by mainstream culture inside and outside of academia, they were determined to construct a college that would help to drag their Mennonite people, some of them kicking and screaming, into the enlightenment of modern life. Such an agenda had by its very nature much potential for conflict with church traditionalists, who were likely to see it for the potentially dangerous course that it was.

In the end, however, what saved most of these leaders from sending the college along the fork toward secularization was their deep commitment (Hirschy possibly excepted) to their own Mennonite people and denomination. They dialogued with the traditionalists, sometimes rose to fight them, but never fully broke off relations. Because of such commitment, Bluffton never lost its basic orientation as a Mennonite college, a fact sometimes overlooked by conservatives who were quick to attack any semblance of secularization—or, to use their own parlance, "modernism."

Potentially more seductive for the college was the opportunity to move more completely in the other direction. At the moment of its founding, anyone could see that the college's basic constituency—a dozen churches with 3,000 baptized members—was inadequate to sustain an institution of higher learning. Partly because of this, Mosiman and others would labor to broaden the college's base with a great "union movement" among the Mennonite colleges. By the World War II years, however, BC's president Lloyd Ramseyer plainly acknowledged that such a movement was dead, killed by economic depression and fundamentalist opposition. The college once again stood where it had before 1913, underfunded and underenrolled, with an inadequate ethnic and denominational base to propel it into the future.[6]

The moment seemed ripe, then and later, to reorient the institution, in the manner of so many other colleges, toward the culture of American evangelicalism. In the world of Christian colleges in the postwar years, there lay both the money and the students. For a college scratching out a bare survival and in dire need of both, the evangelical option must have loomed up as mighty tempting.

What held BC leaders back from taking it was their refusal to accept the compromise that segments of the evangelical world held out as the price of admission. They refused to separate Mennonite ethical precepts from the doctrines they had in common with other evangelicals. They refused to treat peace and service as if they were add-ons, "nonessentials," extra-chrome options. Christ's theological

and ethical teachings were all of one piece, Mennonites have insisted, and a proper Christian college would be built on the firm integration of the two. Guided by such precepts, even while rejecting the
evangelical option, Bluffton's leaders arrived at a sense of mission
and purpose for the college that could propel it strongly forward
anyway.[7]

For lack of a better term, I have chosen to call this sense of mission and BC self-understanding "progressive Anabaptism." Because
the term gets much play through this analysis, it bears a brief expli-
cation here. The term is a loose one and must be allowed some flexibility. In fact, both halves of the phrase serve to encapsulate in themselves vague but markedly different phases of the college's history.

"Progressive" works better for the first half of the college's history, when its leaders were progressives in the sense that they were
both innovators in the church and also enthusiastic participants in
the national political movement of the same name. The college they
created would serve as a vehicle for the deliberate and at least par-
tial assimilation of their Mennonite people into national progressive
culture. By the midcentury decades, however, the national political
movement had about played itself out. Lloyd Ramseyer was a firm
Republican in a time and place—Ohio of the Robert Taft era—when
such commitments took on quite conservative political hues. Subsequent college leaders of the college have been more discreet in terms
of their political leanings, and, at any rate, an overtly political reading of "progressive Anabaptism" diminishes the term.

In the hands of later leaders such as Ramseyer, Robert Kreider,
and Elmer Neufeld, the proper stress is on the second part of the
phrase. The college became an explicitly Anabaptist place partly
because of commitment and partly because of pragmatic necessity.
Lloyd Ramseyer grasped the fundamental idea in 1944, suggesting
that "we enlarge our constituency by making this a center of a certain type of thinking . . . which is different." Its guiding "distinctive
things . . . must coincide with Mennonite principles, but not be confined to Mennonites."[8]

Instead, college leaders would invite all sorts of people to come
to the college for instruction both in the liberal arts and also in Mennonite precepts such as peace, service, and matters of justice—
understandings that, in true Anabaptist fashion, students would be
invited, but not forced, to accept. Once such a momentum became
fully established in the 1950s and 1960s, someone like Elmer
Neufeld could even turn the college partway in an evangelical direction in the years that followed, but do so without fundamentally

endangering its quite conscious understanding of its own Anabaptist mission.

• • •

Altogether it was quite a journey, and one with some interesting twists and turns along the way. To unravel it, one has to travel way upstream—not to the marshes on the edge of soybean fields in a corner of Allen County, but to other rich headwaters. One has to begin with the world of General Conference Mennonites in the American Midwest at the turn of the century, a people just making the transition from German-speaking Amish and Mennonite farmers to English-speaking American Christians.

The flow of Little Riley Creek could serve as an apt metaphor for the development of the college that these people founded. So would a small stone statue that, much later on, college leaders would set in a prominent place on campus. It depicts a seated and burly man, a Ukrainian folk minstrel, in fact, strumming something that looks like a lute. Such minstrels were traditionally seen as possessed with great healing and sacred power. More that that, the placement of such a statue on the Bluffton campus could symbolize the college's determination to engage the world beyond the boundaries of Mennonite peoplehood.

On a campus that long ago has shed its ethnic ambience, most students and faculty hurrying by the statue today probably miss its cultural significance. But set in the context of the figure's ethnic tradition, his own people would have called him a Kobzar.

DANCING
WITH THE
KOBZAR

CHAPTER ONE

Central Mennonite College and the Trials of Noah Hirschy, 1900-1908

At noon on Monday, November 5, 1900, Noah Hirschy mounted to the chapel podium. He gazed out at the five faculty and nineteen students of Central Mennonite College, assembled as a group for the very first time. "Today," he told them, "the pulse of a new institution begins to beat."

Five days before, the founders of the college had hosted a gala event, the momentous and long-winded dedication of the college's first and only building. A thousand people—most from the large Swiss Mennonite community nearby—had gathered to listen to a large choir and five different speeches, all of which celebrated the construction of a handsome, three-story brick structure appropriately named College Hall.[1]

Now, however, the president of the college had a different purpose. That fall afternoon they would inaugurate the functioning life of the college. It seemed fitting to Hirschy to begin with a less grandiose appraisal of where they stood and what their collective purpose was. He reminded his audience that they began their efforts with a clean slate. "We have no history back of us either to help or to hinder us," he noted; the college as yet had no traditions, no stone engravings boasting its history, no ivy on its walls. "All is new."[2]

Hirschy outlined their meager resources. "The beginning is of necessity small and apparently insignificant," he admitted. "There are only a few teachers here and a handful of students." Their one building was small, the funds back of the institution "but a trifle," and the supporting constituency of the college limited. Not one per-

son in a hundred in the larger society had heard of it. They had to realize, he said, that "this is a modest beginning on a very small scale."[3]

"And yet," he enjoined, "despise not the day of small things. . . .
It is ours at the beginning to lay foundations." This was the task of
their day, he declared, along with one thing more. The college they
began that day would not be concerned with "the acquisition of mere
knowledge." It would pursue a higher calling. Its aim would be to
produce stalwart Christian men and women of "life and character,"
who would stay true to the principles in which they were thoroughly
grounded. And so, Hirschy proclaimed, "let this school be right with
God, firm and decided against all the threatening evils of the day,
and it will be a power for good and a mighty impulse to the kingdom
of God. In matters of intellect let us be modest," he entreated his audience, "but in matters of righteousness let us be firm and right with
God, true to the high ideals represented here and to the highest conceptions of truth and virtue."[4]

In such comments, the president effectively laid out the agenda
that would dominate the first decades of the institution that would
become Bluffton College. But the road would not be easy. Behind the
college was a diminutive constituency of three thousand people,
grouped into a dozen or so different Mennonite congregations. Many
found the very idea of a college threatening and heard in Hirschy's
talk of "high ideals" dangerously suspect and "worldly" notions.

More problematic were signs of discord that soon emerged closer
to home. The next eight years would witness the deepening of this
discord into open conflict that would rage between the college and
the largest church in its constituency—a congregation that stood in
the countryside just a few miles away. Six years into the life of the
college, this conflict had so intensified that it was unclear whether
the institution would survive. Throughout the dispute, the figure of
its embattled president could be seen at the very center of the storm.

Inheritances: of Menno and of Wadsworth

The historical factors that would ultimately give birth to the college had begun to gather at the turn of the century. More specifically,
these forces were born out of the creative ferment occurring as
Mennonite churches in the Midwest became caught up in the winds
of sociocultural transformation. A conservative ethno-religious people, traditionally resistant to change, Mennonites would greet these
changes with varying degrees of receptivity. The institutions that
emerged among congregations as a result of this ferment—the new

Sunday schools, missions agencies, and schools—were born out of the energies of a new cohort of leaders, leaders who had most fully embraced the new currents from outside that were beginning to enter the Mennonite world. Their opponents saw these currents in more threatening terms. Although the conflict between these two viewpoints slowly built to a climax in the days of Hirschy's presidency and later, the roots of the conflict had been laid decades earlier.[5]

East of the Mississippi, three subgroups of the emerging General Conference Mennonite Church (GCMC) had begun to form. They would take on central roles in the birth and development of BC. In the years after the Civil War, progressive Mennonites in eastern Pennsylvania had formed an eastern wing of the church called the Eastern District Conference (EDC). Because of close proximity to Philadelphia, the EDC had an urban, cosmopolitan orientation and an openness to acculturation atypical for Mennonites. In the Gilded Age this openness meant receptivity to progressive and urban ideas. A few decades later, it would ease the acceptance of other outside forces—such as religious fundamentalism.[6]

In the 1890s, another new conference began to form in the cornfields of central Illinois, calling itself the "Central Conference of Mennonites." It consisted of Amish who had broken away from the Old Order Amish because of their refusal to accept progressive innovations, such as Sunday schools and mission endeavors. In ethnicity, culture, and practice, most members of this group remained Amish through the nineteenth century. However, in naming themselves "Amish Mennonites," they signaled their intention to participate in the larger Mennonite world and to adapt to other innovations judged appropriate. With some careful wooing, they could become a firm pillar of a new Mennonite college in northwest Ohio.[7]

At the same time, a third group emerged from a dozen or congregations scattered from Ohio in the East to Missouri and Iowa in the West. This was the Middle District Conference (MDC). Two congregational centers were especially important. One was the large GC Mennonite congregation in Berne, Indiana. By the years after the Civil War, this group of Mennonites was just a generation removed from the immigration of ancestors from the Jura Mountain region of Switzerland to the flat plains of the American Midwest.[8]

A new pastor would push a second generation of these Mennonites in more progressive directions. Chosen pastor by lot in 1868 at age twenty, Samuel F. Sprunger pursued more training at Wadsworth Institute. There he absorbed high German, refined dress, and an evangelical, emotionally charged worship style. He arrived home with a burning desire to share his newfangled but demonstrably Christian ideas, such as revivals, Sunday schools, Bible studies, and missionary and temperance societies. Though meeting some resistance in his congregation, in several decades as pastor, Sprunger reoriented the church along these lines. Before long the clannish Swiss Mennonites had begun to participate in retail and civic affairs of the town of Berne, and led the successful, eight-year campaign to banish saloons from the town. They also began to take on important leadership roles in the new General Conference church, managing a church bookstore and publishing the German-language GC newspaper *Christlicher Bundesbote.*[9]

A second Mennonite center was to play a dominant role in the GC's Middle District Conference. This center came into being around another group of related Swiss who had migrated to northwest Ohio in 1833 and settled in the open countryside east of the Great Black Swamp, along the border of Putnam and Allen counties. By the 1890s, later generations of these settlers had fully drained the land and carved out prosperous farms. Some had moved into farm-related trades such as lumbering. Others had begun to establish small business enterprises in the small town of Bluffton to the southeast.[10]

These Swiss were as industrious in building their church, which had grown into substantial proportions well before the turn of the century. In 1864 they elected respected farmer John Moser as preacher and elder. He would judiciously guide the church until his death in 1908. In the 1870s, the Swiss Mennonite congregation established Sunday schools without much wrangling, even hosting a Sunday school convention in 1885. In 1881 they sent money to the new mission efforts of the GCMC and soon after, they joined the denomination. They also systematized its internal proceedings, creating a constitution in 1893 that dropped the selection of ministers by lot.[11]

These three key Mennonite church conferences thus harbored a wide variety of ethnic and cultural understandings, but all shared one basic trait. Each was caught up in a process of social, economic, and cultural change that even the traditional walls of Mennonite rural isolation could not entirely exclude. Town life, for example, was proving increasingly attractive to Midwestern Mennonites.[12]

As such everyday social contacts increased, many Mennonites had begun to forget German. In the Eastern and Middle Districts this shift had begun to occur well before World War 1. By the turn of the century, the GCMC's leadership had appointed a regular English secretary and had begun to publish conference minutes bilingually. Individual congregations, beginning with those in the towns, had begun to navigate this difficult transition. Components of the Swiss congregation near Bluffton turned to bilingual services in 1910-1915 and switched to only English in the 1920s. The youth in particular forced the issue. In 1904, the "German correspondent" to the *Bluffton News* called for English services because "the majority of our young people understand English better than the regular German."[13]

In the 1890s, most Mennonite communities remained intact and were only beginning to face pressures toward assimilation. Even the relatively benign innovations of Sunday schools as well as mission and educational ventures were resisted by many conservative people in the pews. For GC Mennonites east of the Mississippi, the ensuing conflict was centered on the denomination's first venture in higher education, begun at Wadsworth in 1868. Its students received a thorough grounding in theology and also were taught English and some sciences, with all classes held in German. This agenda lured a growing number of students. Thirty arrived at the school's single building in 1868, and that number grew to nearly fifty a few years later.[14]

Yet the tiny college had trouble achieving other purposes the church had assigned it. It achieved little evangelistic success. And its efforts to provide a unifying effect failed miserably because, from its beginning, Wadsworth was immersed in conflict. Its two major leaders—the principal and the theology professor—immediately launched into bitter personal antagonism. This dispute soon dominated the life of the school, with each professor courting a coterie of student followers and attempting to undermine the influence of the other. District churches soon lined up on either side. Passions were so inflamed that one disgruntled combatant once made an unsuccessful arson attempt on the school building before financial uncertainties brought the school to a less violent end in 1879.[15]

The Wadsworth debacle was altogether an inauspicious beginning for higher education efforts in the General Conference Mennonite Church. The legacy of failure haunted the church for decades. Even so, Wadsworth Institute was precedent-setting in a number of ways. For one, its history included an ominous record of meager financial contributions from the churches, a lack of support certainly connected to the nasty conflict rocking the institution. By 1875, in another lesson for the future, financial matters had reached such a head that the college took the unprecedented step of admitting women to the student body.[16]

Moreover, the short life of the Wadsworth Institute provided a clear object lesson for anyone interested in the kinds of tensions that a Mennonite college could have with its conservative constituency.

Mennonites in Berne, Indiana, experienced the new zeal their pastor, S. F. Sprunger, brought with him when he returned from Wadsworth—a style and passion that disturbed many in the congregation. The large Jura Swiss congregation of Sonnenberg, in central Ohio, found the changes induced in its Wadsworth students so threatening (they returned home in finer dress, speaking the more formal High German instead of Swiss, and wearing mustaches) that the students were forbidden to attend. When the Wadsworth graduates of the congregation ignored such signals and pushed the formation of a missionary society and Sunday school, pro- and anti-Wadsworth factions formed. The church soon splintered in half, with the liberal group forming their own congregation. Higher education could clearly be an explosive issue for conservative Mennonites.[17]

Wadsworth indicated something not just of the conflict but also of the contributions denominational higher education could offer the church. In eleven years it had trained a nucleus of progressive leaders for the next several decades. Sprunger of Berne; Nathanial Grubb of the Eastern District; dominant preachers such as A. S. Shelly and Bluffton's John B. Baer; pioneer missionaries like S. S. Haury and H. R. Voth: all had been Wadsworth students. Throughout their lives they remembered what they had learned at the school and what ventures like it could mean for the church. Grubb summed it up, noting, "that institution has gone down . . . but from that time we can date the upward movement of progress in our church."[18]

Years later S. F. Sprunger visited the sole building of Wadsworth Institute, standing vacant on its ten-acre campus. Accompanied by the young assistant pastor of First Mennonite Church of Wadsworth, Sprunger stood silently in the empty building, clearly thinking of days gone by and what the school had promised the church. Finally the aging minister spoke, encapsulating his thoughts in one word: "*Schade!*" (too bad). Sprunger's sense of missed opportunity struck a sympathetic chord that day with his companion, a high-toned pastor and promising young scholar in line with Sprunger's direction for the church and determined to harness higher education toward the same ends. His name was Noah Calvin Hirschy.[19]

"Young people under his influence will be constantly elevated in noble education and character"

Much of Hirschy's life course had perfectly positioned him to nurture the seeds Sprunger and other church progressives had planted. He was born in a log house on a farm south of Berne, Indiana, two years after the end of the Civil War, tenth child of an Amish immigrant from Switzerland. From early on he hungered after education and would sometimes buck church authority to get it.[20]

The country schools Hirschy attended as a child inspired him to teach. On graduation he worked as a teacher in such schools for four years, dutifully turning his earnings over to his father until he came of age. Then he enrolled for two years at Tri-State College in Angola, Indiana, where he performed brilliantly. He took a fairly demanding smattering of general education courses—a heavy dose of mathematics, sciences, and history, plus an immersion in Latin and Greek—and performed smartly enough that its president sent him on his way in 1891 with a glowing letter of recommendation. "Mr. N. C. Hirschy is a gentleman of ability and good education," the president declared, "and we recommend him *without reserve*. He is a man and can govern and teach, and young people under his influence will be constantly elevated in noble education and character."[21]

That autumn of 1891 Hirschy made what appeared later to be a truly fateful move: he obtained a job as the principal of the schools in Berne, where he came under the telling influence of Pastor Sprunger. Soon he transferred his membership to Sprunger's church and even joined the choir. He had, moreover, been sufficiently persuaded as to the magical atmosphere of Sprunger's alma mater that after a year in Berne he moved to Wadsworth and took classes in the academy still run there by the First Mennonite Church.[22]

There he simply blossomed. In a year he had exhausted the offerings at the tiny school and had begun to study at the seminary at nearby Oberlin College. He immersed himself in classical languages and Old Testament studies, then branched out to take courses in the college leading to a B.A. degree. In the college he followed his childhood passions and took a heavy concentration in German language and literature as well as botany. Before 1900 Hirschy completed both a B.A. degree and a Bachelor of Divinity degree at Oberlin. Meanwhile, within a year of his arrival, the local church in Wadsworth recognized his talents and called him to be their assistant pastor, partly because of his ability to preach in English. But there was no doubt that the senior pastor, Ephraim Hunsberger, favored his new young assistant. So did his daughter: Hirschy and Augusta Hunsberger were married September 1894.[23]

Such strategic contacts only aided the young Hirschy's meteoric rise in the church. Through the later 1890s, church leaders recognized his enthusiasm for progressive innovations and assigned their young charge positions of increasing responsibility. He served on the GCMC's home missions committee, then in 1898, at age thirty-one, became Middle District Conference moderator. At the same time he pursued further academic achievement. At four different periods, beginning in 1900, he managed to squeeze in stints of extensive work at the University of Chicago Divinity School, studying Old Testament under prestigious scholars William Rainey Harper and J. M. P. Smith. A master's degree was to be followed by a 1906-1907 sabbatical year in Switzerland, where Hirschy would graduate with a doctorate in Old Testament from the University of Bern.[24]

But this would come later. Even without such fancy and almost unprecedented levels of higher education for a Mennonite, by the dawn of the new century Noah Hirschy was clearly an up-and- coming young church star. And he knew what to do with this kind of capital. By the 1890s, he had joined other ambitious young people in a concerted effort to push their church to build a college.

"The school question is becoming a very live one"

Gaining church approval for another attempt at higher education by the church actually turned out to be easier than many of these leaders would have supposed. Their people were aware of the need for church-based education; by the 1890s the MDC had already started a number of parochial schools.[25] With top leaders inspired if not dominated by Wadsworth graduates, in a few years activists parlayed this enthusiasm into MDC approval for a college.

The opening push in the campaign came from Hirschy, who was reminded of the potentialities for such an effort every time his eyes drifted out of his church study and fell on the vacant Wadsworth building next door. Hirschy was a man of action: he sent a paper to be read at the 1894 MDC meeting advocating that the conference construct a college, then kept raising the idea.[26]

Hirschy rehearsed his case for the influential MDC minister J. H. Tschantz in 1897. He argued that "*Christian, positively Christian* schools is the need of the hour," and that "the time has come to strike the blow." Tschantz borrowed from Hirschy's letter in his long paper (later published in *The Mennonite*) advocating a college to the MDC meeting that fall. To overcome conservative suspicions, aroused by the Wadsworth experience, that such education would encourage acculturation, Tschantz and Hirschy portrayed the college as another means of defending Mennonites against change. Look at the public school teachers, reasoned Tschantz, to whom Mennonite parents innocently entrusted their children. One could point to a few Christian teachers in the public schools but also to "a large number of *skeptics, lodgefellows and dangerous characters*" teaching there as well. If Mennonites would "wake up to our children's spiritual interest," he posited, they would need a college to train their teachers.[27]

Undoubtedly these statements were simply the more public manifestations of private conversations that had begun to reverberate around the conference. The effect was to establish a momentum that became irresistible. "The school question is becoming a very live one among our brethren of the Middle District," editorialized *The Mennonite* in 1898. In fall 1896 the MDC appointed a small committee of three leaders to officially begin exploring the notion of establishing a college. Consisting of Hirschy, Baer, and Berne's J. F. Lehman, who would later lead the college's board of trustees for nearly three decades, the committee met at Bluffton in January 1897.[28]

The makeup of the committee assured its findings. They issued a ringing call for the conference to establish a college, though in carefully qualified language. There was no doubt, they maintained, that the conference wanted a school; a "general harmony" about this point came "from every quarter." But they would start small, with a preparatory school slated only gradually to become a college. The shadow of the Wadsworth failure still hung over their efforts. Management of the enterprise would remain with the conference, they assured. "The beginning shall be on a small and reasonable scale," they pledged, "without great expenses, and entirely without debts." The school would devote special attention to the training of teachers, and "Bible instruction shall have a prominent part."[29]

By the time of the MDC's next conference session, the next fall in Trenton, Ohio, there was enough consensus to allow the church to commit. The education committee's report was accepted. This made it clear to Hirschy that the fundamental approval had been secured. He noted in his diary that night the events of a "Great and Historic day." The question of the school had come up, he recorded, and it had been "warmly greeted" and "enthusiastically discussed . . . all on safe footing now." Another committee was established, this time with seven members, Lehman, Hirschy and Baer among them, to start establishing a school; they were to begin fundraising and make plans to be presented to the conference for approval a year later.[30]

The most immediate and momentous decision charged to the committee was location. Deliberations on the issue would continue for nearly a year. A century later it remains unclear exactly why Bluffton was chosen. The committee solicited church leader opinions, and word leaked out as to major contenders. Clearly the college would need to be established in a major MDC church center, which meant Bluffton, Berne, or Wadsworth. The prospect of having a college nearby was alluring for small towns, and the committee soon received flyers from all three sites, praising each town's qualities.[31] Late in the process, in September 1898, the small town of Goshen, Indiana, suddenly made an attractive offer: a town setting that rivaled the others plus an offer of ten acres of land and $10,000 besides. But probably unknown to the town boosters, Mennonite politics had already eliminated Goshen from serious consideration.[32]

The previous summer, Sprunger of Berne had buttonholed Hirschy and Lehman and argued strongly that they ought to merge their educational efforts with those of Mennonite Church leaders, who had already established an MC school in Elkhart, just northwest of Goshen. The group made an exploratory trip to Elkhart, where they met with MC publicist John Funk and dined at the home of another school promoter, J. S. Coffman. Dinner conversation that evening made it clear to all concerned that church politics—one suspects the theological and cultural gulf between GC and MC Mennonites emerged quite loudly that evening—would not allow for such close collaboration. Goshen would get its own Mennonite school soon enough anyway; in 1903 the Elkhart Institute would relocate there and eventually become Goshen College.[33]

With three good offers in hand, the committee took several votes. Berne and Bluffton tied on the first two ballots and Berne won a clear majority on the second two. However, the committee had previously agreed to accept Lehman's advice and refrain from any recommendation that was not unanimous. Accordingly, it left the decision to the larger Middle District Conference, which would meet amid the Amish Mennonites in fall 1898 at the North Danvers Church in Illinois. By that time, the decision had already been made behind the scenes for Bluffton; the college history of 1925 simply noted in passing that even though conference delegates took a vote, "the slate was fixed."[34]

It was an enigmatic decision, especially since Bluffton's offer did not match Goshen's and Wadsworth could offer a twenty-five-thousand-dollar building already constructed and paid for. Perhaps H. P. Krehbiel's arguments won the day. A year before he had told the committee that though there were strong arguments for Berne, the nod ought to go to Bluffton. The town was bigger, its railroad facilities better, and "above all Bluffton has the advantage of having the largest Mennonite settlement in its immediate vicinity which will almost insure the largest Mennonite attendance of the three places under consideration." The fact that Bluffton had not yet ponied up as attractive an inducement could be managed; apparently MDC delegates used Goshen's offer to extract a matching deal from Bluffton.[35]

The announcement that the college would be in Bluffton allowed town boosters to crow. "Bluffton has so many advantages over its competitor . . . that nobody who has half a glass eye and common horse sense will dispute," declared the *Bluffton News*. The locals were a bit miffed at the proposed college name; a local planning committee pushed the board to change it from Central Mennonite School to Bluffton College. The board compromised with Central Mennonite College, a grandiose title in itself for a school that would in its first years remain a college-prep academy.[36]

Meanwhile, the conference appointed the first board of trustees, nine men, including both Krehbiel cousins, Tschantz, Lehman, and a prominent Bluffton Mennonite leader, Jonas Amstutz. This group busied itself with the practical matters involved in giving birth to a college. In January 1899 they met at Amstutz's home in Bluffton to accept the town's offer and lay plans for a "brick building containing a basement, four to six recitation rooms, a chapel, a library and an office." They began thinking through a course of study, pledging that "German shall be thoroughly taught and that in the public exercises German and English shall be given equal prominence." Then came what would loom as a significant expansion of the college's mission, particularly in light of what came later. These nine founders added quietly that the college would be Mennonite but "shall be open to all." Articles of incorporation were filed December 1899.[37]

At a meeting in Bluffton in January 1899, the trustees took a break from deliberations and trudged through six inches of snow to the ten-acre cow pasture west of town that a local citizen, Judge Eaton, had donated as the college grounds. It must have appeared a pretty spot, sparkling with crystal that cold December morning. Much of Eaton's gift was a floodplain for Little Riley Creek, including a brackish backwater that students later would fondly call "the lagoon." The ground slowly rose up northwest of the creek to a natural stand of hardwood trees, hickories and oaks, a grove townspeople enjoyed as a picnic grounds for much of the year. Stomping around in the snow and envisioning the angles of the building they had authorized, the trustees decided then and there that the structure would fit nicely on the crest of the rise in Eaton's Grove.[38]

On a warm spring day the following June, a large crowd gathered to lay the cornerstone for the hall. They were in a festive and generous mood. When one speaker noted that a better grade of brick would greatly improve the appearance of the building, someone passed the hat among the crowd and right then raised the extra $500.00 needed. The aged John Moser oversaw the laying of the cornerstone, H. J. Krehbiel preached in German, choirs from several local Mennonite churches sang, and the principal English address fell to Hirschy. It was, he recorded later in his diary, "the great day," with "a heavy burden on me. Poured my life and strength into it."[39]

He had a task both demanding and delicate—inaugurating a process that would concern the college for much of the next three or four decades. What Hirschy needed to perform that June day was, in effect, a marriage, joining Mennonite culture and consciousness with that of progressive, democratic American society. Mainstream culture was ready for the union, but Mennonites were shy and reticent. Hirschy would need to proceed carefully.

He began by sketching the Mennonite history that had led to their efforts, listing Menno himself among the "mighty cloud of witnesses" who "stand forth from historic records to cheer us in this task." But as they stood at the close of one century and the dawn of another, they faced an even larger responsibility. The "wheels of progress" now "moved with accelerated speed," he declared, demanding that Mennonites take part in the progress. He outlined problems of the day: political and foreign policy crises that gripped the nation and social problems of hunger and want. Here was a young Mennonite preacher in tune with progressive political currents of the day, noting brutalities inflicted on Cubans and Filipinos, crying that "the oppressed must be set free" and government made "servants of the people." And so, he declared, "let our college be an American college." It would prepare young men and women to take up an activist Christianity "adapted more closely to the needs of the age." From such efforts, Hirschy concluded, "let us expect great things. . . ."[40]

There was talk afterward that Hirschy's address helped secure him the BC presidency, but the truth was that Hirschy was the board's third choice and didn't want the job anyway. Top pick was the widely respected minister A. S. Shelly, who had served on a wide range of GCMC committees and as MDC moderator for eleven years. But Shelly turned down the offer, to the disappointment of many, including Hirschy, who thought "his amiable way of dealing with the people . . . would have put our school on a good basis." Likewise the board's second pick, Rev. H. H. Ewert of Gretna, Manitoba, rejected the call. Soon the board wooed Hirschy, but it would take some doing. He said no in spring 1900, and they pressed him again.[41]

The negotiations were demanding, and shed light on dynamics already at work that would later shroud Hirschy's presidency in difficulty. They revealed that a rift had begun to open, already by spring 1900, between Hirschy and more conservative members of the Swiss church. Before the offer had even come, he told H. J. Krehbiel he had no desire to leave Wadsworth and that "still less have I any love for Bluffton. Should I ever go there, then it will be under the pressure of the *ought*." Hirschy was not merely playing coy; he turned down the offer the first time partly out of a sense of his own inability to "command the necessary support and cooperation of the churches and of the public in general to make the school a success."[42]

Hirschy must have known of rumors that questioned his theological soundness. Krehbiel privately noted the response from one board member who refused to sign on to Hirschy's appointment until he publicly explained his views on the "higher criticism" of the Bible or else pledged to remain silent on the subject in his teaching.[43]

Krehbiel pushed Hirschy hard to take the position anyway, gently trying to soothe the hurt incurred by his being passed over twice. Board member J. C. Mehl of Goshen appealed to his strong ego and his sense of duty to God's call, two items Hirschy sometimes conflated. Becoming the college's first president, Mehl admitted, "means *sacrifice* and *toil* and *responsibility*, but it also means joy and honor and fame and above all the approval of high heaven."[44]

Perhaps equally convincing were signs of support Hirschy received from parties at Bluffton. P. D. Amstutz of Pandora, Ohio, a member of the board of trustees of the Swiss Mennonite congregation, wrote to assure Hirschy of his own support and also that of Pastor Moser. "There may be a few" in the church who "might object" to his coming, Amstutz admitted, but "rest assured the great majority would like to see you here." In August Hirschy gave in and accepted the presidency, pledging to "make the very most of it," though all understood that he would need to govern affairs from Wadsworth for the first year. He was thirty-four years old.[45]

Following another big event, the late October dedication of College Hall, Hirschy delivered an eloquent little address to faculty and students on November 5, 1900. He promised the small group that "if we benefit those who would otherwise pass through life ignorantly, if we can increase . . . the number of well-trained men and women, and if we can in this way hold up before the world our con-

ceptions of truth and righteousness, then we have a right to exist and
. . . look for success." Under this banner, students marched off to
begin classes in the sparkling new building in Eaton's Grove.[46]

"This is a modest
beginning on a very small scale"

When the college opened its doors to students that fall day, it did
so in a town of about two thousand people just beginning to absorb
the new century's technological and communications revolutions.
The town's boasting of its new municipal water and lighting systems
to the committee deciding where the college would be located was no
idle chatter. The first house in town to receive municipal water did so
in 1896, and electrical current and telephone service had become
available to village residents two years later. Until the Inter-Urban
(an intracity street car) rail line tracks were laid down the center of
Main Street in 1906, most students and faculty arrived in town at the
Lake Erie and Western Railroad depot, then proceeded to the college
by foot or horse and buggy. Automobiles were still such a novelty in
1900 that the *Bluffton News* judged newsworthy the appearance in
town of two cars. Ten years later, the paper announced the beginning
of an automobile "craze" in the village; seven more residents had just
acquired them, bringing the count to "at least seventeen."[47]

In many ways, the Bluffton of 1900 remained a nineteenth-century village. One could stand on Main Street on a warm day and absorb sights and sounds which in a few decades would be lost in a
haze of nostalgia for a simpler and golden age. Before the street was
paved, the sprinkling wagon would have trundled by, dampening
the dusty streets, along with the ice wagon that rescued overworked
ice boxes and delivered ice slivers to a gaggle of children following
behind. The ragman would come by calling out for junk while farmers peddled fresh vegetables to passersby or even delivered them to
kitchen back doors. Medicine men parked their wagon on a corner
and with music or magic aimed to lure customers into trying one of
their cure-alls. The countryside was still covered with miles of original forest, and long wagons heavy with logs would creak toward the
sawmill on East College Avenue.[48]

In summer, gangs of gypsies in colorful clothing camped at the
edge of town, and tramps wandered from the railroad to Main Street
seeking a promising neighborhood. In 1900 there would have been
some real affluence in town to beckon them; that year marked the
height of the Bluffton oil boom, with over 500 wells being pumped in

the immediate vicinity. Wages for day labor doubled, then tripled, and oil workers were famously free spenders. With Lima or Findlay a day's buggy journey away, they spent their savings locally, particularly at the town's dozen or so saloons, where poker games raged for hours.[49]

For a college aiming to turn sheltered Mennonite youth into educated Christians of noble character, this environment was fraught with potential danger. With no dorms, the students either lived at home or boarded with private families for $1.50 per week, $1.75 with heat, but this arrangement was inadequate for the long term. Hirschy continually pled with the trustees to provide a residence for young women because many good Mennonite parents were reluctant to let daughters board in private homes in town. He reported with some weariness in 1905 that he had urged the construction of a "Ladies' Hall . . . so often that it becomes monotonous to repeat it."[50]

Meanwhile, BC did its best to protect students from the world's evils. Even when the college was in the planning stages in 1898, Hirschy had pushed the committee of seven toward a unanimous ruling that students would "keep themselves free from the lodge, the saloon, tobacco, and card playing." Ladies and gentlemen, other early rules stipulated, could eat but not room in the same house. In 1904 the faculty passed a 10:30 p.m. student curfew.[51]

Students came anyway and managed to create a sense of student life and spirit that did much to shape the new institution. Enrollment reached forty-eight students by the end of the first year, fifty-nine by the end of the second, and approached seventy in spring 1904, with seven taking junior college work. These numbers were still small enough that the entire college functioned as what a later history called an "extended family." Hirschy characterized personal relationships in the college as "most cordial and friendly," partly due to the fact that except for sports events, all activities and functions—college administration, classes, worship, faculty-student consultations, student activities, studying in the library—took place in one three-story building. Classes by nature were small and relationships quite personal. Faculty teas and receptions as well as daily chapel services reinforced the familiar atmosphere.[52]

Sometimes the level of intimacy seemed unfathomable to outsiders. In 1904, for example, students of Northern Ohio Normal School in nearby Ada (today's Ohio Northern University) rose up in unrest because an African-American student, John Sloan, intended to enroll. Hirschy invited Sloan to dinner, then admitted him to Central Mennonite College, where he stayed four years, earned a diploma, and charmed many fellow students with what the 1925 college history later described as his "refined manners and manly conduct."[53]

Campus atmosphere was mostly characterized by hard work and serious study, despite the fact that the vast majority of the students were enrolled in high school classes. In 1904 there were just two full-time college students and four years later only eight had completed the junior college course. Nonetheless, in his speech inaugurating their work in November, 1900, Hirschy had urged that "'thoroughness' should be written over every classroom door and should characterize the work of every teacher and student." The faculty took him at his word.[54]

Their efforts took shape around a curriculum strongly devoted to teaching the classics, subjecting the students to a general introduction to Latin, English, and German language and literature, history, algebra, geometry, and physics. Students received a general introduction to the sciences through introductory classes in botany and chemistry. Already by 1904 the college had secured "simple and compound microscopes, worktables, and such apparatus as will enable students to pursue this study to good advantage." They had begun an herbarium as well. The academic courses were supplemented for academy students by courses in more prosaic subjects, such as penmanship, bookkeeping, and commercial law.[55]

Gradually college courses were added. By 1904 college students could take courses in Hebrew, ethics, and education theory and practice. A Bible school had organized a three-year program for academy graduates that offered courses in Old and New Testaments and New Testament Greek. High school classes or not, many of these young people were initiates to serious academic life. They soon realized they were engaged in a momentous business. "We . . . knew that we were enrolled in serious study to learn something worthwhile," recalled one. "There were no easy courses." Between classes, students cracked books in a library that could point to over 400 titles in 1902 and had, the *College Record* remarked, "still room for more."[56]

But it was not all study. These students created a rich associational life, most of it contributing to the "high ideals" the president held up for the college. They founded Lowell Literary Society in 1902, which met weekly to engage in orations, debates, recitations, and both instrumental and vocal music. All these activities were intended, declared the college catalog, to promote "a high standard of literary excellence."[57]

Already students and faculty had begun to lay the foundation for what would be a solid college heritage of musical excellence. Both men's and women's Glee Clubs were born in the 1902-1903 school year. A year earlier, Professor Guy Latchaw took up his baton in front of the College Choral Society, a group that would bring vocal music to the college for over half a century. They began to offer two classical religious productions annually, beginning with an ambitious production of Mendelssohn's *Hymn of Praise* in June 1903. In January 1906, the society was ready to tackle Handel's *Messiah*. The production was received with such local acclaim that it has been offered on the campus every Christmas season since. The college orchestra began to accompany the Choral Society in 1903 and gave its first symphony concert in 1910 under the direction of Sidney Hauenstein.[58]

The aim of much of this music, of course, was to contribute to the larger religious purposes of the college, purposes strengthened and deepened throughout its first years. "The college believes with many others," stated the college catalog forthrightly, "that religion is an essential ingredient of all complete manhood and womanhood." Daily chapel attendance was required, as was attendance at daily vesper services. Consisting of hymns, prayers, short addresses, and readings, these vesper services were introduced in winter term 1902-1903 and "proved so successful," Hirschy noted, that they would be continued in the spring. They were moved soon after to Sunday afternoons and continued for decades. In addition, student attendance was required on Sunday mornings at any of Bluffton's eight churches the students or their parents might select, including the Roman Catholic church.[59]

Extracurricular activities were not just confined to matters of mind and spirit. "Physical strength and vigor form the basis of mental achievement," the college catalog recognized. Soon after the college was founded, students began to toss around a baseball and a pigskin in the cow pasture between College Hall and the creek. Before long they had organized teams and begun to seek competition. Informal games of tennis and baseball appeared on campus not long after the first students arrived, and the *College Record* of June 1903 observed the formation of the school's first baseball team.[60]

In fall 1905 the *Record* noted that "a great deal of interest is being shown in the college foot-ball team." With Professor Daniel Jantzen as coach, the men had commenced practices and performed well in a rough scrimmage against a town team in which John Sloan made a "sensational tackle." They played their first regular game November 3 against a city team from Leipsic, Ohio. Leipsic team members were bigger and heavier and included a player who had suited up for the University of Michigan, explained the *Record*, but by the end they had the college team down by only a 12-0 score. They played well and were driving toward a score when the clock expired. For the time being, the games would have to be informal; the college administration regularly stipulated that "no intercollegiate contest games are to be played."[61]

Nonetheless, such activity pointed toward a lively student body. There were even glimpses, in these early years, of the spirit of rowdy mayhem that would percolate through the student body for much of its life. In these years as later, that spirit was manifested in intense competition between different classes. The gradations from lowly freshman to sophomore to exalted upper class status became a fixed channel of student life early in the college's history. Students' consciousness became devoted to the well-being of their assigned group.

Already by 1903, when a senior class at the college had not yet come into existence, this rivalry had mounted to the point where apparently intense scuffles erupted over the capturing of flags of rival classes. There was enough wildness to cause faculty concern about damage to College Hall. At a special meeting in June 1903, faculty unanimously declared that "since our building is constructed that 'flag rushes' endanger it, and since rushes are liable to lead to disturbances and confusion in the halls," no class flags would thereafter be hoisted on the building. Four years later, with a senior class having come and gone and left a memorial to the college, the faculty fined three students who had placed their own class colors on it.[62]

The professors charged with shaping these young spirits into proper intellectuals came from a variety of places. Hirschy scoured both the Mennonite and the local academic world for faculty and seemed to have much more success finding professors from the local scene. Faculty recruitment was an ongoing process because many stayed at the college just a short while, turnover surely related to abysmal salaries. Central Mennonite College professors usually received a lower yearly salary than first-year teachers at Bluffton High School, a condition that lasted well into the 1930s, when, if anything, salaries worsened. Hirschy still managed to assemble a strong faculty. These included local doctor John Sutter teaching physiology and hygiene; Laura Muir teaching piano; John Bixel on voice and composition; and Daniel Jantzen from Kansas, who covered German, history, and the natural sciences for seven years.[63]

Some new faculty stayed longer. Isaiah Beeshy began teaching penmanship to the first class and served on the faculty for nine years, most of the time working also as business manager. After he resigned, Beeshy, his house bordering the college on Spring Street, remained for another half-century a close friend and neighbor of the college. He could be seen walking the campus well into the 1960s.[64]

Hirschy began to develop an eye for faculty talent. He informed the board in 1907 of a Dr. S. K. Mosiman who was available and ought to be hired if possible; such a move "would help greatly to strengthen the faculty." It would take a full year of negotiations to induce Mosiman to come; for unclear reasons he turned down the job but then accepted it in 1908.[65]

In 1903 Hirschy had secured the services of Edmund J. Hirschler to teach mathematics. He seemed to anchor himself to the college with his subsequent courtship and marriage to biology professor Elida Zepp. Like Mosiman, Hirschler was one of the developing core of solid faculty who slowly embedded themselves into the institution until they seemed to become a part of its very physical structure. For nearly four decades, until his death at the eve of World War II, Hirschler taught mathematics and, more informally, what came to be called the "Bluffton Spirit." In an address to begin the 1903 school year entitled "Education as a Preparation for Service," Hirschler assured the study body that "the consciousness of having done your best to serve humanity and your God will be worth more to you, when you look back on a completed life . . . than all the fame and all the riches of this world."[66]

Generations of students later testified to the teaching strengths of this early faculty. Hirschler, recalled one, was "a very capable man indeed." The president himself was a powerful influence. One former student testified later that Hirschy was simply "the best teacher I ever had." Another remembered his eloquence less than his ability to expound the mysteries of botany. Nearly eighty years later, Bertha Goetsch still recalled the thrill she experienced, as a young girl from a farm, when Hirschy placed a single drop of pond water under a microscope and showed her all the bustling life it contained.[67]

The faculty worked hard, meeting monthly in the president's office or his home to rule on most student matters, personal and academic, and discuss pedagogy. In addition to teaching loads that appear astounding by today's standards—in 1903-1904, for example, Hirschy taught twenty-four hours a week, Jantzen twenty-five, Beeshy a numbing twenty-nine—the faculty all passed the extra jobs around themselves. In that same year Jantzen edited the *College Record*, Hirschler worked as librarian, and Beeshy served as college business manager and secretary.[68]

Underpaid and overworked, the college's first faculty managed nevertheless to nurture an extracurricular academic life that still appears impressive for such a tiny place. In 1903, they initiated traditions by stating that the school colors would be "royal purple and cream." Other set practices followed. In January 1904 the college began a regular feature of campus life that would endure until the 1950s: a weeklong Bible conference with visiting pastors and scholars preaching and leading prayers. The first conference, Hirschy noted in his diary, was a week of "great enjoyment and spiritual gain, a break such as one does not deserve." Individual faculty began participating in the speechmaking at the Intercollegiate Peace Conferences, organized by Goshen's president Noah Byers, a tradition that would continue for years. They also nudged students to develop their own powers of oratory, creating a student speech contest in 1905 with cash awards for winners.[69]

These and related efforts of students and faculty in these first years testify above all else to the creation of a sense of common life of the college, an excitement with each other, and a zest for learning that even the passage of a century cannot conceal. Take, for example, some activities of commencement week 1905. Closing exercises began on June 15 with an impressive concert by music students, followed by a reception for the student body by the faculty, held outdoors in brilliant moonlight the next evening. President Hirschy delivered a stirring baccalaureate address entitled "Intellectual difficulties."[70]

The next day, Monday, students gathered in various rooms and also on the front lawn outside of College Hall to take final exams. These were followed by "class-day exercises" Tuesday, when the students were addressed by the first and only graduate of the junior college, H. R. Luginbihl, president of the class of 1905. That evening three speakers participated in the oratorical prize contest. S. D. Basinger took the $8.00 first prize for his review of the Spanish-American War "with its last beneficent results." J. P. Owens' effort attacking anti-Semitism placed second, and G. A. Lehman won third place for his address defending racial justice entitled "The American Negro."[71]

Wednesday featured the actual commencement exercises, where Dr. Herbert Lockwood Willett of the University of Chicago lectured on "Some Ideals of Education." This gave way to the annual alumni banquet, where Professor Jantzen led the forty-some assembled alumni and guests to a full hour of toasting following the feast. The week finished with a rendition of Sullivan's "The Prodigal Son" by the College Choral Society. Five years into its life, the college could offer High Ideals and Noble Character in abundance.[72]

Just a few darker developments were quietly undermining these high and heady times. One had to do with money. Finances started on a rough basis and worsened over the years. Even after College Hall had been completed, the town of Bluffton was still nearly $3,000 short of the $10,000 it had promised the MDC to secure the college; many wealthy people, reported the *Bluffton News*, "have given nothing or little." A year later Hirschy privately told Krehbiel that finances had reached the point where "public confidence is destroyed" and "the work is hampered." Hirschy agitated for a number of items the college desperately needed—for a women's dorm, more land for future expansion, an increase in the endowment fund—but the funds were not there. Like all college presidents, Hirschy extensively toured and preached in churches of the constituency. He had periodic success: a thousand-dollar gift here, a few acres of land there. By 1908 the school could point to a $10,000 endowment.[73]

But that was later. In the interim, the board continually monitored college financial health, in a manner resembling, quipped the seventy-five-year BC history, "a team of doctors monitoring the college's signs of life." Their prognosis was increasingly bleak. Behind the sparkle of the 1905 commencement festivities, financial woes brewed. Krehbiel worried later that year whether BC could even survive. The hot air heating system collapsed, forcing construction of a new $1,700 heating plant. Subscriptions in the churches for a second five years came in at half the rate of the first five years, a drive that itself remained $1,500 short. Enrollment in fall 1906 was way off; only forty-two students showed up, and the college suddenly faced a $4,000 deficit.[74]

It seemed like the Wadsworth experience all over again, a comparison that seemed apt in more ways than merely financial. The problem was not just money, Krehbiel told Tschantz privately; "the great trouble is that our own people have not enough interest in their own school."[75]

Read between the lines, it seems clear that beneath all the high culture, the teas, the choral productions, and the academic achievements of the college, there brewed a deeper problem. In 1905 Hirschy referred to "a certain hesitancy and reserve brooding" and "anxiety and fear" that existed "in the minds of some people who should be more aggressively interested in the work of our College."[76] When the president used such phrases, any Mennonite in the countryside between Bluffton and Pandora could translate. They meant that Hirschy had gotten into a nasty and destructive fight with leaders of the Swiss Mennonite congregation.

The Beast without and the Devil within

By and large the public has a positive view of Mennonites. They appear a gentle, productive, simple people who live quietly in rural communities without harming others and certainly not themselves. The Mennonite heritage of plain dress, simple living, and dedication to pacifist nonresistance has helped foster such generalities.

Perceptive scholars of Mennonite life, however, have known better. Although Mennonites have mostly avoided confrontations with outsiders, in their church structures, and particularly their congregations, they have fought each other tooth and nail. Historically the most common kind of conflict, the sociologist Fred Kniss has argued, occurred between two different protagonists. On the one hand, there were progressive innovators, the institution builders and free spirits, who insisted that Mennonites adapt more creatively to outside society while weakening the power of church hierarchies. They were opposed by traditionalists, who saw such innovations as dangerous compromises of Mennonite charter values. A particularly bitter period of Mennonite conflict along these lines, Kniss argues, occurred 1877-1910, when the disputes grew so heated even the mask of cordiality and civility was sometimes removed.[77]

The kinds of controversy that swirled around Bluffton College for much of its history have demonstrated the accuracy of such analyses only to a point. Certainly the college's history has witnessed a continual tension between progressive college faculty and administrators, eager to embrace outside political and cultural currents, and more conservative constituents in many supporting congregations. However, these generalizations only partly explain the discord infecting Central Mennonite College. Although the local church tended to distrust the high-flown ideals of the college, in these years the president's principle antagonist was a Wadsworth graduate and fellow innovator, a man probably just as progressive as Hirschy. Mapping out the ruinous encounters of Hirschy's day also thus requires an excursion into the more tricky and subtle terrain of personality conflict.

Given the rather damning things Hirschy wrote about J. B. Baer, it is helpful first to take his words at face value and consider the possibility that much of the trouble came from Baer. Old-timers in the town of Bluffton still suspect that Baer thought the presidency ought to have gone to him. Then when it did not, they suspect, he set out to wreck the college. A graduate of Union Theological Seminary in New York City, Baer had spent years traveling extensively in GC churches across the West as preacher, teacher, church builder. In 1900, he had just as impressive a set of academic credentials as Hirschy, was at least as well connected in the wider conference, had been voted into leadership in the important local church, and was thirteen years Hirschy's elder.[78]

In 1901, college business manager Jonas Amstutz recorded Baer as blasting Lehman and other trustees as "infamous liars." Amstutz cried that "there has been nothing mean and low enough for 'Bear and Co' that they would not resort to." That "would-be dictator" was "doing his dirtiest to get control." Yet Amstutz was not an impartial observer; at the time, he was locked in his own bitter row with Baer for other reasons. College founder H. P. Krehbiel, a seasoned church infighter himself, described Baer in different tones. To him, Baer was "a good judge of human nature" who possessed an "amiable disposition" and "a good supply of mother wit and tact."[79]

It is also necessary to admit the possibility that much difficulty lay with Hirschy. His potential for conflict was rooted in a number of areas. One was that his stances on the politics and theology of the day were increasingly removed from those treasured by more traditional Mennonites. Politically Hirschy was deeply in tune with the middle-class crusade of progressivism then reshaping national politics. In one local debate in 1903, for instance, he supported government ownership and operation of public utilities. He made headlines in one local paper with his ringing endorsement of women's suffrage. In fifty years, Hirschy predicted to the Putnam County Teachers' Association, women would rule every profession, and men would have to "bow to her for a position," ascribing this dominance to male sloth and feminine perseverance.[80]

It would be inaccurate to call Hirschy a theological liberal, at least as the term has been understood in the history of U.S. theology. Admittedly, at times Hirschy himself claimed the title, as in a 1907 letter to an old Oberlin professor explaining he had lost his Bluffton job because many local preachers judged him "too liberal in my biblical views." That claim, however, came in a letter in which Hirschy was angling for a job at Oberlin. Thus the claim appears a self-serving explanation for why he would want to go to Oberlin, framed in terms his old professor would appreciate.[81] To use a term just beginning to come into Mennonite parlance, Hirschy was no modernist.

Having said that, it is also necessary to recognize that Hirschy's theology was cutting edge for Mennonite theological understandings at the turn of the century. He had run into problems along these lines before he had even accepted the presidency. There would be more. In 1902 he somewhat innocently delivered an address before a local

Sunday school convention titled "Faith and Reason in Bible Study," in which he dismissed "weak, flimsy, babyish interpretation and teaching of the Bible" as a basic reason "why so many thinking men want nothing to do with it." He called his audience instead to develop a "rational" faith. To Mennonites whose tradition said that one merely accepted the faith of the ancestors without engaging in intellectual exercises about it, these were dangerous ideas. A paper Hirschy published on "The Historical Method of Studying the Bible" expressing similar ideas evoked a like outcry.[82]

Still, such explanations do not fully explain Hirschy's troubles. If there had not already been a breach with the Swiss church, these accusations might not have been made, nor would they have mattered much if they had. Perhaps a deeper explanation for the series of crises the college underwent with its mother church is found in Hirschy's style and personality.

Undoubtedly Hirschy's tastes and operating mode grated on the nerves of many rural Mennonites in the area. This was a community still on guard for signs of pride and worldliness. By contrast, a photo of Hirschy shows him clad in a three-piece suit, with a smart bowler hat and his customary white bow tie, the epitome of the fashionable man-about-town. It was dated June 1, 1901, about the time he moved to the area to stay. Having spent the previous ten years in the relatively open climate of Wadsworth, it was a difficult transition both for him and many local Mennonites. To them, he must have appeared somewhat of an upstart and a dangerously modern young man.[83]

Hirschy privately recorded his impressions of them in return. That September he attended the Sunday school class run by the Swiss Mennonites in town and, in the pages of his diary, termed it "cold, colder, coldest." "Can we endure it?" he wondered. "What can we do to change it?" Returning to Bluffton in 1902 from one of his study summers in Chicago, he prayed for God's assistance to "bring the larger life to those people!"[84]

Differences of style were compounded by the problems Hirschy had adjusting his free spirit to hierarchies of the Swiss Mennonite community. That the young president had personal difficulties submitting to established church authority seems clear. Unleashed for graduate work in Chicago in the summers, he sent letters to Augusta that sounded like those of a man released from prison. "You can hardly imagine how I feel since I am out here," he wrote his wife. "I almost shout for joy all to myself. . . . Why should mortals whose life is short be chained down to trivialities by a narrow people who will not be helped to a larger life? . . . I do love freedom."[85]

Once he finally resigned the presidency, Hirschy's relief fairly jumped from the pages of his letters. Had they taken the presidency of another Mennonite college, he wrote Augusta from the Middle District Conference sessions in 1908, "we would have the whole mob on our necks. Now they all wish they could exercise authority over us but they can't."[86]

Nor was the president aided by his grandiose sense of his own life mission, a sense of purpose repeatedly frustrated by Bluffton-area Mennonites' inexplicable resistance to his efforts to bring them the "larger life." Hirschy wrote with the assurance of a man confident that history's judgment would vindicate him. In his diary and correspondence he would often close descriptions of conflicts with other leaders with phrases like "Let the future tell," or "Let the years to come tell the story." Knowing future historians would be tracing his actions, he tried to make their job easy. Often when he spoke at conference churches or school functions, small-town papers would provide brief reports. Hirschy was careful to clip and paste them in his dairy, sometimes briefly referring to different published accounts of events in case future researchers wanted a more complete record. For their convenience he also provided an annual index to his diary.[87]

More importantly, Hirschy was careful to supply the proper interpretive angle. Whether battling external forces like the liquor trade or malevolent influences in the church, there seemed to be few shades of gray in his world. "We filed our petition for a local option election last night," he wrote Krehbiel, describing his efforts on behalf of prohibition. "Now the fight begins. The forces of darkness and sin are on one side and those of light and righteousness on the other. By the grace of God we hope to win."[88]

A serious man engaged in the weighty business of God's kingdom, he had little patience with individuals who stood in the way. As the president repeatedly remarked to his friend I. B. Beeshy, "anyone who stands in the way of progress is going to get run over." Accounts from his encounters at church conferences read like dispatches from a military strategist, though almost always Hirschy's efforts for righteousness seemed to prevail. The forces of the "bitter opposition" were "decidedly checked" or given "a terrible blow." Describing his response to one individual who had dared oppose him on the floor of one conference session, Hirschy wrote home to Augusta that "I flayed him alive, without much credit." Forced to leave the presidency in 1908, Hirschy instructed his wife to dismiss any sense of regret, reasoning that "we have at least saved our spiritual lives" and "have shown our approval of right and disapproval of wrong."[89]

Perhaps if the president had been different in some ways—less quick to judge, less sure of his own sense of moral virtue, more willing to bend a bit and defer to the authority and wishes of others—things might have gone easier for him and the college. But matters would still have been difficult. While Hirschy may bear blame for the conflict rocking the Mennonite world of Putnam and Allen counties a century ago, a large part of the trouble occurred independently of him and only involved the college tangentially at first. Unfortunately for the college, the mother church in whose midst it was born had become locked in severe and acrimonious conflict all of its own making.

The factors that triggered it came not from any outside preacher or new doctrine but from the more intimate force of Mennonite demographics. Put simply, the Swiss Mennonites had been productive of both corn and children, and their church had begun to expand beyond a point that a single congregation could adequately serve. The congregation had constructed two more churches—Ebenezer in 1868 and St. Johns in 1889—each several miles south and north, respectively, of the original "Old White Church" building. Services were held in each building on alternate Sundays.[90]

By the later 1890s, as the settlement expanded, this arrangement was proving unsatisfactory. Mennonites who moved farther from these buildings had to make a longer trip to church. They began to petition the congregation for regular services in town, ideally in buildings the church would construct. The elders tried compromise. By 1895 they began holding Sunday schools at the Lutheran church in Bluffton, led by Jonas Amstutz. But this concession was inadequate. In 1897 and 1901 members from outlying areas, especially Pandora, increased their agitation for Sunday worship services at the St. Johns' church. Rev. Baer was particularly open to these pleas.[91]

Even if these compromises had been accepted, they would merely have postponed the ultimate reckoning. Already by 1899 grounds for compromise were closing fast. The dissidents from Pandora, led by church trustees P. D. Amstutz and P. C. Suter, also raised the question of church authority and advocated more tolerance toward intermarriage with outsiders. On these issues Baer and Moser stood firm, insisting on the supremacy of church hierarchical rather than congregational authority.[92]

The event that ultimately resulted in schism was triggered by college business manager and founding trustee Jonas Amstutz. In 1898, when the town of Bluffton agreed to raise the $10,000 necessary to obtain the college, Amstutz had been one of ten members of a committee charged with soliciting the funds. The Swiss church had pro-

ceeded under the assumption that committee members were volun-
teering. Amstutz had understood he would be paid for his efforts. He
presented the church with a bill for over $2,000. When the church re-
fused to pay, Amstutz sued.[93]

The specter of Mennonite church members suing others in court
for what was essentially a congregational matter escalated tensions
dramatically. Four days after Amstutz's suit was settled out of court
in October 1903, members of the Swiss congregation filed a com-
plaint with the Church Council against four members who had supported Amstutz. In a series of explosive meetings, the four members
refused to answer charges and were expelled from the congregation.
Then these members, along with supporters, countercharged that
their expulsion was contrary to the church constitution. When the
church refused to relent, they sued and won a favorable ruling from
the Allen County Court of Pleas. In January 1904 the Putnam County
sheriff nailed a restraining order to the door of the St. Johns church,
forbidding the congregation to conduct a business meeting in which
they planned to ratify the expulsions.[94]

It was a sad and painful turn of events for the large, old congregation, indicating divisions too deep to patch. The disputes, moreover, were all of a piece. The Amstutz supporters the church council
tried to expel were members of the same faction in the church that
had been agitating for separate services for years. They were led by
Pandora-area residents P. D. Amstutz, P. B. Hilty, and P. C. Suter. With
the assistance of Berne's Sprunger, these men led 141 departing
members of the old Swiss Mennonite congregation to form their own
congregation in Pandora, Ohio; the *Bluffton News* reported in
December 1904 that they were "working like tigers" on their building. It was called Grace Mennonite Church and was soon admitted
into the Middle District Conference as a separate congregation.[95]

Into this delicate setting in 1900 stepped brash young Noah
Hirschy, supremely confident of his calling to Bluffton. Even if the
new president had come equipped with the ecclesiastical authority of
Menno Simons and the reconciling love of St. Francis, he would have
encountered difficulties establishing a college in such a troubled environment. As it was, Hirschy possessed little authority and even less
peacemaking ability. Ego he did have, and soon after taking up the
college's presidency, he was engaged in bitter and personal conflict
with the lead pastor of the Swiss Mennonite congregation.

Hirschy and Baer had worked together on church committees in
the 1890s, especially the one that led to BC's founding. Their relationships had apparently been cordial at first. In 1898 Hirschy judged

Baer a "smooth article," reporting that in their work that day they had engaged in "some rubs, but no clashes." Periodically his diary made fleeting references to entertaining Baer for dinner or enjoying him as guest preacher in the Wadsworth church.[96]

By the fall of 1902, however, in the private pages of his diary, Hirschy began to refer to Baer in terms that can only be described as venomous. His most common name for Baer was "the Beast," as in "the Beast is still wrangling and tearing things to pieces." In other instances, he was that "old devil" engaged in "fiendish work" who periodically retreated with his "underlings" following a setback. He was a "rotten rascal" with a "hideous face," a "hypocrite and liar, not to be trusted," who would, if he could, "grind the college to dust." "J. B. Baer is wrong at heart. Sin is embittering his life," Hirschy cried. "Unless he repent I do not know how I can ever work with him. He is meanness embodied in human flesh."[97]

Baer had similar feelings for Hirschy. On one occasion in 1903 when Hirschy preached at Bluffton's Lutheran Church, Baer sat on the platform behind him and made mocking faces to the assembled congregation as Hirschy proceeded. "Miserable, awful, pitiable wretch!" Hirschy raged later that day in his diary.[98]

Several incidents had precipitated the hostility. Early in 1901 pastors of the Swiss congregation came to Hirschy with a seemingly innocuous request. For some years they had been renting a room in the Lutheran church to provide Sunday school for members living in Bluffton. Now that they had welcomed and funded a denominational college nearby, they wondered if they could move these services to its brand new chapel. Hirschy refused. Back in 1898, in the presence of Jonas Amstutz, he had extracted a promise from Baer to build a separate church building for Swiss Mennonites in Bluffton. In January 1901 he urged the board to turn down their request to use the chapel, arguing that "it will not be best for the school. Will it not be easier to *keep* them out than afterward to *put* them out?"[99]

When the pastors "had the gall" to go over his head and appeal to the MDC conference sessions that fall, Hirschy pulled enough strings to get the request referred back to college trustees. Days later, Moser and Baer came to see him in his office and again asked if they could use the chapel. Hirschy matter-of-factly recorded in his diary that he "finally persuaded them to stay away from the college for always with the church. What a victory!" he cried, though he did feel "ashamed for my own lack of faith and confidence in the right."[100]

Perhaps Hirschy, already allied with dissidents in the Swiss congregation pushing for separate congregations, thought that by denying chapel use to the church leaders, he could force them to do as the dissidents demanded. If so, he was directly inserting the college into a bitter local church fight, thus needlessly alienating important local church figures in a manner the new school could ill afford. Equally astounding was Hirschy's naïve assertion that "this was the turning point for me in Bluffton. From now on all will go better."[101]

Things did not go better at all; relationships, in fact, soured quickly. There was a stormy session at the MDC meeting in the fall of 1902 where Hirschy was called to task both for his views on the use of reason in Bible study and also for his solemnizing of the wedding vows between Isaiah Beeshy of the faculty and a local woman who was a member of the Lutheran church. The outcome of this confrontation was "gratifying all around," Hirschy crowed in his diary, a "decided victory for the college" where the "bitter opposition of the wild beast" had met "practical defeat."[102]

The college still needed a supportive local Mennonite congregation and the president moved to provide one, working with faculty and allies in town to create their own congregation in 1903. Called the Bluffton Mennonite Church, it easily obtained Hirschy's permission to meet in the college chapel. Hirschy secured its admission to the MDC over the vehement opposition of Baer. The Swiss congregation, in turn, took up the challenge. In short order they voted to withdraw from the Middle District Conference, and their pastors suddenly overcame their reluctance to offer regular services in town, approving the construction of a handsome, two-story building that would be called First Mennonite Church. Dedicated in 1906, it had beautiful stained glass windows and a level of elegance uncommon for the plain Swiss Mennonites. It was located on a corner lot just two blocks from the college.[103]

Because this conflict occurred against the backdrop of the splintering of the old Swiss church, it was inevitable that the college line itself up with some church factions, thereby earning the enmity of others. From opening day Hirschy enjoyed warm relationships with many dissidents who later broke off to form the Grace church in Pandora. Encouraging Hirschy to accept the presidency, P. D. Amstutz had told him, "If you come we will stand by you." Hirschy in turn lent his verbal support to their cause.[104]

Hirschy and others of the faculty felt particularly close to Jonas Amstutz. So much did Amstutz treasure the college that he bought land at the edge of the original campus and built a home on it. Upon college expansion after Amstutz's death in 1908, the property was absorbed into the campus. The old home, which was on what is today the central college lawn just east of the traffic circle, served as a men's residence hall and president's home until the 1960s. Later genera- tions of students knew it as "Amstutz house." In the wake of his law- suit against them in 1901, the Swiss church pastorate excommuni- cated Amstutz and demanded that Hirschy in some way discipline or dismiss Amstutz from his post as college business manager. Hirschy refused, and used the occasion of a sermon at Ebenezer Mennonite Church forthrightly to tell them so.[105]

In such an incendiary environment, it was not hard for hotheads to use minor issues to widen the breach. The admittance of an African-American student to the college alarmed many in the church, as did the alumni banquets BC hosted once it had alumni. Swiss church members looked up the dictionary meaning of *feast* and found it defined as a lavish affair. Only people who were proud and worldly, conservative Mennonites declared, would engage in such celebration. Another bone of contention emerged when word reached the church that two faculty members had attended a local Halloween party, for which the board of trustees scolded them.[106]

All these episodes served thoroughly to estrange the pastorate and a fair proportion of the members of the old Swiss church and also, no doubt, Mennonites in a wider circle beyond. In making an enemy of Baer, Hirschy alienated not just one prominent local Mennonite leader, but someone who had toured and preached in Middle and Central District congregations for over two decades. Baer certainly would have told a wide range of GC Mennonites of his angry encounters with the president of Central Mennonite College.

By 1906, the college realized something of what this alienation would cost. A fundraising appeal was sent to ten churches that had been solid college supporters. In a month, five had turned the request down flat; board trustee J. F. Lehman from Berne wrote Hirschy that "we have to obtain the necessary funds to carry on the school from sources outside the denomination or quit." Hirschy agreed that keep- ing the college in Bluffton meant "a continued fight against unpleas- ant opposition. . . . Hence to continue here seems to me both impossi- ble and even if possible not wise." But he offered a third option: he pushed Lehman to consider moving BC to Berne. Lehman was un- sure. Many in his church were completely opposed to continuing the college in Bluffton, he admitted, but others were afraid of bringing it to Berne, given the pain the college had brought the Swiss church.[107]

The leaders of the Middle District Conference had gotten wind of the dire financial straits of their new college and the personal battles that lay behind them. They called a special conference session to grapple with the troubles. Held at the new Grace Mennonite Church in Pandora in March 1906, the building was packed with townspeople, local Mennonites, college faculty, and much of the student body. (The faculty had dismissed classes that day so students could attend.) All knew that the conference met to see whether the school would continue. It did not look as if it would. One participant remembered later that "a spirit of depression and gloom prevailed."[108]

On the brink of the vote to close the school, founding board member H. J. Krehbiel stood to speak and played his strongest card. He drew on the memories of Wadsworth, thundering out to the gathering that it had closed because of its lack of financial support, and that its collapse was "the greatest loss that our denomination had sustained in America." If we abandoned this college now, Krehbiel cried, "all future generations would point the finger of contempt and shame at us, the delegates to this conference, and say, 'They killed the college.'" Delegates suddenly began moving to the front of the church to pledge their financial subscriptions. The moment of crisis passed. The following month the supporting backbone of churches came forward with contributions. On April 21, Hirschy heard from the board treasurer that "the required sum of $1,500 annually for the next four years is practically assured and we will therefore go on with the school. Please inform all interested parties in Bluffton."[109]

"The college at Bluffton will never be a college either"

Altogether it had been a near miss. Church higher-ups church decided the situation called for outside intervention. They dispatched three respected leaders to Bluffton to try to effect a reconciliation that would enable the school to go forward. They apparently admonished both sides. In May 1907, Beeshy observed optimistically that "so far seemingly the Baerites have received the worst of it . . . but it is hard to say what the conclusions will be."[110]

Whatever the conclusions were, Hirschy was not around to hear them; he had chosen, perhaps wisely, given how things were going, to take a year's leave and finish his doctorate in Switzerland. The prospect of having Hirschy an ocean away must have appeared an answer to prayer to many on the board. With the college run by an administrative committee headed by Professor Jantzen, in February 1907 the board moved to make Hirschy's absence permanent, informing him by letter that they would keep the arrangement for another year and releasing him from further obligation to the college.[111]

Hirschy supporters were outraged. S. M. Musselman, who was emerging as a prominent minister, wrote to complain of Hirschy's being "sacrificed," arguing that "Bro. Hirschy has thus become the scapegoat for the recent troubles in the vicinity of the college." Hirschy himself seethed and sent blistering letters to the board indicating the personal offense he took at the dismissal. To make matters worse, Jantzen suddenly resigned from the faculty to take care of his ailing wife. With nobody else at hand, the board had little choice but to quite literally beg Hirschy to return. Not until September 1907, back in the country with doctorate in hand, did he consent.[112]

So Hirschy was back, smoldering with a private but disdainful contempt for the board. He would not last long. Many people would have been tempered by the experience of nearly having lost their job, but not Hirschy. Maybe he, like others, had simply grown tired of the fight; yet he was particularly emboldened because he had another job offer in his pocket inviting him to the presidency of Redfield College in South Dakota. At the Middle District Conference sessions in Wayland, Iowa, in August 1908, Hirschy resumed his private offensive. He demanded a salary raise of $500. This was an astronomical increase, at a time when the board had just hired another new Ph.D., Samuel Mosiman, for $750.00 annually. He submitted his resignation in case the board refused. Faced with the prospect of keeping their difficult president at a higher salary or finding another, it is hard to imagine that the board hesitated long. They told Hirschy that they felt "compelled" to accept his resignation. They wished him "success and God's blessing on your future labors."[113]

Suddenly, it was over. "Mama this is our gain, our salvation," he assured Augusta, but he also felt out of kilter; many old allies and enemies in the church didn't seem to know what to say to him. Yet his new position as an ex-college president afforded him some grounds for reflections about his people's ability to accept the kinds of innovations progressives like himself were so strenuously pushing. Hirschy was quite pessimistic. "I am gradually being convinced," he penned Augusta, "that our generation of Mennonites will not reach the liberal stage and not even the tolerant."[114]

Meanwhile, both he and Augusta managed one last parting shot with their old nemesis Baer. Before leaving for the conference, Augusta wrote her husband, Baer had appeared at the college and "made bold" to show some visitors around. She had refused to unlock any doors for him. Baer had apparently heard Hirschy was leaving, and was "feeling sort of an ecstasy," Augusta noted. He was "free more so than usual around me these days. . . . It behooves himself to be a little more reserved, however, or he'll get a dose of the kind of powder he will not like" (a reference to gunpowder, perhaps?). Noah's last words to Baer were, strangely enough, almost pleasant. After the end of the conference and on their separate ways home, they accidentally ran into each other on the street in Omaha. Hirschy grabbed Baer's hand firmly and remarked that "he laughs best who laughs last. The struggle is not yet ended."[115]

As it turned out, it seems neither man enjoyed the last laugh. Within a year after Hirschy's departure, Baer also left Bluffton. He told the church it was due to his "impaired health," but people in town knew of another reason. Baer had helped lead the local campaign to drive saloons from Bluffton. This had alienated many members of his church who quietly enjoyed a good glass of beer. He went west and pastored churches in Illinois and Idaho before retiring in Los Angeles, where he died in 1939 at age eighty-five.[116]

Fewer years were left to Noah Hirschy. His Redfield College presidency ended in disappointment. Part of the lure for him there was the possibility that Redfield would join with another small Mennonite college in the state, and Hirschy toured Mennonite communities raising funds for the merger. When the requisite amount had been pledged, the Redfield board suddenly decided against the move. Feeling that he had both been misled and in turn had misled South Dakota Mennonites, Hirschy resigned in 1913.[117]

For seven years he just drifted. He was financial secretary for a small Minnesota college, principal of schools in Winnie, Texas, then oversaw a fruit ranch destroyed by the great 1917 Galveston hurricane. During World War I Hirschy managed a cotton plantation and pastored a Congregationalist church in Alexandria, Louisiana, but lost his pulpit due to his full-throated opposition to the war. In 1920 an old college chum from Oberlin assumed the presidency of Berea College in Kentucky's Appalachian foothill. He induced Hirschy to be professor of botany. The post combined two of Hirschy's great loves, education and nature; he entered perhaps his happiest years. "The absolute freedom we enjoy is something I have always longed for," he wrote Mosiman in 1923, "but never found till we came here." But it ended too soon: two years later he caught an influenza bug that weakened his heart. He suddenly died in 1925 at age fifty-eight.[118]

In 1919, knowing of Hirschy's teaching ability and desperate for more Ph.D.'s on faculty, Mosiman briefly considered offering his predecessor a teaching position but quickly reasoned that "it might be hazardous, considering all the old difficulties." Hirschy made what would be his last visit to Bluffton a few years before his death, preaching at a vespers service in what Mosiman called "his usual interesting way." If nothing else, the visit indicated to Mosiman that some the tensions that marred Hirschy's presidency still sputtered nearly fifteen years later. Many of Hirschy's old friends came out to hear him preach, Mosiman observed, and "some did not come, I presume for the same old reasons."[119]

When Hirschy left the college in 1908, he felt keen disappointment, he told the student body, so much that "it becomes almost painful to place into other hands so incomplete a piece of work." He had worked so hard, and it seemed to him that "comparatively little has been accomplished." All the effort had yielded a small academy offering a few junior college courses. It consisted in 1908 of only one building, a rented dorm, and a cow pasture for athletic activities. For eight years the college had run from one financial crisis to another, due in great part to the conflict its president had engaged in with the leaders of the local church. Hirschy had undergone many trials in his presidency, trials for which he was at least partly responsible.[120]

Hirschy repeatedly referred to his confidence that history would vindicate him and set all his efforts in proper heroic light. Human realities, of course, are always more complicated; the laurels he craved have proved elusive. But the historical record does indicate that the founders of the Central Mennonite College, Hirschy chief among them, had nonetheless accomplished much. In fourteen years, he and a cohort of visionary leaders had coaxed a conservative and recalcitrant people into agreeing to, planning for, and finally building a college. Success was not assured, given slender resources. These Mennonite leaders had still rallied support for a college that, by 1908, had employed upward of thirty faculty and hosted 300 students. Although they had not realized their grandiose visions, Hirschy had also called his colleagues to lay a foundation for an institution that would endure. At that more modest task, they had done well.[121]

In the context of 1908, however, such gains were not immediately apparent to many people. Still wandering around the conference proceedings in Wayland, Iowa, in September 1908, Hirschy envisioned a very different and much more likely outcome of all his effort. "The college at Bluffton will never be a college either," he stated to Augusta. "It is doomed to fall, if not cease to exist."[122]

CHAPTER TWO

"United Progressive Mennonites," 1909-1929

In the years of Woodrow Wilson's presidency, as a soaring, crusading progressivism reigned supreme in American national life, Noah Hirschy's little academy became a real college. It did so with a name change, a new cast of leading characters, an enlarged body of support, and a bustling, energetic air that matched the idealistic tenor of the times. Churches sent their young people off to the college and received them back—if they came back at all—as remarkably changed individuals, bearing all the hallmarks of a good progressive education. They returned home singing the songs of glee clubs, talking of literary societies and debating rebuttals, and enthused by the technicalities of football.

When confused parents asked what had happened to their progeny, college administrators replied without apology that they had absorbed something of what they called the "Bluffton Spirit." The leading lights of the revitalized college had every reason to take pride in their handiwork. In the space of a few short years they had remade many rough Mennonite farmhands into cultured Christian citizens, ready to take up their part in the larger reform efforts of the day. Their remaining task was to convince startled parents and churches of the appropriateness of the transformation.

One of the brightest and most energetic of these new leading lights was the recently departed president of Goshen College, Noah Byers. In August 1913, on the eve of assuming his new duties as academic dean of Bluffton College, he encapsulated the new spirit at an event called "Bluffton Home Coming and College Day." Clearly a gathering to rally the support of local townspeople, Byers readily admitted that he had left the helm of one flourishing college for a "subordinate position" at another. He had committed himself to the work at Bluffton, he announced, "because of the people back of it. United progressive Mennonites. These are significant words," Byers proclaimed. "The union of different sects in this great work is surely in line with the best spirit of the age, and surely we can count on high heaven to bless this movement."[1]

That fall he and a new cohort of college leaders, faculty, and equally energized students would set out to create what they determined would be the flagship Mennonite institution of higher education. In this effort they would need to secure the blessing of not just high heaven but also, perhaps more difficult to obtain, that of the Mennonite churches.

Northwestern Ohio Aristocracy

When Samuel K. Mosiman assumed the presidency of Central Mennonite College in 1909, he claimed the reins of a school many assumed to be as doomed as Hirschy had predicted. One local Mennonite asked Mosiman if he had come to bury the college. But Mosiman had no intention of digging its grave. During his forty-two years, he had already demonstrated stubborn ability to bounce back from several hard knocks.[2]

Raised a Mennonite farm boy near Trenton, Ohio, Mosiman had pecked away at schoolwork with a gradually growing enthusiasm. He completed some college courses, but a Lutheran minister told him he was too old at age twenty-five to consider further study. His own pastor, Henry J. Krehbiel, counseled differently, encouraging him to further his education and serve the church. Mosiman transferred to Wittenberg College and distinguished himself both academically and on the football field. He received his A.B. degree in 1897, then served the next six years at the Mennonite mission to the Cheyennes and Arapahos in western Oklahoma.[3]

In 1902 Mosiman solidified ties with his old pastor by marrying Krehbiel's sister Amalia. The next year the two moved to Chicago, where Samuel studied biblical languages at McCormick Theological Seminary. He proved to be an adept student, so much so that he secured the seminary's $2,000 prize for study abroad. En route to Germany, however, Amalia sickened and suddenly died, leaving the grief-stricken Mosiman to negotiate with the ship captain for the body. He buried his wife under a marble slab in Hamburg and fought off despondency by immersing himself in the study of Hebrew, Aramaic, Syriac, and Arabic. Somehow he survived and in

1907 was awarded both a B.D. degree from McCormick and a Ph.D. from Halle-Wittenburg University.[4]

On his return from Germany, Mosiman taught for a year as professor of Greek and philosophy at a small college in Lebanon, Ohio. However, as a rising Mennonite intellectual with General Conference roots, he naturally gravitated towards Bluffton. He appeared in town as early as 1905, preaching at Hirschy's Mennonite church and receiving Hirschy's assessment that he was a "scholarly" and "thinking man." Mosiman joined the faculty in 1908. As the board recognized his talent as an administrator, it appointed him acting president in 1909 and to the permanent post a year later.[5]

To students, who dubbed him "Prexy," Mosiman sometimes appeared an austere figure, mustache and goatee neatly trimmed, impeccably dressed in a swallow-tailed coat and striped trousers. Although he could burst forth with warmth and charm, the new president was shy by nature. Hirschy described him as "deficient in speech"; a former student recalled his speech as "halting." Yet he dictated letters with blinding speed and sharp accuracy, his secretary remembered later, never once stopping to redirect his thoughts.[6]

Mosiman was also capable of surprise. His best one came when he assumed the presidency. Attending the 1908 general conference meeting in Beatrice, Nebraska, Mosiman met, wooed, and suddenly announced he would marry a middle-aged, local schoolteacher four years his elder, Emilie Hamm. She arrived back in Bluffton as his bride in August 1909 and soon registered an impact of her own that would last for nearly half a century. For most of that period Emilie Mosiman was Bluffton's First Lady, in every sense of the phrase. Tall and stately, she had been born into a prominent Mennonite family in Prussia and had migrated to Nebraska with her family as a twelve-year-old. All her life her speech bore the lilt of a high German accent and her bearing the stamp of high European culture.[7]

She immediately launched a consuming crusade to spread the joys of that culture to the rustic masses in the college's student body. At numerous teas and receptions as well as through entreaties in the student newspaper, in chapel, and especially through her ubiquitous presence in Ropp dining hall, Emilie prodded the students into an embrace of good manners and refined living. The college had scarcely been reconstituted in 1913 when she spoke in chapel that October on "politeness." For decades after she issued repeated injunctions on such matters as always saying grace before meals and thank you afterward or always refraining from eating the lettuce leaf under one's cottage cheese.[8]

She and her spouse bought a fine old pillared house on Grove Street a block from the campus and opened it to students day and night. There a plate of her famous cookies was nearly always available. Emilie in her flowered hats and flowing dresses and Samuel, a bit shorter next to her in his sharp suits, sometimes held forth on the grand front porch. Donovan Smucker, who grew up across the street, remembered later that the couple constituted a living little piece of aristocracy in his small, Midwestern town. Childless and devoted to each other, for two and a half decades they poured themselves into the college. The words of Mosiman's secretary certainly applied to his wife as well. "He just lived for the college," Florence Diller later stated. "That was his life."[9]

Mosiman quickly mastered the skills of tact and church diplomacy that so notably escaped his predecessor. He moved promptly to heal the rift with the Swiss Mennonite Congregation. Wisely he refused to preach in the college chapel church, and without Hirschy's guiding presence, the little congregation soon collapsed. Most members joined the Swiss Congregation's First Mennonite Church a few blocks away. Already by June 1909 Isaiah Beeshy observed that Mosiman "seems to fit in nicely now especially in reference to the Swiss congregation. They seem to have confidence in him." He had begun to preach occasional sermons for them; in return, they had renewed their subscriptions to the college endowment fund. For nearly a century thereafter college folk such as Mosiman, Hirschler, Emilie Mosiman, J. S. Schultz, and many others would serve as prominent First Mennonite lay leaders.[10]

Fundraising was of course a major part of Mosiman's job; he heartily disliked it. He once told Lloyd Ramseyer that before meeting with a possible contributor, he often had to walk around the block a few times to steel himself for the visit. Emilie spurred him to greater self-confidence. "You be yourself, *no inferiority* complex," she instructed him, before his meeting with the heirs of the McCormick fortune. "Isn't your cause a worthy one? Can't you sell your work? Who then should?"[11]

Under such tutelage, Mosiman gradually grew successful in these endeavors. Already by March 1909 he had launched an extensive local campaign to secure a $60,000 endowment. Ultimately he and the college would do a good deal better than that. He and Emilie scraped up $900 to buy an old Model T Ford. Together they traveled hundreds of miles—Mosiman driving and Emilie navigating—up and down dusty farm lanes and in congregation after congregation to plead the college's case.[12]

By 1925 such efforts had combined with those of the board and also of the college's persuasive field man Boyd Smucker to bring in half a million dollars in the previous ten years alone. In 1910-1911, early fundraising successes enabled the college to undertake some much-needed expansion. They obtained Jonas Amstutz's estate (including what is today the central college lawn and land south of the creek where Ropp Hall sits), then negotiated with the heirs of Judge Eaton for another tract of land to the north and east, where the college would one day build Lincoln and Science (Berky) Halls.[13]

Mosiman worked with matching diligence at solidifying the academic standing of the college. He gradually expanded the junior college to the point that academy work became a minor matter and was done away with after 1914. Student numbers built at a slow but solid pace. In 1907-1908 the college had broken the 100-student barrier for the first time, then fallen back before 153 enrolled in 1910-1911. Thereafter the numbers only grew: almost 200 students by 1913, then 271 in 1915-1916. There was a small decline at the height of the war years, then student numbers leveled off in the 250-300 range throughout the 1920s, roughly evenly divided between men and women. Somewhere between a quarter and a third of the student body hailed from out of state, mostly from Indiana, Illinois, and eastern Pennsylvania. Through the 1920s about two-thirds were Mennonites.[14]

In sum, four years into his presidency, S. K. Mosiman, his bride, and his colleagues had begun to rebuild Central Mennonite into a real college. They had laid the groundwork for future success. Suddenly, in spring 1913, they were overtaken by a series of breathtaking developments and a sudden infusion of new talent. The result would be a further revitalization of the work that would render Mosiman's initial accomplishments minor by comparison.

"You can count on several of our best men"

The idea originated with Goshen's president, Noah Byers. He noticed in 1909 that Goshen was the only one of the Mennonite colleges so far offering an A.B. degree. He wrote a letter to the presidents of other Mennonite schools to inform them so, suggesting they send their graduates to Goshen to complete their degrees. In so doing, these colleges would be performing a real service, he argued, because in bringing together future Mennonite leaders the church would obtain a unity between its different and somewhat competing branches. Already Byers had begun to focus on possible gains from

Mennonite educational cooperation and to formulate nascent conceptions of Mennonite ecumenicity.[15]

Because other Mennonite school presidents were scrambling to offer their own four-year degrees, they read "cooperation" as leaving the field to Goshen. None even replied. But Byers revived the idea in November 1912. Soon he and a number of Mennonite educators—Mosiman in particular—were busily sketching out a new and alluring vision. If Mennonites could throw their scattered educational energies behind one major effort, the result could be marvelous: the Harvard of the Mennonite academic world, offering not just a Bachelor of Arts but also Bachelors of Divinity and master's degrees as well, pulling together the church's academic stars under one roof. They agreed to call Mennonite leaders from a wide circle in the church to a larger meeting later that spring.[16]

Mosiman responded with particular enthusiasm because already in February 1913 Byers had begun to suggest to him privately that the best place for this exciting vision would be Bluffton. All that spring and summer he and Mosiman exchanged letters, sometimes as often as once or twice a week, surveying the academic talent pool like two executives of a sports franchise evaluating an upcoming free-agent draft. Byers knew that Goshen's star history professor, C. Henry Smith, would make the switch, along with science professor Jonathan Kurtz. Paul Whitmer, chair of their Bible department, was likewise planning on it. Goshen's oratory teacher and expert fundraiser Boyd Smucker was "still available," Byers nudged Mosiman in July, "if you take it up with him at once."[17]

Byers shared Mosiman's confidence that Bible scholar Jacob Langenwalter could be persuaded to come from Bethel and so might the Mennonite evangelist-turned-biblical-scholar Jacob Quiring. He himself would be glad to serve under Mosiman. "Personally," he confessed, he had always done his "best work" in the "dean's duties." Altogether, Byers assured Mosiman that "you can count on several of our best men for faculty and some hearty support from progressive members in our branch. I believe the movement is timely and can be worked." Byers was right; in the end, he and Mosiman would get every professor they talked about that year except Kurtz.[18]

They also discussed less prosaic matters. Right before the new board of trustees met in August, Byers floated several phrasings of the new school's motto; he thought "truth and freedom" or "truth and life" might work. Earlier they considered a new name for the institution. The contingent at Goshen suggested "Union College," whereas Mosiman wanted to name the school "Witmarsum College" after Menno Simons' birthplace in Holland. Yet neither name could overcome longtime habit. At the very founding of Central Mennonite, local people had wanted to name the school after the town. They persisted in the practice regardless of its official name, and the writers of the *College Bulletin* likewise referred to their institution as "Bluffton College" in 1909. In the end, the new board accepted the inevitable.[19]

At two important meetings in that spring of 1913, in Warsaw, Indiana, in May and Chicago in June, a wide-ranging group of leaders from five distinct Mennonite groups ratified all these decisions. They created a new board of fifteen members, made up of three representatives from the five founding groups, namely the Mennonite Church, the GCMC, the Central Conference, the Mennonite Brethren in Christ, and the Defenseless Mennonites. Berne's J. F. Lehman, chair of CMC's old board, was named president of the new one. If the churches failed to elect their representatives, they agreed, then the board would fill any vacancies. With the Middle District Conference later agreeing to the changes, the old board and articles of incorporation of Central Mennonite College were dissolved and its property transferred to its successor school. When the new board met in August, they filed new articles and agreed to a new name and motto. The institution would officially be called "Bluffton College and Mennonite Seminary." With Byers' suggestions clearly in mind, they affixed the motto, "The Truth Makes Free," on its seal.[20]

These developments, coming with startling speed in less than a year, rocked the little world of Mennonite academia to its core. Mosiman welcomed the movement, for it made the long-term survival of his institution possible. He knew that the present constituency was too small by itself properly to sustain a college. This new situation was rife with possibility. The GCMC's Eastern District Conference began to regard Bluffton as its denominational school. The Central Conference of Illinois was just organizing itself into a coherent body, and its support could be won. One of its leaders, A. B. Rutt, was on the first board. Others, like Valentine Strubhar and Aaron Augsburger, gradually warmed to the college, and Mosiman began to cultivate a wealthy lay leader named John Ropp as a possible benefactor. By 1920 Illinois Mennonites would make up the college's largest body of out-of-state students.[21]

The new faculty promised to fit neatly into the existing aura at Bluffton. Byers, for example, had committed his life to mission work as an undergraduate at Northwestern and had obtained his master's degree at Harvard, where he had studied under philosopher William James. He was happy to escape the rising power of traditionalists in the Mennonite Church, writing rather caustically to Mosiman from Goshen in 1913 that "they want only 'sound men' here."[22]

Smith appeared cut from the same cloth. Depending on the lens through which they viewed him, for many Mennonites C. Henry Smith was undoubtedly either the most sophisticated or the most worldly Mennonite they had ever met. As a child Smith found farmwork tiresome and meaningless. He gravitated toward the life of the mind, leading to a B.A. and M.A. in history at the University of Illinois, then to a Ph.D. in 1907 from the University of Chicago, obtained while teaching at Goshen.[23]

Smith soon came to stride the streets of Bluffton as the very symbol of the sophisticated intellectual. The "C" in "C. Henry" actually stood for nothing—but was added by the young intellectual to embellish an otherwise undistinguished name. He was quite well-to-do; he wore a Phi Beta Kappa key; he traveled widely in Europe and Latin America, where he had befriended all sorts of important people. He was an habitue of opera and theater. He was an immensely popular professor and lecturer, adviser to numerous student groups, and an ardent scholar. A fanatical bibliophile, his diligence greatly enriched the manuscript collections of the historical libraries both at Goshen and Bluffton. His reputation ranged far beyond Mennonite circles: he was longtime member of the Bluffton village council, member of the Lima Lions Club, and founder and president of Citizens National Bank in Bluffton, a position he held for over twenty years. A large framed photograph of Dr. Smith still graces the bank lobby.[24]

So far this book has defined *progressive* in relation to an emerging set of Mennonites who were more accepting of outside innovations like revivals, Sunday schools, and higher education, distinguishing them from traditionalists who tended to resist change. The Mennonite intellectuals emerging at Goshen and Bluffton nearly a century ago certainly epitomized such progressivism. They had tasted much of the life of mainstream academic and American culture and had found it good. Their life's mission would be to expose their Mennonite people to these fine fruits as well.

To such progressives, Mennonite acculturation was not something to be resisted, as the conservatives held, but was instead a process to be welcomed. "The whole object of education," Smith proclaimed in a Goshen College student chapel service in 1899, "is to break up old habits of thought"; he wanted to destroy "the ruts into which we have fallen." Both his writings and speeches were peppered with disdainful references to images like "superannuated ministers" and "outworn church workers."[25]

The sophisticated Philadelphian Maxwell Kratz put the issue even less delicately in 1919, writing to another Bluffton College board member that "progressive ideas are needed more" among the Mennonites than "anywhere else." "Those of us who are in a position to do anything to help our Church and our people toward a truer realization of the fundamental liberalism of Mennonite principles," he declared, ". . . would be cowards and shirkers if we sought other spheres which might be easier and more pleasant."[26]

In the context of their day, this adoption of mainstream intellectual and cultural life meant that these scholars embraced a progressivism in a second sense as well. They also marched to the beat of the reform-oriented national progressivism that dominated American culture and politics in the first two decades of the twentieth century. Byers, for example, came to his political progressivism as a high school student, when he chanced on and then absorbed the socialist novelist Edward Bellamy's depiction of a classless utopia, *Looking Backward*.[27]

Smith made repeated and approving reference to the progressive writers and thinkers of his day, and their glowing optimism pervaded his thought. For instance, in a speech before the Women's Christian Temperance Union in Goshen in 1910, he confidently asserted that "our growing spirit of humanitarianism has driven the practice of war to its last resort." Mosiman enthused over Wilson's League of Nations and dabbled in Democratic Party politics in Ohio. He befriended the state's stalwart progressive governor (and 1920 Democratic presidential nominee) James Cox, entertaining him at the Mosiman home on Grove street and inducing him, on at least one occasion in 1913, to give a rousing oration on progressive political ideas on campus.[28]

Students readily absorbed the teaching. In 1920 they held a referendum on the Treaty of Versailles and hosted a pastor, called the "fighting parson," who delivered a stirring appeal for prohibition. In 1925 students debated whether a national child labor amendment should be ratified and voted 179-10 in favor of the nation's entrance into the World Court. In the 1920s their political preferences had already swung Republican. Ohio Senator Warren Harding won the student straw vote in the presidential election of 1920, and a crowd of 150 students and faculty motored to Marion to hear him speak.

Student straw votes in 1924 and 1928 likewise favored Republicans Coolidge and Hoover by large majorities.[29]

This Mennonite embrace of national political progressivism entailed accepting patterns of thought even farther outside the tradition. For some Mennonites, at least, it meant affirmation of American nationalism and racism. In a series of articles in 1914, for example, Smith narrated a confident description of "The Hand of God in American History" in which God appeared as the prime mover in the nation's past. Mosiman harnessed similar language in his efforts to raise funds for construction of a men's dormitory in 1921. The building, as he promised one potential contributor, would be "an incentive to the development of patriotism and as a stimulus to the study of good Government." Named Lincoln Hall, it would feature an annual lecture on President Lincoln by "some men of National standing and influence." Mosiman stated that "with our people we are doing a good work of Americanization."[30]

The college would not tolerate vicious racism. Periodically BC hosted events that lauded the African-American leader Booker T. Washington, for instance, or denounced racial segregation.[31] At the same time, college leaders chimed resonance with a national political movement whose leader Woodrow Wilson brought the racist film *Birth of a Nation* into the White House and blessed its ugly mythologizing of the Ku Klux Klan as "terribly true." In like mindset, Smith echoed the progressive call for immigration restriction. He worried about the rising birthrates of "the inferior races of Southern Europe" and stated that "if the American nation is to survive and fulfill the mission for which an all-wise providence has thus far prepared it, it must keep pure both its Anglo Saxon blood and Christian ideals." In 1913 he judged eugenics (selective race breeding) a good idea.[32]

Periodically college speakers echoed such sentiments. One chapel guest lectured in 1918, for example, on the beneficence of California's anti-alien land laws that upheld Japanese exclusion. Another the next year advocated isolating foreigners from the "pure blood of civilization."[33]

Not surprisingly, sometimes these attitudes filtered into the student body. A reporter for the student newspaper, the *Witmarsum*, used an ugly racial epithet to describe the African-Americans on the basketball team from Wilberforce University in 1915. Although the paper apologized for the word in the next issue, such words did not disappear from campus. In the 1920s there were periodic references to "nigger-babies" in the paper. Students mounted a minstrel show as an official college activity to bring themselves "into closer touch with our colored neighbors." A photo of these students in blackface appeared in the pages of the 1918 student yearbook, the *Ista*.[34]

In sum, in electing to embark on the cultural-political current of progressivism, the college would come to some strange and questionable positions. Yet its enthusiastic embrace of the national mainstream also furnished it means for a further grounding in the culture of High Ideals that Hirschy had established in its founding. "With open and willing minds we will search for truth wherever it may be found," Byers promised at the official opening of Bluffton College in the fall of 1913. They would have "no mere working for credits and degrees, no bluffs or short cuts, but thorough work of a high grade."[35]

All this dedicated work, the dean reminded students, would be pointed toward one shining purpose. "We want not mere walking encyclopedias or bookworms but men and women ready to take their place in the work of a needy world," Byers cried, "ready to serve the church and society by doing some useful work." He and his colleagues immediately set out to construct a college towards these ends.[36]

The "Bluffton Spirit" and its Fruit

On a fine fall day in September 1913, the newly arrived chemistry professor H. W. Berky set out on a nature tour of his new campus. He began at the bridge where Elm Street crosses the Riley, then proceeded south along its banks, noting species of plant and animal life for future study by his students. Making his way through the underbrush at the water's edge, Berky met a pretty little creek brimming with life. Crawdads, frogs, and small fish ruffled the water, hiding from the raccoons and herons that came to feast on them. The woods would have smelled of lush undergrowth as well as nearby human presence. On the site where Bren-Dell Hall would later stand was a cow barn. As Berky proceeded upstream he passed a hog barn and slaughterhouse just beyond the site of the future Ropp Hall; hogs slid down the banks to the Riley for water. Another 150 feet upstream, just east of the Bentley Road bridge, he came to "a great social center for that day," a hole in the creek deep enough for good swimming and fishing. It teemed with catfish, carp, and a few bass; as late as the 1930s, one of his summer school students, a minister from nearby Columbus Grove, could carry his tackle to class and catch catfish during coffee break.[37]

Berky carefully recorded the tree species he happened upon: maples, beeches, sycamores, and elms. Especially he noted several huge trees with diameters of ten or even twenty feet. Yet his descriptions were also of terrain with remarkably fewer trees than today. Beyond three small clusters of woods, the land that later became the campus had been heavily logged. Early photos show Ropp, Lincoln, and Science Halls standing starkly alone on bare hills and the banks of the Riley largely devoid of trees as well.[38]

The college today appears as a campus in the woods only because of the determined and careful work of a coterie of college naturalists who had foresight and energy to care over the years about matters like trees. The first president had the heart of a botanist and issued a firm command against cutting down any trees or picking flowers on campus. In his fundraising travels Mosiman picked up a variety of seeds, shrubs, and trees, bringing them home to campus. The later leaders of the science department, Berky and M'Della Moon, worked hard at the task as well. Perhaps the greatest share of the credit for campus reforestation should go to a genuine tree lover named Oliver Diller, who graduated from the college in the early 1930s, then pursued a Ph.D. in forestry. From his position as state forester in Wooster, Ohio, as well as chair of the board of trustees in the 1960s and 1970s, Diller for decades directed hundreds of trees to the college, often arriving in a truck to plant them himself.[39]

More expensive but more necessary for the expanding college were new buildings. By 1929 the patient fundraising of both college leaders and students had resulted in the erection of four. By December 1914 a women's dorm, a grand, three-story colonial structure with stately front pillars, had been erected on the south bank of the creek. Sixty women could be housed in what the *Witmarsum* called its "large, commodious and well-lighted" rooms, and 150 students could be fed in its basement dining hall. John and Mary Ropp of Bloomington, Illinois, had provided most of the funds, and the board was happy to give the building their name. By the time of his death in 1922, John Ropp had given upward of $200,000 to the college.[40]

Because rural parents were more concerned about a proper environment for their daughters, a men's dorm was a lower initial priority. Yet rooming conditions in town were "not conducive to developing the best College spirit" in young men either, Mosiman argued. So with the numbers of women students eclipsing those of men for the first time in 1922, a men's dorm was necessary "if Bluffton

College is not to develop into a girls' school." Through the 1922-1923 school year local workmen, students, and faculty labored at its construction site. A hundred young men moved into the new four-storied brick building, named Lincoln Hall, in January 1924.[41]

In 1915 the college constructed its second academic building, located across the road from College Hall. An energetic campaign had secured the $25,000 cost of the new Science Hall, all of it raised locally in the town and environs of Bluffton. It had a grand front stairway and terraced walkway that led down the hill to College Avenue.[42]

Student initiative and labor was central in prodding the college to provide athletic facilities. For the first fifteen years students had played their basketball games in an unheated old warehouse in town, but when it was closed to them in 1916 they took matters into their own hands. They divided themselves into two teams—the "Purples," led by music professor G. A. Lehman, and the "Whites," headed by Berky—then canvassed the town to raise the $950 for lumber. With it they laid out a wooden gymnasium fifty feet wide and 120 feet long on the Riley floodplain south of what is today Marbeck Center. They built it in a flurry of concentrated labor in the manner of an Amish barnraising. Even Dr. Mosiman was seen on the scaffolding with a hammer in his hand. Students proudly revered it as "the Barn."[43]

By the late 1940s it had become an eyesore and was unceremoniously torn down following the completion of Founders Hall in 1950. In the pre-World War II years, however, the Barn was a first-class facility. It sat 1,000 spectators, was steam-heated and electrically lit, and had dressing rooms with showers. Students and faculty leveled and landscaped the baseball and football practice fields, laid out and poured cinders for the track north of Lincoln Hall, and dug out and painstakingly maintained clay tennis courts. Properly harnessed, the "Bluffton Spirit" could work wonders.[44]

As the institution's physical environment came to look more like a real college, so too did its curriculum and personnel follow suit. The academy courses were dropped quickly after the reorganization of 1913—the Mennonite Harvard would not teach high school— along with the penmanship-type business classes. The 1915 catalog listed only two schools, the College of Liberal Arts and the Conservatory of Music, with G. A. Lehman as its dean. A year later Byers created a new department of education, in accordance with a new state requirement stipulating more professional training for teachers. Students took a fairly demanding general education regimen of courses, including ten semester hours in English language and literature, six of philosophy and education, eight in the sciences, and twelve of ancient or modern language. In 1917 the faculty specified two additional hours of physical education for undergraduates and that same year saw their first two students graduate with masters' degrees.[45]

The faculty also began to hold up high expectations for students. In 1918 they created a system of departmental honors, awarded on graduation, for students who wrote an original thesis under a major professor and demonstrated abilities through a comprehensive exam; that year an honor roll began to be published. Berky moved to infuse the entire campus with the same honor spirit. Borrowing the idea from his undergraduate years at Princeton, he proposed and the faculty adopted an honor system in which students would take exams unsupervised by professors. This tradition has lasted nearly ninety years.[46]

Even with the low salaries they could offer, Mosiman and Byers proved remarkably successful in lining up a solid nucleus of progressive and talented faculty, some of whom would construct their entire careers at Bluffton and influence student generations into the 1960s. Mosiman was especially concerned about the English department, which he considered, he told Wilbur Howe in 1922, "the most important one in Bluffton College . . . the department which challenges all the metal a man has in him." Howe hesitated to come because of the salary but succumbed to the president's entreaties; he stayed until 1939. In 1918 Mosiman had found the other half of the department, a young woman who had not yet finished her master's degree but wanted to teach in a Mennonite college and looked promising. "I shall be glad to give my best to Bluffton," Naomi Brenneman assured him. Until her retirement nearly four decades later in 1961, she did.[47]

Mosiman was likewise able to anchor the science department in several strong and committed professors who, as Brenneman did in English, came to epitomize their field for generations of students. In February 1913, as he and Byers laid plans to transform the college, Mosiman began discussions with a young Mennonite from eastern Pennsylvania who had graduated from Perkiomen Seminary and was in the process of completing his A.B. degree in the sciences at Princeton. The young Herbert Weller Berky did not ooze confidence. He was aiming for a position in a solid high school or maybe a junior college, he confessed to Mosiman in July; teaching at a place like Bluffton made him "feel as if I might possibly be attempting too much." But he agreed to come, despite misgivings, promising Mosiman that "I shall bring all the Princeton spirit I can contain and I am certain that I shall like my stay at Bluffton." He would retire in 1958, as much a part of the institution as the lagoon or Science Hall.[48]

The other half of the department was a young woman who began teaching at Bluffton in 1921 and would continue for forty years. M'Della Moon had graduated from Central Mennonite College in 1912, hoping to become a doctor, but her mentors told her this was an unrealistic course for a woman and steered her toward teaching music. Yet the sciences still drew her like a magnet. She completed her A.B. at Ohio's Miami University, studying zoology and geology while playing on the girls' championship baseball and hockey teams before Mosiman approached her about serving on the college faculty. Like Brenneman, Berky, and others, she would later complete her graduate training in periodic leaves, working hard the whole time. Moon was house mother at Lincoln through the 1940s and also dean of women. Berky coached men's sports into the 1920s. The two would together teach the sciences with an infectious enthusiasm and encourage a disproportionate number of their students to pursue graduate study.[49]

Likewise Mosiman obtained a strong professoriate for the arts. He seized on the opportunity afforded him when Goshen College closed for the 1923-1924 school year, and persuaded their organ teacher, Otto Holtkamp, to come to Bluffton. He would teach organ and theory until 1960. Pearl Bogart Mann arrived earlier, in 1910, and taught piano to BC students for forty-nine years. When G. A. Lehman left in 1926, Mosiman tapped Russell Lantz to replace him. At one point Lantz had not figured he would have much of a future. During World War I he had taken the Mennonite commitment to conscientious objection seriously. He had disobeyed military orders and been court-martialed, receiving a prison term. Pardoned after the war, he would teach vocal music and lead choral groups at the college until 1966.[50]

Already in 1911 the college had grounded itself in the visual arts by establishing an art department under Magdalena Welty. The department would be strengthened by the 1924 arrival of another professor whose vivid work would assume a life of its own. In securing the talents of John Klassen, Mosiman had stumbled across a Mennonite original. Klassen had nearly completed a Ph.D. in art at the University of Munich in 1914, but World War I suddenly engulfed Europe, and Klassen spent nine years as a C.O. in the Red Cross. He was then buffeted in the Mennonite persecutions that followed the Russian Revolution. Mosiman found him amid the Ukrainian refugees in Manitoba in 1923 and pulled political strings to obtain approval for his migration to Bluffton.[51]

Klassen taught art at the college for the next thirty-four years. A gentle, self-effacing man, he resisted many of the ways of academe. He refused to don a cap and gown for commencement ceremonies. He so disliked grading that he sometimes awarded all students the same grade. Meanwhile, in his studio in the college garage and later on the top floor of College Hall, he worked steadfastly at his skill, interweaving his art around two themes, his commitment to pacifism and warm memories of his Russian world.[52]

The number of faculty who came in the teens and twenties and stayed twenty or thirty years is astonishing. In addition to these others, Katharine Moyer came in 1928 and would work to inculcate students in the mysteries of French until 1956. Irwin Bauman graduated from Bluffton in 1923, earned a B.D. from Hartford Seminary and a European Ph.D. before settling down to teach sociology at Bluffton from 1929 to 1968. Jacob Schultz had obtained a B.A. and M.A. from the University of Minnesota and worked a as a school administrator before coming to Bluffton in 1924 to oversee teacher education; he would serve the college in various capacities well into the 1950s.[53]

Besides the College of Liberal Arts and the Music Conservatory, the college held another center of intellectual activity that would periodically shine with promise. This was the seminary. In 1920, it experienced its own little revitalization movement that mirrored that of the college in 1913. It formally separated off into its own institution, receiving the official backing of several branches of the church, and officially became known as Witmarsum Seminary. Its new board hoped for the joint participation of the largest Mennonite group, the Mennonite Church, and MC Mennonites at Bluffton like Whitmer and Byers pressed the campaign. Yet the growing power of MC conservatives ended up killing this possibility after an explosive series of church ecclesiastical battles. Thus the seminary remained primarily a GC Mennonite affair.[54]

Although the seminary was located in a converted house on the corner of College and Lawn Avenues, there were moments in the 1920s when it looked as if the seminary would finally flourish. Strengthening its faculty with the additions of people like Henry Fast and Amos E. Kreider, it attracted student numbers that ranged from fifteen to twenty, peaking at twenty-six students in 1926. The subsequent careers of the seminary alumni—pastors like A. J. Neuenschwander, G. T. Soldner and W. S. Shelly, missionaries like

Aganetha Fast and Samuel Moyer, church leaders like Fast and Kaufman—testified to its promise.

Yet further progress was hampered in the 1920s by several factors. Partly because the seminary did not want to compete with the college, it limited its church solicitation and faced continual financial uncertainty. Equally problematic were issues of its leadership. Mosiman was so concerned about the matter in 1920 that he tried to induce Maxwell Kratz to take over as college president so he could head the seminary. Kratz refused. In 1921 Whitmer finally secured the agreement of former Goshen president J. E. Hartzler to take the seminary's presidency.[55]

This proved a hazardous choice. Hartzler was an able scholar and talented teacher when he gave his full attention, but suspicions of his theological liberalism had forced him from Goshen, and similar accusations would grow in the 1920s. Moreover, Hartzler had a flamboyant personality and a relish for church combat that made him a lightning rod for conservative critics. "Hit him again and hit him still harder!!" he cried to one ally in a fight with MCs in 1920. Meanwhile, his Witmarsum colleagues complained of his "loafing on the job" and general neglect of his presidential duties. As a result, the seminary limped along and was in no shape to face the theological and financial challenges it would encounter in the 1930s.[56]

The college, meanwhile, blossomed with vitality. As they had done in Hirschy's day, the faculty and students together created a rich associational life that developed progressive character both inside and outside the classroom. One of the first faculty actions in the new college was to provide for student government, authorizing the creation of a student senate in 1913. The next year a student organization called the press club began publishing the *Witmarsum*, which slowly progressed from a monthly to bi-monthly to weekly publication and emerged as the voice of the student body. The pageantry of the May Day services, surely reflecting the idealization of European culture as articulated by Mrs. Mosiman, became a regular spring feature on the campus beginning in 1910. Boyd Smucker directed annual productions of Shakespeare plays, held outdoors every commencement season, along with regular plays by the senior and junior class. Intercollegiate debating flourished; the college even joined a regular forensics conference in 1925.[57]

The teens were the golden years of the literary societies. Students flocked to them in such numbers that they divided the old Lowell Literary Society into four separate offspring, the Athenians and Adelphians for men and Alethians and Philomatheans for women. Each was given its own room atop Science Hall and began to engage in spirited rivalry with the others.[58]

The college continued to echo with music. In the single school year of 1912-1913, for example, students were treated to visits by visits from the Metropolitan Opera Company, a renowned cellist, the Cincinnati Symphony, and a touring church choir from Chicago. The Mens' Glee Club, under direction of professors Lehman and then Lantz, became a primary vehicle for communicating the Bluffton Spirit to outsiders. In 1922 the club went on tour, venturing all the way to Mennonite churches in southern California and meeting with a warm reception nearly everywhere. At least one of their songs was an original composition. In 1915 math professor Hirschler penned some words and asked a local high school student, Louella Geiger, to compose the melody. The song became the college Alma Mater.[59]

The college made sure that the student character to which all these activities contributed would be explicitly Christian with a progressive shading. At times the planners of the annual Bible lectures spoke to denominational conservatives, bringing in the orthodox Presbyterian leader Charles Erdman, for example, in 1925. The list of Bible lecturers for other years read like a "who's who" list of progressive Christian leaders. It included the Quaker leader Rufus Jones in 1922 and social gospel advocates Kirby Page in 1927, Francis J. McConnell in 1926, and Harry F. Ward of the Methodist Federation of Social Service in 1918. In 1917 Mosiman even welcomed the fundamentalist nemesis Harry Emerson Fosdick to campus.[60]

The students dutifully turned out for such lectures but deepened their own devotional lives through their involvement in busy campus chapters of the YM and YWCAs. Established on campus in 1913, these organizations served as the focus for student Christian activity on campus through the 1950s. In the 1915-1916 school year, for example, dean of women Edith McPeak reported to Mosiman that the YWCA hosted weekly devotional meetings for the women of Ropp Hall, where "Jesus Christ becomes a real living personality to the girls." In addition, it mounted four Bible study classes, its service committee brought wildflowers to area hospitals, and its social committee organized receptions, hikes, and a Big Sisters program for the proper acclimating of new students.[61]

The Y organizations and another group, the Student Volunteer Band, dispatched gospel teams and organized prayer groups. They also served as another channel through which the college's mostly Mennonite student body could crack their isolation and absorb more currents from the outside. These were national movements that caught up thousands of students across the country, combining warm Christian devotion and missions fervor with a heady American nationalism and a progressive thrust toward reform. Bluffton YM and YWCA chapters regularly sent student leaders to national conferences at Lake Geneva, Wisconsin, and Eaglesmere, Pennsylvania. Many, like A. J. Neuenschwander, experienced a deep religious renewal. During World War I the Ys would also work to funnel pro-war sentiment onto campus.[62]

Beyond classes and these official founts of student activity, the college bustled with a student life that, in comparison with today, seems both extraordinarily confined in some respects and relatively unfettered in others. Each student's day began at 7:00 a.m. with breakfast in the Ropp dining hall. This was followed by chapel an hour later, all students filing into seats that had been assigned alphabetically and segregated by class. One did not dare to miss either chapel or class, because a certain number of absences, usually more than three, could result in expulsion from the college. Faculty led the singing, and an outside speaker or a BC professor—usually Byers or Langenwalter—orated and made announcements.[63]

A busy day of classes ensued before 6:00 p.m. dinner, to which one always appeared in semiformal dress. Again students proceeded to their assigned seats, alternating between young men and women, with each man deferring to the lady on his left before serving himself. A short evening followed, usually at the library in College Hall, before the women scurried back to Ropp to beat their 9:30 p.m. curfew. The men could stay out later, but all students were forbidden to smoke, drink, dance, play cards or pool, loaf around the barbershop downtown, or engage in any other activity that would "violate the ideals and traditions of the college." Mosiman regularly suspended or expelled students who ignored these rules, sometimes with little apology to their parents.[64]

Female students especially felt the strictures. They were required to keep their doors unlocked at all times to permit periodic surprise visits by the house mother. They had to get permission to stay out after 9:30 p.m. All dates were supposed to be accompanied by chaperons. Women wore proper dresses and kept their hair long. They could roll it up but never cut it; two women who did this were severely reprimanded in front of the assembled study body. Chapel speakers periodically reminded them of their domestic role, while the YWCA offered lectures on such topics as "Womanliness" and "Women in Dress." For their part, men were instructed to be more "gentlemanly" and show more "manliness to the weaker sex."[65]

Although such restraints comforted conservative parents back home, creative students found enough ways around them to nurture a social world that still appears remarkably boisterous and free in other respects. Young women and men found ways of getting close to each other. Certain enterprising young men quietly secured their own private keys to one of the stairwell fire escape doors at Ropp Hall, while Mosiman learned in 1925 of a dozen women who were regularly sneaking out of Ropp late at night. Students could escape to Hankish' Ice Cream Parlor on Main Street in town. There they laid down a dime for a tin-roof sundae, and daring students sometimes wound up the player piano to dance.[66]

By the mid-1920s student horizons were thrown wide open as a small number of them began to show up on campus with their own automobiles. The *Ista* noted Naomi Brenneman's appearance on campus in a new Ford coupe. By 1926 sixteen students had registered their cars in accordance with the new regulations Mosiman had drawn up. Before long he found himself extending the college's authority to regulate student conduct in establishments in downtown Lima. He requested that a local judge pull the license of a public dance hall on Dixie Highway south of Bluffton.[67]

Back on campus, the same academic climate that enhanced professors' authority in the classroom also permitted students mercilessly to lampoon them outside of it. The 1918 *Ista*, for example, presented a short play about the banning of football at the college. Its central characters—S. "Knowsaman" and a chemistry professor named "Perky"—generally bumbled around like complete idiots; the speech patterns of "Knowsaman" were punctuated with "ah" every other word.[68]

Much of the student rowdiness that occurred on campus revolved around strenuous competition between different classes. In the teens each class had its own officers, colors, professor, motto, and yell, which were so pervasive the faculty had to prohibit them during chapel services. These symbols had vanished by the 1920s but had been replaced by other traditions, especially ones concerning the initiation of first-year students, a practice that continued into the 1970s. They were made to don beanies, sometimes green, sometimes purple and white, that they were prohibited from taking off their heads until Thanksgiving. If young men were found without them, they could expect to be tossed, clothes and all, into the lagoon.[69]

At some point in the fall, students held a series of initiating events. In 1919 they began an annual tug-of-war over the Riley between freshmen and sophomores, with extra beanie time allocated

for the freshmen if they lost. First-year students met some interesting variations in 1928. The men were made to sing to the women of
Ropp, play leapfrog down the middle of Main Street, then walk
backward to the Barn, where they were paddled by sophomores.
The women were given green bands to wear around their heads as
they sang to the men of Lincoln, then taken individually to Lincoln's
attic for more jokes and humiliation.[70]

As with class initiations, students administered much of the
most severe discipline themselves. The problem that strengthened
their hand was hazing, which had begun to loom as a significant
problem with an apparent intensification of class warfare in the
early 1920s. On one dark evening in 1922, for example, four young
men abducted another from his room and lost him in the woods.
They snatched others out of their beds for a nighttime dunking in
the Riley. Another group of class fanatics gave a fellow student an
involuntary haircut one moonlit night in 1920.[71]

When in 1923 upperclassmen took three freshmen three miles
out into the countryside at midnight and left them to find their way
home, their parents strongly protested. Mosiman had to act. He
invited Irwin Bauman, the student senate president, to his office and
asked him if student government could deal with the problem. The
senate was indignant, especially so one senator named Lloyd
Ramseyer. Byers and Hirschler in particular had been contemptuous
about the prospect of student participation in campus governance,
and the response of the senate, Bauman remembered, was to "let the
Administration stew in its own problems."[72]

But Mosiman sincerely wanted their help. He finally agreed to a
student judicial body with real power—the first one included
Ramseyer and Bauman—called at various times the student tribunal, the honor committee, or citizenship committee. It soon threw
itself into matters of student discipline with gusto, investigating
possible violations and dispensing punishments it thought fit the
crime. Students who snuck off unchaperoned were confined to campus for months or prohibited from dating; those who were caught
dancing were suspended from school. Miscreants who missed
chapel and attempted to hide it saw various hours of academic credit withdrawn. Glee Club members who persisted in smoking lost
their places, as did three members of the 1925-1926 basketball team.
The tribunal remained firm on their expulsion from the squad, even
in the face of a student petition asking them to reconsider.[73]

The tribunal was especially creative in punishments it assigned
to a group who defiantly violated the rule against dating first-year

students. The men were dropped off ten miles out into the countryside one evening to walk home. Meanwhile, the tribunal applied shame to the women. They were clad in long dresses and dust caps and draped with placards reading "I like dates, don't you?" In this garb, Elizabeth Baumgartner and Madeline Bogart were placed in the front row at chapel and made to wash the blackboard and sweep the sidewalk after it, all the while handing out dates to their fellow students.[74]

Battling for Football

Nowhere was the growing student initiative and power seen more clearly than in the realm of sports, particularly in the disappearance and renewal of football. In 1912 the faculty had eased its opposition to intercollegiate games, and all sports began to maintain a full schedule. Baseball had caught up student interest from the earliest days, and by 1915, led by the brothers Ed and Hiram Kohli, began to reap success. In 1920 the squad captured the crown of the Northwestern Ohio League, besting other conference schools as Bowling Green and the Universities of Toledo and Findlay.[75]

In 1921 a green track squad clobbered a vaunted Heidelburg team, and the next year emerged victorious in the first meet on its new track. It would dominate conference meets for the next decade. With the construction of the Barn, the college's basketball teams hit full stride. By 1925 the men had taken the conference crown for three years running and had never finished lower in the standings than third.[76]

In 1923 Mosiman informed the board that he had finally secured a new, full-time athletic director, who had been "a great help in the solution of our problems. Mr. A. C. Burcky has been most energetic and active in all his duties and responsibilities." As a Bluffton student, Burcky had turned in stellar performances on the gridiron and baseball diamond. Mosiman hired him immediately on his graduation in 1922 and sent him to the University of Illinois to sit at the feet of big-time coaches.[77]

Burcky's ebullient spirit would permeate athletics at the college for a half a century. His style was rooted in zealous devotion to the standards of good sportsmanship and a roaring sense of humor that enveloped those around him. Long before his death in 1989 at the age of ninety-three, he had become a legend, not just among students—many of whom came to approach him with affection and respect bordering on worship—but in the wider circles of small college sports in the American Midwest. Many of Burcky's great golden moments would come in the college's financial nightmare of the 1930s, when he would keep its sports life alive on a shoestring and a prayer, but already by 1926 the yearbook reported that he "has been gradually winning his way into the hearts of the student body."[78]

One of his first moves would be to provide a mascot for the college. Up to that point its players had been called the "Purple and White" or the "Burckymen," but the coach knew the times required a more identifiable symbol. The official debut of the Bluffton beaver came in the 1926-1927 school year. The beaver was the ideal representative of the college's spirit, the *Ista* declared, because it had five important characteristics. It was small, indefatigable, and resourceful, and it "works with twigs, building up large things from small. Fifth, it never does things any worse than its ancestors did." The coach knew his college.[79]

Even with Burcky's talents, women's sports got off to a slower start. Once the Bluffton faculty allowed women to engage in intercollegiate games, women had a hard time finding other colleges that would. In 1917 the college fielded a basketball team of six women who played a total of four games, losing twice to the high school but beating Ohio Northern twice by healthy margins. The 1921 *Ista* recorded more success; the women had lined up six games with the likes of Toledo, Wilmington, Cedarville, and Antioch and won three, due in great part to the efforts of their coach, Marie Ringelman, who had, the yearbook said, provided "a lot of contagious pep and enthusiastic interest."[80]

After a three-game season in 1926, however, the faculty canceled women's intercollegiate basketball. Their practices could only be scheduled in times when the men's team didn't need the gym, and they had a hard time attracting players or opposing teams. Women would have to content themselves with intramural contests until 1968.[81]

The college would have a harder time getting rid of football, which had continued from the early days of John Sloan, sometimes under questionable auspices. At Bluffton and other colleges, enthusiasts stretched standards of eligibility pretty thin. The usual practice was to find a hot prospect, enroll him in a class like penmanship, and insert him in the game. Sometimes not even these niceties were employed. After Central Mennonite and Heidelberg battled to a 0-0 tie in 1911, it came as no surprise to learn that the former school fielded a player who had never attended a class, and the latter's coach had played the entire game. Even these tricks did not seem to help Central Mennonite's fortunes much. In the fall of 1912 it lost four successive games to Wittenberg, Heidelberg, Wilberforce, and Ohio Northern by the respective scores of 46-0, 81-0, 27-0, and 46-0. The next year the board of trustees abruptly banned football.[82]

The board's action came not because the college team was being regularly annihilated, but because many Mennonite churches, particularly those in Illinois, judged it barbaric and worldly; they were especially upset about a game that had been played on Thanksgiving Day. Students were outraged at football's cancellation and brought it back themselves. Calling themselves the "Bluffton Collegians" and operating out of the local sanatorium, they fielded a team on their own for the next three years. In 1916, however, the board also put a stop to this, thereby triggering an ongoing campaign of student agitation.[83]

As an old Wittenberg tailback, the president was sympathetic, but he could also read the sentiment in the churches. He held a meeting with students in the chapel in September 1916 to explain church politics. The students reluctantly agreed on their own to cancel the games they had arranged for that fall but kept the pressure on in other ways. Mosiman was flooded with hundreds of signatures on petitions from students and alumni demanding football's return. At one point they even staged a mock funeral to lament its death, actually burying a football in the ground near College Hall. Sympathetic allies like Kratz wrote fellow board members to uphold the sport as morally uplifting.[84]

Slowly the pressure began to work. At a 1920 meeting the board narrowly voted 7-6 to continue the ban, but after student unhappiness rose to a fever pitch the next spring, it agreed to allow one trial game for the fall of 1921. Enthusiasts quickly pulled a team together from the ninety-some men on the student body and practiced hard for two months to play the University of Toledo, the only school that would grant them a game. Amid snow flurries on Armistice Day, Bluffton smashed Toledo by a score of 22-0, with the *Ista* judging their left tackle, Lloyd Ramseyer, "the outstanding star of the game."[85]

The game delighted fans but left many in the churches fuming. One minister warned that the Illinois Mennonites had drawn the line on the question and that Mosiman would need to take some action to "pacify them." The board reversed itself and reinstituted the ban. For his part Mosiman directed his young coach Burcky to offer soccer as football's substitute. Burcky grumbled that the move "puts a crimp in the athletic program," but he dutifully began to try to interest students in the game. They would have none of it and kept up a drumbeat of criticism before the board finally relented and approved a four-game football season for fall 1923.[86]

Football was there to stay, to the immense delight of students and alumni like Ramseyer, who wrote to Mosiman in 1926 to urge that he establish a six-game schedule for that fall. "Such things," he promised, "certainly will make for a bigger and better Bluffton." Of course there was a price to pay with the churches. Influential Central Conference leader Valentine Strubhar resigned from the board in protest. The chair of the conference's mission board informed Mosiman that he would no longer support the college.[87]

They understood what had occurred. When forced to choose, Mosiman would sometimes move to placate students and alumni over other elements in the college's constituency. As a result, a gulf gradually began to appear between the college and many conservatives in the churches. When national progressivism mounted its greatest crusade and called on its followers to fall in behind the effort, this distance would grow wider.

Progressive Mennonites and the Great War

In 1917, as the United States embarked on holy war against Germany, it correspondingly launched into a vicious and high-strung offensive against anyone it deemed as dissenting from that effort at home. The postmaster general routinely banned from the mails any publication he judged threatening, and the Congress passed laws such as the Sedition Act, which made unlawful any statement that might be construed as disloyal. A huge war propaganda machine kicked into high gear, and a spirit of intolerance came to take on a life of its own among the American people. Labor leaders and war dissenters were lynched and beaten, the teaching of German was outlawed from the schools, and vigilante mobs of "patriots" whipped up a frenzy of fear and suspicion against anyone seen as detracting from "one hundred percent Americanism."[88]

As members of a Germanic-derived religious group whose theology rooted them in pacifism, Mennonites appeared doubly suspect. Especially in the Mennonite communities in the Great Plains, where their Germanic culture had held on the longest, individual Mennonites who had attempted to remain faithful to their tradition by refusing to buy war bonds, for instance, were tarred and feathered or smeared with yellow paint. In Ohio and West Virginia, Mennonite leaders were tried and convicted under the Sedition Act.

Two Mennonite churches, in Michigan and Oklahoma, were burned to the ground, as was the administration building at the Mennonite college in Tabor, Kansas.[89]

Altogether this new climate left Mennonite leaders confused about how to advise their young men. Some counseled draftees to take up the position of noncombatant service, in which they would join the army but be assigned to a noncombat position like a medic or hospital orderly. Mennonites giving this advice tended to be more acculturated church leaders east of the Mississippi, particularly those with the General Conference church. This group included a number of Mennonite college professors and administrative leaders. Other church elders told the young men in the camps to retain Mennonite teaching and stay firm in rejection of all military service and orders. Draftees who accepted this advice found themselves paying a high price. Isolated in army camps, they were raked raw with brooms, beaten with fists, and court-martialed to lengthy prison terms when they disobeyed directives from officers.[90]

A Mennonite college would need to proceed carefully in this incendiary environment. Because of its declining sense of German ethnicity, Bluffton's peril was not as great as that of Mennonites on the Great Plains. The *College Record* had not been printed bilingually since 1910; in 1917 Hirschy observed from afar with regret that the college "has largely lost its German life and tone."[91]

Still, students and faculty knew they were being watched carefully. One day in April 1918, for example, two secret service agents arrived at the college from Washington, demanding to know why it had "appointed a censor on patriotic news in the *Witmarsum*." With Mosiman out of town, Smith, Byers, and business manager John Thierstein managed to assuage their concerns and afterward called the paper's student editors in for "very sane advice. The whole matter gave Dean Byers a text for the very best sermon I have heard in a long time," Langenwalter told the president.[92]

Byers was right to be nervous, for the specter of patriotic violence hovered not far away. The next month one of the newspapers in nearby Lima began to encourage mob violence against the pacifists at Bluffton. Vigilantes bypassed the college in June but visited three Mennonite churches in the county, placing American flags over their entrances and leaving notes warning congregants that their removal would be taken as confirmation of their rumored "un-American sentiment."[93]

The college was able largely to escape danger, however, because it mostly rang with war enthusiasm. To be sure, Mosiman defended traditional Mennonite pacifist principles where he thought they applied. He was proud that by May 1917, at least, no Bluffton College man, Mennonite or not, had enlisted for regular combatant service, and two had enlisted with the Friends' war reconstruction unit heading for Belgium. The president affirmed that the college would not give academic credit for army service. Because he feared growing militarism at home, he refused to consider the college's acceptance of a Students Army Training Corps unit on campus, despite evidence that it might attract students.[94]

On the other hand, believing his nation's effort "the cause of righteousness and justice," Mosiman threw himself and the college he led behind the war in every way short of contributing to actual combat, and sometimes did not draw the line at that. Immediately upon the president's declaration of war, he wrote his old friend Governor Cox to offer his services and those of the college. "Believing it to be the duty of each citizen to bear his part of the burden of war and his share of the perils . . . assign me to any work that I can do," Mosiman begged. While suggesting in particular YMCA or Red Cross work, he also assured the governor that the Bluffton's student body stood ready "to do all that lies in their power to alleviate the sufferings of our soldiers and to inspire our young men in camp with high ideals, or to do any other work that they can do and to which you may call them."[95]

No, he proclaimed, "we are not slackers"; like others in the struggle, the college would join the president's fight for a "Christianized democracy" with only a slight and qualified nod to Mennonite peace principles. To an ex-student in an Iowa army camp, Mosiman expressed his own particular pride that "the American boys have been giving a good account of themselves" in battle in France. Because he believed in some variant of his church as a peace church, Mosiman thought the best course for Mennonite young men was noncombatant work, and he repeatedly told them so. "I have consistently urged our boys to be patriotic, and have told them that every citizen owed his country some service in war-time," he assured an assistant secretary of war in Washington.[96]

Mosiman had little patience with Mennonite draftees who did not fully cooperate with officers. He damned as "wicked and foolish" advice from MC and Amish leaders encouraging noncooperation with military orders. He was proud that no Bluffton man had done this, urging them not to engage in "hairsplitting" over military commandments to don "the uniform and such things." He likewise extended this kind of advice to a wholesale embrace of noncombatant activities at home, enthusiastically backing the extensive Red Cross activities and war bond sales at the college.[97]

Properly inculcated into the progressive spirit that now waged total war, students naturally followed where their president led. In 1919 Mosiman estimated that about 150 BC students had served in the military in some capacity, along with five faculty members. Several technically served as YMCA personnel, but Mosiman could not have been under any illusions that this agency remained very separate from the regular army. Former athletic director Oliver Kratz bragged that they were drilled by army officers on board their ship to France and were considered as noncommissioned army officers. May 1919 found Byers in France, teaching psychology at an American Expeditionary Force university there. When the army had assumed the contract from the YMCA, Byers was happy to switch employers. Music Conservatory dean G. A. Lehman was enrolled in the regular army, along with Berky, who served his country doing munitions research for the chemical research section of the Picatimny Arsenal in Dover, New Jersey.[98]

Students greeted such activities with acclaim, particularly celebrating the exploits of Pvt. Edwin Stauffer, who had won the Croix de Guerre for gallantry in battle and returned home in March 1919 to a heroes' welcome from fellow students. Throughout the war the *Witmarsum* breathlessly reported on the adventures of former student Pvt. Clayton Welty, following his boot camp experiences in the United States, through his embarkation for France, his wounding in the battle of Belleau Wood, and the combat death of his brother, to his slow convalescence in a Brooklyn hospital, still coughing up blood and the bits of uniform that German bullets had smashed into his lungs.[99]

For its part the 1918 *Ista* published a drawing of Woodrow Wilson with his slogan that "the world must be made safe for democracy," printed underneath. The *Ista* proclaimed, "let us pray for peace but we cannot have peace until the 'God of War' is overcome. . . . We are firm believers in pacifism but to attain immortality we must sacrifice." The women of Ropp Hall organized a Red Cross unit in spring 1917 and soon plunged into making thousands of bandages. That fall the students and faculty together raised over $1,000 towards the YMCA's war fund, and the Glee Club periodically traveled down to Chillicothe, Ohio, to entertain the troops training at Camp Sherman. The Science Club found a lecture by the inventor of the "torpedo with ears" stimulating, and enjoyed hearing from Berky on his work making explosives.[100]

Throughout the 1920s, Mosiman and his faculty colleagues continued to solidify the college's peace commitments without blinking an eye. In 1922 they hosted a major conference of the three historic peace churches. Mosiman's baccalaureate address that spring contained a ringing condemnation of warfare. The college joined the larger 1926 movement on college campuses protesting compulsory military training proposals, turning over the chapel pulpit to peace speakers, and distributing pamphlets against this prospect. Mosiman even paid two visits to Henry Ford in an unsuccessful attempt to induce the automobile magnate to endow a professorship of peace for the college.[101]

Nevertheless, the college's extensive pro-war activity, coming as it did on top of its acceptance of football and what appeared to be discomfiting directions in its theology, signaled a growing distance between the institution and many in the churches. The Bluffton Spirit enraptured the students and alumni, but its fruits had begun to taste strange and somewhat bitter to many conservative Mennonites.

During the war, for example, the important Central Conference leader Aaron Augsburger had sent Mosiman a series of sharp letters accusing the college of betraying Mennonite peace principles. In the years that followed, he directed more comments to the president that indicated his growing sense of alienation from the college. "We hear much about the Bluffton Spirit, but as yet we have not learned what that spirit is," he told Mosiman somewhat acidly. What he and his fellow ministers did see they did not like: an "aping after others for popularity's sake," as exhibited in the college's sponsoring of intercollegiate athletics and its traveling Glee Club, "which has not met general approval" in its appearances in conference churches.[102]

Augsburger was even more concerned about the seemingly liberal direction of the college's theology and was unmollified by Mosiman's patient dismissals of his concerns. "A majority of us feel that the administration and faculty is simply trying to play horse with us, and are just going ahead with their own notion and ideals," he told Mosiman bluntly. "We may be block-heads out here in Ill[inois]., but there is one thing which we refuse and that is, to be softsoaped and swallowed whole."[103]

The tone and length of Mosiman's responses to such charges indicated that he had been stung rather deeply. As the unhappiness represented by words such as Augsburgers' echoed in the churches, the progressives at Bluffton began to realize they faced an escalating crisis.

"The citadel of religious modernism"

Already by the early 1920s this kind of unhappiness had cost the college the support of two of the denominations that had contributed in a small but important way to its revitalization in 1913. In 1920 the Mennonite Brethren in Christ members on the board could no longer contain their dissatisfaction and withdrew their official support from the college. So did the Defenseless Mennonites, at about the same time.[104]

Although these withdrawals were regrettable, the college could get by without support from these two small denominations. More dangerous were forces that promised to alienate segments of the Eastern District, Middle District, and Central Conference. Some Mennonites from many different groups had begun to resonate with the larger movement of Christian Fundamentalism rampaging through American Protestantism in these years. People so inclined began to identify Bluffton as a major headwater of currents of theological liberalism threatening the church. They were helped toward such a conclusion by determined individuals in circles both close to and farther from Bluffton. Although issues of theology riveted this intertwined coalition of Mennonite fundamentalists, a closer examination of their perspective and motivation reveals that part of their agenda in attacks on the college, as had been the case in the struggle between Hirschy and Baer decades before, had much to do with issues of power and personal rivalry.

Suspicions of BC tolerance for dangerous theology had arisen at the school's founding and percolated for the next two decades. The MC denominational organ, the *Gospel Herald*, for example, drew the church's attention to the fact that the college's 1910 commencement speaker held to such conceptions. And in 1913 L. J. Lehman feared that the revitalized institution was so "tainted with 'higher criticism'" that the Mennonite Brethren in Christ could not participate. Quite early in his presidency Mosiman honed his skills at damage control, and the board helped as well, appointing a separate subcommittee in 1921 to investigate and then clear biology professor A. S. Stauffer of suspected openness to teaching evolution.[105]

By that time, as Augsburger's alarm indicated, such rumors had grown more widespread and powerful. In 1920 a sympathetic ally summarized them for Mosiman: the college was prejudiced against the Bible Institutes, discriminated against Moody students who had transferred to the college, opposed revivals, and quietly approved of higher criticism of the Bible.[106]

Such rumors were fed by local sources, especially William Gottschall, pastor of nearby Ebenezer Mennonite Church, where critics of the college nursed grudges going back to Hirschy's day. He was joined by allies such as Berne's pastor, P. R. Schroeder, and fundamentalist ministers in Kansas like P. H. Richert and Peter Unruh, all determined to break the power of the church progressives—centered at Bluffton—and return their denomination to what they defined as the fundamentals of the faith. "There is a tremendous current in the general conference at the present time to prevent any progressive movement of any kind," Mosiman observed in 1919.[107]

In 1922 Mosiman received a questionnaire from this group demanding that Bluffton and Bethel Colleges answer specific doctrinal questions regarding the virgin birth and perfection of Christ, the inerrancy of Scripture, and the like. In his seven-page reply, Mosiman left no doubt that his college held to a conservative evangelical theology but would not buckle under to what was clearly a fundamentalist litmus test. He complained at length that such a questionnaire could not fairly examine an educational institution. Any attempt to do so would have "demoralizing tendencies." No, he did not subject faculty candidates to a rigid statement of faith, Mosiman confessed, preferring to examine the whole of their spiritual, moral, and intellectual character. He quibbled with his questioners' phrasing of doctrinal principles and refused to answer their questions with the fundamentalist formulations they sought.[108]

The president knew what the game was. He simply refused to play. "Personally, I am not interested nor do I feel under obligation to join in the fight of the Baptists and the Presbyterians with the 'Fundamental Party. . . ,'" Mosiman declared. "I feel that the Colleges have a mission to guard the faith delivered to the Saints from being mixed up with all sorts of modern fads." In terms of both their theology and their personal style, the president and his colleagues could not comfortably don the fundamentalist mindset.[109]

Moreover, even if so inclined, Mosiman knew, the student body and alumni could not be easily shifted to a different track. The Bluffton Spirit had assumed a momentum and trajectory of its own. Even the minor concessions the president made to his denomination's conservatives had provoked an outcry from the opposite quarter. "I am constantly warned that I am giving in to conservatism and that I am guiding the College on to the rocks," Mosiman complained to one fundamentalist detractor.[110]

Mosiman and others at the college were inclined simply to put their heads down and try to ride out the storm. Yet there were movements afoot in the wider Mennonite world that would render this an increasingly difficult course to pursue. They emanated from the Mennonite Church, particularly the MC intellectual centers of Goshen, Indiana, and Scottdale, Pennsylvania.

The rising power of MC fundamentalists that had driven Byers, Smith, and others from Goshen in 1913 had intensified in the later teens and subjected that college to further turmoil. In the five years that followed John Hartzler's resignation from Goshen's presidency in 1918 for similar reasons, the conservative old guard that dominated the MC hierarchy installed four successive presidents in an effort to cleanse the college of its progressivism. Finally they closed Goshen College for the 1923-1924 school year to purge it of such influences, creating an institutional and psychic shock that would reverberate in MC circles for years.[111]

What looked like catastrophe at Goshen, however, glittered with opportunity to people at Bluffton. Mosiman began to receive letters inquiring about a "proposed union" of Bluffton and Goshen, rumors he did not entirely dispel. Quietly he expected upward of seventy-five Goshen students to transfer to Bluffton, along with several more faculty and much of its funding base. After Goshen's alumni association recommended Bluffton to its students, seminary president Hartzler nearly panted with excitement. Here suddenly loomed the chance to fulfill the great vision of the union movement of 1913 by finally welcoming significant numbers of MC Mennonites to the all-Mennonite college at Bluffton. "This is the year that we win or lose with the Old church," he trumpeted to MDC ministers. ". . . No one 'rock the boat.' . . . We may have their students and their money for Bluffton. . . . This is our day, let us not miss it."[112]

Hence it was no coincidence that about the same time, MC publicist and historian John Horsch dramatically escalated his all-out assault on Mennonite modernists and focused his blasts in the direction of Bluffton. Back in 1913, when Bluffton rose to prominence partly at Goshen's expense, Horsch had suddenly begun decrying Bluffton's theological soundness, but Byers had ignored him. His and Smith's "standing in our branch is fully as good as that of Bro. Horsch who has never been given any responsible work," Byers reported to Mosiman. "Our people don't take him seriously." Mosiman was assured enough by Byers' assessment that he even tried to recruit Horsch's daughter Elizabeth to study at Bluffton in 1917.[113]

Horsch must have shaken his head in disbelief, for he had long ago emerged as the leading Mennonite fundamentalist of his age. In

1924, when Bluffton's peril to his denominational school seemed greatest, Horsch focused on the modernist threat to his own people. He published an explosive polemic, *The Mennonite Church and Modernism*, which blasted the dangerous liberalism he saw running rampant among Mennonites. His critique was devastating not for its accuracy and truthfulness—areas in which Horsch's polemics often fell short—but because he identified enemies and named names. In this account, many of these "traitors" were Bluffton names— Hartzler, Byers, and Smith prominent among them. Horsch had no doubt as to where the enemy's headquarters were located. In 1925 he refused to share a podium with Smith at a historical meeting because of Smith's place of employment, informing his son-in-law, Harold Bender, that "Bluffton is the citadel of religious modernism among the Mennonites of America."[114]

Scarcely had such charges finished reverberating in the churches before Horsch attacked again. He rattled off another pamphlet, "Is the Mennonite Church Free from Modernism," which he mailed at his expense to every Mennonite minister in the country. This move in itself seriously escalated the fight, taking the destructive charges beyond MC circles and directly into Bluffton's constituency.[115]

To inflict maximum damage on Bluffton, Horsch forged warm and productive connections with GC fundamentalists like Gottschall and Schroeder that were to become mutually beneficial relationships. Gottschall forwarded to Horsch information he had received from informants he had planted in Bluffton college and seminary Bible classes. Horsch reciprocated by serving as wise counselor to their anti-Bluffton efforts, mailing Schroeder a dozen copies of his pamphlets for distribution in the Berne church. In 1929 the Berne deacons collected a variety of antimodernist and anti-Bluffton material, including Mosiman's response to the 1922 questionnaire as well as Gottschall's, Schroeder's, and Horsch's sermons and letters. Then they published the charges in another pamphlet, "Evidence of Modernism at Bluffton College," and endeavored to spread it widely throughout the church.[116]

What made these attacks so maddening to the Bluffton leaders they targeted was that if they were progressives, they were not modernists. In fact, nearly all held to a theology that by any standard remained quite conservative. The theology of someone like Samuel Mosiman, for example, took its bearings from a warm Christian piety that spoke to generations of students.

Mosiman and others produced a central pronouncement of such sentiments, a sort of an early mission statement, that spoke amply to their Christian commitments. "Bluffton College, as a Christian institution," they insisted, "stands for. . . . a practical Christian religion, expressed in terms of life and service rather than in dogma." Perhaps laying themselves open to fundamentalist attack was just the price that Mosiman and others quietly realized the college would have to pay for retaining a faith that was tolerant and inquisitive but solidly Christian nonetheless. Their institution, they proclaimed, "endeavors, through intimate association with scholarly, Christian teachers, to lead students into conscious daily fellowship with the risen Christ."[117]

The only BC faculty member who smelled even faintly of the "modernism" that Horsch, Schroeder, and others obsessed over was Jacob Quiring. Oddly enough, he was a scholar who had arrived on the faculty as a veritable hero of rural conservatives across the church. Quiring had been born in the Mennonite settlements in East Russia and ordained as a traveling "Home Missionary" for all Russian Mennonites at age twenty-two. In 1905 he came to the United States and performed the same function for the Home Mission Board of the GCMC, spending the next two years hosting revival meetings and preaching in dozens and dozens of Mennonite communities across North America.[118]

After he threw himself into academic life with the same vigor at Moody Bible Institute, McCormick Theological Seminary, and then the University of Chicago, Quiring appeared a rising church star. Mosiman pursued him for the faculty as early as 1915. After spending seven years at the University of Berlin researching semitic languages, Quiring finally arrived at Bluffton in 1921 to rave reviews. Mosiman thought him "one of the best preachers . . . I have ever heard"; students flocked to the chapel talks of a man Edmund Kaufman recalled as a "very kind, helpful and saintly person."[119]

One student remembered him as a stout, sandy-haired man with a twinkle in his eye who was capable both of energetic "showmanship" in class—deliberately provoking students with "sweeping generalizations and also daring prognostications of biblical interpretations"—and also of markedly liberal political views. These stemmed from his sympathy for the peasants and anger at their Mennonite oppressors in old Russia.[120]

Except for this latter characteristic, Quiring sounded like a prescription for a conservative champion amid the "modernists" at Bluffton. Yet he had one more hugely important defect: in his years of advanced study in Germany, Quiring had learned much from the newest methods of the historical study of the Bible. He naïvely assumed he could share these insights with his students, never imagining the uproar such efforts could create in the church. By the middle 1920s he had become the chief target of the college's fundamentalist critics, to the great dismay of Mosiman, who personally treasured the absent-minded Russian scholar.[121]

Altogether the fundamentalist offensive left the president besieged and bewildered; his usual talents at damage control proved fruitless. Privately the onslaughts left him sputtering with anger. "I am at a loss to know where all the bunk comes from," he wrote a supporter, "unless it be from a diseased, debased, or perverted imagination." Most of the time Mosiman refused even to answer the charges. He realized that "as soon as you have answered one new ones will be 'trumped-up' and one could waste all his time answering false charges."[122]

When Mosiman spoke to the critics, he usually regretted it. Attempting to placate dissidents at Berne, for example, in 1929 he wrote a long letter laying out "in very simple and plain language . . . what we believe and teach." The Berne deacons immediately submitted Mosiman's statement to national leaders of the fundamentalist movement, who excoriated it as doctrinally insufficient. Princeton's Greshem Machen judged it "bad throughout." William Bell Riley of the Christian Fundamentals Association denounced it as "sadly deficient," adding, "if this is your college, I am sorry."[123]

Certainly people like Gottschall and Horsch were sincerely convinced that dangerous theological currents were eating away at the spiritual fabric of their church and mobilized their energies to stop them. At the same time, there were other agendas at work, for, as Mosiman's words of defense and the analyses of later historians have illustrated, the "modernism" against which these men fought was largely illusory.[124] Searching for other explanations of Mennonite fundamentalism, some historians have posited that the movement was a necessary byproduct of the Mennonite denominationalizing process. Others have suggested it was one way in which Mennonites worked at cultural transitions accompanying their increased acculturation and trials during World War I.[125]

These accounts partly persuade, but viewing the phenomenon through the lens of church progressives at Bluffton yields another explanation. These fights were certainly about theology and may have indicated cultural tensions, but they were also about personal rivalries and power. Applied to institutional politics, such power rivalries transferred damage to a larger frame. Seen in the context of Mennonite higher education, Horsch's deliberate smears—no other word quite works—had a theological agenda but may have also been fueled by a desire in MC circles to damage or eliminate a rival institution. Goshen's Bender identified in 1926 "the strong competition Bluffton is giving us in Ohio," worrying that Bluffton aimed to become "an all-Mennonite college which would ultimately take the place of Goshen College." He performed a cheerleading role as his father-in-law moved repeatedly to the attack.[126]

Yet because of the two very different denominational contexts in which these two colleges operated, each responded quite differently to the rising fundamentalist campaigns in their respective groups. Partly because of the more hierarchical structure of the MC church, Goshen had to give much quarter to its fundamentalists in very direct ways. Faculty were saddled with dress codes many disliked. A conservative church board of education hired and dismissed presidents on a nearly annual basis and even closed the school for a year.

In the strongly congregational polity of the General Conference Mennonite Church, fundamentalists in this denomination could only grasp for power in slippery coalitions of different congregations. As a result, Bluffton never had to buckle under to the power of any bishops or larger church boards. Mosiman and his colleagues needed the partnership and funding of these individual congregations and periodically found it politic to attempt to satisfy the conservatives. They slapped a half-hearted ban on football; they rationalized their enthusiasm for World War I; they told the Glee Club to exercise more care; they patiently explained to their fundamentalist critics that, periodic appearances to the contrary, they still did believe in and teach a conservative Jesus at Bluffton College. While Mosiman and his colleagues were unfairly maligned, they had also given their critics much material to work with.

But Bluffton leaders clung to their Christian progressivism without apology. This course saved them from making the kinds of steep concessions to the conservatives demanded at Goshen. However, it would exact its own toll, a very costly institutional price, as the college would discover in the 1930s.

"A Clarion Call for Christian Education!"

In the meantime, throughout the 1920s the college continued to blossom with vitality and potential. As the school year opened in September 1921, Mosiman found the dining hall filled to a greater capacity than ever before, with thirteen tables of ten people at a table and every chair taken. Ropp Hall itself was "crowded to overflowing." Student numbers hovered around 250 throughout the decade and broke the 300 mark with the transfer of many Goshen students in 1923-1924. In April 1929, the entire campus tingled to the electrifying news that the wealthy Pennsylvania apple grower C. H. Musselman had followed his exploratory visit to the campus with a pledge of $100,000 to build a new library.[127]

If frustrations led Mosiman to overlook accomplishments, others reminded him. "Your constituency seems far on in the line of mental evolution as compared with the audiences I had to face in a similar capacity twenty years ago," Hirschy wrote with admiration from Berea in 1923. "You are really achieving wonders. I congratulate you."[128]

One ambition remained for the college to achieve, a final elusive goal that increasingly appeared within reach in the bright days of the 1920s. This was the legitimizing seal of academic accreditation. Without it, BC graduates had experienced periodic difficulty obtaining admission to some graduate programs or securing high school teaching posts. In 1922 the college had been on the verge of obtaining approval from the high priest of accrediting agencies, the North Central Association (NCA), when the agency had suddenly upped its financial ante, raising the required endowment of its member schools from $200,000 to $500,000. Mosiman learned from an NCA official that Bluffton qualified for admission in every way except for its low endowment. The matter suddenly took on increased importance in 1929 when Ohio's Department of Education stipulated that it would not honor teacher certifications of graduates from schools not approved by the NCA or the Ohio College Association.[129]

The needs of the hour led Mosiman to overcome his distaste for high pressure solicitation and sign a contract with a professional fundraising agency, the Hancher Organization. Under its guidance, BC swung into a full-bore fundraising effort, "A Clarion Call for Christian Education!" Aimed at churches, students, alumni, and people of means anywhere within a wider radius of the college, the campaign used a variety of emotional appeals. Its dominant and ever-resounding rationale for funds was increasing the endowment so as to render Bluffton "An Accredited A-Grade College." "To Qualify It Must Have By September 1, 1930 An Invested and Paying Endowment Fund of $550.000," screamed the BC *Bulletin*.[130]

"Have you pledged? Can you increase? Even double?" read a Mosiman letter entitled "A Last Call to Splendid Triumph." "Please pray! Then sign for your largest and mail at once." The old example of Wadsworth, then a half century in the past, was dusted off and reemployed. "Will Bluffton fail as Wadsworth failed?" asked the *Bulletin*.[131]

By late summer 1929, Mosiman was convinced enough of the campaign's success to issue a "Victory Number" in the *Bulletin*. Reporting on money pledged, he announced grandly though prematurely that it "gives us more than the amount demanded for standardization. It means that Bluffton degrees are at par, that its alumni have the advantage of accredited diplomas. . . . Bluffton has proven itself." On paper it indeed appeared as if all associated with the college had cause for celebration. Once all the pledges rolled in, as they surely would in the flush times of the twenties, the college would receive the seal of approval of the accrediting agencies, the first of all the Mennonite colleges to do so.[132]

With Goshen still recuperating from its year of closure and Bethel locked in a severe battle of its own with GC fundamentalists, perhaps the hour loomed for the fulfillment of the dreams of Bluffton's union movement in 1913. This group of "United Progressive Mennonites" had remained true to their principles and now seemingly stood ready to reap the fruits of their labor. As the "Victory Number" proclaimed, "A new day is dawning . . . thoughts of leadership among Mennonites, like smoldering embers, through sacrifice have been fanned into a glowing flame of hope." The future seemed as bright and golden as the leaves dropping from the trees around College Hall.[133]

Only two nagging problems threatened to undermine the shimmering vision. One was the small technicality of pledges versus actual dollars. Of the $550,000 goal, a total of $466,644 had been promised; the college had on hand a little over $5,000 in actual, unrestricted money.[134] The other problem was the date. As college officials set out in rural Ohio to transform the pledges into cash, far away in New York City the stock market began to flash small signals of distress. It was the fall of 1929.

CHAPTER THREE

"One Can Hardly Imagine Bluffton College without Some Unrest," 1930-1938

For Bluffton College, the spring and fall of 1930 appeared a bright period strangely disconnected from the darker backdrop of national economic collapse. That March, Mosiman and Byers appeared before a meeting of the North Central Association in Chicago and reported that the college's chances for admission seemed solid. On April 5, exciting word came of the college's official admittance to the smaller of the two accrediting agencies, the Ohio College Association. May saw a bustle of preparation as the campus community readied the new Musselman Library. Staff and students together conducted a huge "moving day," transferring the books by hand from College Hall and across the lawn to the shelves in the elegant Georgian colonial structure.[1]

In June BC hosted a memorable commencement week. Myers Cooper, Ohio governor, gave the main address, and the college awarded an honorary doctorate to one of its founders, H. J. Krehbiel. Library dedication was the highlight. The A Cappella Choir sang several numbers, Charles Musselman presented the key to Dr. Mosiman, and librarian Edna Hanley gave a short address. Altogether, reported the *Witmarsum*, the event signified "the realization of many hopes and aims." Even as the Great Depression and Midwest drought deepened, the next September saw a surprising 12 percent increase in students, to a total of 287.[2]

From the standpoint of the college's administration and faculty, however, these sunny events were scattered bright moments in a dark time. They were followed by year after year of unrelenting dis-

97

aster. The college would face continued attacks from fundamentalist critics. Combined with financial devastation, the attacks would kill the seminary and threaten the college's life. BC would stare bankruptcy in the face and watch as power over its future was transferred to creditors. Its attempt at NCA accreditation would be rudely and contemptuously rejected. Its faculty, riven by bitter factional infighting, would be plunged into nasty and personal dispute.

Altogether, the 1930s would bring Bluffton College enough crisis and discord to chew up two successive presidents, bringing one to a forced and angry resignation and a second to the edge of emotional collapse. The only consolation for those connected with the college would be found in its increasingly assertive and committed student body. In their hands the college's initial vision would be both preserved and deepened.

"A faction in our General Conference is moving heaven and earth to brand you a damned heretic"

Throughout the last years of his presidency, S. K. Mosiman penned more patient replies to the college's theological critics, who continued to find them unsatisfactory. The charges, Mosiman stated flatly to one minister, "are absolutely without foundation." Nonetheless, retorted another pastor, his students returned from the college "with modernism in their breast and cause much disturbance." By the early 1930s, the cumulative weight of a decade of such charges had begun to threaten the life of church institutions. Shortly after receiving the condemnation of the BC statement of faith by national fundamentalist leaders, the Berne deacons ceased communicating with Mosiman and "somewhat hesitantly," argues Paul Toews, formally charged the college with teaching modernism. This happened at the 1929 GCMC general conference meeting. The conference responded by passing a declaration of loyalty to "the faith of our fathers" and appointing a committee to investigate the charges and report to the next meeting.[3]

Suddenly here was a threat that could go beyond the unhappiness of individual congregations and result in official denominational damage to the college. As Mosiman's old ally Silas Grubb wrote him, "a faction in our General Conference is moving heaven and earth to brand you a damned heretic (I use the word ecclesiastically and not profanely)."[4]

Even in better financial times, Witmarsum Seminary had never found solid financial footing, and it could not survive this tough new climate. In the later 1920s Hartzler's annual statements to the board sounded increasingly pessimistic notes about inadequate facilities, poor faculty salaries, and a scanty financial base. In August 1930, the seminary's alumni association reported on a plummeting student morale and frankly admitted that "the Seminary is very sick."[5]

When Hartzler resigned the presidency in summer 1930 and student prospects for the fall declined still farther, the seminary board reluctantly agreed to close the seminary for no more than five years. It would never reopen, in Bluffton at least, and Mosiman recognized why. "One dare not overlook the systematic efforts that have been made to discredit Bluffton as a suitable place . . . for the seminary," he wrote a sympathetic pastor in 1931. Goshen historian and ideological leader Harold Bender avidly hoped that Bluffton's "seminary will die a natural death." If so, conservative attacks had certainly hastened it.[6]

Given this ominous development, it became all the more imperative to Mosiman to do something about the chief target of the fundamentalist anger at the college. Bible professor Jacob Quiring, with his open teaching of the new, critical approaches to biblical scholarship learned in graduate school, continued to spark sharp words from many pastors. Mosiman's assurances that the Russian scholar was a "Christian mystic" satisfied no one. At least one suspicious minister, student Arthur Friesen remembered, stopped in Friesen's dorm room one evening to elicit more damaging information about Quiring. Even supportive pastors like Wilmer Shelly wrote to complain of the professor's regular classroom denials of the virgin birth of Christ. They warned that if this continued, allied ministers could no longer defend the college against its many detractors.[7]

Mosiman wrote Quiring a tough letter. "As I have been telling you for weeks and months past," Mosiman reminded his friend, such criticism has "been coming to me more and more." He pled with Quiring to "leave the critical rot and rubbish to others" and do the "large work" rather than accepting "the way of crucifixion, as you so often suggest." If Quiring would avoid such teaching, Mosiman declared, it would make him "the happiest man on earth." If he refused, the president made clear, he would have to leave the college.[8]

As with so much else in the 1930s, events moved to their conclusion in a manner that brought Mosiman little happiness. Quiring would not silence the teaching his conscience directed him to deliver. The result was inevitable. One Saturday morning in late spring 1930, several carloads of ministers pulled up to the college to demand the Bible professor's dismissal. All that morning and long afternoon Mosiman wrangled with the pastors but could not dissuade them. They even refused to allow Quiring to appear in person to defend himself. By that evening the president had acceded: Quiring would have to go.[9]

Mosiman found the decision so difficult that he refused to deliver his annual baccalaureate sermon. As his own public protest, he asked Quiring to give it in his place. Quiring based his remarks on the Protestant reformer Martin Luther's famous words before the Diet of Worms, crying out, "Here I stand; I cannot do otherwise. So help me God!" The Bluffton dean and future Bethel president Edmund G. Kaufman found the address to be "masterful and moving," and delivered entirely without bitterness.[10]

That summer Quiring packed his goods and family and moved to New York City to finish a Columbia University doctorate in Semitics. But he did not have long. One day in 1933, as he stood at a New York street corner waiting for the light to change, a hit-and-run automobile threw him into the center of the street. His promising academic career wrecked, the brilliant professor lived nine more years as an invalid before his death in 1942. His wife Dorothy brought his body back to Bluffton. There former faculty colleagues spoke at his funeral at First Mennonite Church, then carried him west of town to Maple Grove Cemetery. They laid him to rest there a stone's throw from the grave of his old friend Sam Mosiman. Jacob Quiring had traveled half a world since his boyhood in Russia and still, with all that had happened to him here, Bluffton spoke of home.[11]

Meanwhile in 1933, after a one-year postponement because of the Depression, delegates gathered at the GCMC's next general conference meeting. Passions had eased somewhat, as had the threat to the college from the larger denomination, partly because the Depression seemed to have sobered combative spirits. In any case, the investigative committee delivered an inconclusive report that generally condemned the teaching of modernism without any mention of a particular context. A markedly more conciliatory atmosphere prevailed.[12]

In like spirit, the college faculty and board soon delivered statements of faith and assurances that would soothe conservative fears of liberalism. In June 1934 the board "emphatically" approved "a strong emphasis of evangelical Christianity and the development of vital Christian life in every student," aims which the faculty faith statement passed that October reaffirmed. The statement once again explicitly expressed Bluffton faculty devotion to such conservative theological doctrines as the deity of Christ, his virgin birth and atoning death, the divine inspiration of Scripture, and the Holy Spirit as "the divine presence in human life."[13]

In contrast to the earlier statement by Mosiman, this one was ratified by the entire faculty. "The more liberal-minded" in the college constituency, noted incoming associate president Arthur Rosenberger, "expressed a slight surprise that we would go quite as far as an expression of faith as our statement goes." However, after he explained church politics to them, they understood "the necessity of being pretty explicit." Under the pressures of economic collapse and church sanction, even the liberal wing in the college's constituency grasped the need to satisfy the conservatives.[14]

Altogether the dispute reverberated in church politics for several decades. While there is no denying its fundamentally theological character, one must again be careful to recognize as well the personal nature of the conflict. It was due, J. H. Langenwalter asserted, to "selfishness and jealousy and not unbelief," and also to "men who bear an old grudge."[15]

Late in life, Berne's old crusading fundamentalist pastor, P. R. Schroeder, testified likewise. In December 1939, as he lay in a hospital bed in South Dakota, he scrawled what would be his last letter to S. K. Mosiman, a fellow cancer patient whose prognosis was more gloomy than his own. It was a remarkable letter of apology. Schroeder had apologized before, in the heat of church battles in the 1920s, but this time the apology was private, personal, and achingly sincere. "The Lord in his great mercy has dealt kindly with me, despite my unkind and unfair dealings with you," the pastor confessed. "While I felt that I was acting in a righteous cause, that gave me no justification to use unbrotherly means of attack. I hope you can forgive me."[16]

No doubt Mosiman, who at that point had about six weeks to live, was moved. Perhaps he found grace to forgive. But the damage had been done. The Berne church was no longer the firm financial prop of the college it had been for decades; although individual members there continued their support, its deacons would no longer allow the college officially to canvas the congregation. And the loss of church confidence resulting from the modernism charges ranged way beyond Berne. In 1934, sometime college field man and business manager Harold Alderfer informed Mosiman of what he probably already knew: about half the ministers in the Eastern, Middle, and Central Districts of the GC church—nearly all the college's constituent churches—were "placing question marks in back of Bluffton College." Even in normal times this would have been a severe blow. In light of the other financial calamities visited by the Depression, it spelled unmitigated disaster.[17]

"We must save the college in God's name"

From the fall of 1929 until the nation's entrance into the Second World War at the end of 1941, the American economic system largely collapsed. Millions suffered from hunger and want; thousands stalked the streets of cities all across the country desperate for work; searing heat combined with wind and severe drought in the Midwest to produce huge dust storms that deposited soil from the nation's heartland onto ships a hundred miles at sea. Like all the country's institutions, colleges suffered. When parents lost their jobs, college tuitions for children became unaffordable. Those who did graduate often accepted menial jobs as box boys and elevator operators and considered themselves lucky to be working. Even tiny Bluffton distributed relief supplies, welcomed the construction of a football stadium as well as a hospital by the Works Progress Administration, and experienced something of the public disorder of the era when gangster John Dillinger and his men robbed C. Henry Smith's bank on Main Street in 1933.[18]

The new economic and emotional climate permeated the college. They lived in "one of the most bewildering hours in the history of the world," Mosiman told 1931 graduates, and "fear of another kind is creeping in." In a 1933 publication for the alumni, he boldly called for complete accreditation; a new music hall, dining hall, and gym; and a million dollars added to the endowment fund.[19]

This was only public posturing; the more realistic goal became survival. In 1929 the college had celebrated completion of a huge fundraising campaign that had purportedly raised a half-million dollars. But that money had merely been promised; with the crash, most pledges vanished into thin air. The college found itself quickly and deeply in debt. Already by June 1931, the board committed the administration to "a policy of vigorous retrenchment . . . wherever possible" to reduce debt that seemed to grow by the day. In July 1932, the board noted that the college had received a grand total of $1,300 for the previous month and was forced to pay half salaries to faculty and issue notes for the rest. Creditors received even less. Describing his everyday duties as college business manager in 1933, S. F. Pannabecker jotted to his brother that at 11:00 every morning "the mail is in by then and I go over the many letters calling our attention to overdue accounts etc."[20]

Old friends could help little. Wayland, Iowa, minister Elmer Basinger, for example, whose affection for the college had begun with his tutelage by Noah Hirschy, wanted to respond to the college's latest "urgent appeal." But with the liquidation of the major local bank, he told Mosiman, he had been unpaid by his church for a month. Another supporter managed to send ten dollars from his flour mill in Geary, Oklahoma, even though the local bank had crashed, tying up their available cash and costing his daughter her life savings.[21]

College fundraisers engaged in a nearly impossible task. As capable as he was, and even with a wealth of goodwill built up from two decades of church travels, field man Boyd Smucker often found himself unable to raise enough to cover his own salary. Donovan Smucker later remembered his father sometimes returning from fundraising trips with just several dozen eggs. Even so, other than Mosiman, Smucker was the best person for the job. Then in 1936 he suddenly died after a short bout with cancer.[22]

Subsequent fundraisers, like Grover Soldner, leaned hard on college supporters who had promised funds in the 1929 campaign, promises then considered legally binding. People paid when they could; as late as 1950, pledges were still trickling in. But the college was prepared to engage in other desperate and hard-edged measures with pledgers who were less forthcoming. BC sold at least some pledges as promissory notes, leaving some (former) supporters of the college to face legal threats from collections agencies. This created small pockets of ill will that would last decades.[23]

As incoming funds dried up, the college discovered that regional banking failures substantially escalated its difficulty in making bond payments. As early as 1915, to help finance its expansion, BC had authorized bond sales. It did so again two years later and yet again in 1926. Some bonds had been paid off in the 1920s, but many others had not. In the early 1930s they began to fall due. By October 1931, fifty banks had failed in northwest Ohio, seven of them in the immediate vicinity of Bluffton. Two of these were depositories of the college. Not only did these failures destroy an early plan Mosiman had hashed out to refinance the college's debt, but local banks holding college notes called in those notes for payment.[24]

Worse, outstanding bonds with an interest totaling $10,000 fell due. This emptied the treasury at the beginning of the academic year, leaving salaries and other debts unpaid. College administrators were similarly strapped in meeting other bonds that came due with depressing regularity in the early 1930s. In the end there was only one option: the college defaulted on its bonds. In fall 1933, Mosiman issued a general letter to all college bondholders, informing them that BC could not meet the interest nor principal on bond obligations falling due October 15.[25]

The announcement occasioned a barrage of letters, some heartbreaking, from concerned parents desperate for money to buy clothes for their children or facing the cutoff of credit at the local grocer's. One came from Chicago, pleading for payment "as I am in great need, not working and being very sick." Other letters bristled with officious threats from lawyers. To all creditors Mosiman could only respond with varying degrees of sorrow that the college could not yet pay and would meet its obligations as soon as it could.[26]

With possibilities of a governmental loan vanishing, Mosiman turned to a new refinancing plan. It consisted of a small group of "underwriters," among them J. E. Hartzler, as well as Smith and the financial weight of his bank. They came together in August 1934 to purchase some bonds at forty cents on the dollar. Some bondholders took this option grudgingly and some even happily (in an era when the alternative may have been getting nothing). Others, however, remained adamant in demanding the full amount. The danger such creditors posed to the college became increasingly clear. As Rosenberger delicately explained to one substantial bondholder, "the college must either liquidate" or recognize that "its existence without liquidation is dependent on the generosity of its creditors." For they faced a debt that by 1935 amounted to a staggering quarter-million dollars (over $3 million in 1999 dollars).[27]

To help meet this crisis, Mosiman and later Rosenberger assembled an uncommonly strong board of trustees. Some, like Alvin C. Ramseyer, Oliver F. Gilliom, Jerry Sauder, and J. S. Slabaugh, would serve the college in this capacity for decades. To represent the Eastern District Conference, Bethlehem, Pennsylvania, industrialist W. H. Mohr came in 1932. The Berne banker Elmer Baumgartner became a trustee in 1934, beginning a chain of Baumgartners on the board that (with son Howard and grandson David) would last nearly unbroken to the present.[28]

There were also notable losses. In 1932 the college mourned the passing of its last founding board member, the redoubtable Berne businessman J. F. Lehman, who had helped guide the affairs of the college for thirty-four years, twelve as board president. Incoming trustees quickly understood both BC perils and the magnitude of the recovery task. As Baumgartner stated to Mosiman in 1935, "we must save the college in God's name."[29]

Various emergency plans of the early 1930s had stipulated cutting back expenses to the bone, but this by itself was inadequate. By October 1937, the college creditors had agreed by 90-percent majorities to what the *Bulletin* announced, relief fairly screaming from its pages, as "Financial Reorganization Completed." Under the deal, creditors agreed to a lower percentage of the amount owed them. Bondholders agreed to a due date a decade hence and a lower rate of interest. All terms depended on payment of at least some of the pledges from the 1929 campaign. The old pledges would settle the old debts, the argument went, affording the college an "opportunity to build new. A new day is therefore possible."[30]

Nevertheless, as the 1938 school year began, the college was only barely afloat financially. Even making this minimal progress had subjected it to tremendous strains and tensions.

Old Faculty and New Trials

Somehow amid the financial crises, the faculty continued their work. They further developed the curriculum and welcomed important new additions who would place their own indelible stamp on academic and student life.

The curriculum underwent much tinkering. With Byers on sabbatical in 1930-1931, Acting Dean Edmund Kaufman directed a process of curricular revision, reducing fourteen college departments to five divisions. This was partly to please the NCA. Bringing all divisions under the Liberal Arts College eliminated the separate school of music; at the same time the college offered a Bachelors of School Music degree. In 1934, administrators and faculty created a department of economics and business, separate from sociology.[31]

Due to growing student demand for academic areas with more explicit vocational value, by 1937 the college had added a complete four-year course in business as well as several pre-courses in engineering, agriculture, medicine, and law. Likewise, to meet new mandates from the state of Ohio, it had begun a separate training program for elementary school teachers.[32]

The faculty nudged students toward heightened academic seriousness by requiring seniors to pass a series of written and oral comprehensive exams before graduating. At the same time they fostered "well-rounded" students by requiring ten and later twelve "activity credits" for graduation as well. This had the effect of giving academic credit for student involvement in physical training and extracurricular esthetic, social-civic, and religious activities as well as clubs and the like.[33]

The 1930s saw more development of several departments through the arrival of several key faculty members. The department referred to as Home Economics had been established in 1914 and prospered under the guidance of Elizabeth Boehr from 1916 until her resignation in 1936. To replace her, Rosenberger secured a loyal BC alumnus who would further root the college in a consciousness of Christian service and provide a model of a superbly capable professional woman to generations of female students.[34]

Edna Ramseyer came from a deeply devoted BC family: her father A. C. Ramseyer served on the board 1927-1948, and her seven siblings all attended the college. She herself had already left a strong mark on campus affairs as "Most Popular Woman" and as a leading member of the class of 1932. Even during the humiliations of freshman initiation in 1928 she had distinguished herself with a fair rendition of the popular dance the "Charleston," and the 1932 *Ista* dutifully recorded her involvement in a long list of student activities. Accepting Rosenberger's offer to teach Home Ec and serve as dean of women was surely not a difficult decision for her; as she wrote the president, "if I can help Bluffton College in any way it is my duty."[35]

More difficult was finding a new Bible professor, a need opened by the 1936 resignation of Quiring's replacement, Irvin Detweiler. President Rosenberger wooed Eastern District Conference minister Ernest Bohn for the job. He would have been perfect: a progressive thinker and stalwart pacifist but also evangelical enough to satisfy church conservatives. "There are some men in the conference whom you and I cannot fully please," Rosenberger wrote him, "but this we can do and that is to take the 'wind out of their sails' so to speak." Bohn agreed that after seventeen years of fundamentalist attacks, the post was "the most critical position on the faculty, not even excluding the president," but he turned down the offer for the time being. Rosenberger could not risk hiring a liberal Bible scholar who might trigger more modernism charges, so he appointed A. C. Schultz, a conservative Defenseless Mennonite pastor completing a University of Chicago doctorate.[36]

Bluffton hired few new professors in the 1930s, however, because the college had every incentive to reduce rather than to increase faculty numbers, which hovered around fifteen through the decade. In 1933 the faculty agreed to accept students' tuition fees as payment of their salaries; any new faculty additions would thereby reduce the amount each received. These were supremely difficult financial times for college faculty and staff. At different points throughout the thirties they agreed to accept half or two-thirds of salaries that—ranging between $800 to $1,000 annually—had been barely adequate to begin with. Since faculty were on nine-month contracts and faced declining opportunities for summer school teaching, many received no summer income.[37]

Peoples' lives showed the toll: one faculty member gave up his life insurance; another seriously considered accepting government relief; another could not obtain medical treatment for a sick child. They survived, as did other Americans, on the edge of financial ruin. Faculty pushed credit limits with grocers on Main Street. H. W. Berky's daughter Esther later remembered that faculty families were allowed to pick up fallen fruit at the college orchard. Many cultivated large gardens on the hillside below. They cut expenses to the bone. The Berky and Klassen families could not afford cars; H. W. Berky never obtained a driver's license. Surveying faculty needs for the board in 1935, J. S. Schultz testified that "there are very few if any for whom their salaries have paid for the bare necessities of life over the last four years."[38]

Nor could Bluffton's faculty and staff find much solace in other developments, for they faced a series of blows. One was the complete and swift rejection of NCA accreditation, a goal they had been working toward for a decade. Nobody should have been surprised. The officials sent by NCA to inspect the college in 1931 quickly saw through the clever smoke-and-mirrors of Mosiman's budget numbers. They recommended that, for financial reasons alone, accreditation be denied. But surely nobody expected the cavalier and sarcastic tone in which Drs. Johnston and Gardner, the NCA inspectors, delivered this rejection.

They had no use for Mennonites, "a small and weak church" devoted to "sectarian narrowness." They admitted to bias against small "so-called colleges," which were "extravagant of resources and wasteful of student abilities." Specifically, the two visitors found the gym's equipment "very meager" and the lab facilities "on the whole poorly developed, as is frequently the case in small colleges dominated by religious interests." Inspecting the physical structures, they noted the exposed wiring in the Barn, poor lighting in most places, and the "constant disturbance" created by music practice in two nonmusic buildings, Lincoln and Science Halls. They dismissed beloved old College Hall as a "fire trap."[39]

The experts reserved their harshest words for faculty and administration. The faculty, they opined, "has not shown the spontaneity, initiative, imagination and drive which are necessary . . . for the intellectual development of youth." The board of trustees appeared to them "an acquiescent body." In their judgment, "the President dreams dreams and if his plans seem fantastic . . . and his conduct of business characterized by child-like simplicity, it is because the President is not fully aware and his constituency not sufficiently interested in what higher education really means."[40]

"A Storm of Protest Here"

Amid desperate and self-sacrificing efforts to save the college, one can only imagine the manner in which Mosiman and his faculty received such words. The report stung so deeply that the college would not make another serious attempt at NCA accreditation for over two decades, and only then after years of carefully balanced budgets and intense self-preparation.

In the meantime, in the 1930s, this rejection served as the harbinger of other hurts, some quite personal in nature. Mosiman's own faculty seethed with discord, much of it originating in a public and damaging affair his own dean apparently conducted with a woman half his age. In Mosiman's personal papers lies a letter from him to the librarian Edna Hanley, probably never mailed, detailing seventeen separate instances involving her and Byers. By January 1932, the campus buzzed with rumors of improper conduct between the two: they were seen kissing in public; they were found behind locked doors or caught in embarrassing positions behind doors they had assumed locked.[41]

Mosiman was stopped on the street in Cincinnati and asked about the affair by a businessman associated with the college. Board members wrote him about it, and individual faculty members complained that "we can stand the sacrifice of salary, but we can no longer stand the hurt that comes from scandal." No doubt the whole affair was immensely distasteful to Mosiman; doubly so, perhaps, because his wife was close to Hanley. But he had to do something, for the affair came at the very moment the college was getting attacked as the bastion of liberalism.[42]

The president resolved the manner in a way that reveals much about issues of gender and power in Mennonite institutions seventy years ago. In May 1932, the board gave Hanley a leave of absence for the following year, a move that became as permanent as intended when she accepted a position at Agnes Scott College in Georgia. Byers received nothing but public embarrassment, perhaps a private reprimand from Mosiman, and a painful separation from Hanley (which would last until 1950 when, with Byers widowed and seventy-six years old, the pair married).[43]

The inequality of discipline was apparent to many. To faculty spouse Sylvia Pannabecker, for instance, "it never seemed right to ask the girl to leave and not the man"—and left much room for more trouble. Byers' continued employment in the face of his disgrace (he relinquished the deanship in 1934 to J. S. Schultz but continued teaching) polarized the faculty. The original Goshen transfers and other MC Mennonites like Detweiler rallied to Byers' defense, Pannabecker wrote in 1933. "The rest" grouped behind Mosiman and especially behind Byers' principal combatant, science professor Berky, who had initially informed the president of Byers' misbehavior, then further invited the dean's wrath by attempting to have him dismissed. The dispute simmered through the mid-1930s, so openly that one alum writing about other matters to Rosenberger in 1935 could simply refer to the "Byers-Burcky Feud" (though identifying the wrong Berky). Both sides dug in. The major casualty of the fight became the college's old leader, the sad and solitary figure of Samuel Mosiman.[44]

By 1935, many people had begun to suspect that the president's financial mismanagement had worsened if not caused the disaster. Among the suspicious ones was German professor Dr. Peter Epp, a capable scholar and Russian Mennonite refugee whose services Mosiman had secured in 1925. His gratitude and the college's need for Ph.D.'s amid the endowment campaign of 1929 had induced him to turn down an excellent position elsewhere, but soon his relationship with Mosiman had soured. Through laborious and painstaking efforts on his own he assembled an explanation of the college's financial crisis. Somehow he went around or above Mosiman to report to the board for fifteen minutes in January 1934.[45]

The portrait he offered was potentially devastating. According to Epp, the president had wasted and otherwise misspent all the monies raised for the endowment in the 1920s, including nearly $90,000 raised in the 1929 campaign. Plenty of faculty had realized this, the professor charged, but Mosiman had let them know that if they objected they were free to leave and would forfeit back salaries. Epp noted later that the board's reception to his report had been "decidedly hostile." Afterward Smith "attacked me vehemently" for his seeming ingratitude. From Epp's new position at Ohio State University, he filed a lawsuit for his back wages that sputtered for years.[46]

However well Mosiman contained Epp's charges, the entire episode certainly would have helped the efforts of Byers' faculty faction, who had been aiming at Mosiman's removal since at least 1933. Whispers grew of Mosiman's "unwise spending," which escalated into "mis-spending" and then, most unfairly, to "misappropriation of funds." Events quickly moved to their natural and painful conclusion, though the institution put on a sunny face.[47]

At the end of chapel services one Tuesday morning in February 1935, students learned of what the student newspaper called a "startling declaration." At the board meeting the previous week, the president had announced his "retirement," effective immediately. He had been succeeded by Associate President Rosenberger. *Witmarsum* editor Donovan Smucker hoped that Mosiman "may continue to cast his Christian influence and distinctive leadership on our beloved Alma Mater." In April the board designated him "President Emeritus," and the college pushed on. But it was window dressing; behind the scenes, events percolated at full boil.[48]

Mosiman knew, as he told the faculty, that he had been replaced because of the clamor "of certain faculty members that a change was demanded . . . without any defense on my part." Too late for him, the board finally took action to curb the conflict, appointing a subcommittee to investigate "certain damaging reports circulating concerning certain faculty members." Mosiman assumed a public grace, pleading for faculty and alumni to give full support to the new president. Privately, however, he was furious. He had planned on retiring soon anyway, he penned his brother, "but it finally came in a way that was not pleasant, a la Mennonite of the cruder sort." With his resignation announcement he pledged to his loyal faculty supporters that "I will not go out with a besmirched character." Over a year later, still smarting, he fumed to Alderfer that "I resent from the bottom of my heart the calumnies maliciously spread."[49]

Of course word of the faculty coup soon filtered out to constituents. Many of them responded with angry letters and telegrams denouncing the seemingly shabby treatment meted out to "the only 'Prexy' we recognize." The Alumni Association president sent a mass mailing urging alumni to express themselves. One alumni member of the board resigned in dissent. A collection of Cleveland alumni telegrammed that news of the forced resignation and their "reverence for him who is Bluffton College in our hearts has aroused a storm of protest here."[50]

It remains a testimony to Mosiman's character that he looked past his hurt and invested the years he had left into the cause that had consumed his adult life. President or not, he would do his best to pull the college out of the desperate financial straits for which he felt, he confessed privately, responsibility and some guilt. In the end, only the acquiescence of the college's creditors saved it from going under, and this goodwill was largely maintained by the intervention of the former president, who visited each claimant personally and persuaded most to sign onto the 1937 accord. Once they did and the college future was secured, Mosiman could finally retire—on an annuity from the college for his estate that he felt hard-pressed to live on—and try to enjoy the years he had left. But they were few.[51]

Mosiman underwent surgery for cancer in summer 1938, soon realized it was incurable, and quietly passed away in January 1940. His people buried him on a snow-blanketed knoll in Maple Grove Cemetery that afforded a clear view of the college a quarter-mile to the east. Emilie lived more than a dozen more years as the stately old grand dame of the college before her body finally gave out, at age ninety in 1953, and she was laid to rest beside her spouse.[52]

At the commencement celebrations of 1939, Mosiman consented to accept an honorary doctorate from the college as an official statement of its gratitude. The real testimonies, however, were seen in the generations of students whose lives the couple had shaped for three decades. One was Winfield Fretz, who later articulated something of what that influence meant to him as a student. One cold rainy night in December he found dorm conversations stale, his mind unwilling to study, his spirits low. A friend suddenly announced, "let's go over to Prexy's." The two dropped into the Mosiman home unannounced. They were met with a gracious reception, warm conversation, and a plate of Emilie's cookies. They returned to Lincoln feeling much better and settled down to their books. The incident remained "a fixed memory," he wrote later, "of a repeated experience during my student days." Given what Samuel and Emilie Mosiman had done with their lives, the reminiscence would have been as fitting an epitaph as they could have asked for.[53]

In 1935, however, the mourning lay still ahead. More immediately the college greeted its first new president since 1909. As a graduate of the class of 1921 and the first alumnus to be president, Arthur Rosenberger appeared the perfect candidate to pull the college upward. He had turned in a star performance as a student, serving in leadership positions that included senior class president, student senate president, *Wilmarsum* editor, and captain of the debate team. Mosiman informed Rosenberger's pastor that the lad "stands head and shoulders above everybody. We hope he will be an intellectual giant." After college he received a B.D. from Witmarsum Seminary, then pastored churches in Ohio and especially Pennsylvania, where he gained the confidence of Eastern District Conference conservatives. Already by 1928 Mosiman identified him as "one of the men I have felt like grooming to become my successor." That process began in earnest when Rosenberger arrived in Bluffton in the fall 1934 as associate president.[54]

The new chief executive moved quickly to douse the fires of faculty discord. At the next board meeting Rosenberger presented a declaration of "Policy and Principles Governing the Bluffton College Faculty." The ten items stipulated, among other matters, that "each faculty member shall lend his fullest cooperation to administrative officers," "each faculty member should have a willingness to forgive," and each "must refrain from speaking about other faculty members in any unfavorable terms." He then convinced all professors to sign the document as a condition of their future employment at the college. The board's subcommittee charged with investigating the faculty feuds called on "certain faculty members concerned in this investigation" to appear before it (a moment doubtless uncomfortable for someone like Byers).[55]

In the ensuing months, Rosenberger's soft-spoken, conciliatory personal style seemed to bring real healing. Slowly the combative atmosphere dissipated. Thanks in part to the dedicated labor of his predecessor, the college's grim financial skies slowly brightened as well. With the acceptance by the college's creditors of the financial deal of 1937 and contributions slowly picking up, the president could happily report that the institution "is fundamentally in better shape than it has been for a long time."[56]

"I am convinced that the Soul of Bluffton College can be brought back"

The previous eight years had been difficult, Mosiman told his supporters at the moment of his resignation, so much so that "it seems to me sometimes that the spirit and soul of Bluffton College has been well nigh crushed." Yet the resigning president said he was "convinced that the Soul of Bluffton College can be brought back."[57] What kept that spirit alive, both transforming and preserving it for a reawakening in better days, was an energetic, assertive, vibrant student body.

The depression hit students as hard as it struck everyone else. In the banking crisis, on the eve of President Franklin Roosevelt's inaugural, the bookstore refused credit to students, though the junior class allowed students to pay for tickets to their play with IOU's. The NCA inspectors criticized the business office for advancing students credit on their bills. Business manager Pannabecker admitted, "I have to get after them and insist that something be done about their account," but he knew that "it's hard for some of them to pay."[58]

Eventually federal funds became available from New Deal agencies, and students readily applied for them. In 1935 seventeen students secured campus jobs through the National Youth Administration. Under the direction of Ropp Hall matron Louisa Yoder, students canned thousands of quarts of produce raised at the college farm for their later consumption in the dining hall.[59]

The composition of the student body changed only subtly from a decade before. Enrollments dropped drastically after peaking at 371 in the spring of 1930, hitting a low of 185 in April 1936 before stabilizing in the range of 210-240 students throughout the rest of the 1930s. Enrollments were about equally divided between men and women, though late in the decade men began to gain a majority by 20-30 students. With the Depression making it more difficult to go farther from home, the overwhelming majority of students came from Ohio.[60]

Early in the 1929-1930 academic year, the college surveyed the occupations of students' parents, rendering it possible for the first time to gain a glimpse of student social class origins. The great majority of students (76) were from farms. The next biggest categories of student parents were businessmen (15) and ministers (11). In terms of religious orientation, just under 50 percent of students were Mennonite, representing significant losses from 1920s levels. In 1933 Byers blamed the declining Mennonite percentage on the Depression rather than modernism charges. Meanwhile, the college prepared to make adjustments. Because a small but increasing number of Catholic students began to object to religious classes taught under Mennonite auspices, the faculty agreed to excuse them from biblical literature class and substitute courses in philosophy or sociology.[61]

Student social life appeared much the same as in earlier decades, but there were adjustments to Depression realities. "Senior Sneaks," for example, were toned down. In this tradition, begun in 1921, the senior class secretly planned a single day when the entire group would arise early one morning and vanish from campus with no one, especially juniors (whose job it was to foil the plan), catching on. Usually they went to a big city, Detroit or Cleveland, and enjoyed restaurants, plays, and the like. The senior class of 1932 bowed to financial constraints and managed to sneak away successfully for a day of picnicking along the nearby Ottawa River.[62]

The economic downturn did little to lessen the intensity of student initiations or discipline. First-year students continued to wear beanies until their homecoming tug-of-war with the sophomores, and if they lost, until Thanksgiving. In 1936 they were assigned another hurdle, an extensive test on college history and traditions. New students in fall 1932 endured the sophomores making off with their shoes, putting salt and pepper in their pillowcases and beds, then later abducting their mattresses altogether.[63]

Discipline remained strict. Rules included an 8:00 p.m. weekday curfew (10:30 p.m. on weekends) for all women except seniors, demanded that chaperons accompany all couples, and required that students sign out for any trips off campus at night. The student tribunal (or honor court) reinforced such strictures with energy and dedication. One student found guilty of "entertaining two ladies" in his room for a half hour late one Sunday evening found himself suspended for a semester. In 1935 the tribunal briefly considered, then firmly rejected, student appeals to lift the prohibition against dancing and to make chapel attendance voluntary. (These changes were still three decades away). At the same time, the tribunal had a difficult time resolving whether students should be prohibited from keeping guns in their rooms. They finally decided, in the manner of the old West, that students should be required to check their revolvers in the Lincoln Hall lobby.[64]

Increased student access to cars created additional discipline problems but also new possibilities for student interaction. Each student had to obtain a permit for his or her own car, signed by the president himself, and agree to strict rules against "pleasure driving or associating in automobiles with persons of the opposite sex" unless with explicit permission from the dean of women. Yet the rule left a large loophole—permitting "short trips around town on legitimate business"—and students exploited it. The college brought in a dean from an Illinois college to warn students against necking, but the 1930 *Ista* selected one couple as "Mr. and Miss Automobile Necker" of the year.[65]

Student extracurricular activities proceeded apace. The faculty approved a drama club, and annual productions of Shakespeare continued under the direction of new speech professor Paul Stauffer. Fifty years later, Harry Yoder remembered the performance of one classmate, Tim Shenk, as "something that lives on in our memory forever." Intercollegiate debating sparkled with intensity; the 1936 team was anchored in the skilled argumentation of Ralph Locher, Hiram Hilty, and Donovan Smucker.[66]

College musical activities likewise flourished. The A Cappella Choir managed some extensive bus tours, and the men's Glee Club won the 1936 state title. Faith activities involved many, with the YM, YWCA, and something called the "College Church Society" all indicating what Dean Schultz termed "a deeper concentrated evidence in things spiritual." Students continued an impressive level of involvement in campus affairs and management. The student senate managed May Day activities, instigated an annual campus clean-up day, and organized a student work day, where each student volunteered a day's labor for a college project.[67]

Schultz noted in 1937 that "our students are in general more government conscious." That year they reorganized student government from a bicameral (student senate and tribunal) to a unicameral body (student council). Throughout the decade students seemed blessed with especially strong leadership from people like Harriet Criblez, James Creel, Roy Wenger, Eleanor Worthington, Ray Heiks, Wilbur Berky, and Russell Mast. Especially prominent in student governmental affairs was Ralph Locher. He launched himself from BC student tribunal president and football star into a political career that proceeded through a law degree and smaller elective posts to culminate in a term as mayor of Cleveland in the 1960s, then election to the Ohio Supreme Court.[68]

The 1930s were particularly strong years for the *Witmarsum*, which sparkled with wit, good editorship, and probing reporters who cherished many values except personal privacy. The college was still a place, as William Stauffer later recalled, where "we all knew each other including all the professors, their wives and children, and the dogs and cats." In 1936-1937, to cover this small field, the *Wit* assembled a staff of thirty-four students. The result was a campus paper that considered few issues too insignificant for public purview. Especially prominent in this regard was a regular column that appeared in the mid-1930s, then continued for decades. It was called "Around the Horn," student parlance for the longer walk couples often preferred around the edge of campus from the library to

Ropp Hall, rather than the more direct route across the Krehbiel (Adams) bridge. In effect, the feature was a tell-all column about professorial foibles, student hijinks, and campus gossip.[69]

A number of *Wit* writers handled the column over the years. Two in particular deserve mention here. In 1937 the column fell into the hands of "Lil' Dil," Milburn Diller, whose trained eye let few rumors pass without a public airing. For example: "Hop(e) Eberle gave Connie some stamps to use when she wrote him during vacation—it's a shame she didn't use all of them on him."

When students wrote the paper to complain about Diller's "too personal" remarks, he informed his critics "that I shall continue to abide by the college maxim—'the truth makes free.'"[70]

In fall 1939, Diller moved up to the *Wit*'s editorship and passed the column on to a Lima native who had transferred to the college after three years of music school in Chicago. "This Driver lass," he assured readers, "certainly presents a clever line of gab." He was right. Even in her application for a summer kitchen position, Phyllis Driver had described herself as "an expert dish drier . . . in fact I am authority on the subject—may write a treatise on its method and system." A number of students soon noticed her gift as a raconteur besides her dazzling musical ability. Noted one, she "does us proud with her histrionic antics" and also "really has an I.Q. to write home about, but she's always hiding it under a bushel."[71] Driver kept the *Witmarsum* hopping to campus gossip before her graduation and her marriage to a brother of Milburn Diller's named Sherwood. What happened later became the stuff of Hollywood legend. When she was a thirty-seven-year-old mother of five living near San Francisco, Sherwood talked her into preparing a nightclub act for a local club. She stayed eighty-nine weeks and in five years was performing at Carnegie Hall. She was Phyllis Diller, the famous comedienne.[72]

The trials of the Depression could not seriously derail BC sports but did present challenges for Coach Burcky. Since his arrival he had performed herculean feats of endurance as a one-man athletic department. He coached all the sports and taught all the college's physical education courses. He drove the team bus and oversaw the grading of the athletic fields, sodding the old baseball field himself with the help of a neighbor's team of mules. He served as athletic director, scout, recruiter, trainer, groundskeeper, and equipment manager, patching uniforms himself late at night. Now as financial austerity cut deeply into his budget, Burcky made more adjustments. He took "sample" football helmets from equipment companies and repainted them. A friend in the athletic department at the

University of Toledo donated castoff equipment which Burcky pressed into service. The 1937 *Ista* showed a photo of the baseball team dressed in parts of at least five different uniforms.[73]

Still Burcky's teams kept playing. Sometimes they even won. In 1932 only nine students reported for the first football practice, but Burcky squeezed a few more bodies out of the 133 male students. He molded them into a good enough team to win the college's first championship of the old Northwest Ohio Conference. Behind the swift passing of Walt Diehl to able receivers like Melvin Lora and Jim Miller, the 1936 team shut out its final five opponents, outscored the opposition by the combined total of 90 to 25 points, and won a second crown. The coach called it his best gridiron team ever.[74]

Basketball had some golden moments, too. Led by such athletes as Jim Creel, Galen Leatherman, and the aptly named Harry Jump, they won league championships in 1932 (climaxed by a win over arch rival Findlay College), and also in 1935 and 1936. The 1935 team went 11-5 and won seven straight games (a record that stood until the 1970s), and the next year did even better, finishing at 12-4.[75]

As always with Burcky, the stories of his personal warmth and zany sense of humor persisted long past the victories and defeats. There was, for instance, the time in the late 1930s when he stood in the dugout at the start of a baseball game and signaled his leadoff batter, Chet Tetlow, to bunt. Tetlow beat out the bunt safely, then watched, somewhat astonished, as Burcky flashed the bunt sign to the next three batters in a row. Two reached base safely. The Beavers scored a run and finally won the game. Afterward Tetlow asked the coach why he finally quit bunting. Burcky "slapped his thigh in his usual way," Tetlow remembered later, and chortled that the opposition was "about to catch on to what I was doing."[76]

Seen through one lens, student life seemed to differ little from the more halcyon days of the 1920s. Seen through another, however, students appeared to be developing a wholly different campus tone, one that refastened the college to conceptions of peace and service that had sometimes slipped off their moorings in earlier decades.

The faculty were central in nudging students toward peace commitments. Especially C. Henry Smith's influence lived on for decades in the careers of GC church activists. Half a century later, Harry Yoder remembered "Smith leaning on the window sill on his right elbow and letting the dates and descriptions of historical events flow in such a way that helped many of us fit life together."[77]

But pacifist energies at the college ranged way beyond Smith. In the early 1930s, student activists pulled together a wider organization called the Mennonite Peace Society (MPS) that began to attract the energies of Mennonites throughout the eastern states. Led by students like Maurice Troyer, Carl Landes, and Martha Graber (Landes and Graber later married), it gained additional momentum when it secured Vivienne Musselman as its executive secretary upon her 1932 BC graduation. The society had a busy agenda. It promoted short, unofficial college classes on peace. In 1932 it organized seven students, Yoder, Fretz, and George Stoneback among them, into a "peace caravan" that brought a pacifist message into a wide number of Mennonite churches in summer 1932.[78]

Peace convictions reverberated on campus through the decade, again in resonance with progressive national elements. By 133-2, in 1933 the student body endorsed the Oxford Pledge, an international movement sweeping college campuses in Britain and the United States. By signing the pledge, students promised never to participate in war. When seven Ohio State University students were expelled for refusing to participate in student military training, student senate president Carl Smucker sent them a telegram pledging BC student support. BC students in 1935 participated in the national "antiwar strike" occurring in hundreds of U.S. college campuses. Knots of students participated regularly in regional peace conferences hosted by Quakers and the Church of the Brethren, and hosted peace institutes themselves. In 1936, for example, Gandhi disciple Richard Gregg spoke to a large crowd in the chapel. In November of that year the Mennonite Peace Society held a four-day peace retreat on campus. The society's chief, Mennonite minister Carl Landes, made regular visits with an impassioned peace message.[79]

At the same time, against the backdrop of the Depression and prodded by activists of their own, many BC students deepened their sense of social conscience. Admittedly, one must be careful not to overdo this point. In February 1932, when millions hovered on the brink of destitution and the ragged "Bonus Army" marched on Washington to demand payment of their veterans' bonuses, the YWCA hosted a merry "Bum Party." Students came dressed as "hoboes," sang little ditties to their fellows, and "bummed a handout" at the refreshment table. The national trend of political support for the party of Roosevelt hit the college somewhat belatedly; the Democrats won the student straw vote in the 1934 Ohio senate race, the first time the Democrats had won such a poll, and student sentiment swung solidly behind Roosevelt in 1936.[80]

A number of students received a firsthand introduction to the economic conditions that imprisoned millions. In November 1930, sociology professor I. W. Bauman took nine students for a fact-finding trip into the heart of Appalachian poverty. They visited mineworking families in eastern Kentucky. Two years later he accompanied students on a visit to the relief headquarters of the city of Toledo, an operation that fed 50,000 people daily.[81]

Such experiences worked a sea change in the lives of some BC students, who then worked as leaven to nurture similar developments in others. A few examples stand out. Four sons of Boyd Smucker all graduated from the college—Orden in 1931, Carl in 1934, Donovan in 1936, Bertran in 1942—then went on to distinguished academic, church, and service careers. Carl served as student senate president in 1934 and would have the longest formal association with the college, but in mid-decade, the most public and provocative voice belonged to Donovan.[82]

He arrived at the college in fall 1932, having played a leading role on a high school debate team that had won a state championship. He would graduate four years later having accomplished such a sterling record as *Wit* editor, student governmental leader, and debater that Rosenberger would nominate him for a Rhodes scholarship. More important for his later intellectual and political development were less publicized experiences. He learned much in the classroom from people like Smith and Byers, he remembered later, and even more from his summertime participation in Quaker work camps in a factory district in Philadelphia and among poor coal miners in southwestern Pennsylvania.[83]

Out of such experiences Donovan Smucker anchored his Mennonite faith in a cry for social justice. He did not hesitate to express such convictions in the *Witmarsum*. One editorial on behalf of Roosevelt's plan to expand the Supreme Court—"something must be done to stop the autocratic legalism of these kimono-clad grandfathers!"—triggered angry letters to Rosenberger from no less than three board members. O. F. Gilliom thought such convictions were "penned by someone with an immature mind"; F. J. Wiens complained that "such half-baked socialistic sentiments . . . will only antagonize many sincere friends of the college." Rosenberger hastened to assure such weighty men that "we are moving in general in a sane and conservative direction."[84]

J. Winfield Fretz arrived at the college in fall 1930 against the advice of his home pastor, Daniel J. Unruh of Lansdale, Pennsylvania. Unruh had denounced the school as a fount of modernism and urged young Fretz instead to study at Moody Bible Institute. But Fretz had been impressed with a recent visit of the college men's glee club, with their exciting songs and shining black tuxedos, and Boyd Smucker had followed up with literature and personal solicitation. At Bluffton Fretz found a mentor in Smith. His "discussions were always on a high level," he remembered a half-century later; "he was just an interesting fellow." Fretz grew active in peace agitation, chaired the campus YMCA for a year, toured churches in the peace caravan in 1932, and plunged into late-night Lincoln Hall bull sessions on the labor movement and socialism.[85]

He learned a lot from his professors, Fretz knew, but later he said, "the person who influenced me more than any single teacher was John Keller." For it was Keller who "introduced me to social ethics." A fellow student who lived across the hall from Fretz in Lincoln and a central player in these late-night discussions, Keller was the son of a railroad laborer from Lima. His passionate Christian socialism reflected both his firm Methodist childhood and the tough, Irish-German working-class neighborhood of his youth. From that background, Keller became a YMCA officer and also, as Donovan Smucker remembered, "the official socialist on campus," one who was "very articulate about socialist theory." In 1931 he was instrumental in bringing socialist presidential candidate Norman Thomas to campus. Thomas delivered a ringing condemnation of industrial capitalism to a good crowd in chapel.[86]

Smucker recalled Thomas as "sort of a regular visitor to Bluffton," but on campus, the greater influence may have been Keller himself. The *Witmarsum* reported that it was Bauman *and* Keller who took students to Appalachia; he organized a socialist student group (which quickly collapsed following his graduation in 1932). Sometimes he ushered two foreign students from China back to his Lima neighborhood, where they learned much about "the American social environment."[87]

Keller caused a commotion on campus when, in 1931, he asked that his name be removed from the student honor roll because it neglected to honor accomplishments of less prominent students. "Most of the students on the campus have entered a stage of intellectual complacency," he stated bluntly. The charge occasioned a series of hot replies in the *Witmarsum*. "Young people in general must abandon and combat a type of individualism my critics so well represent," Keller responded. "Jesus was a revolutionist."[88]

Of course, at a time when conservatives across the church were quick to label the college as a dangerous liberal hotbed, it was somewhat perilous to let such words appear in the student newspaper. Fretz's pastor Unruh sent Mosiman a "formal protest against the apparent trend to socialism in Bluffton College," objecting to Keller's influence in particular and calling the college to "definitely disavow the socialistic theories of Norman Thomas and his communistic cohorts." In his response, the president indicated his growing grasp of a potentiality that later generations of BC leaders would not only recognize but begin to build on: non-Mennonite students could sometimes nudge Mennonites to think again about what was most attractive and usable in their own tradition. Keller had a burning Christian conviction to "help those who are what you might call the underdog," Mosiman replied to Unruh. "John Keller did do this for the students at Bluffton College. He gave them an insight into the working conditions of our people."[89]

Finally, as much of the above activity indicated, the student body continued another informal tradition which had been established early in the college's history: persistent assertiveness. Perhaps it was that assertiveness that prompted a remark by Paul Whitmer. In 1936, by then a pastor in nearby Pandora, Whitmer visited Lincoln Hall and suggested to Mosiman that its residents should have "more respect for law and order." In any case, at one time Mosiman and the board both received an unsolicited two-page list of suggestions for improvements from seven students—Fretz as well as Don and Carl Smucker among them. In plain and unsparing language, the seven identified problem areas important to students. For example, they advocated lower tuition, "more personal appearances by president in churches on occasions other than drives for money," a "strong man" for the economics department, and a permanent dean with a "vigorous and inspiring personality and *public speaking ability*" (emphasis theirs).[90]

BC women were assertive too. In 1931 the annual YWCA banquet featured Ellen Wilkinson, a member of the British Parliament, who urged her listeners to "save the civilization from men's influence." Many women students did their best. The college formulated especially restrictive rules for women and reaffirmed its prohibition of women's intercollegiate basketball, but many young women pushed hard on a variety of other issues. Thirty-two attached their names to a petition requesting the college to hire a trained woman coach and allow female students the same use of the gym the men enjoyed. In 1934 they organized their own soccer team. They created their own women's student organization in 1930, which the college finally approved and placed under the auspices of the YWCA. In 1938 the *Witmarsum* finally welcomed its first woman as editor, Mareen Bixler.[91]

The Presidential Meat-Grinder

However much this reinvigoration and creative reapplication of the Bluffton Spirit cheered college supporters, it was not enough to save the presidency of Arthur Rosenberger, who battled hard against the pressures that had ended the tenure of his predecessor. He was haunted by continued financial uncertainty. Field man G. T. Soldner wrote from the church circuit in 1936 that "my efforts to get funds simply do not seem to bear fruit. Last week was very poor—almost nothing." One wealthy New York financier apparently offered to buy the entire college. To this Rosenberger replied with a terse six-word letter: "Bluffton College is not for sale."[92]

Nobody could conceive of making another serious attempt at NCA accreditation, yet the new president knew that the college desperately needed more Ph.D.'s even while it could not pay the salaries needed to attract them. In the spring of 1938 Rosenberger began to consider the possible loss of the college's thin remaining prop of academic legitimacy, accreditation by the Ohio College Association. That body, he noted, was still "holding us in grace" for two more years.[93]

Nor could the president entirely soothe faculty unhappiness. Some faculty members, Schultz wrote him, remained quite dissatisfied with their summer school salaries, to the point where even the gentle art professor John Klassen had begun to grumble audibly about filing a lawsuit. Rosenberger could only respond with a resigned and weary sigh, replying that "one can hardly imagine Bluffton College without some unrest of some kind." He did warn Klassen against filing suit.[94]

By spring 1938 the pressures had become too much for the president to bear. In a state of "nervous exhaustion," he abruptly submitted his resignation. The board refused to accept it and gave him a two-month leave of absence to rest and recuperate. After that they hoped he could continue. Dutifully Rosenberger returned to the office and attempted to carry on, but his own mental and emotional health would not permit it. In late September, telling the board that "I can no longer serve in this capacity," he requested an immediate release from his presidency. Taking the helm of the college at that critical time had exacted a steep price. For the rest of his life Rosenberger quietly pastored churches in Ohio and Pennsylvania. He served for a decade on the board but probably never completely recovered from the strains his three-year presidency had placed on his health.[95]

After appointing a committee of three faculty members, headed by Schultz, to guide the college in the interim, the board scurried around seeking a new president. Their prospects were not good and darkened further when two of the leading candidates, college professors and BC alumni C. O. Lehman and Harold Alderfer, quickly took themselves out of the running. The problem soon appeared as tough as any the college had faced in this most difficult of decades. S. K. Mosiman knew the kind of person the times required. "A man is needed who has ideals," he suggested, "who can put his ideals into a workable program, and who has the determination to do a lot of things that can't be done!" But where could such a miracle worker be found?[96]

CHAPTER FOUR

Prexy Ramseyer's College, 1939-1959

In college fellow students nicknamed him "Tank" because, commented the 1922 *Ista*, "he hits mighty hard in football." A barrel-chested farm boy from Illinois, he took to most aspects of college life in the same full-bore manner he plowed through blockers on the gridiron. "He is a mighty man in various ways," the yearbook observed. He served as president of the student tribunal, the Choral Society, the Oratorical Association; as business manager of the *Ista* and the *Witmarsum*; and as treasurer of the YMCA. He sang bass in the men's glee club and discussed literature with the Adelphians. As captain of the debate team, commented one admirer, he "literally smothered his opponents with his rapid-fire arguments."[1]

Once he became Bluffton's president, students recognized a kindred spirit and came to love him. They noted his fanatical rooting at sports events, serenaded him outside his house on his birthdays, and for almost three decades fondly called him "Prexy"; no BC president has worn the title since. At the same time, many students viewed him with awe and a little fear. He tolerated most pranks but had little patience with academic laziness or misbehavior. He warred ferociously against student consumption of alcohol. Tact was not a value he always prized; years later, faculty member Edna Ramseyer remembered him as "probably a little blunt." Students, staff, and faculty alike sometimes felt the sting of his tongue.[2]

He was intimidating and warm, plainspoken and inspiring, and for nearly three decades, Lloyd Ramseyer personified Bluffton College. In an era of strong leadership at many Mennonite institutions—one thinks of Bender at Goshen and of Bethel's E. G. Kaufman—Ramseyer dominated this college more completely than

124

anyone ever had before or has since. Partly this was due to his hierarchical leadership style. Robert Kreider remembered how the president "just ran things," a characteristic never demonstrated more clearly than in Kreider's own selection as dean of faculty. Ramseyer called Kreider into his office in spring 1953 to ask how his first year of teaching had gone. In the course of the conversation, Ramseyer asked whether the impressive young history professor would be interested in the deanship. Kreider replied that yes, in an abstract way, someday he would. Shortly after, Ramseyer sent out a notice to the faculty informing them that Kreider had replaced Jacob Schultz as dean. This was the first word of the change any of them, including Schultz, had received.[3]

Ramseyer's own spirit permeated the college as well. He never pushed others harder than he drove himself. For years he combined his presidential duties with the tasks of a development office and student recruiter in addition to a significant teaching load. Beneath the tough exterior, Kreider remembered a "marshmallow center" and a genuine humility. Ramseyer regularly and sincerely told his board that if they ever found his performance as president unsatisfactory he would readily step down from the post.[4]

Although Ramseyer confronted forcefully, he backed down readily, holding no grudges. He often defused tensions with his flat Midwestern sense of humor. When certain denominational conservatives objected to his ordination as a minister in 1940, for example, he confessed to Paul Whitmer that he felt "some irritation" but decided to "take it in the same spirit as the man who was kicked by a mule—I consider the source and let it go."[5]

It would not be entirely accurate to claim that Lloyd Ramseyer single-handedly saved Bluffton College. When he began his presidency in fall 1938, that miracle was already underway. Likewise the remarkably good shape of the college when he exited the office in 1965 was due as much to a favorable economy and student demographics as to his own efforts. Nonetheless, Ramseyer's accomplishments were remarkable. Out of the ashes of the Great Depression he laid a solid foundation for the college's later expansion and guided it through an uncertain era of hot and then cold war.

Moreover, Ramseyer took the progressive Anabaptism that had nurtured him as a student and reshaped it into a durable vision for the future. As he assumed the presidency, he declared to a friend that "I do not associate Christianity with an anemic type of living but with a dynamic force and red-blooded activity." For decades afterward, the college would reverberate to such understandings.[6]

"I thought I would live longer in some other position"

In 1938, after two other prominent candidates for the college presidency had removed themselves from consideration, Ramseyer increasingly appeared the logical choice for the job and was not entirely happy about it. For the ten years following his graduation from BC in 1924, he taught, coached, and served as school principal in rural Illinois. In 1927 he married Ferne Yoder, whom he had met in college. Originally from MC Mennonite circles, she had transferred to Bluffton with other students from Goshen when Goshen closed for the 1923-1924 academic year.[7]

By mid-1938, Ramseyer had earned an Ohio State University doctorate in education and joined the BC faculty as temporary teacher of biology. But he knew that something bigger was in the works. He later recalled that "both sides" of the divided faculty soon approached him to be "on hand" in case of Rosenberger's resignation. Mindful of the fates of recent BC presidents, he "told both sides that I thought I would live longer in some other position." At the last minute one faculty faction (presumably Byers' followers) began pushing the candidacy of Goshen professor M. C. Lehman. But once BC alumni deluged the board with over 200 letters demanding Ramseyer, the board could not resist. They announced their choice at a homecoming banquet on November 5, Ramseyer's thirty-ninth birthday. He began functioning as president the next morning.[8]

Ramseyer accepted the job dutifully, thinking he would serve for two or three years "until it became respectable to leave." He knew he inherited a college in critical condition. Ministers in the college's constituent churches would be watching carefully, warned a friend, "to see if you speak their language . . . you still have to sell yourself to the church." The new president knew this meant convincing minds that had turned against the college long ago. In two months, Berne's Board of Deacons unanimously reaffirmed their decision to keep the congregation closed to the college. At the same time, a college fundraiser reported that "the smoldering antagonisms from the Mosiman, Smith, Byers feud" still hindered his efforts. Indeed, college finances were still in desperate straits, even as the nation began to recover from the Great Depression. By mid-December 1939, salaries had still not been paid for the month, making it a bleak Christmas for faculty and staff.[9]

The new president was an apt student of recent BC history, and memories of the disastrous 1930s influenced him throughout his presidency. "I suppose we are over cautious [sic]" in financial management, he admitted to Don Smucker, but this was "because daring ran the college almost to the point of bankruptcy." To Ramseyer, further extensive bond sales appeared as the financial equivalent of drinking rat poison. Like many Americans scarred by the Great Depression, he bore a lifelong aversion to debt. College indebtedness should not be refinanced, he pled with the board in 1943, "*but paid off. Let there be no more mortgages!*" (emphasis his)[10]

Studiously he avoided the mistakes of the past, instructing the college financial agent to quit legal proceedings against one of the unpaid pledges from the 1929 campaign. Such procedures, he told D. W. Bixler, were inconsistent with church teaching on nonresistance. As a way to erase the hurt and distrust such practices had caused, he directed his aide Harry Yoder to personally visit each of the pledge holders and tear up the notes in their presence.[11]

Instead, the president would raise money the old-fashioned way: through honest reporting of college financial needs and heavy reliance on the church to meet them. With the Depression ending and wartime prosperity settling in, the church did come through with the required sums. Today the college has several buildings named after generous donors. While proper, such recognition may obscure the hundreds and hundreds of more modest donors: the Sunday school classes in Mennonite churches from Pennsylvania to Iowa who dutifully forwarded the contents of their "Penny A Day boxes" to the college; the women's groups who laboriously canned fruit and vegetables for consumption in the dining hall; and the hundreds of alumni and other individuals across the church who sent ten- and fifteen-dollar checks month after month.[12]

In 1939 Ramseyer moved to regularize such gifts by creating the "Friendship Group," college supporters who would each commit themselves to a monthly contribution of $25. The idea came from a college fundraiser, Guy Cutshall, who candidly told Ramseyer that "it is going to be a *terrific battle* to put the college over—but you can do it if your health and nerves hold out." By June 1940, the Friendship Group had 202 members, providing a regular and reliable source of income.[13]

By spring 1940, BC finances had improved to almost unbelievable levels when compared to the preceding decade. The college completed the academic year with a surplus of $41.29—the first black ink at year's end since 1922. By January 1946, the college finally paid off all bonds and other accumulated long-term debt, although some creditors accepted less and the college never completely paid the faculty their Depression-era back salaries. In every year of his presidency, Ramseyer would achieve a balanced budget, except for 1952-1953. It was altogether a testament to the dedicated labor of a host of college leaders backing the president and also to a committed body of church and alumni supporters who repeatedly responded to their call.[14]

Chief among these leaders was Harry Yoder, a capable Mennonite minister whom Ramseyer persuaded in 1946 to become the college "field secretary." Soon Yoder was more than a mere fundraiser. For nearly two decades after, he was the president's loyal aide, his jack-of-all-trades, and even his alter ego. Already by 1951 Ramseyer told one church official that "without doubt Rev. Yoder is the best field man that the college has ever had."[15]

As the 1940s began, the college suddenly faced better prospects than it had in at least a decade. The largest freshman class since 1931 had arrived in the fall of 1939, boosting the student body to its highest enrollment in eight years. The following spring the Ohio College Association restored the college to "good standing." But the upturn was only illusory. Just as the skies around the college began to brighten, they darkened across much of the rest of the world and threatened to drag all into an endless downward spiral.[16]

Total War, the Home Front, and Bluffton College

Throughout the later 1930s many on campus had cocked a keen eye toward the increasingly ominous events transpiring on the world stage. When the Mennonite Peace Society dissolved, in 1939 students organized their own equivalent, the Peace Action Club. Led by activists like Bert Smucker and Betty Keeney, the club spearheaded student agitation on peace and justice issues through a number of venues. They sent deputations to schools and churches to speak of peace; they mounted fasts, forums, conferences, and peace institutes on campus; they held offerings for war relief; they directed protests to Congress and to the White House. They pulled together a play with peace themes, "Let My People Go," and sent it to tour Mennonite churches in the spring vacations of 1940 and 1941. In February 1941, the Club discussed and then condemned President Roosevelt's "Lend-Lease" bill.[17]

Meanwhile, faculty members such as Peace Club sponsor Russell Lantz added their voices to the agitation. Chapel addresses rang out with peace-related themes from scholars like C. Henry

Smith, GCMC Peace leader Emmet Harshbarger, and Harold Bender of Mennonite Central Committee. Edna Ramseyer led by example. In 1940-1941 she took a year off teaching and served in southern France, working with refugee children still displaced from the Spanish Civil War. Some of the most public words came from the president. In his June 1940 baccalaureate address, for example, Ramseyer condemned war as "one of the greatest enemies of man. It is not Hitler, Mussolini, or Stalin that is our chief foe; it is war itself." With the peacetime draft bill of 1940 obviously in mind, he warned that "we are in danger of letting a vast military machine control our lives and our resources."[18]

Such emphases surely must have affected individual students who had to make their own decisions about war and peace. In the fall of 1940, Ramseyer noted that even quite a few non-Mennonite students leaned toward pacifism. Yet a sense of duty to the national community pulled strongly in other directions. In a questionnaire distributed by the Peace Club in March 1940, half the students indicated willingness to serve in the military if drafted.[19]

Less and less were these abstract questions. When the coming storm finally broke, students, faculty, and college leaders alike would have to choose from a variety of difficult choices that would send them in opposite and sometimes dangerous directions. The war also promised a different kind of difficulty for the functioning of a college. In the dark summer of 1941, as the U.S. lurched toward war, Don Smucker phrased the key issue clearly to Ramseyer, hoping that "the Army, Navy, Marines, CPS, and plain ordinary cranky Mennonites do not get the college down."[20]

Two days after Pearl Harbor, Ramseyer realized that colleges "primarily interested in maintaining Christian principles" faced a difficult year. One critical fact was that their young men might be drafted at any time. In a special meeting early in 1942, the faculty voted to cancel all vacations and set commencement several weeks earlier. They also decided that seniors drafted before the term ended could take comprehensive exams that might substitute for remaining classwork. And to seize the initiative and declare their own position, the faculty instituted two new courses. These were entitled "Biblical Teaching on War and Peace" and "The Economics of War and Reconstruction." They also reaffirmed "the position of the Mennonite Church in relation to participation in armed conflict . . . as the belief and practice of the College."[21]

The most direct and inescapable impact of the war on the college came not in new classes or hurried graduations but in the more fundamental matter of enrollment. With no student deferments, colleges and universities across the country quickly saw most of their young men leave. Lured by well-paying defense jobs, young women also deserted the colleges. Already by April 1942 Bluffton's student enrollment had fallen by one-fourth, and that was only the beginning. In March 1944 Jacob Schultz informed the board that they could count on ninety-three students taking classes. The next year the number dropped even lower, to seventy-seven, enrollment totals the college had not experienced since its earliest days. Professors commonly addressed courses of five to ten students, and individual classes could barely round up enough members to work up a loud cheer. The class of 1944 had consisted of sixty-seven freshmen in fall 1941, but by the time they became juniors, their numbers had dwindled to sixteen full-time students.[22]

The president gamely observed that the students "are of an unusually fine caliber, with a smaller percentage of rough necks than usual." A brighter fact was that, with the farm prices soaring and the wartime climate inducing Mennonites to turn inward, many Mennonite churches stepped up their support of their college, both financially and in other ways. Ramseyer and other professors would do their best to carry on. "In many ways it is just as you left," he assured scattered former students in December 1944, "Smith talking politics, Schultz speaking in terms of centile ranks, Coach telling stories, Miss Amstutz delighting in the Romans, Miss Brenneman striving to have folks appreciate Shakespeare, and Byers trying to get inactive minds to think."[23]

Faculty members found themselves engaged in other activities too, for a student body of less than a hundred could not keep them all busy. By spring 1945, only half the regular faculty and staff were working for the college full-time. Smith busied himself with his bank; music professor Hauenstein, speech professor Stauffer, and Coach Burcky taught at the high school. Bauman took a year off to work for the Ohio Department of Public Welfare. Besides her teaching, Naomi Brenneman ran the library.[24]

Students also tried to proceed with college life as before. The 1943 *Ista* chattered gaily about the same old student foibles: water fights in chemistry lab, future preachers sleeping through Bible class, the library as a "scene of serious study and last minute cramming" and a "perennial dating bureau for the not so studious." Finding dates became a problem, however, because the war quickly transformed the college into a largely all-female institution. In fall 1942 Burcky scraped together eighteen men for the football squad;

two had never before seen a game. Two years later he was reduced to organizing a game of six-man football, frosh versus upperclassmen, before dispensing with sports altogether until war's end. Without enough male voices, Lantz discontinued the Vesper Choir and created a fifty-member Women's Chorus that made around twenty-five appearances in 1943-1944, mostly in the vicinity of Bluffton due to wartime travel restrictions.[25]

Women were quick to capitalize on their new dominance. *Witmarsum* editor Christine Burkhard led student agitation against some of the college rules, such as the ban on dancing and women's smoking, and editorialized for better use of student activity fees. Her campaign irritated Ramseyer, who privately grumbled that she wanted to "do away with all rules" and "apparently has no conception of the ideas of the church nor of its rights in this institution."[26]

Altogether the *Witmarsum* continued to reflect the diversity of viewpoints that had characterized the campus before the war. Editor Margaret Berky signaled the nation's entrance into the war with a firm plea for gracious tolerance of diverging opinions, and certainly the campus responded in kind. The paper published regular letters and guest articles from former students, whether they were like conscientious objector Don Gundy, who called the college to a steadfast adherence to peace principles, or Johnnie Leathers, who wrote from Navy boot camp to express his pride in his own version of service.[27]

At the same time, many students held fast to the peace and service commitments that continued to characterize the college. Student Senate organized a War Relief Committee, which threw itself into activities like blood donations and collecting clothes and gauze. With Ramseyer's warm approval, the Peace Club expanded its energies considerably. These came to include providing assistance to the men in the conscientious objector labor camps (the Civilian Public Service [CPS] system) as well as bringing to campus such national pacifist leaders as A. J. Muste and J. Nevin Sayre.[28]

The peace-minded students were following the lead of their president, who created a very different model of college commitment to nonresistance in wartime than had its leaders in World War I. This president did not promote war bond sales or join such campaigns. He turned down a request from the Navy to run an advertisement in the *Witmarsum,* and no war recruiting posters or slogans appeared in the *Ista.* In contrast to Mosiman's open advocacy of the noncombatant position twenty years before, Ramseyer refused to counsel young men about how they should respond to the draft. Instead, he pointed to the BC peace position and urged them to serve their country "in the manner in which your own conscience dictates."[29]

Still, when he heard word that a former student was considering transferring from CPS into the military, he penned a scarcely disguised attempt to dissuade him. And when three former students did transfer to noncombatant service, the president wrote to a CPS administrator wanting to know why.[30]

In a nation at total war, continued dedication to peace principles was a sometimes risky business. In fall 1942, despite signals of opposition from many in town, the college admitted three Japanese-American students who had left internment camps. Even more hazardous was a decision by the board of trustees, prodded by the president, to deny the request of a local defense plant, the Triplett Corporation, which wanted to use empty campus buildings for its work. The decision alienated a powerful local leader who had previously been a generous contributor to the college.[31]

Meanwhile, the college consciously strengthened its ties with the CPS system. Some graduates rose to key positions in CPS. Roy Wenger of the class of 1932, for instance, helped to found the "smoke-jumpers" program, made up of conscientious objector (CO) firefighters who parachuted into hot spots. Art professor Klassen toured the camps extensively, giving demonstrations in wood carving and ceramics. Schultz and Bauman taught a number of courses to COs at the Ypsilanti, Michigan, unit. Edna Ramseyer helped create a women's equivalent of CPS, the "CO Girls." She also taught dietetics in a CPS camp in Virginia and at MCC's relief training program in Goshen. The president visited COs in Florida, returning home from one trip with a chameleon that he had caught himself. He turned it over to Miss Moon, who lodged it in a glass cage in Science Hall.[32]

Quite soon Ramseyer realized the wealth of future faculty talent in the CPS camps and began to focus his recruiting efforts accordingly. Equally important for the future vision of the college, he also grasped something of the impact the war years would have on an entire generation of Mennonite young people. "We hope that out of this experience of college in the war years you would have received a new vision of service," Ramseyer told the graduating class of 1944. For if "your education has not made you more discerning of human needs, more concerned about them, and better prepared to meet them, then your education has failed its purpose."[33]

Writing to a former student then in the military in fall 1944, the president exclaimed, "My but it will seem nice when the athletic field is full of men again. The baseball field seemed so quiet last spring, one wanted to hear the crack of a bat . . . it made one lonely." But the BC men who used to be hitting baseballs or singing to the women of Ropp Hall had long ago departed for different pursuits. When the choice finally came, most opted for military service. Of the 167 men listed in the "Bluffton's Boys in Service" chart in the 1944 *Ista*, 38, or about 22 percent, were in CPS. In the context of 1944, these were not surprising totals, not even for a college that had upwards of 45 percent of its students listed as Mennonites. In fact, they indicated a higher CO percentage than did the college's constituent churches. The Middle District Conference sent only 15 percent of its young men to the CPS camps.[34]

While remaining clear about his own pacifism, Ramseyer did his best to maintain cordial relationships with BC students who had entered military ranks. He admitted to one that during World War I he had desperately wanted to join the heavy artillery; only his father's need for help on the farm had kept him home. His peace commitments had developed later, during the national disillusionment with warfare in the 1920s, but still he understood the young men who decided the same way he would have. He readily wrote letters on behalf of their promotion to higher military rank, responding to the news of one that "it is always encouraging to hear of alumni who are making good." In return, numbers of such men sent small checks in support for the college, along with expressions of warmth for the president and for their alma mater. "My hat is off to you," Russell Fellers wrote Ramseyer, along with a ten-dollar check, "because I think you are a man."[35]

Throughout the 1930s an increasing number of non-Mennonites had been coming to the college. Some wrote back to Ramseyer indicating that they had absorbed something of the college's mission, even as they bent themselves to the task of war. Calvin Workman had wandered into the library at his air base and picked up a volume of Shakespeare, he reported to Ramseyer in 1944, mostly because all the popular magazines had been taken. But Shakespeare's words immediately took him back to images of Riley Creek in October and Naomi Brenneman's "astounding patience in trying to get me through one of her courses," he wrote. Influenced by such memories, he thought he "almost understood" something of Shakespeare.[36]

Workman had other, more sober thoughts about his job at hand. "The job I am preparing to do myself I do not believe in, so I can imagine how religious people would look on it," he confessed.

"Whenever you hear and read of the glory of the Air Corps, you can be assured that quite a number of those heroes (so called) flying in our bombers shall hate and be ashamed of that part of their lives, forever. . . . I am just a small cog in the machinery that must deal out the destruction." Assigned to a bomber crew and stationed in England, Fellers penned Ramseyer between missions that "sometimes as I am flying over enemy territory and the flak is terrific and at the same time I'm trying to drop bombs, I think, 'How silly and childish the entire thing is.'" Dale Francis said it more simply, telling the president that "next time I'll stand with the objectors."[37]

With some 160 ex-students plunged into the war, surely some would not come home. Arthur Naffziger of the class of 1934 died in a German POW camp. Former student Homer Gratz turned up missing in the South Pacific. Ralph Althaus disappeared in the heavy fighting in the Battle of the Bulge. Robert Clippinger was killed in action in Italy. Harold Twining died in a plane crash in Texas. In the early 1940s Minard Deeds had been a popular figure on campus, mostly due to his reputation as a tenacious defender on the football field. In July 1944 the college received word that he had been killed in action in the Marine assault on Saipan. Ramseyer preached at his memorial service, though his body rested in a military cemetery on the island.[38]

About the same time, news came that Cal Workman's plane had been shot down over Italy, on his fortieth bombing mission. Only later did the college learn that he had survived. He spent the rest of the war in a German POW camp, where the literary enthusiasm Brenneman had inspired in him served him well. There he helped mount productions of Shakespeare that played to packed crowds of fellow prisoners in a makeshift playhouse.[39]

Altogether, both in terms of personnel and ideology, the war served as a watershed in the larger history of the college. Mosiman's death as the decade began signaled the final passing of the founding generation. In July 1941 the venerable old math professor E. J. Hirschler, who had begun teaching at the college in 1903, passed away after a three-year illness. Noah Byers retired from full-time teaching in 1938 and taught a class here and there until he moved to Georgia in 1950 to join his new wife Edna Hanley.[40]

As the war drew to a close in 1945, C. Henry Smith retired. Three years later, at age seventy-three, he underwent an operation for a malignant tumor and died shortly after from a heart attack. More bewildering was the sudden death of psychology professor and college business manager Jesse Loganbill, then in the prime of life, who discovered his cancer in summer 1942 and passed away that November.[41]

At the same time, the 1942 *Ista* pictured the bright young faces of what would soon become a worthy successor generation of the BC professorate. Between the covers of that single yearbook smiled the photographs of Richard Weaver, Delbert Gratz, William Keeney, Leland Lehman, Richard Pannabecker, Earl Lehman, Mark Houshower, and Darvin Luginbuhl. As the war's end approached, their day was not far off.[42]

The war years also pushed college leaders to rethink their entire vision for higher education. Because Ramseyer had learned much from the "practical Christianity" of Mosiman and Byers, the emerging vision would not represent a clear break with the past. Instead, he would simply attempt to refine the Bluffton Spirit that had nurtured him as a student, eliminating its flaws, such as its haphazard nationalism and its too-easy assimilation, and enhancing its better elements. Particularly by seizing on commitments of peace and service and phrasing them in a way that students inside and outside of Mennonite circles could absorb, the president and his colleagues would further create an eminently serviceable vehicle of progressive Anabaptism that could carry the college forward.

"You are choosing between two paths"

The new vision would be expressed in a variety of ways. However, it was best encapsulated in two statements the president delivered to the College's Board of Trustees in spring and fall 1944.

Ramseyer had little to do with the more explicit ideological formulations of Mennonite identity developed elsewhere, especially Goshen, during the war years. His writings and speeches include nothing more than a passing mention of Bender's monumental "Anabaptist Vision" or of Guy Hershberger's seminal work, *War, Peace and Nonresistance*. The central premise of those works—an insistence that Anabaptist-Mennonite history was the fundamental point of reference for the church—would have invited his immediate and forceful rejection. "Are we to believe something just because Menno Simons believed it?" he asked Don Smucker. "We must go to the Scripture itself for our theology."[43]

Dogmatic quoting of Anabaptist forbears reminded the president of the blind ancestor worship of the Daughters of the American Revolution. Although he agreed, in June 1944, that "the interpretations of the great men of the church can well be studied," he insisted that "the source of the Mennonite faith should not be Menno Simons, but Christ." Ramseyer was suspicious of the Mennonite Community Movement of the 1940s which, as articulated by Hershberger, Winfield Fretz, and the like, called for strengthening the Mennonite rural community. To Ramseyer such arguments appeared, perhaps inaccurately, to represent a dangerous and irresponsible withdrawal from a world in pain and need. "We must not be so intent on saving ourselves," he told the class of 1944, "that we forget to save others."[44]

At the same time, however, from the very beginning of his time in office, the president determinedly fastened the college to its founding church. In 1938, when just a presidential candidate, Ramseyer insisted that "this should specifically be a 'Mennonite school,'" whose "first responsibility must be service to the Mennonite church." By that he did not mean "narrowness or dogmatism." Indeed, having non-Mennonite students on campus "would help give our students an open-mindedness which they need." As for faculty, he declared in 1943 that "the kind of faculty member we need in Bluffton is the conservative, Bible centered type, who is tolerant . . . and exhibits the love of Christ to others."[45]

Christ's love was a topic the president particularly liked to dwell on. Like his predecessors and successors in BC's president's office, Ramseyer shared a biblical and conservative theology that took concepts such as sin, repentance, personal piety, and biblical authority quite seriously. Students who listened to chapel talks he delivered weekly for over two decades heard the president elaborate on such concepts nearly endlessly. If there was a particular lodestone in his theology, however, it was expressed in the ending of the first chapter of Ramseyer's book, *The More Excellent Way*, a compilation of his chapel talks he published in 1965. "Love is the greatest thing on earth," he reasoned. "It must be extended in two directions, toward God and toward man."[46]

In such phrasings and others, the president made it clear that he would steer the same theological course that Mosiman had charted: a close adherence to a firm evangelical piety, rooted in experiential Christianity, and an avoidance of the doctrinal rigidity that the college's fundamentalist critics insisted on. Hence, as with his predecessors, he would face the same potential for serious friction with conservatives in BC's constituent churches.

For nearly six years Ramseyer watched the storm build and tried to avoid it with remarkable self-restraint. He knew from personal experience how destructive such conflicts could be. As a young adult he had observed how conservative attacks had riven his home congregation in Illinois. His participation in the BC Alumni Association in the 1920s and early 1930s had kept him attuned to BC's internal religious battles in a manner that further reinforced the lesson. He thus worked hard to satisfy conservatives, even though sometimes swallowing hard as he did so.[47]

Ramseyer's greatest challenge in this regard was college Bible professor—and new Ebenezer pastor—A. C. Schultz, who had become a darling of church conservatives. After years of the "cold and modernistic teaching" of former BC Bible professors, Mennonites "in the east idolize this man" with his "clear and fundamental teaching," declared one easterner in 1941, writing in protest of the college's reduction of Schultz's teaching load. Any attempt to deliberately reduce the professor's influence, the easterner warned, was "simply committing suicide" with the churches.[48]

But Schultz increasingly became a problem for the president. The Bible professor saw himself as "defending the conservative group among the students and the constituency," summarized William Mohr, an important BC trustee whom Schultz tried hard to cultivate. Schultz felt it his duty to report to the EDC governing ministers when the college brought in speakers or entertained ideas he thought inappropriate. He also warned students of the dangerous currents of theology he perceived at the college. Such actions dismayed many of the liberals in the constituent churches; undoubtedly, they infuriated Ramseyer. Privately he found Schultz arrogant, intolerant, and worst of all, disloyal to the college. Still, as he told Mohr, "I have never yet seen a church or school fight which did not end disastrously for everyone concerned." Determined to "avoid a 'show-down,'" he kept his tongue. Yet as tensions continued to build, he quietly realized that Schultz would have to go.[49]

The initiative, as it turned out, came from Schultz. In January 1944, he mailed the board a three-sentence letter of resignation as "a protest against the liberalism, or modernism, that dominates the college under the leadership of President Lloyd L. Ramseyer and Dean Jacob S. Schultz." Meanwhile, a number of the Bible professor's supporters in the student body circulated a petition to the board in support of his charges.[50]

The big confrontation Ramseyer had tried to avoid had exploded anyway. Now the president scrambled to contain it. He held a long heart-to-heart chat with one conservative, the prominent EDC minister and BC trustee Freeman Swartz, even though Swartz had come to campus to express his outrage over Schultz's resignation.

The president knew his board well enough that he never really worried about keeping his job. Still, he grew increasingly concerned when the trustees indicated they would invite Schultz to appear before the board's March meeting to document his charges. For several months Schultz had refused to provide specific evidence to board chair J. S. Slabaugh in support of his claims, but in person, Ramseyer knew, he could be persuasive.[51]

Now that the confrontation was here, Ramseyer instinctively threw himself at it head-on. He seized on his semi-annual report to the board, on March 24, 1944, to throw down the gauntlet in regard to the future direction of college teaching on matters of faith. "You are choosing between two paths," he candidly told the trustees. The bulk of his lengthy address served to lay out these two alternative directions. It was not a decision between fundamentalism and modernism, because "both groups firmly believe in the fundamental statement of faith as printed in our catalog." It was instead a choice between two different temperaments.[52]

For three pages the president described the viewpoint of his conservative critics with scarcely concealed indignation. Members of this "first group" (he never used the terms "conservatives" or "fundamentalists") were self-righteous, judgmental, and intolerant of any other view than their own. They thoughtlessly classified peace and social concern as fruit of the social gospel. Their attitudes rendered it "impossible" to have them on a college faculty, he declared flatly, "since the very attitude causes strife and confusion in the student body."[53]

There was, the president said, another way, "the path which Bluffton College has attempted to follow throughout the years" and which "the main stream" of the larger Mennonite church has tried to follow. It is just as conservative in its theology as the other group, but it "is given to tolerance of thought" and is "more critical of ideas than of men." "I am interested in working for and sacrificing for this second viewpoint," he told the board, "and in trying to remedy its defects." Hence, he recommended that the board accept Schulz's resignation. Even more, he warned, the board must decide which direction to take. "For too long we have gone as a ship without a rudder. It is time that we describe our goal, and chart our educational experiences accordingly."[54]

It was altogether a compelling tour de force, presented before a board already inclined to side with Ramseyer anyway. On the other hand, in his own hour before the trustees, Schultz seemed to have botched his case. He never did produce the specific instances of the president's or the dean's "modernism," as Slabaugh had requested. His repeated vague charges of theological deviance and what trustees saw as his general air of self-righteousness further alienated them. Ramseyer had called on the board to choose between two paths. As the meeting ended, they clearly did. With only Freeman Swartz abstaining, they voted to accept Schultz's resignation and followed it by passing a unanimous vote of confidence in the administration.[55]

It was not a surprising choice—given the basically progressive orientation of the board since the college's founding—but it was important nonetheless. The trustees reasserted they would stand with their president in the ongoing effort to place a Mennonite college in the nebulous middle ground to the left of fundamentalism.

All that remained was to face the chorus of dismay from church conservatives. Schultz had his letter of resignation, and word of its acceptance, published on the front page of the Pandora *Times*. An allied minister then had it reprinted in small-town papers throughout the college's constituency, in order, said the pastor, that "our innocent people who have been pan-handled all these years" could "know the truth." The next month Ramseyer rather bravely journeyed to a "stormy" meeting of the Eastern District Conference, where Schultz's supporters, he reported later, "spent nearly two hours cussing and discussing the college." But the president resolutely faced the accusations, accompanied by trustee Mohr, who "stood like a rock," Ramseyer said, in the college's defense.[56]

The damage could be greatly minimized, Ramseyer and the board knew, if they could secure a new Bible teacher who was conservative enough to please the critics but also committed to the second path the president had mapped out to the board. The list of such notables was woefully small. The ideal candidate was former president Rosenberger, but there seemed little chance of bringing him back to such a hot spot. The board extended a call to the old seminary professor Amos Kreider, but he quickly declined.[57]

Soon Ramseyer began to consider a suggestion from Rev. Swartz about an earnest young EDC minister then studying for his doctorate at Columbia in religious education. His name was Paul Shelly. He appeared "the combination which we need," Ramseyer told Harry Yoder, "basically conservative yet open minded and cooperative." Shelly prayed over the call, felt assurance that God was leading him to accept it, and arrived that summer of 1944.[58]

Until his death from cancer twenty-five years later, Shelly would place his own indelible stamp on college religious and student life.

Along with his regular job as Bible professor, he was informal admissions adviser, campus pastor, counselor, and confidante to hundreds of students. He never married and lived in Lincoln Hall for years as dean of men; the students became his extended family. Generations of them came to cherish his own personal idiosyncrasies, his loose suspenders, his cluttered office.[59]

Equally important was Shelly's ability to blend his warm evangelicalism with an ardent commitment to the larger mission of the college that the president and others had begun to sketch out. As he told Ramseyer when he accepted the job, he believed that "our Mennonite colleges should in a real sense be pioneers in stressing both our heritage as Mennonites" and in "discovering new methods to perpetuate this way of life."[60]

With Shelly in Schultz's place in the religion department, Ramseyer was soon able to put church battles pretty well to rest. There were periodic complaints about matters such as "folk dances" (square dancing), but for about two decades no serious fight with church conservatives threatened the college. In 1946, for example, college trustee and Berne deacon Elmer Baumgartner wrote Ramseyer that "I could hardly believe my ears" when he heard Berne's new pastor Olin Krehbiel suggest to the deacons that the congregation take up an offering for the college. Before long, such contributions picked up again, Ramseyer had preached in the Berne pulpit, and Krehbiel had become a regular speaker at the college, where he sent his children to study.[61]

"A certain brand of educational and religious philosophy which is different"

With the Schultz matter behind him and the war drawing to a close, the president looked ahead. The college had again rejected fundamentalism. But where would it head? In fall 1944, Ramseyer began to articulate a postwar vision for the college. Speaking to the board that November, he openly acknowledged that the great "union movement" inaugurated in 1913 was finally dead. The twin calamities of fundamentalist attack and economic collapse had done it in. Already in 1939 the board had revised its regulations to make it answerable to only three church conferences: the Eastern and Middle Districts and the Central Conference of Mennonites.[62]

Now, the president told his board, trying to build on a constituency of three small conferences with a total membership of 12,000 people would mean an uncertain future. The bulk of the

resources of the General Conference Mennonite Church would probably flow west toward Bethel. The possibility of the Mennonite
Church providing any significant amount of students or funds was
so remote that Ramseyer did not mention it. He briefly mentioned a
different option—to remake the school into a "work college" like
Berea, which let students work for their own tuition—but he quickly
dismissed that idea. It would draw students primarily interested in
the work plan, he said, and divert the college from its "greater
aims." In the face of such obstacles, what kind of future could the
college construct?[63]

The president had just one glittering idea. He suggested that
"we enlarge our constituency by making this a center of a certain
type of thinking, a certain brand of educational and religious philosophy which is different." The guiding "distinctive things . . . must
coincide with Mennonite principles, but not be confined to
Mennonites." Ramseyer seemed to be thinking out loud. "Having
found these principles," he wondered, "how can we capitalize on
them to attract others than Mennonites who would be interested in
these ideals?"[64]

The vision was hazy but shone with promise. Other Mennonite
colleges could build from substantial nearby populations of ethnic
Mennonites who came to regard these institutions as their official
denominational schools. Lacking such advantages, Bluffton had to
turn toward attracting Christians outside the denomination. Doing
so held the potential to return BC to a particular conception of
Anabaptism that its progressive heritage had always pointed to anyway. The original Anabaptists had not relied on an ethnic base either.
What had drawn people to them, as Harold Bender's *Anabaptist
Vision* had pointed out, was the strength and integrity of their own
Christian commitments. Ramseyer left it to the scholars to quarrel
about the different shape and content of that Anabaptist vision.
Instead, he and his colleagues busied themselves with constructing a
college on what they identified as the most usable precepts of the
vision: tolerance, inclusiveness, and unswerving commitments to
peace and social justice.

Because this formulation, like the college it spoke to, was a work
in progress, Ramseyer never set it down in clear or capsule form. He
came closest in two different kinds of documents. One was a history
of the college written by different faculty members for the college's
half-century celebrations in 1950. In it the president elaborated a bit
on the fundamental principles that must guide the college. Among
other items, those principles were peace, plus "individual responsi-

bility to God, freedom of conscience, absolute authority and trust-worthiness of the Scriptures and respect for civil government."[65]

In upholding such precepts the college had sometimes suffered, Ramseyer wrote, but it would never violate them. Moreover, the institution would continue to cater not to a wealthy elite but to "the average American family." Its ability to attract students would necessarily be limited, he admitted, because of "the number of students who will really fit into the philosophy of the college." It tried to blend a conservative theology with broad-mindedness and tolerance, and its commitment to Mennonite nonresistance would further limit its appeal.[66]

A second place Ramseyer expounded his vision was from the pulpit, especially during his annual baccalaureate addresses and weekly talks in chapel. He denounced the consumption of cigarettes and alcohol, relentlessly condemned war, and called students to life-times of service. Long before Little Rock or Birmingham, Ramseyer rehearsed the evils of American racism. For example, he asked the class of 1944, "how can we as Christians look on this field with serenity when the God whom we serve has made us as one all nations and races of men?" As the Cold War deepened, he also resisted its mentality. He urged students to empathize with the Russian people, railed against the buildup of nuclear weaponry, and challenged students to break the conformity of the era by becoming "fanatics for that which is good and against that which is evil."[67]

Taken together, such exhortations amounted to a powerful ideological foundation on which the president and his colleagues could build the future. Soon into the postwar years, the college began to see some of the vision in practice.

Collegiate Anabaptism and the Cold War

Most immediately, as did so many other colleges and universities across the country, the campus lost its empty look as the young men came home. GI's were generally released earlier than CPS men, a cause of concern to Ramseyer, who thought "we need the leavening influence of the latter." The college did its best to recruit ex-COs: along with other Mennonite schools, it offered free tuition to CPS veterans. But students of all stripes returned soon enough and filled the college to its rafters. Beginning in 1946, enrollments steadily climbed until they peaked at more than 300 students in spring 1949. The president should not have worried; in the fall of 1947, Mennonite enrollment shot back up to over half the student body.

The large influx led to some marked class imbalances. Of the 264 students taking classes in November 1946, 135, or over half, were freshmen. Suddenly there were 40 more men than women students. With upward of 60 students enrolled in survey courses like Introduction to Sociology, for the first time the college offered multiple sections.[68]

Administrators scrambled to find space for all. They bought three houses next to campus (quickly named Hirschy Cottage, Lehman Cottage, and Sauder Home). They added two prefabricated duplexes and ten trailers. These were parked at the corner of campus where Hirschy Hall now sits. They were designated for student veterans and wives, who proudly began to call their little community "Beaverburg." Because Ropp Hall was bigger than Lincoln, staffers solved the new gender imbalance by switching the populations of the dorms. "When one hundred and one girls moved in," commented the 1947 *Ista*, "Lincoln Hall, so long a paradise for men, acquired a femininity that was entirely foreign to it." Meanwhile, Coach Burcky gathered the few men who had returned early, shaped them into a football squad, and sent them out in October 1945 to tackle the Polar Bears of Ohio Northern University. It was the college's first homecoming game in three years.[69]

With enrollment and finances improving, administrators began planning for what would be the college's first new building in twenty years. BC desperately needed a new gymnasium. Most high schools had better facilities than the old Barn. Fundraising began in the fall of 1946, and the plans were quite ambitious. The new building would double as an auditorium, with a stage large enough to be a girls' gym; moveable doors would enable men and women to exercise at the same time but in proper privacy. The building would also include a kitchen for alumni or booster banquets and a room under the bleachers that would serve as a much-needed student union.[70]

Supporters supplied the funds, but postwar inflation slowed down the construction schedule. Finally in November 1949 dignitaries gathered to lay the cornerstone. The board named the edifice "Founders Hall" and engraved the cornerstone with a quotation from Hirschy, "Let us expect great things." Only in June 1952 was Founders Hall officially dedicated. But a few months earlier a crowd of over 1,800 had filed into it to watch the basketball team inaugurate the gym with a thrilling 61-59 overtime win over Ashland.[71]

In 1958 Edna Ramseyer designed and funded the construction of the college's other new building of these years. She decided she would call it the "Mara-Alva House," after her parents and the farm where she had grown up. The house still serves, as she intended, as a laboratory for the home economics (later, family and consumer sciences) department.[72]

Student intellectual life responded to the crises that continued to pervade national and international events in these immediate postwar years and did so in accordance with the peace and service commitments that permeated the campus. Chapel speakers regularly hammered away at such issues: Scott Nearing on war resistance, Bayard Rustin on racial injustice, Elmer Ediger and Orie Miller vigorously pushing Mennonite Voluntary Service and Mennonite Central Committee (MCC) work. Students responded. The *Witmarsum* editorialized against complacency about relief needs in Europe and regularly advocated disarmament as the key to world peace. The voice of H. W. Berky's son, *Witmarsum* editor and war veteran Richard Berky, seemed particularly compelling in peace advocacy. By May 1947 the diligent work of a student relief committee had finished a soap drive, raised $265, and collected over 500 pairs of shoes for the needs of European war refugees.[73]

Cold war again gave way to hot war in Korea and played havoc with student enrollment. From spring 1949 to spring 1950, enrollment dropped 15 percent, then another 10 percent the next year. With President Truman's 1948 peacetime draft bill, the promise of conscription became a constant presence in lives of young men until 1973. Again the college would have to make adjustments, some painful. In October 1952, during the Korean War, word came that the draft was taking Charles "Choo-Choo" Spencer, the Beavers' star halfback, in his senior year. Spencer returned in fall 1954 with his remaining season of eligibility restored, but in 1952 the loss hurt. Like other wars, the Korean conflict cost the college. In 1952 the faculty voted to terminate a student work-study arrangement with the Triplett Company because of the plant's involvement in defense work. Meanwhile, at least one local supporter canceled his regular contributions to the college because of Ramseyer's blistering public opposition to Universal Military Training proposals.[74]

BC's most prominent confrontation with the political realities of the Cold War came spring 1949, with the trial and conviction of its young history professor, Larry Gara. A soft-spoken Quaker who had already served three years in prison during World War II for his refusal to register for the draft, Gara was also hall director for Ropp Hall. As the 1948 school year started, he came to know one of the students in Ropp, Charles Rickert.[75]

A Presbyterian, Rickert had already made up his mind to resist registering for the 1948 draft. Gara's general attitude had been to counsel young men to follow their own conscience in regard to the draft, but once he had learned of Rickert's position, he gave the young man some literature and expressed his private support. When FBI agents showed up at Ropp in September with an arrest warrant, Gara led them to Rickert's room. As the agents handcuffed and led him away, Gara told the student not to "let them coerce you into changing your conscience."[76]

On the basis of that comment, despite the fact that Rickert had long before decided on nonregistration, in January 1949, the Justice Department indicted Gara for aiding Rickert's nonregistration with the draft. The presiding judge at Gara's trial in Toledo in March, Frank Kloeb, seemed determined to see Gara not only convicted but also discredited. Kloeb told the jury that the legal principle of "clear and present danger" applied. He remarked that Gara was "obviously mentally unbalanced"; he asked the young professor to submit to a psychiatric examination. On Gara's conviction, the judge denied bail and sent Gara immediately to prison to serve his eighteen-month sentence.[77]

The case became something of a *cause celebré* in pacifist circles. The American Civil Liberties Union condemned the conviction, four hundred ministers and others signed a letter of protest to President Truman, picketers appeared in front of the White House, and a stream of angry denunciations appeared in publications like the *Christian Century* and *Catholic World*. Whatever their personal opinion on nonregistration, the Bluffton students and faculty alike simmered with indignation. About 150 students, half the student body, appeared at Gara's trial in support, along with Ramseyer and Dean Schultz.[78]

The president disagreed with draft nonregistration, but Gara's case seemed to him a monumental injustice. Characteristically, he did not hesitate to voice his opinion. In angry editorials in the *Witmarsum* and in the larger denominational organ, *The Mennonite*, Ramseyer warned that the case indicated that "freedom in America is precious" and "we must be constantly on our guard" in defending it. Privately he thought the publicity from the trial "will probably do the college considerable harm." Indeed it quite clearly did cost the college both financial support and enrollment. Even so, "we would be something less than men," he told a friend, if Bluffton people let such consequences deter them from supporting Gara's stand for conscience.[79]

Building a Postwar Faculty

Against the stressful and uncertain backdrop of the Cold War, college student and academic life still gained momentum. One strength was its faculty. Despite the handicap of meager BC faculty salaries, Ramseyer and his academic deans, Schultz and Kreider, were nonetheless able to assemble a core of solid faculty who would further elevate the college's academic pursuits.

Salaries were embarrassingly low for male professors and lower yet for women, a disparity Ramseyer refused to change or apologize for. Naomi Brenneman in particular voiced her objections, even vaguely threatening to accept a position at Goshen. "Try to look at it from the woman's point of view," she pled with the president. "Bluffton has my affection, but it is extremely hard to suffer year after year of discrimination." An equal pay standard, Ramseyer retorted, was a "modern tendency." Whereas such equity seemed commendable, Bluffton would continue to offer men a higher salary because most men had families to support.[80]

Ramseyer calculated that Brenneman's fondness for the college would keep her on the faculty, but others without such a bond were harder to attract. Late in the 1940s, with the postwar baby boom beginning to put pressure on the nation's school system and with the state of Ohio eager to certify teacher training programs, Ramseyer realized it was high time to begin a program in elementary education. He began corresponding with Ada Lapp, a Goshen graduate at work on her master's degree. With twenty years of school teaching experience in Illinois, Lapp gulped hard at the salary Ramseyer offered. But she consented to come anyway, hoping she could "be of real service in the fall." She would stay until her retirement in 1973 and lay the foundation for a college program that soon became dominant.[81]

Early in the 1950s, Ramseyer's heavy recruiting of future faculty in the CPS camps began to pay dividends. Admittedly, there were budding scholars he was not able to get. William T. Snyder of the class of 1940 preferred an MCC post, and to Ramseyer's great personal disappointment, Winfield Fretz took a job at Bethel College in Kansas. In 1940 Donovan Smucker penned the president a florid paean to Christian pacifist education as basic to saving Western civilization. Ramseyer signaled agreement by trying to recruit him for the faculty.[82]

Smucker turned him down several times but in 1944 had a better idea. He had been talking with MCC chief Orie Miller, who was heavily involved in planning postwar church relief work. Miller had said the church needed trained social workers more than any other professionals. He had pointed to Donovan's brother Carl as the only Mennonite in the country with such training. Bluffton ought to pioneer a social work program among the Mennonite colleges, Donovan stated, and get Carl to head it up.[83]

Ramseyer jumped on the suggestion; his letter to Carl went straight to the point. Three sentences into the letter, Ramseyer asked whether he could make "a permanent break with the state Welfare department and make this here your life's work?" Smucker would not begin full-time teaching until 1958, but by 1951 he had a social service major established and was expanding fieldwork placements for students.[84]

As Smith began to talk of retirement at the war's end, for the first time since 1913 a vacancy loomed in the history department. To fill the spot, Ramseyer had his eye on another BC graduate serving in CPS, Delbert Gratz. But for the time being, Gratz elected to plunge into postwar relief work. Soon the president trained his sights on one of the biggest prizes in the entire CPS system, camp educational director Robert Kreider. Kreider was a Bethel graduate but with Bluffton ties. Son of Witmarsum Seminary professor A. E. Kreider, Robert had spent his boyhood in Bluffton. He had completed an M.A. in history at the University of Chicago, then rose to important CPS administrative positions. It was in line with those duties that he had come to speak at Bluffton in 1945, where he had met, wooed, then married a bright BC student named Lois Sommer.[85]

Yet to get Kreider to Bluffton, Ramseyer would have to pull every string. As Kreider directed postwar MCC relief work in Europe, then pursued a doctorate in history at Chicago, his stock rose even higher. Goshen wanted him, and in 1951 rumors flew that Bethel insiders fancied him to replace Kaufman as president.[86]

Ramseyer lacked Kaufman's eloquence in faculty recruiting, but he tried every conceivable angle to attract Kreider. He insisted that "Bluffton is the institution which needs your services most." He used flattery, telling Kreider he was the logical successor to the eminent Smith. When Smith died, Ramseyer even tried guilt, remarking that the old professor had gone to his death wishing he could have heard Kreider would be his successor. Ultimately, the hard sell worked. The president could hardly contain his satisfaction. Kreider, he wrote an NCA examiner, was "a real find, equal in ability and religious commitment to the late Dr. C. Henry Smith."[87]

For his part, the confident young professor scarcely flinched at the large shoes he had to fill. Not long after he arrived in Bluffton in fall 1952, he informed a friend that "we are at long last in a community where we intend to live out our days." As it turned out, the college secured Gratz's services as well, though in sadder circumstances. In 1949 the college librarian, Lenore Myers, was tragically killed in an auto accident. In a month, his MCC stint ending, Gratz consented to replace her.[88]

The president met with solid success in his location of a solid professorate for mathematics, the sciences, and business. Luther Shetler arrived in 1950 to teach math; he would chair the department until his retirement in 1984. Ramseyer began courting Richard Weaver almost immediately upon the student's graduation from Bluffton and induction into CPS in 1942. Of course, Ramseyer suggested to him, he would soon be interested in "establishing a permanent home and raising a second generation of Weavers." But Weaver also grasped the bigger idea, that Bluffton would be, in his words, the ideal place for maximizing his own possible contributions "toward the realization of the kingdom."[89]

On arrival in 1950 Weaver joined an uncommonly strong department. In 1951 the prestigious journal *Science* reported on a study that ranked undergraduate science departments according to the number of graduates who pursued doctorates. Bluffton's science department was fourth in the state and twenty-fifth in the nation. The department maintained its strength through several notable transitions, including the additions of S. F. Pannnabecker's son Richard, who came to teach biology alongside of M'Della Moon in 1956, then Arden Slotter, who in 1958 replaced retiring professor Berky.[90]

Searching for new faculty to teach business, in 1948 Dean Schultz managed to locate a young businessman from Iowa who was also an ordained GCMC minister, a farmer, teacher, school administrator, and enrolled in graduate school to boot. Howard Raid originally feared that, without his doctorate, he might be "discarded" by the college in a few years. When Schultz laid those fears to rest, Raid arrived in 1947, convinced that "we Mennonites have a way of life which the world needs and we hope that through our college contacts we can aid in spreading it." Over the next three decades, he would shepherd 445 graduates through a business program he came to personify.[91]

The new dean Bob Kreider similarly located a fresh infusion of faculty talent for the arts. For three decades or more the music department had been anchored in the capable but aging hands of professors like Mann, Lantz, and Holtkamp. Now in 1954 their efforts would be augmented by the genial enthusiasm of a 1944 graduate they had trained, Earl Lehman. College vocal groups would respond to the beat of Lehman's baton through a career that was to last until 1987.[92]

The abilities of new professors such as Lehman, Weaver, Pannabecker, and Slotter, BC alumni all, also spoke to the college's increasing ability to draw faculty from its growing pool of graduates. When estimable old sculptor John P. Klassen retired from teaching in 1958, Kreider turned to one of Klassen's former students, Darvin Luginbuhl, as his replacement. Luginbuhl would teach until his own retirement in 1984, when he yielded to his own son Greg of the class of 1971. Similarly, searching for a director of student recruitment in 1950, Schultz tapped recent graduate Dale Dickey. Eventually Dickey turned to teaching speech, and except for a period in the early 1960s, stayed until his retirement in 1990. Already by 1956 he had greatly expanded the college's drama program and during the 1950s guided students through a number of annual productions.[93]

The keen eye Ramseyer had focused on CPS camps and alumni lists also resulted in the arrival of key staff members who would serve the college well for years. In 1944 Winfield Fretz told him of a young CPS man from Berne who had served as business manager for several camps and could well do the same for the college. In fact, Fretz said, he "would give Carl Lehman the number one rating for the job." Lehman approached the possibility carefully. He respected Ramseyer's commitments to the church, but from his background at Berne, he was unsure the college had the support of its church constituency. Did Ramseyer really think "there is enough real Mennonitism left in Bluffton's supporting constituency to make possible a strong Mennonite college?" He would come to work as business manager anyway, spending nearly three decades finding out.[94]

Finally, when Harry Yoder left the position of field man to pastor a church, Ramseyer managed to persuade William Keeney of the class of 1948 to replace him as field man. Keeney was reluctant not due to lack of affection for the college but because he felt more of a call to teach than solicit funds. When Yoder returned in 1956, Keeney was happy to shift to teaching philosophy and religion and would do so through 1968.[95]

"Its excellences are imponderables"

The faculty, old and new, carried heavy teaching and committee loads. With a much smaller staff than in later years, many also had additional student life responsibilities. Yet together with the dean and president, the faculty also took on several long overdue and integrally related tasks. One was renewing the old quest for NCA accreditation. Throughout the war years, the college's lack of credentials had continued to hurt. Some prospective students shied away from the college; now and then, alumni were denied entrance into select graduate programs. Yet through the first years of his presidency, Ramseyer had scarcely mentioned the problem. His silence, he told the board in 1946, was because the college's still precarious finances ruled out NCA acceptance anyway. Further discussion only depressed people. But after a half-dozen years of balanced budgets and the ending of the war, the president considered renewing the old dream.[96]

The first step in what would become an eight-year campaign was a thorough reexamination of BC's general education curriculum. BC had worked at this in fits and starts over two decades, with some successes. One was H. W. Berky's "General Science," which he had created in 1925 for his own majors. Then ten years later, BC required all students to take the course. Berky blended scientific principles with philosophical and religious speculation. In doing so, he may have created BC's first real interdisciplinary course. His aim, he reasoned later, was for the course to become "a witness for the God which created the universe." Into this heady brew of theology and science he added sociological and psychological perspectives, and, after 1945, reflections on Hiroshima.[97]

In 1932, the history department added a course, "Comparative Civilization," required for all first- and second-year students. Modeled on a similar course at Columbia University, it treated the interrelated development of European and American cultures in historical perspective. About the same time, the English department added an "Introduction to Literature" course.[98]

In midcentury years, a larger general education movement swept through academe as colleges and universities across the country began consciously to rework their core curriculums. Part of the impetus came from the NCA. With an eye focused on accreditation, Bluffton obediently dispatched faculty representatives to a series of NCA summer workshops and redesigned its departments into four basic divisions in line with the new thinking.[99]

From such developments, and from their own faculty discussions dating back at least to 1944, BC professors came to endorse a theme for their general education curriculum that could carry them a long way toward NCA acceptance. Originally the brainchild of

Dean Schultz and clearly inspired by Berky's general science course, the theme became "God as the Integrating Force in the Students' Curriculum." A series of institutional self-studies ensued, faculty redesigned courses under the banner, and in 1948 a new, heavily interdisciplinary program emerged.[100]

Building from the core classes of the 1930s, the program emphasized Christian reasoning, explored through a number of disciplines. For example, a course called "Human and Spiritual Resources" plunged first-year students into an interrelated exploration of psychology and religion, principally New Testament Christianity. The new Division of Social Sciences came up with a course called "Fundamentals of Social Sciences" which required first-year students to approach modern social problems from the various fields of politics, economics, and sociology. In his enthusiasm for the new conceptualization, at one point Berky even proposed (unsuccessfully) that the very name of his general science course be changed to "Science and the Imminence of God."[101]

Soon the watchful eye of NCA examiners began to view the college in more favorable light. In the late 1930s, two NCA officials had suggested that the college face the inevitable and become a junior college. Now in 1946, those same two urged Ramseyer to apply for NCA admission. So did NCA official Harry M. Gage, who was particularly impressed with the new core curriculum theme and with the firm sense of mission it reflected.[102]

Wary of another NCA rejection, Ramseyer and Schultz held off applying until they were sure the college was completely ready. Ramseyer first wanted to strengthen their staff, and he began an informal program of financial assistance to help BC faculty or prospective faculty speed up the completion of their doctorates. Three years later, with professors like Shetler, Shelly, Weaver, and Kreider nearing completion of their doctorates and Raid and Edna Ramseyer working on theirs, Ramseyer still deferred applying to NCA. He worried about low faculty salaries. Rather than apply to NCA immediately, in the autumns of 1951 and 1952 the college launched instead into yet two more exhausting self-studies.[103]

Finally, in fall 1952, the president and dean worked through the details of applying to the NCA. For two days in January 1953 they hosted two NCA officials who put the college under a magnifying glass. Late in March, Ramseyer journeyed to the Palmer House hotel in downtown Chicago to receive official word of the NCA's decision. Back home, faculty and staff waited in what Richard Weaver remembered later as "considerable suspense." The NCA's Board of Review had not offered any particular encouragement. Ramseyer knew at least one president whose college had recently been rejected, and Gage had informed him of others. Altogether, the juncture loomed as important as any in the college's history. If the NCA had turned down Bluffton again, after eight years of intense preparation, the result would have been devastating.[104]

Thus the college came to a moment that still leaps out, nearly half a century later, as an especially shining one. Early in the afternoon of March 25, 1953, President Ramseyer made a long-distance phone call from Chicago to Dean Schultz in his office in College Hall, then caught a train heading east. A moment later, the dean—a man, Von Hardesty wryly noted later, "not given to emotional excess"—hustled across the lawn to Musselman Library and shattered the sleepy decorum of the reading room with his joyous shout that "we've been admitted to the NCA!" As he told the board later with only slight hyperbole, "there has been no greater reason for rejoicing in the history of Bluffton College."[105]

This must have been particularly satisfying for Schultz, who had begun his career amid mid-1920s optimism, stuck with BC through the dark 1930s, then worked so hard for NCA approval. In the rush of congratulations that ensued, all faculty signed a statement of appreciation to him as "our field commander."[106]

Meanwhile, the news traveled around campus as if by telepathic current. That evening a jubilant crowd of banner-waving students and faculty gathered at the Pennsylvania Railroad Station in Lima to await Ramseyer's train. With the accompaniment of a pep band, they escorted the beaming president back to campus in a noisy motorcade, then filed into the chapel for a special celebration. With "the doxology" blasting from the loudspeakers atop the College Hall tower, a series of speakers proceeded to the podium to thank God and the hard work of so many who had made the achievement possible. Hopes were high for the future. Years later Robert Kreider remembered one alumnus who called for a doubling of the student body to a total of over 400 students. "Some of us conservatives thought that a little extreme," Kreider recalled, "but it did reflect the heady enthusiasm of the occasion."[107]

Congratulations poured in from friends near and far. Far away in Georgia, one who could truly appreciate the accomplishment, Noah Byers, wrote Ramseyer that he had "looked for this day for over thirty years." Perhaps the most revealing words of praise came from NCA official Gage, while the college still awaited word of acceptance. Well-versed in the cold calculations the accrediting agency relied on, Gage realized BC offered something more, if intangible. "The thing that I feel so deeply and keenly about Bluffton," he penned Ramseyer, "is that its excellences are imponderables, and do not submit readily to objective measurement."[108]

Watching Dubenion Run

NCA approval did not immediately usher in a golden age. Financial conditions remained tough, at least through the mid-1950s. Agriculture continued in a slump, Ramseyer reported gloomily in 1955, an important consideration to a college depending on a constituency that was still primarily rural. Inflationary pressures still bit hard. The president noted that half the nation's colleges and universities had failed to balance their budgets that year. BC managed to raise about $50,000 annually, but with its terribly small endowment, most of that money went to everyday operating expenses. Nor, Ramseyer thought, could the college anticipate substantial enrollment increases. National birthrates had been low in the early 1930s. That fact, combined with the draft and the lure of jobs in booming defense industries, would surely keep small colleges struggling.[109]

Thus it was that enrollment increases the college began to register in the mid-1950s were a surprise. Already by March 1954, Kreider reported a 10 percent increase in student numbers. In fall 1956, the registrar recorded a 17 percent gain, resulting in a student body of 278. The numbers kept increasing. By November 1958, Kreider could report to the board that the college had seen a gain of 10 percent or more each of the preceding four years. From 1956 to 1957 the total enrollment had jumped from 295 to 328, never again to dip under 300.[110]

The college's facilities began to feel the strain once more. In fall 1958, Ropp Hall was filled to within nine students of capacity (all women once more), and Lincoln Hall had room for only six more men. With only 361 seats, the chapel was filled to bursting. Kreider called for additional desks in the library reading room. He also suggested that the college rethink its admission policies. It had traditionally tried to steer a middle course between highly selective institutions like Oberlin and other schools who accepted any high school graduate; perhaps now it was time to be a bit more selective.[111]

BC tuition would not have presented a great obstacle to most prospective students. Tuition in 1955-1956 ran at nearly $400 annually, with room and board another $800, costs that, compared with today's numbers, appear eminently reasonable. Translated into 1999 dollars, BC tuition in 1955 cost about $2,500, and room and board about $5,000 yearly.[112]

In surveying the life beyond academia that such students found, Von Hardesty's perception in the seventy-fifth anniversary history still appears on the mark. "For nearly two decades after 1945," he observed, "the established contours of campus life remained relatively unchanged." Students still operated by the old class hierarchies, with seniors looking ahead, juniors running things, and sophomores lording it over the lowly freshmen. They filed into required chapel four times a week, arranged by class with freshmen at the back, and stood as a group when the faculty entered. They still dressed for formal dinner nightly in the Ropp dining hall and took their assigned seats. The gentleman still served the lady to his left before serving himself. Amid postwar affluence, more and more students owned cars and could find more entertainment off campus.[113]

There may also have been a change in the general tone of student priorities and pursuits, in accordance with larger societal shifts. These were years, charged cultural critics, when not just students, but all sorts of Americans, rapidly accommodated themselves to a conformist, homogenous, and somewhat vapid popular culture. "The great majority" of college students, complained political scientist Philip Jacob in a widely cited study, appeared "unabashedly self-centered," "politically irresponsible" if not "politically illiterate," and focused almost totally on narrow vocational concerns.[114]

A surface look at BC student life in the 1950s seems to offer at least modest support for such a view. Certainly students focused on their future professions. A variety of new campus clubs sprang up in these years, including the Investment Club, Commerce Club, Future Teachers of America, and a Science Club. Robert Kreider, among others, was somewhat shocked at the limits of many students' horizons. In 1952 as a newly arrived professor, he gave his History of Civilization students a map quiz and was "soundly disillusioned" to learn that many could not locate the Nile, Black Sea, or Saudi Arabian Desert. Similarly, in another quiz he gave to 103 entering freshmen enrolled in the same class in 1957, vast majorities could not identify such persons as Norman Thomas, Charles DeGaulle, Karl Marx, or Pablo Picasso (fewer than twenty of the 103 students could place them correctly).[115]

Worse, only sixty-six of Kreider's students could correctly spell the last name of the current U.S. president, Eisenhower. This was particularly surprising in a student body that, as early as 1944, had reassumed a trend towards political conservatism. In the student straw poll that October, Republican presidential candidate Thomas Dewey took 69 percent of student votes, as opposed to 16 percent for Roosevelt and 15 for Norman Thomas. Regardless of whether they could spell his name, Eisenhower likewise garnered the majority of student votes in a 1952 election eve campus straw poll.[116]

Under scrutiny few generalities seem as true, and a closer look at BC student extracurricular life in the 1950s diminishes the perception of a "silent generation." The mission the president and faculty articulated for the college had taken hold. The Peace Club remained active, holding annual Peace Institutes and bimonthly programs that debated issues such as the draft and conscription. Among its speakers were Don Smucker, African-American pastor Vincent Harding, and Mennonite theologian John Howard Yoder.[117]

Racial acceptance at the college went beyond the strong words in Ramseyer's sermons. By the late 1940s BC had a small number of minority students, mostly African-Americans, partly due to the enthusiasm for his alma mater of a Youngstown African-American civic leader, Hugh Frost. After a stellar student career, he had graduated in 1951, then sent a stream of young African-Americans to Bluffton. Neither the president or Frost could detect that these students experienced much racial discrimination. Once, Bill Ramseyer later remembered, the football team was returning from a game and stopped at a restaurant in northern Kentucky. When it became clear that the establishment would not serve the African-American players, without much discussion the entire team stood and left.[118]

At the same time, African-American students may have felt some isolation at the college. Members of the student Citizenship Committee noted in 1956 that "the social life of our negroes [sic] on campus seems to be apparently nil because they seek elsewhere for their entertainment. We should try to get the fellows interested in our school activities and clubs."[119]

Through the 1950s, student devotional and governmental activities percolated on with renewed emphasis. The annual Bible lectures continued to attract crowds. Vespers services declined to once a month, but daily chapel continued to be required for all students. In 1949-1950 the old YMCA and YWCA organizations combined to form a new group, the Student Christian Association (SCA). As an umbrella organization, the SCA oversaw a variety of Christian activities such as the annual Christian life week on campus and sent gospel teams and other deputations on tours into the churches. The fall of 1948 found forty-five students, almost a sixth of the student body, preparing for church vocations.[120]

Minutes from SCA cabinet meetings ten years later hum with interrelated activities that would have cumulatively exerted a telling impact on a campus of fewer than 400 students. Meanwhile, by 1949 Ramseyer had initiated and the college agreed to a procedure that other colleges would adopt only after massive student agitation in the 1960s: faculty and student mutual representation on significant committees of both groups. Such a policy helped the rise, as in the 1930s, of strong leaders in the structures of BC student government. Student councils in the late 1950s, for example, were led by such individuals as Don Pannabecker, Romaine Clemens, LaVerne Schirch, Jerry Shenk, Glenn Snyder, Martin Strayer, and Marilyn Weidner.[121]

Student social life likewise continued to be shaped by traditions of earlier generations. Freshman initiation remained a focal point of the fall semester, with first-year students subjected to (mostly) gentle humiliation by the exalted upper classes. They were still sentenced to campus cleanup or thrown into the Riley when caught without their beanies. All through the fall of 1948 the sophomore women in Lincoln Hall engaged in feuding with the first-year students that built up to a wild waterfight before peace negotiations ensued.[122]

The close-knit campus continued to invite a wide variety of student pranks. The most famous, perhaps, occurred in 1939, when four students, Richard Weaver among them, borrowed a cow from a pasture across Bentley Road and coaxed her into Dr. Bauman's classroom in the basement of College Hall. There students arriving for their 8:00 class the next morning found her waiting for a sociology lecture. Weaver and comrades received an appropriate sentence, cleaning out the chicken house at the college farm.[123]

Students in the 1950s placed alarm clocks set to go off during chapel, snatched hymnbooks, or broke into College Hall late at night to broadcast records from tower loudspeakers. Bill Ramseyer remembers being wakened at 4:00 one morning by an endearing chorus of "Don't Kill the Bartender, He's Half Shot Now." Late one night in 1949, an intrepid soul led a party of eighteen young men into the women's dorm to set off firecrackers and upset paint cans "which," read the report of the Citizenship Committee, "were not quite empty." One whole group of adventurers in 1953 managed to lift a car belonging to football coach Ken Mast and deposit it in the library. Another set of pranksters that year piled snow in front of the doors of College Hall, wired them shut, then poured water on the sidewalks to make a solid sheet of ice. As penalty, they were assigned to shovel snow for thirty-five hours each.[124]

As in earlier years, college administrators imposed strict rules about dancing, smoking, chapel, class attendance, and the like. As always, some students defied them. Faculty discouraged students from wearing jeans to class, chapel, or dinner. In 1957 the administration forbade first-year students to bring cars to campus. The president especially exhibited little tolerance for incidents involving student alcohol consumption. Early in 1948, for example, nineteen men and women students went out to a tavern, where several had a few drinks, nobody drank in excess, and all came home in good order. Ramseyer pushed hard for two-week suspensions for twelve, including students who planned the party but drank nothing. Nor did he back down in the face of objections from students, parents, and even a board member who thought the penalty severe.[125]

Still the disciplinary cases came. Men and women snuck out late at night to go swimming in the town quarry. One student broke into the dean's office and destroyed chapel attendance records. Dean of women Edna Ramseyer had to police the curfew regulations. She remembered hearing a scuffling as students detected her approach. She found young women under the covers but their feet sticking out of the bottom of their beds with their shoes still on.[126]

Yet students also had a number of favorite and legitimate local hangouts. These included the Horseshoe Grill; the Pine Restaurant on Main Street (which advertised itself as "the Beaver Feeding Ground"); Pat's Barber Shop, where students obtained a haircut from the 1920s to Pat's retirement in 1973; and cheap movies at the Carma Theater, the antecedent to the Shannon Theater of today.[127]

BC sports continued to stir student, faculty, and staff passions. The rivalry with the University of Findlay was especially intense for both sides, and midnight emissaries sometimes left painted messages in evidence of their enthusiasm. "Findlay College's initials will be on our Science Hall steps for years to come," Ramseyer complained to Findlay's president in 1942. "We need paint, but we would like to suggest the color and the place to put it."[128]

A number of different sports enjoyed bright moments. The 1953-54 basketball team went 11-8 and finished as runner-up in the Mid-Ohio League, highlighted by Joe Collingwood's thirty-five-point game in the victory over Huntington. The baseball team went 8-2 in 1952, 9-3 in 1953, and shared the league title in 1958. In May 1958, track won its eighth consecutive league championship, four due in great part to the speed and hurdling of Martin Strayer. Despite lack of college direction or funding, in the early 1950s BC women formed their own basketball team, the "Beaverettes." They scheduled games with the likes of Heidelberg and Ohio Northern. The 1952 squad managed to post a 5-1 record.[129]

The sport that seemed to dominate the decade, however, was football. In fall 1950, with Burcky deciding to limit himself to the duties of baseball coach and athletic director, Ramseyer needed to find a new football, track, and basketball coach. Somehow he came across the name of Ken Mast, a twenty-four-year-old Mennonite young man from Sugar Creek, Ohio, who had just graduated from Heidelberg with All-Ohio honors in basketball. Mast agreed to take the job, privately hoping his teams could perform well enough in basketball and at least adequately in football to win him a promotion to head coach at a big high school.[130]

Instead, he stayed seventeen years and led the BC football program to what still appears as one of its two golden ages. Already in fall 1951 the Beavers chugged up enough yardage through the efforts of their halfback "Choo-Choo" Spencer and the passing of Leland Garmatter to grab a share of the championship of the Mid-Ohio League (M.O.L.) with a 4-1 record.[131]

But that was only the beginning. Because the college offered no athletic scholarships, Mast asked each player to recruit a friend. The biggest dividend from that policy came when quarterback Garmatter received a visit from an old army buddy named Elbert Dubenion, who had just been turned down for a position at the University of Minnesota. Garmatter convinced Mast to have a look at Dubenion's speed. The coach lined Dubenion up beside his fastest back, Willie Taylor, for a forty-five-yard dash, then watched as the newcomer beat Taylor by five yards. "I tried not to smile," Mast remembered later, "but inside I was laughing out loud."[132]

The next four seasons the sensational halfback rewrote league record books. In his freshman season, fall 1955, Dubenion ground out 1,236 yards in 107 caries, an average of 11.5 yards per carry. In one game with Defiance, he managed four runs of 68, 65, 82, and 79 yards. The next year he and his team were even better. The Beavers won eight games, and only a season-ending loss to Centre College in Kentucky kept BC from an unbeaten season. Beginning with Dubenion's sophomore season, and aided by the immense talents of fellow backs like Taylor, guards like Bill Ramseyer, Ron Lora, Larry Raid, and C. K. Steiner, as well as the passing of quarterbacks Spike Berry and Joe Urich, the Beavers won four straight M.O.L. championships. They dominated the league into the early 1960s.[133]

If there were moments that epitomized the golden 1950s, they occurred while sitting in the stands at Bluffton's Harmon Field, watching Dubenion run. As the back hung up his spikes and prepared for what would be a successful eight-year career with the Buffalo Bills of the National Football League, the college's good years were apparent nearly to all. Against the backdrop of the football and track teams regularly winning league titles, college administrators plunged into planning for what they came to recognize would be a permanently larger student body. They had begun to openly talk of enrollment over 500 students, a goal inconceivable when Ramseyer had begun his presidency two decades before.

In October 1957 a crowd gathered to break ground for a sixty-six-bed expansion to Ropp Hall, the college's first new permanent expansion of dormitory space since the completion of Lincoln Hall in 1924. A year later, as part of homecoming festivities in early October 1959, officials turned the first spadefuls of earth for a building S. K. Mosiman had begun dreaming of back in the 1920s. Soon girders began to appear for what would be a new music hall, named for the college's second president.[134]

At the same time, in the later 1950s, Bob Kreider felt a little frustrated in his role as dean. Despite the slow additions of younger professors through the decade, BC's faculty was still dominated by an older group who had arrived decades before. They were fine teachers, he remembered later, but tended to resist the smaller innovations Kreider and younger professors had begun to push. He enjoyed a solid and respectful working relationship with Ramseyer. Yet he sometimes found himself bucking against the president's innate conservatism, a tendency that still reflected the crisis atmosphere of the Depression years. Prexy Ramseyer's "instinctive" initial response to an idea, Kreider recalled, was to say no.[135]

Kreider's frustration would soon dissipate, however. A new decade brought winds of change to American society, Bluffton included, blowing in directions few thought possible. Take, for example, the students and faculty occupying positions of academic and student governance in 1958-1959. By the end of the 1960s, two student leaders of 1959-1960, Martin Strayer and Marilyn Weidner, would be married and living through the Tet Offensive as volunteers with Mennonite Central Committee in Vietnam. Others such as Don Pannabecker (married to Romaine Clemens), LaVerne Schirch, and Glenn Snyder would be serving on the BC faculty. There they faced a new, assertive student generation who would offer Bob Kreider all the change he wanted—and then some.

CHAPTER FIVE

Freedom and Order, 1960-1972

During the first three weeks of January 1968, the students and faculty of Bluffton College interrupted their usual patterns of academic pursuit and launched into a community-wide exploration of a single subject. They called the endeavor the "Interterm." That month they devoted themselves to examining the theme of "freedom and order." Students opted for different seminars that applied the theme to particular disciplines, enrolling, for example, in mini-courses such as "Authority and Freedom in Education," "Free Enterprise and Controlled Economy," or "Man's Freedom and God's Sovereignty."[1]

The entire academic community gathered twice weekly in Founders Hall for convocation addresses on the topic by a variety of speakers. They heard from church historian Martin Marty, from Czechoslovak pastor Bohimur Sedlinsky, from psychologist Bruno Bettelheim, and from Haverford philosopher Douglas Steere. The avant-garde composer John Cage delivered a jarring performance of new electronic music. BC's own bright young history professor John Unruh lectured on "Freedom and Order on the American Frontier."[2]

For their part, students watched films, plunged into assigned readings, and discussed new perspectives late into the night. Some were frustrated by the seemingly abstract nature of the theme, but many confessed to a new understanding of the two concepts at the opposite poles of discussion. "In our seminar," summarized one professor, "we agreed that freedom was a 'hurrah' word and order a 'boo' word, but we discovered that freedom needs order."[3]

The entire experience served as a metaphor for the larger story of Bluffton College in the watershed decade of the 1960s. Students pushed for new freedoms, professors and administrators readjusted the conventional mechanisms of order, and nearly everyone learned to navigate a complex and unfamiliar new terrain. In a few short years, the process had worked some fundamental transformations in the traditional formulations of Bluffton College life. The changes partly emanated from the vigor of a new generation of faculty and administrative leaders. In 1965 the college welcomed a warm and capable new president who would leave a mark as its greatest visionary. His abundant energy and enthusiasm was augmented by a new coterie of restless and inquisitive professors who reconsidered many established ways of doing things and pushed the college in new directions.

But the larger engine for change came from the student body. Student assertiveness had been an important factor in other eras of college history, but never before with the intensity that accompanied it in the 1960s. Many of the traditions, mores, and ways of thought that had governed student life for decades were discarded in a few short years. Amid the freedom, however, there was also an unmistakable continuity with elements of an earlier Bluffton. Even the angry young rebels sometimes found themselves acting, intentionally or not, in harmony with the traditional mission of the college that Ramseyer and others had restated to carry the college forward in the postwar world.

New Landscapes

A third engine propelling changes at BC was simple numbers: both the campus and student body were rapidly growing. This was, of course, connected to changes beyond Bluffton; in many ways, the school merely reflected the revolution occurring in American higher education in the 1950s and 1960s. A new generation of GI Bill-educated parents combined with the maturation of their baby boom offspring to result in a huge and dramatic expansion in college enrollments across the country. In 1946, for instance, about 165,000 faculty at the nation's colleges and universities taught over two million students. A quarter-century later, in 1970, over half a million professors faced eight million students, three-quarters of them now enrolled in public rather than private institutions. In the process, college education was transformed from an elite privilege to an economic necessity and a normative experience in the lives of young, middle-class Americans.[4]

Throughout the 1950s, as Ramseyer's reports to the board and the alumni bulletin repeatedly testified, BC's leadership saw the flood of new students coming and did their best to prepare. "This is not hypothetical," Ramseyer repeatedly reminded people. "The children are there. It's not as though they weren't already born." Indeed, as college enrollments steadily increased in the later 1950s, it became clear that the oncoming waves had already begun to arrive. The president and board confidently projected the number of students they wanted, planned new dorms, and held grassroots meetings throughout the constituency to hear from the churches about how big the college should be.[5]

Not everyone regarded the prospect of open-ended growth as an unmitigated blessing. As he led the board in 1963 through a consideration of a student body he projected could reach the unheard-of neighborhood of six hundred, Dean Kreider acknowledged some of the concerns: that even more dorms would be required, that the student-faculty relationship would be "less personal," and that "the feeling of a Christian academic *community* with the *family* atmosphere might be impaired" (emphasis his).[6]

Such slight hesitation detracted little from the enthusiastic welcome mat the college laid out for the coming multitude. And the students did come. Already in 1960 the enrollment jumped the old barrier of 400 students, then took off from there. Each fall for the next eight years would see a new enrollment record set as student numbers increased by an average of 10 percent a year before peaking at 789 students in fall 1969.[7]

This growth rate would have had faculty like Lantz and Bauman shaking their heads in wonder. As the venerable old professors prepared to retire (in 1966 and 1968, respectively), the 261-member freshman class of 1967 was bigger than the entire BC student body had been through many of the early years of their careers.[8]

Tuition increases had nearly matched enrollment leaps. In the ten years previous to 1966, Kreider wrote a former student that year, enrollment had increased 132 percent, operating expenses 253 percent, and tuition 135 percent. By 1965, student fees for room, board, and tuition totaled over $1,400 annually (or about $7,400 in 1999 dollars). Yet with student aid (from government and BC sources) rising 662 percent over the same period, such expenses did not appear a major obstacle. The potential for growth seemed boundless. At one heady moment in 1965, Kreider wondered to the college's landscape architect Jim Bassett whether they might start planning for a student body of 2,000, with 1,200 students as an intermediate goal.[9]

With ever larger first-year classes arriving each fall, the most pressing need was for new student housing. Repeatedly through the decade, girders for new dorms rose into the sky over campus. In July 1960 trustees approved a new dorm for women, built next to Ropp on the corner of College and Spring Streets. All quickly agreed that the 100-bed building should be named after two BC longtime female faculty members, M'Della Moon and Naomi Brenneman. It fell to a faculty committee to marry the names. They considered variations of "Brennamoon" and "Naomadell" before finally arriving at "Bren-Dell Hall." "Overwhelmed and deeply moved" at the honor, Brenneman wrote Ramseyer that she was also pleased with the name, given other possibilities. "What if," she wondered, "apropos of the 1962 orbiting, you had hit on *Moonman*!" At the same time, the board moved to rename Science Hall after the recently retired professor Berky.[10]

In September 1963, BC dedicated its second dorm in two years, this one for men. Constructed next to Lincoln Hall on the "male" side of Riley Creek, the building bore the name of the college's first president. In 1965 the trustees okayed an addition to Hirschy that would house another 112 men, and a ninety-five-bed annex to old Ropp. Finally, in May 1969, BC completed what would be its last new dorm for a quarter-century, dedicating the complex of modular dormitories named Riley Court. The name was appropriate for buildings set on a brow of a hill on a newly bought tract of land east of the creek where a chicken farm had stood.[11]

More students also required more places to study, play, and eat. In April 1966 the college dedicated a huge new expansion of Musselman Library by having Edna Hanley Byers lead participants through the same litany the college had used for the dedication of the original building. To staff the expanded facility, the college hired a number of capable new librarians, led by Harvey Hiebert and Mary Ann Moser. At homecoming festivities in October 1970, alumni celebrated a huge new expansion of the college athletic complex. Coach Burcky had finally retired in 1968, but he was there in person to beam his approval at the dedication of a new gym, locker rooms, weight room, and faculty offices in the A. C. Burcky addition to Founders Hall.[12]

With the old Ropp dining hall taxed beyond capacity by mid-decade, an even bigger project would be the construction of a new dining facility. Kreider coaxed the trustees into envisioning a much more ambitious building than a mere cafeteria. The structure should be located in a central location, he argued in 1965, "which is not more than three or four minutes walking distance from any residential area." It must be "a setting which will contribute to grace and dignity in dining, but particularly to good conversation and a solid sense of community"; it should "encourage student-faculty conversation" and "ease of mingling," even of dating.[13]

Like so many of Kreider's visions, this one was exciting and irresistible. As plans developed, the center managed to incorporate nearly all the threads from the burst of ideas he had floated in 1965. It would be located overlooking the creek and floodplain in the center of campus, just to the east of Founders Hall, and approached through a handsome plaza studded with the art of sculptor John Klassen. It would have a bookstore, post office, snack shop, loft, and dining facilities that could accommodate up to 900, with room for future expansion. All activity would radiate outward from a sunken lounge with a jazzy name, the "Kiva."[14]

Better was Marbeck Center, the name for the entire complex, which could only have come from an Anabaptist historian like Kreider. "A bit of steam seems to be building up here among students and faculty," Kreider reported in 1966, that as "the major arena of good conversation on campus," the building ought to be named after the Anabaptist "engineer, theologian, public servant, earnest conversationalist," Pilgram Marpeck. Television personality Hugh Downs appeared on campus to dedicate the complex before an enthusiastic crowd of 1,000 people in March 1968.[15]

With the completion of Burcky Gym in 1970, the college's big building expansion was finished, though few people realized it at the time. Other buildings awaited construction. There was to be a chapel erected on the central lawn of the campus, south of Berky Hall. Particularly exciting were plans for a new facility designed to showcase the talents of a department that had traditionally been one of the college's strongest. In 1967 trustees promised a new science center that threatened to rival even the architectural elegance of Marbeck. It would be a five-story, 42,000-square-foot hexagonal structure built in front of Founders Hall, housing a separate library, classrooms, faculty offices, and state-of-the-art research facilities. All the science faculty had to do was wait for the students and money to keep rolling in—as they certainly would, in flush times that few could imagine ending.[16]

New Frontiers

The large influx of new students by itself worked a revolution in BC student life. One significant new difference seemed to be an increased level of student ability. With 240 applicants for 145 spots in

August 1961, the college could suddenly afford to be more selective about whom it admitted. Average student ACT scores hit 21.9 in 1966 and stayed at about the same level through the decade.[17]

Professors were quick to note the difference. Reflecting back on his thirty-seven years as a BC faculty member, Richard Weaver remembered that his students accepted a heavier workload in these years than at any other time in his career. "I could give them very long assignments," he recalled, "and they wouldn't bat an eye." Librarian Delbert Gratz found the library filled with students on Friday afternoons and Saturday mornings in 1963, a marked change from just a few years before; he also witnessed an increased circulation of classical record albums. Hordes of newly serious students packed lecture halls for visiting speakers and musicians. Dorm halls appeared to be quieter, with more students studying.[18]

BC professors may have toughened requirements. At least some students rose to the challenge. Departmental honors candidates in 1972-1973 included, for example, such budding intellectuals as Neal Blough, William Hawk, and Morris Stutzman in philosophy, as well as George Rable in history, who wrote a 275-page treatise on "The Impeachment and Trial of Andrew Johnson: A Revisionist Study."[19]

There were other important shifts in BC students. The percentage of out-of-state students declined. As late as fall 1959, 35 percent of BC's students hailed from outside Ohio. Eight years later the proportion had fallen to 17 percent, and to 11 percent in 1971, a trend caused at least partly by sources of state aid that began to stipulate that students attend schools in-state. Students appeared more affluent and middle class than in earlier generations and as devoted to vocational pursuits as earlier students. At one point in 1967, an NCA official estimated that "at least" 70 percent of BC students were pursing teacher certification. Increasing numbers of students arrived on campus with their own cars. This further eroded the cohesive, residential character of the campus.[20]

Equally important, the percentage of Mennonite students declined. Like Americans generally, Mennonites had experienced their own postwar baby boom and educational surge: from 1960 to 1964, GC Mennonite young people increased their rates of college attendance by 21 percent. And from 1962 to 1965 the number of Mennonite students at Bluffton increased from 158 to 200. However, the *percentage* of Mennonite students remained about level in the early 1960s, then began to drop. That was because numbers of non-Mennonite students were increasing even faster. The Mennonite baby boom peaked and then ebbed. Moreover, more and more

Mennonite high school graduates elected to attend nondenomina-
tional and public colleges. By comparison, in 1971-1972, 65 percent
of BC's faculty were members of one Mennonite group or another.
But by that year the percentage of students who were Mennonite
had dropped to 15 percent; in contrast, in 1967 the figure had been 24
percent.[21]

Of course, BC officials were concerned about the percentage
decline in Mennonite students. They cultivated relations with their
church as attentively as ever. Yet they also saw the trend as a positive
opportunity. Here was another avenue for the college mission that
Ramseyer had begun to redefine for the postwar era. At one point
MCC chief William Snyder wrote to suggest that Mennonite colleges
not encourage their students to serve with the Peace Corps.
However, Ramseyer responded with some vehemence. With nearly
65 percent of BC's students non-Mennonite, he rejoined, "we here
believe that the Peace Corps program is a program in which many of
our students could well participate."[22]

Such developments were accompanied by a marked change in
student cultural and political styles. At the dawn of the new decade,
the national political community had replaced an older chief executive with a younger and more dynamic one. John F. Kennedy promised to lead the country into a "New Frontier." Many BC students
took his message to heart and pressed toward frontiers of their own
beyond the realm merely of new buildings.

Culturally, students moved to new rhythms. Many crowded into
Founders Hall for a concert by the "New City Lost Ramblers" folk
group in 1963. Others journeyed to Ft. Wayne the next year to catch
folk musicians Peter, Paul, and Mary. *Witmarsum* reporter Jo
Davidson reviewed beat writer Jack Kerouac's new work, *Big Sur*,
and found it "a lyrical, powerful novel."[23]

There were new political stirrings. As at many other campuses
in these years, in the early 1960s Bluffton harbored its own noble
young liberals. Only 25 percent of the students had voted for
Kennedy in the student straw vote October 1960 (compared with 59
percent of the faculty). Grief nonetheless enveloped the campus on
his assassination; over a thousand students, faculty, and townspeople packed into Founders Hall to listen to faculty and staff read from
Kennedy's speeches and in other ways remember the slain president. Like the rest of the country, students chose Johnson over
Goldwater in a massive landslide in the 1964 straw vote. Because of
peace and service commitments previous generations of students
and faculty had woven into the very fabric of the institution, new

expressions of such commitment did not appear as radically out of kilter at BC as at some other campuses. All the same, the pulse of student activism began to pick up tempo early in the new decade.[24]

Civil rights emerged as a new focus of concern. In 1960, the Peace Club conducted an extensive survey of racial attitudes in the town of Bluffton, discovering a fair local commitment to racial equality (at least in the abstract). Jan Emmert eagerly stepped forward as an exchange student to Fisk University for the 1962-1963 academic year. Back on campus, seven students sent a polite petition to Dean Kreider to request that the college "secure competent Negroes to serve on the faculty of our institution" as a means of removing racial stereotypes and of reinforcing BC's commitment to racial justice. In 1964 they fasted to raise both funds and student consciousness about civil rights efforts.[25]

Guided by strong new student leaders such as Keith Kingsley, Jim Roth, and Judy Hilty, the Peace Club became even more active than it already was. Members pondered the morality of the death penalty. They mounted a play demonstrating the futility of the arms race. They brought in speakers such as Nashville sit-in leader James Lawson and pacifist activist Albert Bigelow. One evening the club focused on dangers of governmental anticommunist propaganda by showing the anti-House Un-American Affairs Committee film, *Operation Abolition*.[26]

In November 1961, fourteen BC students expanded their activist energies to a wider level, journeying to Washington, D.C., for a three-day picket and fast in front of the White House and the Soviet Embassy against the resumption of nuclear testing. In the context of the early 1960s, even this mild level of activism became a weighty public issue. The students found themselves featured in a number of local newspaper stories and TV news broadcasts, an exposure that brought the inevitable queries regarding possible inroads of "communism" at the college. Professors followed where students led, voting in 1962 against allowing local civil defense officials to designate the new Bren-Dell Hall a fallout shelter.[27]

There were also initial rumblings, in these years, of significant student agitation against the college's in loco parentis mode (that is, the sense that colleges replaced students' parents as the legal guardian of their personal behavior). Students such as Marji Hazen and *Witmarsum* editor Ron Conrad repeatedly took to the pages of the newspaper to question the policy of compulsory class attendance. Early in 1964 a student/faculty review committee was appointed to recommend changes.[28]

About the same time, partly to head off a student "strike" that had been organized, the student council held an open meeting to hear complaints about quality of food and service at Ropp dining hall. That spring the student council formally asked for more responsibility over a number of student life issues. BC's student government, proclaimed council president Phil Kingsley, should "become recognized by the Administration as a legitimate influence on their policy decisions." Later in the decade, such agitation would rise to a crescendo.[29]

Amid signals of change, BC sports life continued to chug along as before. The decade would not go down as another athletic golden age, but it did have highlights. Led by such standouts as Lynn Martin, Alex Clark, and Jim Sommer, the men's basketball team finished 17-5 in 1966, including 9-1 in league play, earning its first Mid-Ohio League championship and a spot in the NAIA national tournament. Winning basketball seasons were few for most of the next twenty years, but the Beavers fielded strong teams in the early 1970s under leadership of athletes like Clair Recker and Denny Lane. Recker was the highest scoring player on three of the highest scoring teams in BC history, 1970-1973. He set career and season scoring records that lasted thirteen years. Lane set an all-time scoring record himself and was even more impressive in his performance on the baseball diamond, where his pitching prowess landed him a spot on the All-District NAIA team for two years running, then a professional contract from the Kansas City Royals.[30]

The 1960s also saw the establishment of new intercollegiate sports. A BC golf team began intraschool competition in 1958, as did wrestling in 1963, soccer in 1967, and cross-country in 1968. The new soccer team, coached by Frank Porter, managed to win four league games in its inaugural season.[31]

The decade also saw the establishment—or rather reestablishment—of women's intercollegiate sports. Women's intercollegiate basketball reappeared at BC in the 1968-1969 season. Coached by Kate Little and anchored in the athletic skills of individuals like Yvonne Niswander, Barb Boutwell, and Phyllis Moyer, the "Beaverettes" managed to go 5-3 in their first intercollegiate season, though not until 1979-1980 would they post another winning record. In 1968-1969 Mary Lou Fretz led the new women's tennis team to astounding success. At one point in 1969 they had won thirteen straight matches, and Fretz herself finished undefeated in her entire collegiate career. Fretz's success inspired another new women's sport in which the college would later dominate. Coached by Lavera

Hill, the new women's volleyball program went 3-3 in 1968 and 4-5 the next year. With four coaches in the next eight years, the program had a difficult time gaining much headway, but the foundation had been laid for later success.[32]

The BC "marquee" sport remained football, but by later in the decade it had fallen into decline. With a stream of new stars and the coaching wizardry of Ken Mast, the football team posted fine seasons in the early 1960s. In 1962, sophomore back Mike Goings put up offensive numbers that rivaled any of Dubenion's. His 132 points, 22 touchdowns, and 1,183 total yards led the nation's small colleges. In each of his four years, Goings was leading team rusher, the first player (of just two) to accomplish this.[33]

But Goings graduated. Mast retired as football coach in 1965 and left the college altogether in 1967 to pursue business opportunities. He was followed by a string of ineffective coaches—five in the next fourteen years—none of whom seemed able even faintly to replicate his success. By 1971 the Beavers had lost twenty-six of twenty-eight games over the previous three seasons, including a miserable stretch of nineteen in a row. In the 1970 season, despite the heroics of one back, Ken Casey, who led the league in rushing, the Beavers were outscored by a total of 267-54, including three straight games to end the season when they did not score at all.[34]

"A new faculty is emerging"

Though unfortunate, losing sports teams did not represent a radical break with BC tradition, nor did active peace clubs, provocative campus speakers, or evidence of student concern for social justice. Instead, many of the more substantial changes the 1960s would usher into BC campus life occurred later in the decade. Some at least were the product of an energetic new cohort of faculty and administrative leaders.

As the student body expanded, so did the number of teachers. The late 1950s and 1960s saw, in fact, a generational turnover in the BC professorate. One by one the old stalwarts called it a career: Jacob Schultz in education; Moon and Berky in the sciences; Brenneman in English; Bauman in sociology; Holtkamp, Mann, and Lantz in music; coach Burcky. By 1965 it was clear to Kreider that "a new faculty is emerging." Each fall through the decade, the college regularly welcomed a host of young professors, sometimes in groups of a dozen or more, many of whom had passed up more lucrative positions elsewhere. Arriving either with doctorates in hand or in active pursuit of them, the new professors tended to be serious about their academic disciplines and endowed with talent.[35]

Take, for example, the new faculty in the humanities. As Kreider's teaching load declined with his increasing administrative duties, he fingered three historians who would serve the college well. Two were alumni: Von Hardesty of the class of 1961 and Ray Hamman of the class of 1949. Although "not a minister, not even a Mennonite," Dean Schultz had observed in 1951, Hamman "is about as loyal to our goals as the best of our products." In 1962 Kreider tapped a young Bethel graduate with a newly minted master's degree to teach United States history. Originally from South Dakota, John D. Unruh arrived with a flaming, infectious enthusiasm for teaching, scholarship, and the history of the western plains that would consume him the rest of his life.[36]

Convinced that "it is crucially important to have an excellent English instructor," in 1961 Kreider secured the abilities of Lawrence Templin, a Bethel graduate who had served in federal prison for his refusal to register for the draft during World War II. Templin would ably fill the post until his retirement in 1984. His colleague, a young Mennonite from Saskatchewan, Linda Falk, would arrive in 1967 and stay even longer, working as English instructor and registrar until 1999.[37]

To help the overworked Shelly in the religion department, Kreider found several impressive young professors. Don Pannabecker, Presbyterian minister and 1958 graduate, arrived in 1964 to teach Bible. As Arthur Rosenberger's son-in-law, Burton Yost was another young Bible scholar from eastern Pennsylvania satisfactory to denominational conservatives. Yet Yost was also well-schooled in BC's progressive Anabaptist mission because he had studied under Shelly and graduated from BC in 1949. Yost would construct a solid career at the college from 1961 until his retirement in 1993.[38]

The arts likewise received a fresh infusion of professorial energy. In 1960 Kreider persuaded Jim Bixel to leave Bethel and return to his alma mater. Bixel was something of a renaissance man; a pianist, conductor, composer, and quick-witted conversationalist, he would help anchor the reconstructed music department for two decades. He and Earl Lehman were joined by Jim and Jean Szabo to teach violin and Christine Purves to teach voice. Earnest young organist Steve Jacoby also joined in 1966. The painter Jaye Bumbaugh arrived in 1967 to begin a career that would span three decades. In theater arts, Kreider found a young Goshen graduate who, though lacking a master's degree, seemed promising. Gene Caskey would make the most of his chance, directing plays and teaching drama at the college from his arrival in 1962 until 1998.[39]

Once again the college was able to draw on its growing alumni list for many new hires. Howard Krehbiel (BC class of 1948) came in the fall of 1970 to teach math. Leland Lehman (BC 1942) arrived in 1968 to join Howard Raid in the business department; their efforts were augmented in 1969 with the arrival of economist Ron Friesen. Due to its sending so many alumni to graduate study, the science department was especially able to increase its ranks with its own alumni. LaVerne Schirch (BC 1958) came in 1963 to teach chemistry and serve as science department chair. The same year, biologist Maurice Kauffman (BC 1952) began a thirty-year career with the department, where he was joined in 1968 by another BC alumnus, Bob Suter (BC 1963).[40]

Schirch proved an adept fundraiser, obtaining a series of National Science Foundation grants for his active research agenda and also monies for his department. By 1971 he had wangled over $200,000 in new equipment, $120,000 of which was for a "new NCR Century 100 computer machine." In March 1970 the department added a physics major, bought a small laser, and began to construct an optical bench. At the same time, partly due to the demands of an expanding student body, the college added a whole new major in Health, Physical Education, and Recreation (HPER) in 1968-1969.[41]

Meanwhile, the home economics department had fallen on harder times, occasioned by the sweet moment in 1965 when Edna Ramseyer, heart and soul of home ec for twenty-nine years, dropped the bombshell announcement that she would soon be leaving the college for a simple reason: after a secret courtship, she and widowed ex-Bethel president Edmund G. Kaufman would be marrying. After years of collegiate turf battles with Kaufman, the best quip belonged to President Ramseyer, who remarked that "we've always had trouble with Ed Kaufman invading our territory." Administrators scrambled to find a suitable replacement for Edna Ramseyer until 1970, when Barb Stettler joined the faculty on a full-time basis and did much to rejuvenate the major.[42]

Yet "the prize" of the new recruits, Kreider admitted privately in 1964, was a young philosophy professor who arrived the next year with glittering Mennonite credentials. Elmer Neufeld had been born and raised on a farm amid dense Dutch-Russian Mennonite settlements of south-central Kansas. He had graduated from Bethel, done a stint in CPS during World War II, and earned a University of

Chicago Ph.D. in philosophy in 1959. Already by 1957 Kreider had noted that "Elmer has great potential as an administrator," talents which he steadily developed through a number of important church and peace leadership posts—associate secretary of the National Service Board for Religious Objectors in Washington, D.C. (1951-1959), chair of MCC's Peace Section (1959-1962), and peace missioner in the Congo with MCC (1963-1965).[43]

By August 1965, Neufeld had settled his large family in a small farmhouse in the countryside six miles west of Bluffton. He was anticipating settling down to a quiet life as a professor. He would shortly discover that things did not always work out as planned.[44]

They were an impressive bunch, BC's new faculty of the 1960s, and would make their own deep impact on academic and campus life. But the biggest staff change, not unexpectedly, came at the top. At the spring board meeting, in March 1964, as he looked to the approach of his sixty-fifth birthday, Prexy Ramseyer announced he would be stepping down following the 1965 school year.[45]

No other BC president (except perhaps Elmer Neufeld) has left on a higher note. In 1938 Ramseyer had inherited an institution on the ropes. Twenty-seven years later, by every conceivable measure—endowment, enrollment, physical growth, and especially refinement of institutional mission—his little college was booming. The accolades soon poured in, a process doubtless somewhat uncomfortable for Ramseyer, because he had no intention of vanishing to a fishing hole somewhere. His "retirement," characteristically, was packed: MCC service in Korea, interim pastorates of several congregations, interim president of the Mennonite seminary in Elkhart. In 1977, at age seventy-seven, surrounded by loved ones at a family reunion, he would suddenly die of heart failure, but long before, the old president could reflect on a life well-lived.[46]

"An intellectual feast"

With Ramseyer's retirement, the college prepared to greet the first new president anyone under age thirty could remember. Though the board conducted a proper search, there was little doubt in many minds who the natural successor was. On a beautiful fall day in mid-October 1965, a large crowd gathered on the sun-drenched lawn between the library and the creek to participate in the inauguration of Robert Kreider as BC's fifth president.[47]

There was something inevitable about a Kreider presidency at Bluffton, not just because his academic and administrative credentials outshone anyone else's (he had already turned down an official invitation from Bethel trustees to be their president in 1959), but because his spirit and energy encapsulated the wider currents moving through the college this memorable decade. Robert Kreider as BC president in the 1960s was a fine fit, a fact he illustrated immediately with a searching, soaring inaugural address that probed interconnections between architecture, scholarship, and Christian discipleship. "The liberal arts also are an invitation—an invitation to dialogue," his strong voice rang out. "And where there is dialogue . . . there are intriguing diversities, varieties, surprises and delights." During Kreider's years as president, these qualities would exist at the college in abundance.[48]

The new president brought a multitude of abilities. He was the college's foremost public intellectual, capable of learned comment in a dozen different fields. He was a voracious reader, an engaging conversationalist, a deft administrator, and a compelling speaker. Blessed with a fertile imagination, Kreider could quickly spin out big ideas, yet he also, Bill Keeney remembered, had the people skills to translate his visions into reality. He knew how to mobilize his troops behind a consensus that his words and enthusiasm had knit together, with little apparent need to grab personal credit.[49]

After the hierarchical style of the Ramseyer years, many older faculty found the presidential change refreshing. To a much greater degree than ever before, faculty governance became a reality at the college. The new president quickly oversaw the creation of a faculty constitution that established numerous committees with real power and that placed an elected faculty chair in charge of faculty meetings. Indeed, so much did faculty governance come to reign at the college that Kreider had to instigate the workings of a "faculty reorganization committee" in 1968-1970 to reduce the number of faculty committees because of professorial overload and possible burnout.[50]

Many of his ideas were big ones, for Kreider was intensely ambitious for his college. Even as dean he prepared a set of "expectations for Bluffton College for the next decade" which he relied on when interviewing prospective faculty members. The memo consisted of twenty-five separate items. They ranged from "well-built," "utilitarian and aesthetically pleasing but not plush" facilities, to a faculty with an active research agenda, to "a college which exposes students to a variety of intellectual experiences—some bewildering, some stimulating, some disturbing."[51]

It was Kreider's fate to preside over a college in heady expansionist times, and he played his role with gusto. Perhaps, as Keeney wondered later, Kreider's own hearty personality rendered him something of a "plunger," but he was also consistent with his own historical context. At one point in the mid-1960s, business manager Carl Lehman remembered, the board was enthralled by a personal visit from the president of Knox College, who described how he had revitalized his institution by spending much money. The ebullient Kreider took his cues accordingly and projected new potentialities in a wide variety of college affairs. He especially cared about things like architecture. He walked the campus with college architect Jack Hodell and landscape architect Jim Bassett, incessantly sketching prospects and laying out new visions.[52]

Some of Kreider's big ideas, of course, did not quite pan out. Shortly before his inauguration, for instance, he suggested that they acquire extensive mileage of the Riley Creek bottom and floodplain south and west of the college as a permanent "greenbelt," along with half a dozen different woodlots, as "woodland laboratories or biology field stations." This dream did not see fruition. And not until thirty years later did the college even begin to approach Kreider's initial target of 1,200 students.[53]

Yet it remains remarkable how many of Kreider's dreams saw quick and successful realization. There was the interterm, for example, and the huge and impressive list of speakers he brought in to enrich the academic climate. These included Supreme Court justice William O. Douglas, journalist John Howard Griffin, Nobel Prize-winning scientist Linus Pauling, and poet Karl Shapiro (all of whom came while Kreider was still dean). Though the college never established an expansive "greenbelt," Kreider oversaw the rapid transformation of the old college farm into a "rural life center." Included were a retreat center called "Der Hof," a naturalist onsite with a full program of activities for school groups, and a new seven-acre lake and nature preserve constructed with the active financial partnership of the National Audubon Society. A more important legacy of his administration is much of the BC landscape of today, especially the contained elegance of Marbeck Center, which stands as permanent testimony to Kreider's initiative and foresight.[54]

Finally and most importantly, long before Kreider's arrival at the college, he had come to embrace a progressive reading of Anabaptism that dovetailed with the college's own ideological foundation. He did not overlook or slight the bedrock Christian theological understandings that had guided the college since its founding. "To be a follower of Jesus is to be a disciple," he proclaimed in his inaugural address, "—one who accepts the discipline of Christ." Yet even as a young relief worker in Europe in 1947, Kreider had realized that "today we as Mennonites stand on the threshold of a new era of prophetic vigor." Such a voice had long been inherent in the Anabaptist tradition, he argued, but had been silenced by centuries of persecution and ensuing Mennonite isolation. In such "quietude," Mennonites were in danger of losing the light they might offer the world. It was time to hold that light higher, he declared, and "to reach out beyond our group." In his presidency at Bluffton, Kreider would pursue such a vision with immense and focused energy.[55]

The new president immediately moved to assemble his own capable staff, which came to consist of people like women's dean Lois Rodabaugh and development director Jack Purves. For his own faculty dean, Kreider managed to enlist the abilities of Mark Houshower of the class of 1942, who came equipped with a doctorate and fifteen years of experience as a school administrator and education professor. Under such leadership, the curriculum underwent nearly continual tinkering. Already by the late 1950s, Kreider had done away with granting academic credit for student extracurricular achievement. In 1968 the college entered the computer age with the approval of its first course in the field, "Introduction to Computers." That same year Kreider had begun pushing hard for student cross-cultural education and dispatched Houshower to Columbia to set up what would be a successful program there.[56]

Yet Kreider's biggest contribution to curricular revision was a huge and ambitious enterprise that by itself left an indelible impact on the wider campus climate of the era: the interterm. Though the concept itself had become a staple of the national educational enterprise—upward of thirty institutions were experimenting with various programs by 1967—BC's project appeared pioneering and received national publicity. Articles about it shot out over the AP and UPI wires. Students were intrigued to encounter a reporter from *Newsweek* on campus for a story.[57]

The interterms could not help but generate excitement. The themes by themselves underscored Kreider's confident description of the program as an "intellectual feast." In 1967 the college focused on "The City." BC offered forty movies and two plays on urban themes and brought over sixty resource persons to campus as speakers and panelists, including the mayor of Detroit, Jerome Cavanaugh. The 1969 interterm focused on "The Poor." The 1970 study of "Revolution" brought to campus such diverse and engaging speakers as right-wing columnist William Rusher and Illinois politician Paul Simon.[58]

In 1972 student demands for freedom of choice did away with the larger campus study of a single theme. Students favored independent studies, and the college shifted to a series of interdisciplinary seminars. With the college entering a more difficult financial era, undoubtedly the heavy financial cost of the program also played a role in its demise.[59]

In retrospect, the interterm was a product of and reflection of its times, both in terms of its expense and in its all-encompassing approach. It seemed to speak to increased student demand for more autonomy and authenticity in education—but could only contain these energies for a time. For six decades BC administrators had served up small measures of student freedom within the order they maintained. Now in the later 1960s, students and faculty worked together, sometimes harmoniously and sometimes not, to provide some means of order in the vast expansion of student liberties. Change was in the wind.

"Intriguing diversities, varieties, and surprises"

One arena where this wind blew with particular intensity was termed "campus conduct," particularly in relation to BC religious life. A number of younger faculty quickly demonstrated a willingness to think along new lines. This soon put such matters as required chapel attendance in different light.

The impetus for some of the rethinking emerged from an NCA self-study process in 1964-1965. The study focused on BC relations with constituent churches and sent teams of faculty and administrators out to congregations for grassroots meetings. There they met with interesting news: many in the churches would support some changing of traditional campus conduct rules. Firm Mennonite majorities remained unalterably opposed to tolerance of student drinking or smoking, but many churchgoers had themselves begun to give in to their teenagers on social dancing. Some might accede to the specter of dancing at a Mennonite college.[60]

There also might be space to change a rule that increasingly discomfited many younger faculty. Compulsory chapel attendance, declared individuals like Bill Keeney, was inconsistent with the teachings of Anabaptist ancestors who had given their lives to the principle of Christian worship as a voluntary decision. The issue seemed all the more pressing now that the college included larger numbers of students from outside Mennonite and even Christian circles. One memo of the time reemphasized the church-relatedness of the college but also acknowledged that it was "a mixed community," including those who were committed, some who were uncommitted, and some "uncertain about commitment." Meanwhile, the student council kept its own pressure on, recommending in 1966 that the college allow dancing on campus and drinking off campus and eliminate its prohibition of female smoking.[61]

Several more years of discussion followed, but the trend was clear. There would be no student smoking or drinking on campus. Three years later the faculty still resisted strident student demands for a smoking lounge. Convocation attendance rules were tightened, if briefly. Students who missed more than three convocations were called in for counseling. If they missed over six, they were suspended for a semester, a policy the college firmly enforced.[62]

But in June 1967, Kreider informed students of fundamental rule changes approved that April by trustees. Dancing would be allowed, along with moderate off-campus drinking and smoking. About the same time, a strictly worship chapel was separated from informational programs (called "convocation" and, later, "forum") and made voluntary. Professors would set their own class attendance requirements. By the following November, the college had hosted three dances, an activity that became a regular feature of campus life. Then the president braced himself for what would be the inevitable negative reaction from many in the churches.[63]

Already alarmed at many of the wider cultural changes of the 1960s, Mennonite church conservatives readily perceived the changes occurring on campus and did not like them. All around they could detect the signs of seeming religious decline: students dancing and smoking, increased reports of students drinking, attendance at chapel dwindling down to scarcely more than a dozen or two. In 1966 the traditional Bible lectures, a staple of campus life stemming back to Hirschy's day, were reduced to barely more than two days because of declining attendance.[64]

Kreider heard increasingly pointed criticisms in the later 1960s from influential pastors like Berne's Gordon Neuenschwander, who wished the conduct code "would have been tightened some instead of making it more liberal." Again the Berne church decided to cancel planned financial giving to BC. One BC trustee from eastern Pennsylvania was removed as the EDC's representative following his defense of the new standards in conference sessions. In his efforts at damage control, Kreider used all of his considerable charm and did his best to patch things up. Yet in the later 1960s, the momentum toward further change was too great to be easily resisted, even if Kreider and his staff had been so inclined.[65]

They were *not* so inclined. Whereas conservatives could highlight any number of developments as evidence of the college's seeming secularization, Kreider and others could point to other realms of college activity that suggested the endurance of student Christian commitments of other valid kinds.

There was, for example, a new staff position on campus. Late in the decade the college culminated a series of discussions among the students, faculty, trustees, and many in the churches by approving the position of a campus pastor. Kreider quickly secured a young Methodist seminarian, Richard Moman, in 1971. The larger reason for the new position was the sudden and sad cancer death, in June 1970, of Paul Shelly, who had performed so many pastoral duties for so many years.[66]

More to the point, there was the legitimate Christian transformation that had swept over the college's central vehicle of student spiritual life, the Student Christian Association. The SCA had voted early in 1960 to sever its longstanding official ties with the YM and YWCAs but continued to sponsor a busy potpourri of religious activities: Bible studies, outside speakers, and the like. By mid-decade, however, student interest in SCA activities was at "an all-time low," Ramseyer noted in 1964, with abysmal attendance at meetings. To student Judy Palmer in 1966, the SCA seemed a "dead or dying duck" for a number of reasons. So many students had distanced themselves from the "organized, structured church" that any association with the SCA itself carried a "stigma that throws cold water on anything it touches." Moreover, the degree to which SCA was perceived as standing with the administration in perpetuation of restrictive rules appeared further to alienate students.[67]

Hence, one reason the SCA redirected its activities may have been, as phrased by the *Witmarsum*, "an attempt to be more relevant." But a bigger reason may have had to do with the powerful currents produced when the college's longstanding mission combined with the peculiar *zeitgeist* of the times. In the middle 1960s, both Mennonites and other Christians inside and outside of SCA began to understand issues of peace and social justice as integral to their expression of faith. By fall 1964, SCA had begun to send regular student deputations to a variety of service sites—an orphanage, various local retirement homes, the rescue mission and mental hospital in Lima, the state mental hospital in Ypsilanti, Michigan—to try physically to demonstrate something of Christ's love.[68]

Led through the mid- and later 1960s by energetic Christians such as Gerald Wingard, Gayle Preheim, and Ed McIver, SCA activists also conducted a series of seminars, taught by faculty/student teams, that generated some student interest. Over 110 students came out for the seminars in the fall of 1964 and seventy were still participating five months later. Some of these seminars dealt with more traditional topics, such as "the Spirit-filled life" and "the church," but seminars in 1967-1968 included studies of the racial revolution and Vietnam as possible areas of Christian concern.[69]

Contrary to conservative assumptions, the transformation of the SCA did not indicate that large numbers of BC students had ceased to live by Christian precepts. It did suggest, however, that many students had begun to demonstrate their Christian commitments in new and radical ways.

For decades the college had called students to integrate considerations of peace, justice, and Christian service into their traditional understandings of faith. Though their particular expressions of this had varied, from Hirschy's day onward college leaders and faculty had increasingly interwoven such imperatives into the very fabric of the BC mission. Partly because of his own inclination and partly for reasons of institutional survival, Lloyd Ramseyer had both refined this call and also reinterpreted it to make it more readily assimilable by those non-Mennonite students who had begun to appear at the college in increasing numbers. Now in the 1960s, a new generation of activist students, within Mennonite ranks and without, began to manifest the mission in word and deed and to do so with a greater intensity and zeal than their mentors had dreamed possible.

New Offshoots of the Bluffton Spirit

The college was never a hotbed of protest, at least as compared with many other campuses in the decade. A BC senior told a reporter from the Toledo *Blade* in 1970 that "the faculty here is more progressive and liberal than the students," an observation echoed repeatedly by writers in the *Witmarsum*. Throughout the era, although conservative students repeatedly posted angry accusations on the opinion board in Marbeck about the perceived liberal bias of the college, they also demonstrated that hawkish perspectives struck a deep and responsive chord in the student body. A BC campus poll conducted during the national uproar over the Cambodia invasion and the killings at Kent State in 1970 indicated that nearly half the student body agreed with Nixon's policies in Indochina. For their part, antiwar and justice activists engaged in continual hand-wringing about the apathy and conservatism of their fellow students.[70]

Even so, midway through the decade, the campus seemed almost literally to explode with expressions of student social concern. A large number of students, for example, threw themselves into agitation for social justice. In 1967 a new "Social Action Organization" sprung into being and devoted itself to internal campus education and outside activism issues of racism, poverty, and the war in Vietnam. Over 200 students, better than a fourth of the student body, volunteered in 1967 to tutor deprived African-American children in south Lima and flooded representatives of church voluntary agencies when they appeared on campus. The work in south Lima soon took on a life of its own. Students served in a variety of voluntary positions in the black ghetto: as recreational directors, Boy Scout leaders, and English teachers. They endured some hostility as white outsiders but kept coming back.[71]

These experiences pushed some to begin asking pointed questions about the racial and power structure of the community that contributed to the poverty they witnessed. Students in the seminar taught by radical sociology professor John Mecartney in the 1969 interterm on "The Poor" launched into an extensive study of such conditions. They concluded that such factors as the "white church" and "white power structures" lay behind much of Lima's poverty.[72]

A number of BC students, drinking deeply at the wells of Christian nonviolence, found in such efforts material for a life's work devoted to social justice issues. One was Mubarak Awad. A young Palestinian student who had come to Bluffton from childhood study at a Mennonite orphanage in Jerusalem, Awad learned much of the potent combination of social work and Christian nonviolence from the tutelage of Carl Smucker. After graduation he put his training to work on new frontiers of his own. He founded the Ohio Youth Advocate Program as a means to reach troubled youth before their incarceration, then took his training and commitment back to his homeland. He mounted a nonviolent campaign for justice in Palestine before his expulsion by the Israeli government in 1988.[73]

Baldemar Velasquez provides another example of the creative Christian ferment Bluffton experiences helped induce. Born in south Texas to a family of migrant workers, he had come to northwest Ohio as a seven-year-old, settling with his family near Pandora. There he "grew up seeing my mom and dad cheated, stripped of their honor, dignity and pride" in their work in the fields.[74]

As a BC sociology major and graduate with the class of 1969, Velasquez organized area migrant workers into a union he and his father formed, the Farm Labor Organizing Committee (FLOC). Before long, his marches, picketing, and civil disobedience had begun to garner press attention as well as opposition of local farmers and especially the large Campbell Soup plant of nearby Napoleon. Throughout this process, his BC experiences helped nurture a growing commitment to Christian nonviolence. Fellow BC students like Lyle Henry and Sara Templin threw themselves into the struggle. Velasquez was also influenced by faculty like Smucker, Mecartney, and especially English professor Templin, a relationship that deepened when Velasquez married Templin's daughter Sara. BC faculty raised money for him to go to Atlanta in 1968 to work with Martin Luther King, Jr.'s Poor People's Campaign.[75]

At one point, Velasquez and others prepared a campus demonstration to demand the college participate in the boycott of table grapes but arrived at Marbeck to discover that Kreider had already ordered the removal of grapes as a measure of college solidarity. Thirty years later, FLOC continues to pursue justice for migrant workers. Velasquez is a nationally recognized labor leader. In May 1999, his alma mater would award him an honorary doctorate.[76]

As for Vietnam, it was inevitable that many BC students would follow the national opposition movement on college campuses. Given its increasingly middle-class orientation in a time when America's soldiers in Vietnam were increasingly blue-collar, the college lost few students to the war. (There was at least one. Pfc. Larry Van Meter, who had studied at the college in 1966-1967, died when his helicopter was shot down southwest of Da Nang, Vietnam, in 1968).[77]

As early as 1964, student Mary Smucker sent a lengthy letter to the *Witmarsum* denouncing the war. Gradually such voices of dissent increased in volume. BC student Joe Sprunger, for example, denounced the college's hypocrisy for its advocacy of "a policy of pacifism" on one hand, and its ready furnishing to Selective Service of the class ranks of male students on the other. Students like Sprunger and Gayle Preheim followed their antiwar convictions to service with MCC in Vietnam shortly after their graduations. Back on campus, students like Phil Sommer and Nathan Habegger agonized over whether to destroy their draft cards. Of course, such positions perhaps came a bit easier to Mennonites like Sprunger, Habegger, and Preheim. Yet the era also witnessed significant extensions of BC's mission to its non-Mennonite students, many of whom voiced, Neufeld remembered later, some of the most strident and vocal campus denunciations of the war.[78]

Later in the decade, antiwar activity on campus hit full stride, as it did on other campuses. Students listened closely to the passionate antiwar speeches during the visits to campus of national activists like David Harris and Art Gish. Some students, like Tim Kruse and Ernie Diller, staffed information tables on campus in support of Eugene McCarthy's presidential campaign. The vast majority of student votes in the 1968 straw poll went to antiwar presidential candidates McCarthy and Robert Kennedy. Activists entered an antiwar float in the town of Bluffton's 1969 Memorial Day parade, an event traditionally dominated by patriots. The float, Greg Luginbuhl remembered, was met with some cheers but also boos. Already by 1968 Kreider admitted to the board that strains had appeared in Town-Gown relationships (as interactions between a school and neighboring community are sometimes described), partly as a result of student antiwar expression and Velasquez's activities.[79]

Compared to what happened elsewhere, BC's antiwar activists were relatively calm. The huge, national "Vietnam Moratorium" demonstrations of October and November 1969 proceeded in an orderly manner at the college, marked with three days of discussion, poetry readings, discussion groups, debates, and miscellaneous speakers on campus. Students then gathered in groups to pen antiwar letters to congressional representatives and solemnly marched from Marbeck to the post office downtown to mail them.[80]

Following the killing of four students at Kent State in May 1970, BC faculty voted to cancel classes for a day to discuss the violence at home and in Indochina. BC alumnus and Kent faculty member Roy Wenger came to speak of the shootings based on personal observation. Both the faculty and the student council issued condemnatory statements. Meanwhile, the numbers of students voicing opposing perspectives sparked *Witmarsum* editor Pete Ceren to cry that "the polarization in this country and this school frankly frightens me. . . . My God! What is happening to us?"[81]

Certainly, it was no surprise that, as college campuses across the country shuddered to intense student concern about matters of peace and social justice, students at Bluffton would do likewise. The fact that such concerns had resounded for decades as the natural expression of the college's mission, however, embosses them with special significance. What made the 1960s an especially interesting time at Bluffton was that students found a number of creative ways to apply this teaching to new spheres of campus life. With Earth Day

1970, for example, a student environmental consciousness blossomed. Led by Don Ernst and Larry Crooks, one team of students hauled refuse out of Riley Creek, while Mark Steinmetz and Jim Simcox worked with another group to check the Riley's water for phosphate content. Yet in a campus that had inherited the environmental legacies of Moon, Berky, and Hirschy, this consciousness did not appear entirely out of place.[82]

The model of competent, professional women presented by scholars like Brenneman and Edna Ramseyer had only partly paved the way for what would be the emergence, about the same time, of BC's own feminist movement. Several outside speakers had nudged it along. Radical feminist Ti-Grace Atkinson appeared at convocation during the "Revolution" interterm in 1970 to describe marriage as an arena of legalized slavery and rape. She occasioned deep thinking and hot replies (including one sharp response by the gentle Steve Jacoby). Feminist leader Shelia Tobias highlighted the issues with a softer touch in 1972. More influential were voices within BC. English professor Elizabeth Yoder, for example, wrote on "the Biological Tragedy of the Woman" in an issue of the *Centaur*, an "Interterm Journal of Opinion," in 1970. Sara Templin Velasquez offered an impassioned analysis in the same issue, arguing that the women needed to show men "that Women's Liberation is serious business and that they should begin to liberate themselves also."[83]

Emerging BC feminists would have plenty of targets for their fire. As late as 1966, a woman student had been dismissed from the college because she had become pregnant. By 1975, partly as a result of the U.S. federal government's antibias decree, Title IX, the budget for women's intercollegiate sports had tripled in the previous three years. Even so, it remained less than a tenth of that allocated for men's sports. Female athletes suffered from discrimination in other ways as well. The college offered them four sports (compared to six for men), and one fulltime professor (compared to four male professors). In two of the sports women athletes had to purchase their own uniforms. In January 1970, about twenty women began meeting regularly as a "Women's Liberation group." [84]

These students and others produced a fair stream of analyses, some of them quite barbed, of matters pertaining to lives of BC women. One focus for their comments was the particularly restrictive dorm hours for female students. The title of one analysis conveys its tone: "Time to be Tucked in."[85]

Pam Neff and Priscilla Friesen Luginbuhl directed their fire at what they perceived as an aura of sexism underlying the home economics department. They argued that it was "only a tool in continuing the hypocritical system of roles particularly unfair to woman." Acting department chair Leland Lehman issued a point-by-point rebuttal, but the feminist charges had struck a nerve. In September 1972 the college canceled its curfew policy for all female students except those in the first semester of their first year and dropped even that with U.S. President Gerald Ford's signing of the Title IX amendments in 1975.[86]

Through the later 1960s, other students followed a similar process to arrive at pointed new analyses of BC race relations. Partly due to the general student boom of the decade and also to the efforts of alumni and alert athletic recruiters, a growing number of African-American students had begun to arrive. Judy Kingsley remembered only two African-Americans students in 1962, but by the early 1970s, they made up about 5 percent of the student body (a woefully small number but higher than upward of 25 other small colleges in Ohio and Indiana).[87]

These students encountered an overwhelmingly white student body. Many of these whites had come from small Ohio towns with few people of color. A smaller number of the white students seemingly arrived with ugly racial attitudes. The fall of 1968 was marred by several fights between students which had clear racial overtones. That spring several white women students who had been dating African-American men found nasty racist notes slipped under their doors. Off-campus, black students encountered what they perceived as hostile glares and other evidences of prejudice from townspeople.[88]

A month after King's assassination, a large interracial group of students gathered in the Kiva to denounce campus racism. "I'm surprised at the degree of prejudice that exists on our campus," student Steve Swartley declared on the opinion board. For its part, in June 1969 the college hired its first African-American faculty member, Archie Perry in education (who would stay until 1972). That same spring, Unruh and Neufeld began offering a course in "Afro-American" studies. The class attracted a number of students, including some members of the Black Panthers from Lima.[89]

Yet expressions of solidarity from sympathetic whites could not erase the deepening and legitimate sense of hurt and outrage felt by many BC black students. From every facet of the news media came word of racial militance elsewhere: cries of Black Power, reports of Black Panther activism, hostile racial confrontations at Cornell, San Francisco State, and other universities. Before long, BC's small minority of African-American students began to adopt something of these models for themselves. Early in 1970 they formed the Black Student Union (BSU), with participation limited to black students only and secured faculty and student council approval. At a time of financial retrenchment, they received a seemingly generous operating budget of $600, which they applied toward the many activities planned for a special celebration of African-American culture, the "Black Cultural Weekend."[90]

But sparks began to fly almost immediately. The new BSU pushed for scholarships reserved for African-American students, a prospect administrators seriously considered but rejected because of limited budgets. In May the BSU received word that the college would not provide nor allow a separate facility for the exclusive use of black students. Worse, the student council turned down an additional funding request, "one of the most biased decisions in their history," fumed the BSU. Resentment began to fester. Further seeming jibes from white students on the opinion board—"it sounds to me like the Negroes are now wanting segregation," read one—only aggravated tensions.[91]

In spring 1971, the BSU pushed agitation to a new level, sending three representatives—Adah Jones, Larry Miland, Thom Lott—to present Dean Houshower with demands. When Houshower and Kreider "evaded the issue by sending us through committee after committee," in April the BSU announced an official boycott of all classes, organizations, and athletics until the college met five ultimatums: hiring of black professors, increased enrollment of black students to at least 15 percent of the student body (and all black applicants admitted), a black admissions counselor and "black counselor" hired (with his energies channeled through the BSU), and finally, a "cultural house" for use of black students. "We expect full amnesty," the BSU informed the faculty, "and will be ready to take further actions if our demands are not met."[92]

Given the trajectory of decades of college teaching on matters of race, it is difficult to imagine the board responding with anything but nearly abject surrender. Late that month, the trustees held a two-hour meeting with the BSU. Subject to cancellation of the boycott, they agreed to most of what the BSU described as "our package deal." The board pledged the college would search diligently for another black professor, hire a black admissions recruiter and counselor, and hire (budgetary constraints permitting) a black counselor "on a periodic visiting basis." Most significantly, the college would move quickly to establish some kind of a cultural facility (though the use of the center, the college insisted, would be open to all). By the next fall, an "Afro-American Cultural Center" was up and running, tastefully decorated in Pan-African themes and directed by Nate Fields. A recent graduate and BSU leader, he had also been assigned responsibilities in the admissions office with an eye to black recruitment.[93]

Altogether the episode furnished an apt case study of what might be accomplished when an assertive group of students with a determined agenda confronted a flexible administration and board whose very sense of mission and purpose had rendered them sympathetic to such demands. From mid-decade on, similar confrontations played themselves out in a number of interrelated areas of campus life. In half a dozen years, the process would result in the rapid transformation—and eradication—of many of the traditional measures that had governed BC student life for most of its history.

"Negativism is in the air"

The emotional distance provided by the passage of time later gave Robert Kreider some perspective on the tone of student attitudes he encountered while BC president. "If you weren't angry," he reflected, "you weren't with it." Thirty years before, as a major target of that anger, even his own upbeat countenance sometimes reflected the strains. "This is the season of discontent on campus," he apprised the board in 1966, ticking off a litany of gripes with a sigh that was nearly audible: "the opinion board filled with complaints about a variety of issues . . . food in the dining hall . . . restrictive rules . . . crowded dormitories . . . unfulfilled expectations for new facilities . . . poor teaching . . . losing football season . . . chuck holes in College Avenue . . . Authoritarianism . . . Negativism is in the air."[94]

Students pressed for academic reform. By 1968 the student council had initiated regular student evaluation of courses. And sometimes the new student restiveness went beyond the academic. One snowy evening in January 1970, students studying the interterm theme of "Revolution" decided to practice what they had heard preached. Unhappy about what they perceived as unequal penalties handed out by the Citizenship Committee following a snowballing incident, more than 250 students occupied Marbeck one evening until midnight. Fifty spent the night, discussing the concerns they planned to present to the administration, including women's dorm hours, student representation on faculty committees, and smoking regulations. A small group of others broke into and occupied College Hall to accentuate the seriousness of their position.[95]

Given the confrontations occurring on other campuses in the era, where buildings went up in smoke and students shouted down administrators, at BC at least the two sides were talking in a discourse that was usually somewhat civil. Nonetheless, the fact that they faced a new kind of student quickly became apparent to nearly every designated authority at the college. Professors realized it. Students insisted that assignments be "relevant," Richard Weaver recalled, and he adjusted his teaching accordingly. One term he taught a course in which the daily assignment asked students to "go to the library. Read whatever interests you, then report on it."[96]

Even the most venerated figures of traditional authority on campus—sports coaches—faced some student resistance. For example, in fall 1969 the athletic department stipulated that only clean-shaven athletes could represent the college. To runner Mitch Kingsley, this seemed a matter not of hair but of principle. He informed his coaches that he would quit the cross-country team before he would shave his mustache. Soccer player Isaac Riak, international student from Africa, argued on the opinion board that "the Athletics Department is an instrument of the Big System which tries to impose white, middle class, Anglo-Saxon and Protestant cultural values . . . long live student power." Meetings ensued: faculty committees considered the angles, the student council pled on behalf of beards, the coaches talked tough. In the end, Kingsley's cross-country career was over, but the next year, hairy-faced men appeared without sanction on BC sports teams.[97]

In retrospect, the central event seems clear. As at so many other schools at the time, at BC students busied themselves dismantling the in loco parentis mode that had dominated campus life for sixty years. Through the later 1960s and into the new decade, many of the old traditions fell like a row of dominoes. In 1963 students abandoned the old custom of senior sneaks, with all its elaborate rules. As late as 1964, the student body still rose en masse when the faculty left chapel, but this had to be stipulated by the student council. With the switch to voluntary chapel, and attendance dwindling down to several dozen or less, this tradition died. In 1965 the student council resolved that work day and campus clean-up day would be kept, but in two years Kreider recorded that these, too, had vanished as a staple feature of campus life.[98]

Family-style meals did not long survive the change in dining hall to Marbeck from the Ropp basement. Persistent student assertiveness did this practice in. A student poll in 1968 found over a 90-percent student majority favoring its abolition. Until 1970 students ate family style on Sundays only, then even this was discarded, following the appearance of an opinion board petition with more than 300 signatures in opposition.[99]

Neither could the mass humiliations inflicted by freshman initiation survive the changing 1960s student culture. In 1967, opinion board letters questioned the ritual. "Freshmen no longer enjoy initiation," one read. "Rather they quickly learn to abhor it." Two first-year students were considering leaving the school because of their ordeal. Partly such questioning emanated from a 1960s student mindset that prized individualism, autonomy, and personal responsibility. Partly the willingness to rethink initiations may also have come from the fact that they were simply getting out of hand.[100]

BC student culture of the era seemed to have had some particularly rough edges. In the later 1960s, the minutes of the Citizenship Committee (changed to the student Judicial Board in 1971) were laced with references to student fights and other physical confrontations, many involving alcohol—a pattern which, when combined with the initiation rites, made matters worse. In 1967 Kreider offhandedly informed the board that "the most disturbing point in the year to date has been freshman initiation . . . pranks and disturbances prevailed," a statement that, in light of what actually occurred during the festivities, was an understatement.[101]

For years initiations had culminated in the "creaming," where sophomores corralled first-year students on the college lawn and hit them with pies made of materials like eggs, shaving cream, and flour. By 1967 sophomores had come up with an additional twist: first-year students were sent off on a country hayride, where they were pelted with eggs and rotten fruit. Gary Wetherill remembered one student standing on the side of the wagon and flinging hard fruit from a distance of about two feet. One young woman caught a hurled corncob on the back of her head. She spent the next two days throwing up and thrashing about in bed in severe pain.[102]

In 1969 the college announced that "Freshmen Days" would replace initiation and aim to bring all classes together for common games and recreation. Upper classes greeted this substitute with such dismay that initiation was reintroduced the next fall but was gradually replaced with "Freshman Olympics," a milder version without the hazing. This new tradition would last through the rest of the century. For years student memories of the event were cemented by images of history professor Ray Hamman (and later president

Neufeld) initiating the event with a ceremonial lap around the college track, carrying a lit torch and wearing a toga.[103]

At least some church conservatives became convinced in the later 1960s that BC was a haven for student alcohol and drug abuse. Like many rumors circulating in the churches, this one was wildly exaggerated, but it may have contained a kernel of truth. Bill Keeney came to believe, along with many in the faculty, that students had begun to drink more later in the decade. Citizenship committee proceedings of the time seem to bear this out. In 1967 Kreider admitted to the board that there might have been slight increases; Houshower later testified to much more student drinking than this.[104]

Certainly there was some illicit drug use, though the records are even murkier about how much. On the one hand, after a visit to campus, one national expert on student drug use told Kreider that BC students seemed naïvely innocent of the drug culture. On the other hand, thirty years later, Houshower still carried "a lot of pain" over the drug use and abuse of many of his best students. One morning, he recalled, he walked into his office to discover that students had left a marijuana plant sitting in a pot on his desk.[105]

Other student adoptions of the counterculture were more visible. Kingsley and Riak were no different from the mass of their fellow students, many of whom sported blue jeans, long hair, beards, and mustaches. Vociferous student pressure had quickly shattered any semblance of the old campus dress codes. Nor was it just students who appropriated the new styles. The *Istas* in the later 1960s and early 1970s show varying faculty members dressed de rigueur: Elmer Neufeld and Houshower with neat mustaches; John Unruh with long sideburns; Harvey Hiebert and Steve Jacoby with luxuriant, black, Lincoln-esque beards; and Don Pannabecker resplendent in a bushy grey beard flowing down over a black turtleneck, looking like a new member of the Black Panthers.[106]

Of course such images generated some heat from conservatives in the constituency, some of whom voiced dismay to Kreider at the specter of "hippies" and "long-haired professors" at the college. Students periodically acted in ways that set such conservative alarm bells jangling. Every so often, Greg Luginbuhl remembered, "spontaneous demonstrations" burst forth from the dorms at night, expressing no political perspective in particular but accompanied by loud rock music and dancing. County sheriffs showed up a few times to investigate.[107]

In the explosive and tense environment operating in both college and law enforcement communities in the spring of 1970, even little events could be magnified into matters of epic—and ridiculous—proportions. About 11:00 p.m. on the first warm spring evening in early April 1970, for example, an intrepid band of male students finished off a wild waterfight in their own dorm by invading Ropp Hall with water balloons. Merry and noisy mayhem ensued. In another context, this waterfight, like hundreds of others over the years, would have run its course and resulted in little more than a few students appearing late for early classes next morning and perhaps a few sanctions imposed by the CitizenshipCommittee. This particular confrontation appeared tame enough that a number of dorm residents slept through the entire affair.[108]

Yet at a time when the antennae (and budgets) of local law enforcement officials were attuned to campus unrest, the Ropp Hall waterfight assumed sinister dimensions. Someone—probably an irate local resident—called the police. Suddenly over fifty deputy sheriffs from six counties appeared in full riot gear to quell the reported "riot." They encountered about the same number of students innocently throwing water on each other. Some hot words were exchanged between students and police, a few fire hydrants were opened, and an improvised barricade was hastily constructed on College Avenue. Someone lobbed a single tear gas canister before the police went into action, arresting seven students, bystanders all, whose principle offense apparently had been to neglect to flee their approach. The next morning, newspapers from Cleveland to Dayton carried bizarrely exaggerated stories of the "Campus Disturbance" at Bluffton, describing crowds of 600-800 students roaming the streets and engaging in a four-hour "siege" of Ropp.[109]

Viewed as a totality, the 1960s at Bluffton College have the air of a wild, confusing, yet exhilarating ride. A major expansion of buildings, finances, student numbers, and quality had unfolded. BC had seen exciting curricular developments, led by a dynamic president and progressive faculty. Their energies had been overtaken by the contributions of an activist, engaged, assertive student body. All these actors and factors had together brought sweeping change to the institution along the Riley Creek. Then, in the dawn of a new decade, much of this momentum came to a grinding halt.

"These are perilous times, but we are not discouraged"

There had been moments, as record numbers of new students flooded the campus each fall, when the great expansionist era seemed limitless. As late as the end of December 1968, the *Lima News* still reported on confident college assertions of a 1,200-member student body by the mid-1970s. Perhaps the climate of optimism induced administrators and trustees to overlook demographic reports pointing the other direction. The great surge in student enrollments had leveled off, the experts quietly stated; the boom had to end. At least one BC voice had sounded a small note of caution on another front. As he announced his retirement in 1965, Prexy Ramseyer had warned that "a prolonged escalated war in Asia could have disastrous effects on college plans."[110]

Such discordant notes might be dismissed as more Ramseyer conservatism, but in the end, he and the demographic experts were right. As the building program proceeded with Riley Court and Burcky Gym, the economic foundation crumbled. War-induced inflation combined with declining student enrollments to plunge the college into debt. By 1972 enrollment numbers had dipped back below 700. The college had finished deeply in the red in three of the past four years. Overall, the college's long-term indebtedness increased from $454,000 in 1965 to $3,400,000 in 1975.[111]

Certainly, as Kreider pointed out, BC was not alone; a wide number of private colleges faced severe retrenchment at the same time and for the same reasons. Contemporary analysts of higher education used terms like "grim," "desperate," and "with back to the wall" to describe widespread collegiate financial conditions. Like Franklin Roosevelt in the national Depression of the 1930s, Kreider realized that the times required him to set a proper upbeat tone. He labored hard to sustain morale. "These are perilous times," he admitted to the church in the pages of *The Mennonite*, "but we are not discouraged." When he read in the Toledo *Blade* early in 1971 that BC's administrators were "not sure they and the students will be around to celebrate the seventy-fifth anniversary in 1975," Kreider composed a polite but firm letter to the editor assuring him that the college would survive to celebrate many anniversaries to come.[112]

Still, the college had to act. Kreider and the trustees (and also Mark Houshower, acting president during Kreider's six-month sabbatical in 1970) made hard and painful decisions. New faculty hires were curtailed. Bob Suter later recalled that he was originally hired in 1968 as an addition to the faculty, but by the time he arrived in the fall of 1969, he understood he would replace a departing professor. The next year he watched as departmental budgets were cut, other faculty not replaced, and so many secretaries let go he thought the public might assume they were the graduating class of a vocational school. Kreider accepted with gratitude the offers of seven professors who volunteered to teach reduced course loads, with appropriate salary cuts.[113]

In 1971, as they came to realize the magnitude of the crisis, the board froze hiring, froze wages (in effect this meant a general salary cut, in a time of rampant inflation), and Kreider announced additional budget cuts totaling $112,000. The college's great "brick and mortar" era was stopped dead in its tracks. The principle casualty was the exciting new science center. A special meeting of the trustees in January 1971 stipulated that before any new building could proceed, the budget had to be in balance, enrollment must increase substantially, and the college had to have the requisite cash or pledges in hand. It would take a miracle, Kreider realized, to meet these conditions and start construction on the science center by 1975. Architect Hodell quietly began scaling back the plans.[114]

To the many faculty and staff who had come to hold the college's leader in considerable esteem and affection, perhaps the toughest blow of the era came September 1971, when Kreider announced his retirement. He had said from the beginning, he reminded the board, that he would not have a long presidency; besides, he wanted to get back to teaching and administrative work for MCC. In his parting statement the following August, he reminded the college and alumni that things were nowhere near as grim as they might appear. In fact, he could identify bright spots. The faculty was immersed in the development of an entirely novel and creative reshaping of the general education curriculum. The Afro-American Center was up and running. The student council had reorganized itself, in impressive fashion, into a Student Senate. There were new stirrings of Christian commitment among the students; gift income from the constituency was up. At the same time, he admitted, a 1,200-member student body was unrealistic. BC indebtedness was daunting. And they faced severe competition from the expansion of junior colleges.[115]

One could read the tea leaves however one liked. Yet one thing seemed crystal clear: the great boom of the 1960s was over.

CHAPTER SIX

Photo Essay

Images evoke memories that speak to the individual on a level untouched by words. The following chapter relates, in visual terms, the story of Bluffton College through photographs gleaned from the college archives.

AERIAL VIEW In 1950, a half-century into BC history, Founders Hall was emerging (left center). Days were numbered for The Barn and nearby heating plant, as well as for the married students' trailer village, Beaverburg. Maintaining their roles as centers of college activity at the time were Lincoln and Science halls (center), College Hall (right center), and Musselman Library (right center), and Ropp Hall (rear center).

Late in life, Bluffton College art professor
John Peter Klassen sits with the Kobzar, his creation.

PRESIDENTS
*(above left) Noah C. Hirschy was
only 34 years old in 1900 when he
accepted the presidency of the
newly established Bluffton College.*

*(above right) From 1910 to 1935,
Samuel K. Mosiman led the college
as president while his wife, Emilie
Hamm Mosiman, influenced the
social life of the campus.*

*(above) A graduate of Bluffton College and
Witmarsum Seminary, Arthur S. Rosenberger
stepped into the presidency in 1935 and resigned
for health reasons in 1938.*

*(right) Lloyd L. Ramseyer, another Bluffton College
alumnus, was president for an unprecedented 27
years, from 1938 to 1965.*

(left) Benjamin Sprunger was inaugurated as Bluffton's president in 1972 and remained until 1977.

(above) A former professor and academic dean at the college, Robert S. Kreider led Bluffton from the years 1965 to 1972.

(left) Lee Snyder was inaugurated as the eighth president of Bluffton College in 1996.

(above) Another former Bluffton professor, Elmer Neufeld, assumed the presidency in 1978 and served as head of the college for 18 years, until 1996.

TRADITIONS

(right) A tug-of-war across Riley Creek at Homecoming decided the length of time the first-year students were required to wear their freshman caps or beanies. In 1963, the sophomores dug in their heels and were victorious.

(below)
Winding of the Maypole has been a part of Bluffton's year-end May Day celebration since before 1915, when this photograph was taken.

(right) An engaged classmate took an enforced dunking in the murky waters of the campus lagoon in this 1961-62 photo. From the early years until the present, this BC tradition has continued.

(above) Former athletic coach A. C. Burcky donned work clothes and gloves to join students in the annual campus Clean Up Day in the mid 1960s.

DINING STYLES
(left) Dining in the lower floor of Ropp Hall was a formal affair for more than fifty years, with table assignments, white-jacketed student waiters, hosts, and hostesses. This photo from the late 1920s gives evidence.

(below) With the expansion of Ropp Hall in 1958 came more informal cafeteria-style meals. Rod McDaniel and Hama Arba (far left) enjoy a meal with friends in 1963.

(left) Today the commons in Marbeck Center affords multiple dining choices in a casual atmosphere.

200

CHAPEL

(right) Weekly chapel services, now held in Yoder Recital Hall, include more student involvement than in Bluffton's early days. Brian Schmidt, Ryan Clements, and Adam Simcox led this chapel service in 1996.

(above) College Hall originally housed a balconied, hemispherical auditorium where daily chapel services, Vespers, recitals, and other programs were held. President Mosiman addressed the audience in this service during the late 1920s or early 1930s.

(right) A remodeling of the old chapel space, as seen in this 1952 photograph, did not alter the schedule of services and programs which drew students and faculty together in one place on a daily basis.

(right) The Barn in Marbeck Center offered another space in which to hold chapel during the late 1970s.

EXTRACURRICULAR

(left) Frances Beckenbach, David Rosenberger, Marcene Blodgett, Phyllis Hartzler, and Howard Baumgartner were dressed for a formal occasion on campus in 1943-44.

(below left) In the early 1900s, Halloween parties (well-chaperoned) were popular outlets for youthful enthusiasm. In this 1913 photo we recognize President Mosiman in the lower right corner and Mrs. Cromer, faculty member, at far left.

(below) The "Faculty Follies" of 1986 found Harvey Hiebert, Bob Suter, Bob Beer, Steve Jacoby, Elmer Neufeld, Ray Hamman, and Linda Suter cheering for BC.

FINE ARTS

(right) During the summer of 1922, the men's glee club made a precedent-setting coast-to-coast trip by train, bus, and car. They presented, over a three-month period, a total of 97 sacred and secular concerts from California to New York.

(above) During Bluffton's history, the theatre department has presented a variety of Shakespearean plays, including As You Like It *with Ruby Bixel and Rosemary Gutridge in 1964.*

(left) Gregg Luginbuhl majored in art in 1971 under the tutelage of his father, Darvin Luginbuhl, and later returned to campus as an art professor.

FACULTY

(below) By 1913 the college faculty had grown to 19 members. Old timers may recognize the names and faces of [back row] Mark Evans, C. Henry Smith, Harold Adams, D. W. Bixler, William Egly, Reuben Detweiler, E. J. Hirschler; [middle row] Waldo Schumacher, G. A. "Dad" Lehman, H. W. Berky, Pearl Bogart Mann, Oliver Kratz, Gail Watson, Sidney Hauenstein; [front row] Noah Byers, Edith McPeak, S. K. Mosiman, Catherine Cromer, and Ruth Easterday.

(above) Eleven professors, who saw the college through the lean years of the Great Depression and served the school an average of 40 years each, were honored in 1956. Pictured are [back row] A. C. Burcky, I. W. Bauman, Otto Holtkamp, J. P. Klassen, Russell Lantz; [front row] H. W. Berky, Pearl Mann, Naomi Brenneman, Katherine Moyer, M'Della Moon, and J. S. Schultz.

ATHLETICS
Although women's intercollegiate sports were not officially sanctioned until 1968, even in 1913 the students at Central Mennonite College had their own women's basketball team which competed with local teams.

(above) There are always plenty of fans to cheer on the Bluffton College teams.

(left) It was a long walk from campus to the high school stadium, Harmon Field, where all football games were held until 1993. Many football players, including those on this 1964-65 team, will remember riding the truck to and from the game.

(left) Clay tennis courts, bordered by Riley Creek to the west and College Avenue to the north, were much in demand from the 1930s to the early 1980s.

(below left) Men played basketball in the first gymnasium, fondly referred to as "The Barn," from its erection in 1916 until the building was replaced by Founders Hall in 1951.

(above) Former women's volleyball coach Kim Fischer proudly displayed the 1982 district championship banner.

(left) Bluffton's mascot, the beaver, is present at all football and basketball games. Here, cheerleader Lisa Brandeberry greeted the Bluffton beaver at a 1987 football game.

TOWN-GOWN

(above) Faculty and students marched down Bluffton's Main Street on November 11, 1918, to celebrate the end of World War I.

(right) Exuberance spilled into Main Street as students snaked their way through town in celebration of Homecoming 1956.

(below) The 1979 Homecoming court rode down Main Street on horse-drawn carts, while student clowns greeted parade onlookers with balloons and chatter.

GONE . . . BUT NOT FORGOTTEN

(above) The construction in 1916 of Bluffton's first gymnasium, "The Barn," was primarily the work of students who solicited the town for funds and helped in the construction of the facility. Not only athletic contests but large musical events such as the annual Messiah *were presented in the spare wooden structure.*

(left) First purchased in 1910 as a residence for female students, a two-story frame house at the corner of College and Spring was the primary Witmarsum Seminary building from 1920-1931. Then it was remodeled and housed the music department for 30 years until it was moved across Spring Street to end its years as East Hall, a men's residence.

(left) The tall smokestack of the college heating plant was a familiar campus landmark from 1915 until the building was razed in 1965. The plant provided steam heat to all campus buildings for half a century.

(below) Amstutz House was built by Jonas Amstutz, a founding trustee. Located where Centennial Hall now stands, it served as an administration office, a home to two BC presidents, and later as a residence for male students.

BUILT FOR A CENTURY
*(top) Ropp Hall, Bluffton's first
women's residence hall, was
constructed along the treeless
banks of Riley Creek in 1914.*

*(middle) Ropp Hall's massive
porticoed main entrance is familiar
to all alumni, recalling evenings
when women listened from the
second floor balcony as men
serenaded below.*

*(bottom) Built in 1915, Science
Hall offered modern, well-
equipped classrooms and
laboratories for that day. The front
steps also provided a perfect spot
to take the annual wide-angle
photograph of the entire student
body (this one in 1930).*

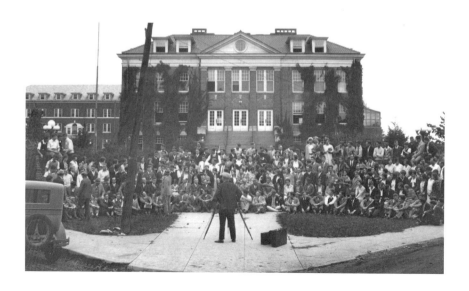

(left) College Hall's stately profile has remained virtually unchanged since its construction 100 years ago. BC's oldest building continues to house classrooms as well as administrative and faculty offices.

The 1920s saw two more structures added to campus. (middle) Musselman Library became a permanent part of campus life in 1929 and remains as such today.

(bottom) Lincoln Hall, a residence hall for men, was built in 1924.

ON WITH THE NEW

(above) Visiting artists and their audiences appreciate the acoustics and intimacy of Yoder Recital Hall, built in 1996.

(middle) Science and math professors Maurice Kaufmann, Richard Pannabecker, Luther Shetler, Laverne Schirch, and Howard Krehbiel watch colleague Robert Suter and retired science professor H. W. Berky break ground in 1976 for a new science facility, to be built primarily underground.

(bottom) A new look and feel came to campus in 1968 with the erection of a modern student center. Ground-hugging lines and a casual atmosphere make Marbeck Center a welcoming home base for BC students.

TRYSTING PLACES

(above) This 1918 photo captured Lenore Miller and her husband-to-be Aaron Myers in a quiet moment together.

(right) Generations of alumni can attest to the romantic draw of Krehbiel Bridge, now Adams Bridge. Whether wood- or iron-railed, the bridge has always been a favorite campus trysting place.

(right) The first college cabin, situated off campus on the College Farm, was destroyed by fire and replaced by a similar structure. New students are still introduced to the cabin and swinging bridge during orientation days in the fall.

(below) Whether in the first small library in College Hall or in the much more spacious Musselman Library reading room, students could always find an excuse to meet.

DIVERSITY

(above left) Bluffton's first international student, Bedros Sharian, came from Armenia and enrolled as a student in 1920. Since that time, hundreds of international students have walked the pathways of Bluffton College.

(above right) Students David Myers, Steve Evans, and Jamie Windau worked at a Habitat for Humanity project in Jamaica while on a cross-cultural trip in January 1999.

(left) Professors Russell Lantz (far left) and Donald Steer (second from right) were advisors for a 1967 group of international students.

(below) Bluffton's Black Student Union was formed in the late 1960s and was an influential group on campus. The 1981-82 BSU posed for a photo at Marbeck Center.

ACADEMICS
(above) The 1901-02 penmanship students were inspired by a drawing on instructor I. B. Beeshy's classroom wall.

(upper middle) Science students explored such intricacies as the anatomy of a cat in this 1918 Bluffton College classroom.

(lower middle) It appears that Elizabeth Boehr's home economics students had few modern kitchen facilities in their 1925 classroom.

The Bluffton Slaw Cutter Co. was operated by the economics and business department from 1961 to 1986. It provided students with a hands-on business laboratory, where they were involved in all facets of running an actual business operation. Dr. Howard Raid is pictured in 1975 with students Jim Sauder and Don Baker.

MILESTONES
(above) An excited crowd of 1,000 well-wishers attended the dedication of College Hall on October 31, 1900.

(above) Fifty years after its founding, BC reached a pivotal point with the construction of Founders Hall, a new gymnasium. Gathered around the cornerstone were J. N. Smucker (pastor), Harry Martz (mason), J. S. Slabaugh (trustee), Robert Miller (contractor), Don Martz (mason), Louis Hermiller (worker) and BC President Lloyd Ramseyer.

(right) Every person at the groundbreaking for Centennial Hall, January 12, 1999, had opportunity to turn a shovel of dirt. Faculty, staff, students, and townspeople relished being part of the celebration.

CHAPTER SEVEN

"The Mood Is Sober . . . But Still There Is Hope," 1973-1989

In the fall of 1975, the college commemorated its seventy-fifth anniversary with a beef roast, a talent show, and a lecture series on some of the college's key leaders through the years. Von Hardesty produced a solid little seventy-five-year history booklet. On November 5, the Bluffton College chorale gathered with the choirs of three area high schools for a joint concert at Founders Hall, followed by a performance of a gospel pop group from Southern California. Though the festivities seemed somewhat modest, due perhaps to budget considerations, participants still had much to celebrate.[1]

Three-quarters of a century earlier, the institution had begun with nineteen students in a single building on the edge of a cow pasture. Now the college appeared in better shape than at most comparable points in its history. Its professors had embarked on an innovative and attractive new curriculum, and its administrators seemed capable of meeting financial challenges.

On the other hand, there was no denying that the college had entered tougher times. It would spend the better part of two decades trying to recover something of the forward momentum of the 1960s. The 1970s would prove to be a particularly contentious and difficult era—not just because of years of uncertain student enrollment and continuing financial crunch, but because a combative young president would try to pull the college in a different direction over strong faculty objections. In 1977 the trustees would turn to a new president with a longer history at the college, who would lead the way through another decade of difficult economic conditions before skies began to brighten again. Under his leadership, many professors, staff, and students alike would once more take their cues from a variant of progressive Anabaptism that had governed the college since its founding.

In 1981, when storm clouds from outside seemed to be gathering with particular intensity, the college's dean and provost, Don Pannabecker, caught the tone of the times. "The mood is sober," he noted in his official report to the president, "but still there is hope, still there is a buoyancy of spirit." He admitted the college faced real threats to its own survival. Yet "still there is a striving," he stated quietly, "sometimes spoken but more often unspoken, for excellence in what we do."[2]

Human Explorations

The college entered the 1980s in a sober mood, in part because the previous decade had brought an intermittent barrage of depressing economic indicators. Enrollments had continued to fall. The student body numbered in the mid-600s through the 1970s and dropped under 600 in the fall of 1975, nearly 200 students below the high tide of enrollment of seven years before. Student ACT scores declined as well, as the college relaxed admission standards; Mennonites fell to 11 percent of the student body in 1973. That year, one reading of the deficit placed it at over $400,000. Three times in 1972 the college came within a month of not meeting payroll.[3]

Even with these uncertainties, the faculty and students carried on. Professors devoted their energies to a complete and creative overhaul of the general education curriculum. The origins of what came to be called the "Human Explorations Program" (abbreviated to HUEX) lay in a number of different developments. All emerged in 1970-1971, including an NCA self-study and a team of four faculty members dispatched to Colorado College under a grant from the Danforth Foundation to rethink the curriculum.[4]

Fundamentally the program was born from an effort to better integrate the BC Anabaptist mission with student demands for academic reform echoing from the 1960s. Students had denounced "assembly-line education," the Danforth team reasoned, and Anabaptism likewise prized individual responsibility. Students had trumpeted the power of their own subcultures, and Anabaptism stressed a similar "belief in the covenanted community and on the insights of the community as a guide to action." Hence the new curriculum needed to allow students maximum choice along with a respectful eye to guidance from the larger academic community. It needed more flexibility in the calendar structure, affording the student an opportunity to "concentrate more single-mindedly on his immediate goal." Perhaps respect for students as individuals might even mean the "elimination of the competitive grade system."[5]

Finally, the Danforth team reasoned, student demands and the Anabaptist heritage also joined in "commitment by the community to the role of living and witnessing in a hostile world." On a practical level this could translate into renewed stress on experiential learning, off-campus and intercultural, if possible. Students would actively engage their subjects of study, all with an eye to practical demonstrations of Christian truth in the real world.[6]

As it finally emerged in the fall of 1972, HUEX tried to accomplish all these objectives. The college never eliminated the grading system, but the new curriculum led to creative calendar revision, helped hands-on learning, and provided an amazing range of student choice. Reflecting clear inheritances from the old interterm, the new calendar plunged participants into three classes in two quarters, interspersed with three one-month modules, a 1-3-1-3-1 pattern. Each student was required to take two courses "or comparable units of experience" in each of the following "five dimensions of the human experience:

1. Exploring Meaning and Faith
2. Exploring the Natural Environment
3. Exploring the Cultural Environment
4. Exploring Creativity
5. Exploring World Peace"

HUEX presented students with a veritable smorgasbord of options. For instance, as the program began, under category 3, "exploring the cultural environment," students could select from eighteen different courses ranging across a dozen disciplines. The list included "Personal Investment" with Howard Raid, "Biblical Archeology" with religion professor Perry Yoder, "Cinema: Religious Themes" with Burton Yost and Dale Dickey, "Aging in the Modern World" with social work professor Carl Smucker, and "The Cultural Implications of Golf in Modern Society" with physical education instructor James Knox.[7]

The program began with considerable enthusiasm in the fall of 1972; one student-faculty preference poll noted high percentages of both students (78 percent) and faculty (83 percent) viewing HUEX favorably. Problems appeared soon enough, however, leading to an inevitable process of curricular tinkering. Even before the program had been launched, Burton Yost wondered whether faculty might be tempted to compete for students with "exotic" offerings. He urged Houshower to "take a hard look at the menu in terms of good nourishing food."[8]

For example, as part of HUEX, Delbert Gratz began to offer a course in mountain climbing that included real-life experiences in the Rocky Mountains. This was a wildly popular course, and Gratz took it seriously. As part of their training, he had students rappel down the sides of Musselman Library. No doubt some participants had "mountain-top" spiritual experiences. But was it really appropriate, some faculty wondered, to allow this experience to count as credit for completing Category 1, "Exploring Meaning and Faith"?[9]

Early proponents of the program like Elmer Neufeld and even some students, like Peter Passage and Eileen Ewing, began to wonder whether the college was shortchanging rather than reinforcing its mission. The college "has always been committed to training men and women with certain kinds of values and commitments," Neufeld argued. Now the wide range of general education courses the college offered, he asserted, enabled many students to escape confronting "the basic goals of Bluffton College as a Christian Liberal Arts Institution."[10]

Other professors complained that HUEX demanded an exhausting regimen of new course preparations, decreased rather than increased course flexibility, and lessened student choice because of scheduling conflicts. In late 1976, the faculty restructured HUEX into two tracks, requiring each student to select one class in the five categories from a list of more traditional surveys ("Fundamentals of Biology," "Introduction to Literature," and the like), including a required course in Bible or Christian theology.[11]

BC professors and administrators launched new academic initiatives in areas beyond HUEX. In 1978 the old requirement of senior oral examinations was switched to a junior-year stipulation. More indicative of the college's straitened economic circumstances were a variety of vocational programs plainly designed as market incentives to attract additional students. By 1979 the college had begun to offer B.S. degrees in medical technology and nursing. The nursing program would last until the late 1980s, when it was phased out because another analysis determined it no longer financially viable. In the later 1970s, for similar economic reasons, the college began offering a series of evening classes as part of a degree-completion program in Lima.[12]

Such programs raised eyebrows of stalwart faculty defenders of the liberal arts. "Are we becoming a 'vocational' institution?" wondered one faculty committee. "Is it appropriate at Bluffton College to be using words such as *marketing, packaging courses, entrepreneur, aggressive,* and *relevant*?" [emphasis theirs][13]

But the college did what it had to. Through their persistent pleading and the support of new president Ben Sprunger, the science faculty finally got their new building. Though economic circumstances of the decade forced it to be only a shadow of the original grand design, it was still no ramshackle affair. It retained the hexagonal shape envisioned in the 1960s plans but was dug into a hillside south of Founders Hall to conserve energy and preserve the environment, key 1970s concerns. It offered 11,000 square feet of space for college scientific endeavors, including room for faculty offices, classrooms, labs, and a new science library. The Kresge Foundation contributed $100,000, but the building bore the name of Gursaran (Frank) Shoker. He was an industrialist who had come to BC as a 1950s international student from India and had pledged a quarter-million dollars for the building. As it dedicated the new Shoker Science Center in December 1978, BC also dedicated a small adjacent greenhouse, a gift of Cloy Miller of the class of 1926.[14]

Even with the excitement of HUEX and new campus construction, there seemed an ambiguous quality to mid-1970s BC student life, especially compared to intense student energies of the previous era. On one hand, extracurricular life seemed to exude (to echo the assessment of the nation offered by U.S. President Carter not long after) a vague sense of malaise. Student senate president Ken Spiert complained of massive student apathy in 1974. He reported to the board that "it has been difficult to arouse student interest in any issue." For several years in the early 1970s, the *Ista* became a much smaller and cheaper affair with a new name, the *Profile*.[15]

Because of student disinterest, it was unclear if the *Witmarsum* would survive. In May 1973 the paper sadly announced its own impending death. It reappeared the next fall, dramatically "saved" by new student energies, but came out only sporadically and in such poor newsletter quality that other students came forward in spring 1974 with a proposal to start a new campus newspaper. It fell to professors such as Unruh and Hardesty to transfer successfully the old name to the "new" paper. So the *Witmarsum* struggled on.[16]

Beyond the malaise there was simple tragedy. In late October 1978, a fire swept through a ground floor room in Bren-Dell Hall, killing student Dan Purdy.[17]

Early in 1976 the BC community was convulsed in sadness over the fate of John Unruh. Already by the early 1970s Unruh had become a legendary teacher: a masterful lecturer, caring adviser, and such a stickler in terms of grading that his students would often find their term papers returned with Unruh having circled matters such as wrong page numbers in individual footnote citations.[18]

Unruh's capacity for work was astounding. Endlessly he reorganized his courses, changing books from term to term, revamping lectures continually, all the while chairing important faculty committees. Through the academic year he routinely got by on five hours of sleep per night or less. An intense perfectionist, summers he immersed himself on a project he came to call "my albatross," his dissertation on the pioneer experience on the Oregon Trail. This undertaking was so demanding he allowed himself only one proper vacation in a packed eight-year period of researching, writing, and teaching.[19]

Feeling ill in early winter 1976, Unruh submitted to medical tests. Three weeks after turning in the final copy of his 880-page dissertation, he underwent surgery to remove a brain tumor. A few days later, mid-January 1976, he was dead of cancer at age thirty-eight. His fellow history department colleague Hardesty and his wife Ellie shepherded the dissertation through to publication three years later. *The Plains Across* received a fair bushel of awards; the eminent Western historian Ray Allen Billington lauded it in the *Washington Post* as "the best book ever written on the overland journey." It was still in print in 1993, having sold over 14,000 copies. But Unruh's passing had left a monumental hole on campus.[20]

There may have been a sense of languor among students, but on the other hand many of the issues and energies of the 1960s did not dissipate overnight. In 1973 young feminists flocked to a class entitled "The Creative Use of Woman Power." They created their own separate "Woman's Student Government Association" and pressed the president about unfair dorm hours. In 1974 a "Woman's Recreation Association" sprang into life.[21]

The Black Student Union continued apace, building from the real efforts the college had invested into recruiting African-American students. In the fall of 1972, nearly 10 percent of the incoming first-year class was black; by the next fall Sprunger could report that BC's enrollment of people of color was the second highest percentage of any college in the state. The BSU focused much of its energy on annual "Black Emphasis Week," complete with talent show, style show, dances, and the election of a separate King and

Queen. Yet in 1976, trying to pare expenses and expand support of international students, the administration changed the "Afro-American Center" into a larger "Inter-Cultural Center" designed for "appreciation of the heritage of various cultures" on campus. Somewhat surprisingly (in light of the militancy of four years before), the move met apparent acceptance by the BSU.[22]

With radical professor Mecartney around until 1976, the campus continued to percolate with an undercurrent of political activism. Following up on a Forum speech by socialist leader Michael Harrington, in 1974 Mecartney and a handful of students formed a campus chapter of the Democratic Socialist Organizing Committee. The group dabbled in local Lima politics, brought speakers to campus, and attended national socialist meetings.[23]

There were other indicators of continued student vitality. In January 1973, fifty-one BC students had embarked on cross-cultural trips to Vienna, Russia, London, and Florida. That June the college inaugurated an honors society named for C. Henry Smith. Discipline-oriented organizations such as the Math-Science, Investment, Social Studies, and Social Work Clubs continued with a full slate of activities. A new group, KIDS, began a regular visitation of area orphanages, nursing homes, and detention homes. The annual spring musicals attracted the energies of a variety of students, many of them talented. There was, for example, the performance of Jeff Boehr and Julie Osborn in the lead roles of Curly and Laury in *Oklahoma!* in 1977.[24]

Rather than malaise, perhaps mostly what occurred among BC students moving from the 1960s ferment to the 1970s was a shift in mood. Both student and faculty participants in a straw poll on the eve of the 1976 presidential election preferred the Democrat Carter over the Republican Ford, with the faculty demonstrating a much higher Democratic affinity than students.[25]

Nonetheless, a change was again underway, as the student senate discovered in 1974. In accordance with sympathies for migrant labor stemming back to Velasquez's day, the senate had committed the campus to boycott lettuce in solidarity with the United Farm Workers. But a student petition appeared on the opinion board, demanding the senate submit the decision to a student referendum. After public debate, with visiting representatives speaking on behalf of both growers and farm workers, a firm student majority voted to reject the boycott.[26]

Even more telling was a reorientation of student religious commitments in a decidedly more evangelical direction. Again this was a trend in line with larger developments. Bethel's student body president noticed "a real generation gap" between students who had arrived at college "before Kent State and Cambodia" and those who arrived later; new students at Bethel and a number of Mennonite schools found more excitement in Bible studies than in politics. The same movement quickly gathered power and momentum at Bluffton. The revivalist Bill McKee and his "Young and Free Singers" had appeared on campus in 1971 to urge "revolution through Jesus Christ." In spring 1972 the *Witmarsum* had heard enough of the "various rumors floating around about the 'Jesus Movement'" that it assigned a reporter to take "a closer look at the God Squad." The Fellowship of Christian Athletes was meeting regularly with roughly thirty active members. On Sundays as many as fifty students began gathering regularly for worship and fellowship.[27]

The more dramatic developments were the unstructured ones. That fall of 1972, for example, a Bible study and prayer group began meeting weekly in a men's dorm. One evening a participant felt "bothered" by his sense of the presence of Jesus. This quickly spread to others in the group. Other men in the dorm woke up and joined a spontaneous prayer meeting. Soon they came pouring out of the building, early in the morning, and proceeded to the women's dorms and then downtown. There dozens of students knelt for prayer in the deserted street. "Religion," one observer commented, "has become an all-campus topic."[28]

The advent of this "Jesus Movement" had its nucleus in the last years of the Kreider presidency and predated the college leadership transition of 1972. But such developments lent steam and authority to the efforts of an ambitious, young new president who arrived that fall determined to pull the entire college in exactly this direction.

"The Christian College of Western Ohio"

In the spring of 1972 a BC presidential search committee wrapped up its work by appearing to break new ground for the college. They recommended the candidacy of Gladstone Brown, a prominent Methodist leader from the Cleveland area. Brown had solid credentials as an administrator and church leader and may have served the college well. But the larger board demurred. Mennonite ecumenicity had stretched widely in the postwar decades, but not enough to allow a Methodist to assume the helm of a Mennonite college, even one with a minority of Mennonites in its student body.[29]

In two months the search subcommittee had produced another intriguing candidate, more acceptable to the larger board, who promised to stretch Bluffton's sense of ecumenicity in other ways. On June 24, 1972, the trustees voted unanimously to invite Dr. Benjamin Sprunger to serve as the college's sixth president. The larger community inaugurated him in a gala ceremony the following October.[30]

Sprunger came with impressive credentials: B.S. in education, M.A. in counseling and psychology, Ph.D. from Michigan State University in personnel and higher education administration. Despite his relative youth—age thirty-five—he had accomplished all that and held a variety of administrative positions besides, including associate dean of students at a rock-ribbed evangelical school, Wheaton College, and more recently as a senior planner for the National Institute of Education in Washington, D.C. Of more immediate BC significance, Sprunger was a child of First Mennonite Church in Berne. There he had grown up under the spiritual guidance of his childhood pastor, Olin Krehbiel, a firm BC supporter.[31]

He arrived saying all the right things. In a sermon he gave more than forty times in his first visit to the college's constituent churches, he called on BC to reaffirm its mission as a church-related college dedicated to "the Anabaptist heritage of love, service, peace, reconciliation and freedom of choice." At the same time, his immersion in the world of education administration provided him with a clear reading of the nitty-gritty task at hand. Beginning his second year on the job, he told the faculty-staff retreat in August 1973 that "I am more persuaded than ever that the major task is survival," and offered ample demographic data on the numbers of high school graduates for the next seven years to illustrate his point.[32]

Besides skills as a financial manager, Sprunger proved to have a keen eye for other administrative talent. Even before taking the reins of the presidency, he managed to woo another young Ph.D. in higher education personnel he had known from Michigan State University circles to serve as dean of students. Don Schweingruber came to Bluffton that same fall of 1972, intending, he remembered later, to stay a few years before moving to something bigger, but in the end he would hang around a bit longer. When Mark Houshower resigned the deanship in 1973, Sprunger recognized the immense administrative potential of philosophy professor Neufeld and promoted him to be academic dean.[33]

Altogether the college community had every reason to take heart. They seemed to have a capable new president with firm back-

ing in the churches. Every sign pointed to another period of successful administrative leadership. The fact that Sprunger's presidency
instead became such a troubled one still shrouds that era in considerable sadness and a sense of missed potential.

Though some in the BC community came to regard the new
president as some kind of rabid fundamentalist, the caricature was
unfair. He could be clearly located with an emerging group of "New
Evangelicals," a theologically conservative but politically progressive group of younger seminarians and intellectuals who had begun
to push the cutting edge of evangelical social concerns in the early
1970s. Sprunger was no right-winger. To a friend serving on the staff
of a congressional representative involved in the Watergate hear-
ings, Sprunger wrote with a plea to "keep the heat on Nixon!"[34]

He had his own criticisms of the conservative evangelical world.
When a prospective student asked whether he should choose
Bluffton or Wheaton, Sprunger characterized the latter school as "a
very closed community" and a "hothouse environment that many
times stifles a student's confrontation with spiritual and behavioral
norms." Bluffton, by contrast, was " an open campus" with "a het-
erogeneous environment that is anything but artificial." Sprunger
voiced private reservations about a local revival crusade conducted
by the National Association of Evangelicals. Instead, the kind of
evangelist he attempted to get to come to campus was Tom Skinner,
a fiery black revivalist who laced his evangelical appeals with cries
for racial justice. Likewise, he expressed admiration and personal
warmth to the progressive evangelical writer and justice advocate
John Alexander.[35]

Still, on hearing of Sprunger's accession to the BC presidency,
Goshen's J. C. Wenger wrote to express his joy "to see a dynamic
Evangelical serve as president of Bluffton," and there is no reason to
doubt the fundamental accuracy of Wenger's characterization. As a
recent Wheaton dean and a proud product of one of the more conservative congregations of the General Conference Mennonite
Church, Sprunger may have been politically progressive but
retained a deep affinity for evangelical theology and subculture.
When asked by the *Mennonite Weekly Review* to list two books that
shaped his life and thought as a Christian educator, he responded
with C. S. Lewis's *Mere Christianity* and a book put together by the
faculty of Calvin College called *Christian Liberal Arts Education*.[36]

Naturally such a perspective would shape the way Sprunger
conducted college affairs. He wrote to former colleagues at Wheaton
and a dean at Fuller Theological Seminary soliciting candidates for

Bluffton's faculty. At the same time, he urged the trustees to enter the college in a coalition of evangelical colleges, the Christian College Consortium.[37]

Sprunger immediately set out to strengthen BC relations with many of the more conservative churches in the constituency who had grown increasingly alienated from the college. From their perspective, conditions at BC had gone from bad to worse. In 1970 the BC faculty had approved a student Bahai'i Association, and not all observers of the college caught the amendment the faculty added to the words of approval ("this does not necessarily mean we approve of the tenets of the Bahai'i faith"). At first under HUEX, students no longer had to take a specific course in Bible or Christian theology, a requirement the faculty had specifically rejected as "counter-productive." One student complained in the *Witmarsum* in 1971, perhaps unfairly, about the "listless Religion Department" and "the number of Revs on the faculty who don't rev much Christian spirit."[38]

For seeming concrete evidence of the secularism predominant at the college, critics could point to the wild student enthusiasm for the rock concert staged in 1975 in Founders Hall by the group REO Speedwagon. It was for good reason that Sprunger circulated so tirelessly in the churches and pointed publicly to matters like increased patterns of student chapel attendance. Slowly he managed to win back at least some support from conservatives disaffected by 1960s changes. Already by 1974 Sprunger had begun to claim that "we have turned the corner" on student spiritual expression and commitment. Relentlessly he pushed forward with his program.[39]

But Sprunger's evangelical agenda quickly began to encounter resistance across the campus from students and faculty. It became apparent to many students that, in the continuum between freedom and order their forebears had widened in the 1960s, the pendulum had begun to swing back toward order. "The work in tightening rules and regulations is a most difficult, frustrating, discouraging and long-pull activity," a battle-scarred Sprunger advised a student dean from another college in 1976. "It almost requires a complete turnover of students before the heat and name-calling dies down."[40]

He had encountered a fair bit of heat and name-calling when he had tried to tighten rules at BC, a campaign he had extended on a number of different fronts. He closely monitored the number of empty beer cans the grounds crew had collected from dorm trash cans, reported to pastors with some relief that recent appearances of campus "streakers" (nude dashes in public places) had been few, and distanced the college from nude drawings in a student art show.[41]

The president's major arena of conflict with students occurred, once again, over the old contentious area of dorm hours. Early in 1974 students presented the president with a proposal to double the dorm intervisitation hours on campus, a proposal that had won approval of the faculty-student Community Life Committee. Sprunger promptly vetoed it as a matter that would "encourage behavior antithetical to scriptural imperatives." The veto, he admitted to constituent pastors, has "made me less than popular."[42]

But sometimes he seemed to be losing the larger fight. A faculty meeting had just concluded one evening when the president told Dean of Students Schweingruber that he wanted to stop in at the rock concert by REO Speedwagon, then underway in Founders Hall. Sprunger was aghast at what he found: ear-splitting music and great clouds of marijuana smoke wafting through the air. But the dean prevailed on Sprunger to keep his cool and let the students work it out. Schweingruber's course proved correct. The student committee in charge of such programming (Marbeck Center Board) concluded shortly afterward that the concert had attracted a huge number of nonstudents, not a good thing for the college, and would not be repeated. Schweingruber likewise resisted repeated demands from Sprunger summarily to expel students caught for violations of the alcohol ban.[43]

As contentious as the struggles were between the president and the student body, already by 1974 they paled in comparison to those between Sprunger and the faculty. That spring, the board wished both students and faculty might be "involved with the administration rather than polarized in opposition to it," but tensions only escalated. Part of the conflict stemmed from a fundamental divergence of opinion between Sprunger and the BC professorate over the proper direction for the college. This divergence was illustrated in faculty reaction to a major paper Sprunger delivered to the fall 1976 faculty retreat, then distributed widely to trustees, students, and ministers.[44]

The paper, entitled "Bluffton College: A Time for Appraisal and Action," began with a long section laying out in impressive detail the extent of the college's fiscal challenges: the coming demographic trough of high school graduates, the likelihood of increased competition from public institutions and declining amounts of governmental aid, the college's still-numbing level of indebtedness, and the like. "The short of it," Sprunger summarized, "is that Bluffton

College . . . is headed for an extremely difficult period of time." He even feared "the institution's ability to survive."[45]

He laid out four directions the college might go, but the way he phrased them (accepting the status quo and certain decline, becoming a vocational-technical school on one hand or an elite institution on the other), there was only one true option. Sprunger pointed to other schools, conservative evangelical colleges like Wheaton, Malone, and Cedarville, who chose none of the above options but were clearly flourishing. The way to future prosperity, he proclaimed, lay in a similar reconstruction of Bluffton as "the Christian College of Western Ohio."[46]

Such a course demanded, the president was clear, "some modifying, delimiting, and recapturing of the College's original intent and heritage." He laid out specific suggestions. Required was redesigning the college to appeal to a recognizably "limited clientele," the 3-5 percent of eighteen- to twenty-two-year-olds identified by the Christian College Consortium as desiring an evangelical college education. The college already had a small minority of evangelical students, but they were "thought of as second-class citizens by the secular majority." The conservative minority, Sprunger proclaimed resolutely, "needs to be a majority even if it makes some faculty uncomfortable."[47]

The president, in fact, took a number of pokes at the faculty, many of whom, he implied, relied on "Mennonite and ethnic pride" as an "excuse for lack of assertiveness, productivity, achievement, scholarship, accountability, piety, and the demand for excellence." Instead, the college needed emphatically to reject the mushy morality of the "progressive education movement" and return to strict discipline and teaching of values. Students caught cheating or drinking should be automatically expelled. The college needed a statement of Christian doctrine to which every professor, staff member, and trustee would be held accountable. Most of all, they needed "a movement of God's spirit through Bluffton's campus that would reawaken and rekindle faith, love, and Christian spirit."[48]

Though Sprunger presented this stunning tour de force without once using the word "evangelical," it was nonetheless a clear indication of the direction he intended to take the college in the future. And it met with decisive and immediate rejection by many faculty. There was a tense and suspicious atmosphere in the retreat following the president's presentation, J. Denny Weaver remembered later. Given the tough words Sprunger had flung at the faculty, it is hard to know what else he could have expected. "While Bluffton College claims to be church-related and Christian, college personnel mostly go about tasks as if no statement existed," the president's paper had read. To many professors, these were fighting words.[49]

Sprunger had asked two professors—faculty chair Bob Suter and historian Hardesty—to respond to his paper. Both stood to offer blistering critiques. "I reject the notion that Bluffton College has simply 'drifted,'" Suter declared. Hardesty took offense at Sprunger's depiction of the college as having "secularized." The college had a deep and treasured heritage of Christian commitment and pervasive sense of Christian mission, Hardesty argued eloquently, which, in his haste to "re-caste" the college into the homogenous "mold of the Christian College Consortium," the president had overlooked. The college had a valuable ethnic and religious pluralism which the president threatened to destroy. Finally, Hardesty observed, "the evangelical option does not reflect the priorities of a substantial number of faculty."[50]

Whatever the response to Sprunger's paper, one thing was clear: the president had signaled a change in orientation. Yet it was not an entirely new option for the college to consider. Since Lloyd Ramseyer's confrontation with Bible professor A. C. Schultz in 1944, the college had successfully carved out a self-identity as an Anabaptist college just to the left of the evangelical world. It had remained wedded to its Christian rooting in the Mennonite grain, but, following the lead of founders such as S. K. Mosiman and his "practical Christianity," had insisted that this Christianity would be reflected in acts of peace and service rather than in doctrinal formulations.

Now a new president pointed to a newer formulation of the older course Schultz, Schroeder, and other conservatives had demanded in generations past. And again many in the BC community gathered to resist. One stalwart alumnus, a Presbyterian Church elder, warned Sprunger that "if you are attempting to make Bluffton another Oral Roberts or Wheaton College, be assured I will never encourage another person to go there." When admissions director Arman Habegger proposed reorienting college admissions marketing more effectively to tap the evangelical youth subculture, faculty raised red flags.[51]

Then the trustees indicated a favorable enough response to Sprunger's paper to appoint a committee to map out its implementation. The die was cast.[52]

Certainly Sprunger's intended reorientation of the college furnished grounds enough by itself for a conflict with faculty and staff who treasured and carefully guarded the legacy of Mosiman and Ramseyer. But another part of Sprunger's series of troubles lay in a more personal sphere. At the faculty retreat in fall 1973, Sprunger acknowledged that his relationship with many was strained. And he had not been in office yet a year when one perceptive outside observer, Mennonite Biblical Seminary president Erland Waltner, penned him his sense that "your relationship to certain members of the faculty may well constitute your greatest challenge." Waltner's words would soon prove prophetic.[53]

The strains emanated from a number of sources. As noted above, some faculty responded with distaste to the marketing approaches Sprunger and his staff selected. These struck some professors as unnecessarily entrepreneurial and unappreciative of the liberal arts tradition. More troubling to many faculty was Sprunger's attempt to tighten the criteria for tenure and also to re-evaluate tenured faculty. This was a complex and demanding initiative that seemed to express a number of different agendas. It stemmed in part from the college's difficult financial condition. Sprunger set up a "Blue-Ribbon Committee" of faculty members to take a hard load at teaching loads and student numbers and recommend tenured positions that might be cut.[54]

Certainly the rethinking of tenure criteria also came, in part, from a recognition of the new possibilities inherent in a changing academic job market. Gradually it became easier to find candidates with a terminal degree or near it, and expectations had begun to change accordingly. In such a context, the new stipulations floated by Sprunger and Neufeld that a terminal degree (in most disciplines, a Ph.D.) would be required for tenure do not seem unreasonable. In 1980, by then as president, Neufeld firmly established that policy, in fact, and the percentage of BC faculty with terminal degrees rose.[55]

But in the mid-1970s the policy engendered much faculty unhappiness and a series of countermoves. Professors created and obtained trustees' approval for a proposal by which faculty working on their doctorates could delay their tenure candidacy. They also established, again with both administrative and board approval, faculty grievance procedures.[56]

Specific consequences were what really exacerbated faculty evaluation and tenure tensions. Sprunger and Neufeld recommended that tenure be denied to two longtime BC professors and that one tenured professor be let go. Sprunger arrived at the decision based on a number of considerations, most supposedly backed by objective market rationales: teaching evaluations, low student enrollment in their courses, the college's larger financial distress, and the like. In the end, the trustees overrode Sprunger in one of the two tenure cases, refusing to cut the faculty position. But fuel had been added to the fire; faculty fought the president tenaciously. "Termination of a tenured faculty member is not in harmony with our tradition of two-way commitment between college and faculty . . . ," professors charged. "Morale is low."[57]

Many professors disputed whether college finances were truly bad enough to justify such decisions. And many suspected that what really lay behind the moves were more personal considerations (suspicions supported by fleeting remarks in Sprunger's private correspondence, such as his grousing to one supporter that the board had "tenured a Catholic"). Instead, professors saw the president threatening the careers of cherished colleagues and watched some of them depart in clouds of hurt and anger. Feeling bypassed and neglected, Mark Houshower resigned as dean in December 1973.[58]

Even more damaging to the president was his encounter with longtime college treasurer Carl Lehman, who commanded deep respect and warmth among the faculty. In 1975 Sprunger assigned him different duties. Lehman saw this as demotion and part of an effort to scapegoat him for financial problems inherited from the 1960s. Bitterly angry and deeply hurt, Lehman publicly resigned his position and sent a scorching letter to board chair Richard Rosenberger. At a tearful goodbye reception he pled with the faculty to refuse to let the college's motto stay so "soiled."[59]

In early winter 1977, faculty met privately to prepare a lengthy list of charges against the president, many of them quite damning, then delivered it to the board. When Sprunger sensed that the support of the trustees had begun to waver, both for his decisions on tenure and for the larger direction he intended to move the college, he submitted his resignation to force the issue. Since "the board believes that reconciliation is impossible," he told an astute *Witmarsum* reporter, "it seems appropriate to provide them the option of my contract at its expiration. You don't stay when you aren't wanted anymore." At its meeting in April 1977, the board accepted Sprunger's resignation, effective at the end of his term in August 1978. Perhaps it was just the easiest way out of the impasse.[60]

It had been a sad and even traumatic episode. Certainly the tumult obscured the financial accomplishments of Sprunger's presidency. Against a backdrop of difficult economic conditions, in each of his years as president he had balanced the budget. The college had completed both a major new building and a $1.8 million capital campaign. It had seen the endowment increase 35 percent and giving from constituent churches rise 300 percent.[61]

Yet this did little to ease the predicament of the trustees. In fall 1978 Sprunger left the college with a considerable feeling of alienation, a sense that threatened to extend to many of the conservative churches in the constituency whose support he had so effectively rekindled. A number of congregations, including Berne, sent letters to the board to express their disappointment. Nineteen pastors of the Eastern District Conference signed a joint statement of regret and sadness at the news of Sprunger's resignation. They requested that the trustees continue to construct a college from which their young people could receive "a definite evangelical orientation."[62]

Embroiled in perhaps its most weighty presidential pick since 1938, the board faced a numbingly difficult set of preconditions. These letters from the churches underscored that the trustees needed to find someone much like Sprunger: a leader who could retain the support of the conservative churches and ably manage the college's fiscal affairs in economic times that promised to be tough for years to come. At the same time they needed a president who could do the above while drawing on the respect and cooperation of the faculty and building on and even amplifying the traditional mission of the college. The board might have searched long and fruitlessly for a leader with such an impossible set of credentials, except that a candidate was right under its nose.

Walking the Highwire

The trustees culminated their November 1978 meeting by announcing that Elmer Neufeld would become BC president. The announcement was no great surprise. The dean had an impeccable résumé as administrator, knew the college and constituency, and seemed ready to hit the ground running. But Neufeld offered more. If anyone could pull off the required balancing act, it was he. For much of his career, Neufeld had shown ability to walk the highwire between different and competing constituencies. In his twenties he and he wife LaVera had brought their young family to live in areas where they stood out as racial minorities, first in South Side Chicago, then amid potentially explosive racial turmoil in Central Africa in the early 1960s. He had won trust and friendship across tense racial lines. Somehow he had retained faculty affirmation while serving as Sprunger's loyal dean through the 1970s conflicts. He had studied under progressive scholar and church leader E. G. Kaufman at Bethel and identified with denominational peace and justice activists. Yet he had also gently objected to what he saw as Kaufman's liberal theology. He retained an ability, inherited from a pious Mennonite childhood, to speak to conservatives in their own language, in a manner that invited their trust.[63]

Gradually Neufeld won such confidence from congregations of all stripes across the church that he became appointed to major positions of church responsibility. At the time of his accession to BC's presidency, Neufeld was moderator of the entire denomination and in 1980 would be appointed chair of Mennonite Central Committee. Periodically he would interrupt his presidential duties with month-long investigative forays to far-flung MCC posts.[64]

There was, in fact, an enigmatic quality to Elmer Neufeld that served him well in his ability to lead. On the one hand he never lost the air of a Mennonite farm boy from the thick Dutch-Russian Mennonite settlements of the southern plains, kicking the sod off his boots before descending into church basements to teach Sunday school. His inherited, instinctive pattern of traditional Mennonite humility rendered him acutely uncomfortable with much highlighting of his own accomplishments. His presidential inauguration was, by his own request, Don Pannabecker remembered, distinctly "low-key." He refused to move his family into the official presidential house, the Mosimans' grand old home on Grove Street. He preferred instead to commute to campus on a motorcycle from his small but working farm west of town, where he could teach his children that "manual labor is dignified" and that "it is an honorable thing to work with your hands."[65]

On the other hand, Neufeld possessed a Ph.D. in philosophy from the University of Chicago. He could converse knowledgeably about Sartre and Nietzsche. He was a globe-trotting administrator and a widely respected church leader. He was committed to racial justice and had courted arrest in civil rights demonstrations. Beneath the "aw-shucks" demeanor was a canny leader who had honed a deft ability to bridge all sorts of gaps.

Take, for example, Neufeld's management of church relations. Neufeld knew well, from recent and painful personal experience, the kind of delicate minuet he would have to perform between the competing claims of conservative churches and more progressive faculty members. He was more successful than Lloyd Ramseyer in avoiding a showdown with conservatives. Even before he took office he had heard from Berne's pastor Ken Bauman concerns about the shaky Christian climate the pastor perceived on campus. Bauman called, in particular, for the religion department to receive a healthy dose of "a more positive and evangelical stance."[66]

Neufeld apparently agreed, to a degree, with such prescriptions. Without prodding, in 1983 he expressed to Yost and young Bible professor J. Denny Weaver the "conviction I have long held that a Mennonite church-related college like Bluffton should have room in its Religion Department for a clearly conservative/evangelical voice." Anabaptism itself, he reasoned, had grown out of such a perspective. It remained "a very strong part of our constituencies' orientation."[67]

Neufeld nonetheless allowed himself and the department a fair bit of wiggle room. When a conservative young pastor and BC alumnus wrote to complain that Weaver's teaching "does not represent the Christian theology of the Bible," Neufeld pirouetted adroitly. "Scriptures continue to have greater and greater significance in my life," he testified. "I accept the Scriptures as God's infallible guide to faith and life; and at the same time it seems to me that some of the Fundamentalist interpretations of literal inerrancy are not only unscriptural but may really be misleading." When Weaver presented his successful case for tenure, the president lent his quiet support.[68]

Most importantly, Neufeld assumed office deeply committed to the progressive Anabaptist mission of the college that had been fermenting for three-quarters of a century. He had never served under leaders like Mosiman or Ramseyer but had fully absorbed their articulation of the larger purpose of the college. Even as a new dean, he had declared that "an ultimate measure of the effectiveness of our educational program must continue to be the Christian service and witness roles of our graduates."[69]

In the early 1980s, with the new U.S. president Ronald Reagan pursuing a massive military buildup and policies that began to widen economic inequalities between the rich and poor, Neufeld told the trustees he sensed that "we also stand in need of the renewing prophetic witness." He hoped that "we might be more faithful to our heritage of peace in a world that is threatening to destroy itself. That we might grow in our historic emphasis on Christian service, in a world that has some 15 million refugees. . . . "[70]

He grasped another key point that harkened back to the Ramseyer era. Neufeld believed, Dean Schweingruber later said, that "we had a unique role to play in Mennonite higher education, that we're here to serve not just Mennonites but all kinds of students." As Neufeld kicked his new presidency into motion, he would take this kind of ideological inheritance and consciously act to extend it.[71]

His immediate task was to deal with a demographic and economic climate that continued to proffer grim tidings for a small and struggling college. By 1984 Neufeld wrestled with projections of a 25-percent decline in high school graduates, a demographic trough that would extend from 1979 to the early 1990s. Other negative factors registered an impact: college costs at Bluffton and across the nation climbed in the face of a sluggish economy and rising inflation. Reagan-era budget cuts slashed federal expenditures for student financial aid.[72]

All across the country, private colleges suffered from enrollment drops; Bluffton was no exception. BC student enrollment fluctuated around 600 through the early 1980s and had some precipitous drops at several alarming moments. In the fall of 1982 Neufeld informed the board of a "major setback in enrollment," down to below 600, something the college had not seen since the early 1960s. Student numbers hovered in the mid-500s through much of the rest of the decade.[73]

In the face of such conditions, Neufeld and his staff scrambled for the better part of a decade to keep the college on an even keel. They would do so in personal relationships that would proceed much more harmoniously than in the 1970s. Neufeld had tendencies toward Ramseyer-style hierarchical management, but his experience as dean in the high-tension Sprunger era, Pannabecker later said, had mellowed him remarkably. He allowed his staff a fair bit of autonomy, remembered Schweingruber, but he also "had his finger in just about everything."[74]

Neufeld and his administrators tried a number of different solutions. The college offered any new student a full tuition refund in 1987 if they remained dissatisfied after their first semester. At least the move garnered publicity. In 1985 each department was assigned to produce their own student recruitment strategies. More effective than gimmicks was a massive increase in the level of financial aid the college offered students, an increase made possible by the generosity of the constituency and the adept fundraising of Neufeld and development directors like Richard Ramseyer and Paul King.[75]

By 1989, when two decades of dark economic clouds had begun to lift, the college could point out some remarkable indicators to

NCA officials. The budget had been balanced every year for ten years but one; long-term indebtedness had declined from $3.4 to $1.5 million. The endowment had doubled to over $3 million in the same period. Already by 1984, the college began to think about the creation of new athletic fields, signaling for the first time an expansion of the campus across its traditional western boundary, Bentley Road.[76]

Lions, Lambs, and Beavers

In March 1985, the college grounds crew reluctantly decided to replace the venerable but decaying old Krehbiel Bridge. Since 1919 it had spanned the Riley in front of Ropp Hall and provided the backdrop for generations of student memories and romances. A more solid and equally handsome structure, Adams Bridge, soon took its place. Though Krehbiel Bridge was gone, in many other ways new faculty and new students in the 1980s demonstrated firm continuities with the college's past while embarking on a number of new initiatives.[77]

By the early 1980s, it was clear that another generational turnover of faculty was underway, as so many of the World War II professorial cohort laid down the chalk. The daunting list included Richard Weaver, Dale Dickey, Ray Hamman, Dick Pannabecker, Earl Lehman, Darvin Luginbuhl, Emerson Miller, Luther Shetler, Lawrence Templin, Howard Raid, Mark Houshower, Leland Lehman, and Jim Bixel. Yet the college persisted in its remarkable ability to attract able professors despite salaries that remained painfully low.[78]

A number of departments received fresh infusions of talent. English and communications welcomed a young, elegantly dressed Texan, Mary Ann Sullivan, in 1972; Goshen graduate Wes Richard in 1983; and an accomplished young poet, Jeff Gundy, in 1984.[79]

The sciences and math departments continued to build their ranks from BC alumni, including the additions of Stan Clemens (class of 1963), Mike Edmiston (BC 1972) and Steve Steiner (BC 1978). Willis Sommer (BC 1967) returned to his alma mater to teach business in 1979. One of that "new generation of Weavers" Ramseyer had urged Richard Weaver to produce, Weaver's daughter Sally, came in 1982 to teach economics. Edith Painter arrived in 1981 to teach education and psychology.[80]

History saw the addition of a fluent linguist, Eastern European specialist and peace activist Jim Satterwhite, in 1984. Appointments to the religion faculty continued to be a touchy business. Given his later contributions to building an Anabaptist—and explicitly nonorthodox—theology, it was somewhat ironic that the hiring of the young church historian and budding theologian J. Denny Weaver came at the hands of evangelical president Sprunger in 1975. Perhaps the enthusiastic recommendation of the conservative Goshen Bible scholar J. C. Wenger, Weaver's father-in-law, had satisfied Sprunger as to Weaver's basic theological soundness.[81]

As with their faculty forebears in the post-Ramseyer era, the incoming new professors could be assertive with their deans. Ronald Rich concluded a difficult, yearlong tenure as dean in 1980 with the observation that "some faculty members may need more of the Bluffton spirit or less emphasis on machismo or whatever." Macho or not, the emerging new faculty were certainly energetic. They created a subcommittee to beef up the academic climate of the campus. As the faculty's academic profile expanded and a widening majority arrived with terminal degrees, numbers of new professors began to put an increased stress on academic publishing. As late as the early 1970s, publishing scholars like John Unruh were rare birds on the BC faculty (many professors were too busy still laboring on their doctorates).[82]

In 1987 the college provided both a welcome push and a financial incentive for more faculty scholarly efforts by obtaining a $75,000 grant from the Lily Foundation for the creation of the "Bluffton College Studies Center." Administered at first by former president Kreider and religion professor Weaver, the center had two purposes: first, to promote microcomputer usage across the curriculum, and second, to provide mini grants for faculty research and creative activities on subjects integrally related to the college's Anabaptist mission, especially peacemaking, notions of Christian service, and cross-cultural issues.[83]

BC's emerging new faculty also subjected the curriculum to intense revisioning through the 1980s. They changed academic calendars nearly as often as some teens change clothes, moving from a 1-3-1-3-1 to a 1-3-3-2 system in 1979, then to a 3-3-1-1-1 system in 1982, partly because of a persisting student demand for more modules. By 1985, they found that the last-quarter series of monthlong modules, the 1-1-1 system, had proved unworkable. The faculty approved the adoption of a straight 3-3-3 quarter system.[84]

Around the same time, the faculty and their academic leaders realized that the old HUEX system had been tinkered with and amended beyond repair. They followed the "back-to-basics" climate of wider academia to a more traditional, distributive general education core curriculum in 1983. Students were required to take introductory courses in the traditional disciplines, along with classes in new areas such as "Contemporary Issues," "Personal Wellbeing," and "Intercultural Studies."[85]

Along with the curricular rethinking came a number of new majors and other initiatives, some a result of faculty efforts and a few emanating from students. The social work department, for example, continued apace, anchored in the strong commitments of teachers like Carl Smucker, Paul Klassen (art professor John Klassen's son), Betty Sommer, and Don Brubaker. In 1983 they became one of the few departments in the state to receive accreditation from the Council on Social Work Education.[86]

Partly to meet a persistent student demand for vocationally oriented programs, in 1985 the college launched a program, later a major, in criminal justice. Another part of the rationale was to somehow envision a peace church approach to criminal justice in an era of rising crimes rites and increasingly draconian penal solutions.[87]

Sociology professor Larry Kay Hardesty came up with particularly creative, real-life ways to teach his students about the criminal justice system. He brought students to the penitentiary in Lima to help his classes with inmates there. He also arranged for the fake "arrests" and incarceration of (volunteer) students. For example, in the fall of 1985 Tim Pannabecker accompanied other students on a field trip to the Putnam County Courthouse and jail, where two sheriff's deputies suddenly appeared to arrest him on the charge of "criminal menacing," for allegedly threatening Hardesty's life. Even though Pannabecker knew charges were fictitious and the arrest was staged (the class observed his handcuffing, fingerprinting, and mugshot, and returned the following day to watch his trial), Pannabecker still spent the night in a jail cell with nine other regular inmates.[88]

Student vocational concerns in a time of economic uncertainty propelled new energies in a number of areas. Besides criminal justice, the college added new majors in computer science; recreation management; and in clothing, textiles, and merchandising. Large numbers of students continued to prepare to teach. When the sciences vacated Berky Hall, home economics (renamed Family and Consumer Sciences) gained new facilities considerably redesigned for the needs of the department, all to accommodate a number of majors (forty by 1980) that had doubled in ten years.[89]

Likewise, student choices reflected the generally pro-business aura of the Reagan era, as the college experienced a flood of new business majors. The economics and business department responded accordingly. Since 1962 the college had provided real-world management experience by purchasing a small Bluffton manufacturing enterprise, the Bluffton [Cole] Slaw Cutter Company. Howard Raid served as president, but students managed the day-to-day running of the operation. In 1984 the college formed the Business Studies Center to help better relations with local businesses and to "foster the appreciation of Christian values to business practice."[90]

Some initiatives related even more directly to peace and conflict studies. Rather surprising for a peace-church college so intensely conscious about its mission, the impetus for what became a program in peace and conflict studies came not from the faculty or administration but from a student, Jim Stutzman, who won the 1985 C. Henry Smith Peace Oratorical Contest in the Mennonite College network with a ringing cry for the establishment for such a program.[91]

But the faculty found additional ways of expressing the college's mission. One noted contribution came from the dedicated energies of education professor Libby Hostetler. A 1969 BC graduate who had joined the all-male education department five years later, in 1985 Hostetler found a way of concretizing her sense that children might best absorb peace teachings through the arts. She floated a proposal and obtained both a sabbatical leave and a $20,000 gift from BC alumnus Herman Parent to, in the words of the original proposal, "develop a Peace Studies Center for the Promotion of Peace Education through Art and Literature for Children."[92]

In two years Hostetler's original vision had taken shape as the Lion and Lamb Peace Arts Center, with Hostetler as its first director. It soon spun off activities in a number of areas. Its first major acquisition was all the original art from the classic book of children's peace literature, *Sadako and the Thousand Paper Cranes*. A number of modest foundation grants helped it develop its library. It brought in a number of noted writers and artists for lectures. It organized volunteer drama troupes to present conflict resolution techniques to local schools. Within two years of its founding, over 2,500 area schoolchildren had visited. By the time Hostetler left in 1998 to pursue a career as a school principal, it was clear to Neufeld that the center had "attracted more off-campus interest in Bluffton's peace emphasis than any other college program."[93]

Hostetler and other members of the emerging new faculty daily faced classrooms full of students who had begun to change in subtle but important ways from a more rambunctious student body of a decade or two earlier. Denny Weaver detected that incoming students seemed less assertive than those in earlier generations, less willing to challenge what he suggested in class (even reticent to object to his questioning of some of their long-held and cherished religious beliefs). At the same time, they seemed to possess slightly increased academic abilities. With the college better managing its student enrollment and able to exercise slightly more admissions selectivity, test scores and high school GPAs of incoming students gradually rose, with a sharp upturn in the later 1980s.[94]

Professors interacted with students who appeared remarkably more homogenous in other ways. In 1989, only 11 percent of the student body hailed from out of state, and the number of minority students had dropped back to a consistent range of 4-5 percent from the temporary gain of the early 1970s. Early in the 1980s Mennonites had risen briefly to a fifth or even a fourth of the student body but by 1989 had again declined to around 14 percent. While the college "of course has long been committed to working with a majority of non-Mennonite students," the president admitted in 1985, "a core or 'critical mass' of Mennonite students seems important to maintain our distinctive Mennonite identity." His staff began pushing a congregational scholarship matching program, but the decline, like the drop in minority students, continued to cause concern.[95]

One key leavening influence on the student body was the small but significant number of international students. Such students had registered a memorable impact on the college for sixty years, stemming back to the student career of Bedros Sharian, an Armenian refugee who had graduated in 1921. One family, the Alemayehus family of Ethiopia, had seen four of its members graduate from BC. The Kawira family of Tanzania had sent three brothers into the ranks of BC graduates. And Phineas Nyangaro of Tanzania (class of 1969) and his daughters Josephine (BC 1980) and Deonestina (BC 1981) had continued the tradition over two generations.[96]

By 1983, 175 international students (not counting Canadians) had graduated from the college. A number, like Mubarak Awad, had gone on to illustrious careers, including Jan Trenite (BC 1951) with the Dutch embassy in Washington and Douglas Mead (BC 1971), who was working for the economic union of Liberia and Guinea with his native Sierra Leone. Through the 1980s, a nucleus of twenty to thirty such students brought a different perspective to campus, especially expressed in activities of the annual International Student Association week.[97]

Like earlier generations, 1980s students enjoyed personable relationships with professors, but perhaps not to the same degree of familiarity as earlier. The larger student body led to a growing gap between students and faculty. In the 1970s and 1980s, this gap increasingly came to be filled by a professional and growing student affairs staff. For much of Bluffton's history, these had been part-time positions held by regular faculty with no preparation for the posts except on-the-job training. For example, Carl Smucker and Dale Dickey had served as dean of men; Paul Shelly had been assigned tasks in student recruitment. Dean of students through much of the 1960s was Lois Rodabaugh, who was competent yet whose professional training was as a nurse. In the mid-1960s Robert Kreider had finally hired a professional psychologist, Otto Klassen, as student counselor. However, the first college staffers specifically trained to work with college students were Don Schweingruber as well as Sprunger himself in 1972.[98]

Thereafter the ranks of such professionals expanded rapidly. They put together not just a full and creative slate of student activities but organized retreats for student leaders, trained and managed resident assistants in the dorms, and provided professional evaluation of student affairs services. For several decades Schweingruber used graduate student interns from Bowling Green State University in student affairs management. Many of them later came to serve in key college staff positions.[99]

Still, in various ways the college marched to the beat of commitments established in earlier decades. Through the 1980s, BC welcomed a variety of speakers, many of whom helped reorient its fundamental mission to pressing political and moral issues of the day. Evangelical peace activist Ron Sider, for instance, spoke as a Keeney Peace Lecturer (a lectureship established by the Keeney family), as did Catholic bishop and nuclear freeze advocate Thomas Gumbleton. Philosopher Ivan Illich and southern church leader Will Campbell met on campus with other activists as part of a "Sanctity of Life" conference in 1986. This conference was designed to widen common ground among foes of abortion, the death penalty, and nuclear weaponry. The faculty likewise paid attention to national and international affairs, voting in 1984 to approve holding a special convocation to map out the college response if the U.S. government escalated its military presence in Central America.[100]

Guided by such able and budding young activists as Paul Weaver, Kathleen Kern, Olin Zuercher, and Iris Neufeld, the Peace Club managed a busy agenda through much of the decade. Efforts focused on internal campus education (particularly in the annual "Peace Emphasis Week") and external activism. In 1981 and 1982, for example, a number of students mounted a picket line in front of Bluffton's post office on Main Street to question the government's new program of draft registration. Women's activists mounted a similar focus on feminist issues during their annual "Women's Week," featuring a host of speakers and activities. For three years running they wrote a special annual issue of the *Witmarsum* devoted to feminist issues entitled *The Lily* and in 1980 created another group called the "Women's Awareness Association."[101]

As in earlier decades, activists provoked some opposition; BC student conservatism continued to run deep. In 1983, for instance, fifteen students signed a joint letter to the *Witmarsum* objecting to what they perceived as the paper's "propaganda" against the draft. By 1988, student sympathies had once again swung markedly Republican in the presidential straw poll. Meanwhile, faculty favored the Democrats by a nearly mirror-inverse percentage.[102]

All in all, a fairly rich extracurricular agenda continued. In many ways student life remained unchanged from past decades: new student orientation and homecoming in the fall, with the powder puff football game and crowning of the homecoming court; junior orals, intense intramural sports, and snowball fights in winter; then the traditional rites of spring—the spring musical, the "Bach's Lunch" of the Music Department, and commencement.

Men who became engaged could still expect to be tossed into the Riley and their future spouses flung into the showers. Students still lined up for May Day ceremonies on the college lawn. Amid all the traditions jettisoned in the 1960s, this one had somehow, inexplicably, survived. Perhaps students did not engage in pranks with the same intensity or regularity as before, but Dan Parent remembers one panty raid in the late 1970s, with the resulting trophies hung on a rope stretching across College Avenue.[103]

The *Witmarsum* rose from its doldrums, flourishing again under the able management of editors like Suzanne Zerger, Kendra Arn, and Darryl Nester. Students continued to elect solid student senators and presidents, such as Nancy Bertsche and Karen Zehr, while the Student Christian Association remained busy, hosting a number of student spiritual activities and also planning annual Christian Emphasis Day (later an entire Christian Emphasis Week). The efforts of the student affairs staff notwithstanding, other student activities persisted as well. For several years in the mid-1980s, students threw an annual picnic/beer bash in the Bluffton village park. This new tradition later died in infancy when village authorities denied them an alcohol permit.[104]

Sports remained a major focus of student interest, and with good reason: in many ways, the 1980s would rival the 1950s as a great age of sports in college history. A number of different teams could point to memorable seasons. The baseball team finished 7-5 in league play in 1980, with Kevin Olds breaking BC's single-season home run record. That spring the college hired a new coach for the team, Greg Brooks, who would stay to guide the program for at least two decades. The following fall, John Zerger, Jim Kirtz, and Bob Alvarez broke time records for the cross-country team.[105]

From 1983 to 1985, the men's basketball team enjoyed its only two winning seasons in the decade. At one point in the 1984-1985 season, coach Glenn Snyder's team was 15-4 and led the Hoosier-Buckeye League with a 5-1 record. Then a cold shooting spell cost the team its first league title. Sophomore center Pete DuMonte set a number of individual scoring records that year, however, and the next year broke Clair Recker's mark to become BC's all-time leading scorer. The women's basketball team struggled through much of the 1980s but had some high points as well. They finished 15-5 in 1981-1982 and at one point were ranked fifth in the state. That year they traveled to France over Christmas break to play top European national teams. With strong shooters and rebounders like Michelle Durand, Paula Slaughter, Tonya Crowe, and Cheryl Althaus, the "Lady" Beavers proved consistently competitive. Althaus finished her BC career in 1983 as the team's all-time scoring leader.[106]

The greatest women's sports teams of that era—or any other in the college's history—were in volleyball. Although a steady stream of remarkable athletes contributed to the amazing success of the women's volleyball team for nearly two decades, the primary credit must go to its diminutive but powerful coach, Kim Fischer. Even at just over five feet, she had starred in three sports in her undergraduate days at the College of Wooster, but no one could have predicted what happened following her arrival at BC and her 1979 appointment as head volleyball coach. In her first year the Beavers finished at 25-11 and went to the state tournament, where they appeared with numbing regularity for the next fifteen years.[107]

Until Fischer's retirement in 1997, the team would fail to win at least twenty games in only one season, and some of their seasonal records still appear astounding: 38-4 in 1987, 34-4 the next year, 31-6 in 1989. For nine straight years they received invitations to the NAIA district tournament. In three of those years—1982, 1985, and 1988— they won the championship. An able recruiter and motivator, Fischer compiled a record that speaks for itself. No one in any BC sport, not even the legendary Burcky or the fabled Kenny Mast, had produced such a pattern of persistent athletic dominance.[108]

However, in 1979, the same year Fischer arrived, the college quietly hired another new coach who would rescue the football program from years of misery and soon have people making comparisons to Ken Mast. Before Carlin Carpenter's appointment, the team had posted only four winning seasons out of the previous fifteen, and his first five years brought more trials. The team won only seven games in that stretch, including two difficult seasons, 1981 and 1983, when they won none. But as the descendant of a coal-mining family from Ohio's Appalachian foothills, Carpenter had long ago learned to plug doggedly along in the face of adversity, and suddenly in 1985 everything changed.[109]

Early in October, a local sportswriter realized something of what had begun to happen. He arrived at the Hanover game in the third quarter because he didn't figure it mattered much. Hanover was ranked seventeenth nationally in small-college football and had been pounding on the Beavers for years. But when the writer happened to glance at the scoreboard, he realized that this time Bluffton was doing the pounding. The Beavers won the game going away, their first victory over Hanover in thirteen years. Soon other teams in the league began to realize, with the sportswriter, that "the Beavers are for real."[110]

Three weeks later the mighty Quakers of Wilmington College swaggered into town. Coached by Lloyd Ramseyer's son Bill and ranked sixth in the nation, they seemed ready to extend their winning streak over BC to twelve straight years. Instead, BC freshman quarterback Cliff Hemmert tossed four touchdown passes and another freshman, Greg Gilcrease, plunged across the goal line another two times. BC stunned the Quakers, 42-28. At season's end, the team had broken or tied twenty-three seasonal or single-game records, stood second in the league with an 8-1 record, and ranked eleventh in the country.[111]

By the time Hemmert and Gilcrease were juniors and seniors, in 1987 and 1988, the Beavers had gotten even better. In 1987 the team again went 8-1, qualified for the NAIA national playoffs for the first time, and saw star wide receiver, senior Ed Coleman, signed with the Detroit Lions. In 1988, helped by a host of talented players—including a new back, Roger Gilyani, who along with Gilcrease broke or tied several of Dubenion's notable records—the Beavers finished 9-2 and went two rounds deep in national playoffs. The team won a bundle of league awards. Carpenter won his coach-of-the-year award for the fourth straight year. It had been a memorable era on the gridiron and on the hardcourt.[112]

A "Buoyancy of Spirit"

In fall 1988, with Carpenter's Beavers gearing up for the NAIA playoffs, the larger college prepared for the visit of an NCA accreditation review team. The administration and faculty could well feel as confident as they had at any moment since halfway through the Kreider years. Certainly they had endured a difficult two decades. An ambitious young president had taken the helm, determined to push the college toward more conservative evangelicalism, but his plan had foundered on the rocks of faculty resistance. For fifteen years following, the college had devoted itself to hanging on, surviving, then making slow progress once more.

Still, Pannabecker had been right. Through it all the college had persisted in a remarkable "buoyancy of spirit," and better days had indeed come. This much and more was readily clear to the NCA review team. In their report delivered the next spring, they had a number of positive things to say. They found the trustees enthusiastic, the faculty and staff better trained and more competent than expected, and college finances in solid shape and with brightening prospects. "The campus is very attractive," they noted, with the facilities "sufficient" and "generally aesthetically pleasing."[113]

Most important, the NCA team perceived that the mission of the college held consistently and with "strong enthusiasm" among faculty, staff, and students. The team recommended a full renewal of BC's accreditation for another decade, reasoning that "Bluffton College is a sound institution, appropriately positioned and possessing sufficient resources to continue to pursue and achieve its mission as a college with a liberal arts orientation, grounded firmly in the Mennonite tradition."[114]

Maybe such positive analyses came more easily from outsiders. Neufeld did often write in happy tones in the alumni bulletin, but others harbored private, nagging doubts. In 1979, for instance, an administrator conducted an extensive series of interviews with faculty as part of an effort to rethink how the college marketed itself. Many professors felt the college had a "mixed" or "passive" image as merely an "average, private, church-related college," little more. Outsiders might be impressed with BC as a "Mennonite college," BC's internal critics suggested, "but we ... don't leave our graduates with a clear definition of what this means."[115]

Of course, this might be dismissed as residue from the emotionally trying and financially uncertain Sprunger years, but a decade later, amid their upbeat comments, the NCA reviewers articulated similar concerns. The college's modest financial resources, "albeit improving," they noted, "severely limit the institution to do anything but meet the needs of the moment, and that, barely. There is little room for innovation. . . ." They had no doubt that the college "has a strong mission, one that is clearly held and pursued by all." Yet the NCA team still detected "a sense of attending only to the demands of the day without the fervor that is present in a community that is consciously pursuing a vision. . . ."[116]

Perhaps the critics went too far. The college had the same vision it had always had—one that, if anything, 1970s challenges had reinforced. Finances seemed the main culprit behind any hesitancy to embark on new adventures (besides reluctance of an innately humble president to blow his own horn too loudly). At any rate, by 1989 the institution stood on the threshold of a new era that promised to address any lingering doubts about a lack of vision. The college had proceeded from years of retrenchment to the arrival of an adept leadership team, competent new faculty, and a gradual increase in students. After a long period spent slowly climbing out of a financial hole, at the dawn of a new decade, the college readied itself to boom once more.

CHAPTER EIGHT

The Dance
of the Kobzar, 1990-1999

In the spring of 1989, roughly when the NCA review team was writing of the college's lack of vision, a host of people in the music and art departments busied themselves with a spring musical. Instead of being another Broadway production, the musical expressed a peculiarly Bluffton story. Written by BC music professor Jim Bixel, the production was titled "The Dance of the Kobzar: Scenes from the Life of John Klassen, Artist as Peacemaker." A cast of forty-six played 146 different roles. Drama professor Gene Caskey starred in the central role of Klassen. Bixel's opera told the story of the artist's ultimately successful legal quest to be granted U.S. citizenship while retaining a claim as a conscientious objector. But the play involved far more than politics. Through dance and dialogue, the musical celebrated Klassen's life and work, building especially on imaginary conversations between the artist and his best-known sculpture, a Ukranian folk minstrel called the "Kobzar."[1]

The open exuberance of Bixel's opera was appropriate for a number of reasons. Just like Klassen's minstrel, in 1989 the entire college prepared itself to bound forward again. Moreover, Klassen's engagement with his Kobzar managed to encapsulate a sense of the college's very mission and purpose—a sense that, as it neared its centennial birthday, BC seemed more conscious of than ever before.

Boom

In contrast to the massive expansion of American higher education of the 1960s—a wave that, due to a huge pool of high school graduates and favorable economic conditions, Bluffton could ride along with everyone else—the BC boom of the 1990s was remarkable precisely because it was *not* so universally shared. In June 1990 the *New York Times* observed that, with the number of high school graduates shrinking, all across the country colleges and universities were "scrambling to fill up freshman classes." Six years later, the *Chronicle of Higher Education* filled in the dark picture, describing how, between declining student populations on the one hand and tuition constraints and cutbacks in federal support for higher education on the other, "private colleges are in a tightening vise."[2]

After twenty years of tossing about on rough financial waters, reports like the *Chronicle's* threatened to make some BC people seasick. Few could imagine an alternative scenario, even as President Neufeld began to report, as early as 1989, a surprising upturn in admission numbers. Two years into the boom, many could still not believe it was taking place. When new dean Bill Hawk delivered the results of a "Long-Term Planning Questionnaire" to a faculty meeting in 1991, he noted that BC had the third lowest enrollment of any college in the state. The fond hopes that many entertained of a student body of 750 by 1995, he warned, would have to come with no increase in faculty.[3]

But the favorable numbers soon became undeniable. Six months after Hawk's sober estimation, Neufeld reported that student enrollment had expanded for the fourth year in a row. In 1994, growth had continued seven years in a row. In fall 1993, the college reached its longtime goal of 200 entering students. In fall 1994, there were 229, and in fall 1995, BC welcomed 247 new students, then reached a high mark of 255 in fall 1997. In fall 1995, the college for the first time had 1,000 students and remained above that level the rest of the decade. Dorms were bursting at the seams: in fall 1995, for example, there were 690 beds filled out of a total capacity of 698. The enrollment leap, moreover, came accompanied by a financial one as well. In the decade following 1988, the college more than doubled its operating budget (from $7 million to $17 million) and tripled its endowment (from over $3 million to more than $10 million).[4]

The explosion left college old-timers scratching their heads in wonder and administrative officials groping to explain. A more pressing matter was the need to provide for the new students. If they realized only a five percent enrollment increase each year, Neufeld told the board in 1995—an annual increase a good deal under what they were actually seeing—then in five years they would see a student body of 1,200, way beyond what the college could accommodate. Already by 1991 the board realized they would either have to build a new dorm, send students off campus to live, or limit enrollment. Staffers engaged in residential and academic space studies, trustees grappled with the numbers, and an army of architects, masons, and carpenters soon invaded the campus.[5]

The result was another burst of campus construction that, in rapidity and scope—five buildings in ten years—rivaled the great "bricks-and-mortar" era of the 1960s. Since nobody had the slightest intention of limiting enrollment, in fall 1994 the college completed a new dorm barely before classes started. Over 100 women students moved into the spanking new building named after President Ramseyer. Permanent new classrooms would have to wait a few years; in the meantime, administrators rented portable bungalows for classrooms, installing them just east of the new Ramseyer Hall.[6]

At the same time, the college found itself able to build structures for the enhancement of arts and athletics it had dreamed of for years. A new Visual Arts Center originally started out merely as a replacement for the old "art barn" but gathered momentum of its own as donations poured in. Located on a bluff overlooking the Riley, the 12,000-square- foot building housed studio space for painting, printing, ceramics, kiln work, and sculpture, as well as a display gallery, lecture room, and darkroom. On its completion in 1992, trustees named it after longtime board member Jerry Sauder.[7]

Two longtime BC supporters, Al and Marie Yoder of Middlebury, Indiana, provided a single gift of $1 million. This enabled completion of a state-of-the-art recital hall. No longer would college musical performances have to echo off the walls of the old gym. Located next to Mosiman in what once was College Avenue, the new Yoder Hall also brought a permanent rearrangement to local traffic patterns when Neufeld persuaded the village council to agree to close the major auto thoroughfare across campus.[8]

Finally, a gift from another donor enabled the college to construct a new home for the football team. After decades of sharing a field with Bluffton High School, a quarter-million-dollar bequest from the will of Dwight and Harriet Salzman helped support construction of Salzman Stadium, in the new Sears Athletic Complex across Bentley Road. With the press box installed on September 7, 1993, the stadium was completed just four days before the Beavers' home opener that fall with Ohio Northern University. The fact that the Polar Bears rudely ran the opening kickoff back for the first touchdown in the Beavers' new home did little to dampen the larger excitement.[9]

Less visible from the outside, the flush times also enabled the college to catch up with the breakthroughs in technology that reshaped not just higher education but so many aspects of larger American life in this era. Primarily, this meant computers. In the mid-1980s, the college had begun to make a small number of micro-computers available for student use. Through the 1990s, this effort expanded incrementally but, ultimately, dramatically. By fall 1996, BC had established additional computer lab space, helped student connections to the Internet, and provided each professor and most administrative offices with a networked computer also connected to the Internet.[10]

"From the individual to the global citizen"

The boom of the 1990s, like the one thirty years earlier, brought new people as well as new buildings to campus. The number of administrative staff grew apace. The academic dean's office expanded to include two assistant deans, and the figure of the dean himself changed, from Bill Hawk in the first half of the 1990s to one last interim appointment of Don Pannabecker, who had performed so many administrative functions for three decades. In 1997, with Pannabecker firmly determined to retire, the college welcomed John Kampen to the deanship. A Mennonite originally from Saskatchewan, Kampen held a Ph.D. in New Testament from a Jewish Rabbinical school and had spent the previous decade as dean of an African-American seminary in southern Ohio. He arrived not only as an active, publishing scholar but firmly committed to the multicultural, Anabaptist mission of the college.[11]

The most important change came at the top. In July 1995, Elmer Neufeld announced he would retire at the end of the term. The following spring the college community gathered in Founders Hall both to roast and honor him in a gala "Celebration of Service," then prepared itself to welcome its first new president in nearly twenty years. The trustees' pick was intriguing. With her Mennonite Church background, Lee Snyder was the first BC president from outside the General Conference Mennonite Church. On the other hand, with the two major branches of the church moving toward integration, her MC ties promised to serve the college well.[12]

Regardless of her particular denominational affiliation, Snyder had a number of abilities that surely rendered her a leading candidate for this or any other Mennonite college presidency. She had a Ph.D. in English from the University of Oregon and had been dean or assistant dean at Eastern Mennonite University for twenty-two years. Through these and other leadership positions, she had garnered enough respect across both Mennonite branches that in 1999 she was tapped to lead the executive committee of the new, united Mennonite Church. Finally, she had one other quality that was insignificant in most ways but symbolically important in another. With her inauguration in October 1996, she became the first female president not just of Bluffton but of any college in the Mennonite network.[13]

The new president signaled from the beginning that she not only understood the BC mission but enthusiastically shared it. In her inaugural address she quoted extensively from N. C. Hirschy's cornerstone-laying speech, rephrasing it to tell the assembled crowd that "the challenge is one of fostering a call to service, of nurturing in our students an appreciation for the way of peace and nonviolence." A similar consciousness permeated the faculty of the 1990s, which, like the student body, steadily expanded through the decade.[14]

Midway through the 1990s, the college faced a faculty shortage. As recently as the 1987-1988 school year, the student-faculty ratio had been in the neighborhood of 10:1; by 1995 it had gone past 17:1. That was the year such figures convinced Neufeld and the trustees to approve fifteen new faculty hires, nine of them new positions. At one point in the hiring process, Pannabecker's office found itself sorting through 1,500 applications for these fifteen jobs. In contrast to the days when Robert Kreider sometimes flew to graduate schools to woo potential candidates, BC's deans soon discovered that despite low Bluffton salaries, the saturated academic job market of the 1990s enabled them to be quite selective. This factor alone boded well for academic strength and also BC's larger purpose.[15]

The result was the development, through the 1990s, of a new, younger, but superbly qualified faculty. By fall 1997, a full 85 percent of the faculty either had terminal degrees or were completing them, the highest percentage in BC history. Women represented over forty percent of the professorate and nearly half the combined faculty and staff (though, with only two people of color, the faculty remained woefully under-represented in that area). Various individual professors glittered with ability. Edith Painter and Mary Ann Sullivan won national teaching awards; chemist Steve Steiner pulled in grant money from the American Heart Association; in 1992 Jeff Gundy published his fourth book of poetry.[16]

The religion department's J. Denny Weaver began to make the first major scholarly contributions to Anabaptist-Mennonite studies that had come from the college since the days of C. Henry Smith. Weaver's book *Becoming Anabaptist* both summarized Anabaptist historiography and laid out some "regulative principles" of Anabaptism for the guidance of their modern descendants. Adopted in many adult education classes across the church, the book represented for many in the constituency the college's attention to its Mennonite tradition.[17]

Even more importantly for the larger mission of the college, the academic deans were increasingly able to select faculty candidates voicing enthusiasm for BC's progressive Anabaptist mission. Extensive faculty surveys in mid-decade conducted in accordance with the NCA-ordered stress on assessment provide ample evidence of this. A full 95 percent of the faculty reported that peacemaking was a high priority in their lives. Eighty-seven percent declared that the peace, justice, and service concerns of the college were influential in their decision to seek employment there. Much higher percentages of BC faculty stressed issues like influencing the social values, racial understanding, and community service of their students than did faculty members at other four-year Protestant colleges. Over half of the 1994-1995 faculty were members in a Mennonite congregation, and over a third had previously been members of or worked for a peace and/or justice agency. (By comparison, in 1995 twenty-two of twenty-five trustees were members of a Mennonite congregation).[18]

Such commitments were soon manifested in a variety of ways across campus, particularly in a new general-education core curriculum. It was implemented with the first-year class of 1995, then on the semester system in 1999. Part of the rationale was weariness with the "cafeteria-style approach" of the old core. A greater impetus was the common faculty perception that many students were graduating without a common core of experience or learning reflecting college purposes. Several years of intense committee work produced a new core stressing three goals: that students grasp interrelationships between disciplines; that they fit the knowledge, skills, and values they gained into a coherent whole; and that they "understand themselves in an ever-widening context from the individual to the global citizen." In its rather strict regimentation and lack of student choice, the new core contrasted with the old HUEX system but resembled HUEX in two keys ways: in its interdisciplinary approach and in its attempt fully to interweave the college mission with academic life.[19]

Nowhere was this agenda better displayed than in the new cross-cultural requirement. Through the previous decade a faculty committee assigned to this topic had often called for a cross-cultural effort that went beyond making programs available to the invariably small number of interested students. These patient efforts were finally rewarded by the requirement in the new core that each student "experience another culture by geographical immersion in it." After spirited debate, the faculty also stipulated that each cross-cultural trip would not only teach students to appreciate another culture but also to "reflect critically on their own location in a cultural context" and to "grow in developing an ethic of justice, service and peace-making."[20]

To achieve these goals, energetic professors soon constructed experiences that ranged from quarter-long stays in Northern Ireland or Poland to shorter, two-week trips to such locales as Jamaica, Miami, or the shantytowns along the U.S./Mexico border in Texas and Arizona. The trip to Washington, D.C., perfectly expressed the common agenda. There student experiences deliberately juxtaposed daily visits to comfortable and interesting places like Capitol Hill, Smithsonian museums, and ethnic restaurants with nightly returns to the bleak homeless shelter where they lived and worked.[21]

Finally, new faculty energies combined with favorable economics to yield a number of new programs. Unlike two decades before, the college managed to create a degree completion program in organizational management without provoking faculty suspicions of an overtly entrepreneurial administration. Led by Libby Hostetler, education faculty generated a graduate program in education, awarding the college's first master's degrees in 1997. By decade's end, a new master's program in management was underway. For several years in the mid-1990s, the college mounted an effort to provide a B.A. degree in a state penitentiary near Marion. However, amid a continuing public opinion shift toward harsher criminal justice policies, the state of Ohio killed public funding for the program.[22]

New Students, Familiar Mission

In what was probably the happiest death of a BC tradition experienced by the student body, in 1996 the faculty did away with junior oral exams. They thereby eliminated what had been a normative part of the junior- or senior-year experience for BC students since the 1930s. In other important ways, however, BC student life in the 1990s continued to reflect, with subtle changes, the college's peculiar student ethos.[23]

As in the 1960s, the college seized on enrollment growth to effect wanted changes in the student body. By 1995 the trustees began considering raising admission standards to slow the flood of new students. Whether or not this occurred, in ten years the average ACT scores of the first-year class rose several points to approach 23, and the number of new students with scores below 19 fell off dramatically. The other major change was in gender balance. By fall 1995, women residential students outnumbered men by 415 to 275.[24]

Yet continuities remained. Nearly 90 percent of students came from Ohio and a majority from rural or small-town Ohio. More than 50 percent arrived from high school graduating classes of fewer than 100 students. They came, like other BC cohorts, with firm vocational pursuits in mind, overwhelmingly clustering in a few majors (mostly business/accounting, education, and, to a lesser degree, social work). Mennonites continued to make up a small percentage of the student body, a persisting cause of concern to administrators. Later in the decade, the prospect of GC/MC integration had begun to nudge the Mennonite numbers up a bit, from about 10 percent up to 14 percent by 1999, with a majority of the Mennonites from MC rather than GC backgrounds.[25]

The campus life these students encountered continued along channels carved by nearly a century of tradition. Certainly, there were some newer expressions of older impulses. An organization called Peer Awareness Leaders (PALS) emerged to educate fellow students about issues of personal health and self-esteem. Other students threw themselves into a Habitat for Humanity chapter or into vocational clubs like the Bluffton College Education Organization or the Social Work Club. With leaders like Gina Goff, James Jones, Jamie Casper, and Bob Daugherty, the student senate remained strong, as did the Peace Club. Members journeyed to Washington, D.C., in 1991 to protest the Gulf War. In 1995 they expressed their peace principles in a different way. When the presidents of Bosnia, Serbia, and Croatia met for peace talks at Wright-Patterson Air Force Base in Dayton, over thirty-five BC students gathered outside the gates to pray silently for peace in the Balkans.[26]

The 1990s brought their own tragedies. A numbing total of seven students or recent alumni—Tara Hertzfeld, Lou Stahl, Scott Nafziger, Tim Suter, Andy Lehman, Theresa Grothouse, and Mandy Burden Shoup—died from accidents or illness. Amid sadness, there were also triumphs. In 1996 the women's basketball team set a school record for most wins in a season, finishing at 16-9, and the volleyball team continued to dominate. They topped off a 34-13 record in 1995 with a trip to the national playoffs. The 1997 team again qualified for the national tournament and at one point were ranked as high as ninth in the country. That was the season Kim

Fischer won game 500 as BC coach. Coached by Guy Neal, the men's basketball team posted memorable seasons, led by talented players like Todd Varvel, Kevin Gump, Jamie Yount, and David Sheldon. By mid-decade, the football team regained its winning form. The Beavers finished as conference co-champs in 1995, breaking or tying thirty-nine school records, and Carpenter was once again selected as conference coach of the year.[27]

"More than Mennonite"

To a significant degree, such continuities in student life were made possible by a basic consistency in the college's mission. For a variety of reasons, the college had become more openly conscious than ever of its basic purpose and identity.

The explicit focus on BC's mission was expressed in a variety of ways. Some were visible, as when in 1997 the college painted the key words of the mission statement on the ceiling beams in Marbeck cafeteria. Some tended to be more rhetorical than substantive, as in the concern to highlight the college mission statement. Here minor adjustments gained full approval of the trustees. Some were structural, as when President Snyder created a representative Council of Church Leaders to strengthen relationships with and accountability to the church constituency. A visiting review team of church leaders in 1995 quickly detected such consciousness. They were "impressed with the clear sense of identity understood and expressed by all segments of the College community. It was abundantly clear that the College is intentional about its mission and has been remarkably successful in its attempts to articulate and apply its vision."[28]

The mission consciousness seemed to emanate from several sources. One was the era's larger intellectual climate, particularly the accounts of the secularization of the academy offered by scholars like George Marsden and James Burtchaell. In his fall 1991 report to the trustees, Neufeld described at some length developments that, as articulated by Burtchaell, led many colleges to sever themselves from their denominational and Christian roots. The next fall the president relayed a similar analysis from a source closer to home, Mennonite sociologist Donald Kraybill, who identified nine factors that, Neufeld warned, "propel colleges away from their parent church denominations." Mennonite higher education analyst Albert Meyer delivered the same message in yet more depth at a well-attended conference on Mennonite higher education held at BC the same year.[29]

There was also new focus on academic assessment, the great "reform" of the 1990s that accrediting agencies imposed on colleges and universities across the country. Sparked by a mistrustful public anxious for assurance that colleges deliver what they promise, the NCA stipulated that by 1995 all member colleges submit in writing their plans to assess student outcomes in line with their professed mission in both academic and nonacademic spheres. Like other schools, BC plunged into an intense internal examination designed to ensure that all aspects of its program—curriculum, staff, faculty, trustees, student life policies—reflected its mission. Its 1998 NCA self-study report, for example, hammered away at this theme relentlessly.[30]

Finally, administrators and faculty focused more explicitly on their mission because of the internal evidence they uncovered—produced as a direct response to the assessment frenzy—suggesting they may be less successful than they supposed in inculcating students with a sense of mission. Through extensive surveying of BC's student body through much of the decade, Will Slater, BC's official director of assessment, uncovered pertinent evidence. He learned that though huge majorities of the faculty enthusiastically backed the college's mission, equally large majorities of students seemed impervious to it. Worse, Slater's surveys revealed that the percentage of BC students agreeing with various statements reflecting the BC mission—peacemaking, gun control, desire to corral military spending—actually declined over their four years at the college and remained lower in comparison to students at other private Christian colleges.[31]

Undoubtedly such trends underscored a tension between faculty and students that may continue. Even so, it was also clear that the college retained a sense of mission that, true to Anabaptist principles, its hearers remained free to accept or reject. And it is possible for the cut-and-dried statistics of assessment gurus to mislead as well as inform. The same students who appeared so resistant to college teaching were actively demonstrating affinity for it, albeit in more evangelical ways.

One irony of recent Bluffton College history is that, twenty years after the faculty and staff decisively rejected Sprunger's attempt to transform the institution into an evangelical college along the lines of Wheaton, much of the campus effectively functioned in a markedly evangelical milieu. By the later 1990s, the indications were unmistakable. Several hundred students had voluntarily enrolled in small Christian fellowship groups meeting weekly in the homes of faculty and staff. Others eagerly participated in Christian ministry teams or expressions, such as Diakonia, the Fellowship of Christian Athletes, or dorm hall Bible studies, led by an enthusiastic new team of hall chaplains. Two to three hundred students regularly packed chapel, which moved to the new Yoder Hall partly to handle the crowds. Campus pastor Randy Keeler estimated in 1994 that 40 percent of students were actively involved in one or another college religious activity.[32]

What made the 1990s so different than the 1970s was that this time such evangelical resurgence occurred with the cooperation, sometimes enthusiastic, of many faculty and staff. Church conservatives could continue to regard religion professor Weaver's theology as suspect, but when Neufeld led the college into the Christian College Coalition (one of Sprunger's old dreams), he did so with Weaver's support. The campus pastor played an important role in this resurgence. A 1980 graduate, Keeler had previously graduated from a Mennonite seminary and spent years in church youth work. His success at BC emanated from his adept harnessing, much in the manner of Paul Shelly years before, of a warm personal evangelicalism with Anabaptist engagements.[33]

Another reason for the college's incorporation of a more evangelical style came from its top leadership. Bluffton did not become another Wheaton partly because Neufeld had no intention of shedding the Mennonite ethos that had so markedly shaped his own life and the life of his institution. Yet—for reasons both pragmatic and theological—Neufeld was willing to steer the college partway along the evangelical tide for both its own survival and renewal.

Hence it was no surprise that visiting teams of church leaders in 1980 and 1995 could detect no significant tensions between Mennonite and non-Mennonite students. Both groups of BC students inhabited a shared and meaningful Anabaptist Christian context. The 1995 team found operative at the college "a peace church emphasis in a more or less evangelical Christian setting." This was a posture Neufeld had stressed. Evangelicals had a needed and valid place at BC, he insisted, along with everyone else. Through such inclusion the college did not forsake its Mennonite roots but seized the opportunity to be evangelical about its own Anabaptism. "Bluffton should not be seen as somehow less than Mennonite for its diversity," he declared to alumni in 1996, "but rather *more than Mennonite*, with a stronger Christian peace church witness growing out of this experience."[34]

As always throughout BC history, the heritage of progressive Anabaptism could not be easily defined or contained. Sometimes, as under Mosiman, it listed toward a pious version of American progressivism. More recently it has bent in an evangelical direction. Yet its fundamental message has remained. In his report to the trustees in fall 1987, Neufeld tried to articulate the basic message. In the world of church-related higher education today, he said, there are at least two different types of institutions. On the one hand there are schools "which have largely given up their earlier church affiliation." On the other hand "there are right-wing religious schools which tend to identify American culture and shallow nationalism with Christian faith." BC's direction has been to chart a different path between the poles. "Bluffton College has been called," Neufeld stated, "to a uniquely interdenominational context to share its Anabaptist tradition."[35]

It was a conceptualization on which, as before, the college could construct the future. For it continued to build. On the morning of January 12, 1999, a good crowd assembled in Founders Hall for the annual state of the college address by the president. Snyder made several exciting announcements: that the college had about completed its $15.2 million fundraising campaign, and that it had received a million-dollar gift for the new academic center from the Cecelia Cornelius Charitable Fund. But the president kept her comments short because there was a bigger task at hand. With bells tolling from the tower atop College Hall, the crowd proceeded down the sidewalk in front of Shoker Hall to a spot near College Avenue, marked with purple and white balloons, where the old Amstutz house had once stood. Behind them loomed the still-handsome face of Berky Hall, looking strangely alone on a hill recently cleared of trees.[36]

The crowd had gathered to break ground for the new classroom and office building that trustees had been planning for much of the previous decade, a building they decided, later that spring, to name Centennial Hall. The moment itself literally shone with promise. The previous week had been bitterly cold and snowy, and another six inches of snow had fallen the day before. But the morning of the twelfth came in warmer, with hazy sunshine, temperatures above freezing, and the earth able to accept the bite of a shovel.

Snyder stood with a host of dignitaries in a semicircle: board chair Ed Diller, President Emeritus Neufeld, Bluffton's mayor, and faculty and student senate chairs Loren Johns and Greg Hartzler. Each took hold of a shovel and, to the sound of applause and cheers, turned over spadefuls of earth, splashes of brown against the white snow. Then came a lovely little gesture. The president invited the entire crowd to come forward and dig some more. Somewhat shyly but then with laughter and a sense of celebration, all sorts of people did so: faculty, students, trustees, townspeople, alumni.

In her speech that morning, Snyder had recalled Hirschy's phrase in the College Hall groundbreaking of nearly a century before by referring to the "mighty cloud of witnesses" surely looking down with approval on the endeavor. Similar witnesses were present that morning once again, both seen and perhaps unseen. Bill Keeney stepped out of the crowd to turn over a shovel of earth, as did Howard Raid, Burton and Elnore Yost, Alice Ruth Pannabecker Ramseyer, and other retired faculty, staff, and trustees who had poured so much of their lives into the college. Leland Lehman leaned on a shovel and remembered his arrival on campus as a scared eighteen-year-old, one fall day in September 1939, when college business manager Jesse Loganbill had met him at the old Beaver Hut and escorted him to Lincoln Hall. Robert Ramseyer cast his mind back too. The events of the morning, he confessed quietly, had prodded him to think again of his father Lloyd.

The Legacy of John Peter Klassen

A century is not such a long time to measure the life of an institution. BC's own history now stands at three or four generations and is not much longer than the span of a single human life. Robert Kreider, who remained an active and regular visitor to campus through the 1990s, remembers something of what seemed to his small boy's eyes a great fanfare accompanying the visit to campus of college founder H. J. Krehbiel in 1930. Or, more to the point, Lois Hirschy was born in 1901, about the time her father Noah arrived on campus to take charge of college affairs. Her earliest memories must have included playing along the treeless Riley Creek or amid the woods in Judge Eaton's grove around the sole building of the new institution. Yet Lois Hirschy Trimble lived long enough to be present at the inauguration of the college's eighth president, Lee Snyder, in 1996.[37]

Several scholars have analyzed the larger histories of institutions like Bluffton. Their conceptualizations seem to help make sense of BC's own historical trajectory. Thomas Askew has summarized the history of evangelical colleges in the United States, and James Juhnke has done the same for Mennonite colleges. Both point to three stages such institutions have undergone. Colleges began as insular affairs, closely tied to the founding denomination in structures that ensured church control. In several decades they entered a middle era of, in Askew's words, "corporate definition, consolidation and credentialing," when they built stronger financial foundations and pursued the academic legitimation bestowed by outside accrediting agencies. This stage, according to both scholars, lasted from the end of World War II through the 1960s. Since then, both Mennonite and evangelical colleges have entered a third stage of further growth, characterized by the growing professionalization of both college staff and faculty.[38]

Through this process, these colleges ran the risk of serious alienation from founding church denominations. Although Juhnke only suggests this possibility for Mennonite schools, Mennonite sociologist Leo Driedger has recently voiced more certainty. Driedger examined fifteen Mennonite colleges and seminaries in the U.S. and Canada, carefully counting numbers of Mennonite students and faculty at these institutions as his primary criteria for determining faithfulness to an original "monastic" vision. By such a yardstick, Bluffton emerged as one of his premier examples of schools which, for demographic and entrepreneurial reasons, have turned instead to a "marketplace" model for its student body, thereby endangering the commitment to founding Anabaptist principles.[39]

Driedger is an able sociologist, but he was wrong about two small matters that may have led him to a larger error. He assumed that BC opened its doors to non-Mennonites in the 1970s and only for pragmatic, entrepreneurial reasons. This examination of the college history has, however, shown otherwise. Bluffton's openness to non-Mennonites was written into the college charter in its first few decades and assumed a greater importance after World War II. Even as its ethnic base eroded, the college's fundamental sense of mission flourished because it remained rooted in Anabaptist conceptions rather than ethnic Mennonite ones—conceptions outsiders were continually invited to consider and, perhaps, accept.

Although this sense of mission resists statistical assessment, the lives of many BC graduates provide ample testimony as to its influence. Various alumni surveys have uncovered remarkably high percentages of BC graduates devoting lives to service occupations: teaching, medicine, social work, church ministry, and the like. Some specific examples underscore the point. Late in what had been a productive life as a Mennonite sociologist and church leader, Winfield Fretz recognized the key turning point in his own journey. "I frequently shiver," he wrote, "as I think of what I might have spent my life doing had I not gone to Bluffton."[40]

Then there was the letter that President Rosenberger wrote in 1935 to a prospective student in Altoona, Pennsylvania, who had initially planned to come to BC but changed his mind, aiming for business school instead. Rosenberger urged him to reconsider, arguing that "we emphasize in this College the Christian values and the Christian interpretations of life." The president's pleading proved compelling. The young man enrolled at BC that fall and stayed to graduate, having plunged into baseball, the YMCA, and a number of other campus activities. His name was William T. Snyder. He would go on to spend forty years in active service with Mennonite Central Committee, including succeeding MCC founder Orie Miller as executive secretary of the organization.[41]

Snyder and Fretz illustrate the impact of the college on individual lives. But given the trajectory of BC's mission, it is significant that some of the better later examples come, unlike the two above, from outside the Mennonite world. People like Baldemar Velasquez and Mubarak Awad come to mind in this regard. So do the life choices made by someone like Kathleen Kern, 1984 graduate, who threw herself into activism with Christian Peacemaker Teams in Palestine and elsewhere, modeling with her own life a nonviolent response to injustice.[42]

In the end, the best symbol of the college's deeper meaning may be Klassen's Kobzar. At first glance, such an emblem, saturated as it is in ethnic understandings, may seem out of place at Bluffton and more appropriate for some college more immersed in Dutch-Russian Mennonite peoplehood. Yet the actual Kobzar of Klassen's memory had only a tangential connection to Mennonite ethnicity. He was based on a real person, a blind singer Klassen found performing in the opera house in St. Petersburg, then paid to sit as a model. In sculpting him, Klassen deliberately tapped into a rich ethnic tradition of Russia rather than a specifically Mennonite one.[43]

Klassen intended his original Kobzar sculpture to be a much bigger affair, a gift from the Mennonite to the Russian people because "they were good to us." As such it represented a remarkable act of Christian grace to a people who later subjected Klassen's Mennonite family and community to intense persecution in Stalin's purges. Nor, to the artist's great disappointment, was he ever even able to complete his contribution. Wary of rekindling Ukrainian nationalism, Soviet authorities refused the piece. Klassen later sculpted a small statue of the seated Kobzar from memory. It still remained his gift to a people outside, a symbol that could bridge the gap between Mennonites and other people no longer beyond their world.[44]

If Klassen's minstrel could be taken to symbolize this outside world that the college had determinedly set out to engage, for nearly a hundred years, Bluffton's own story could be described as a delicate but enduring dance with the Kobzar. Of all the continuities in BC's history, this may be most important in defining what BC was and is and what it set out to do.

Different historical contexts have admittedly sent this engagement spinning in varying directions. For a time, the outside society appeared in the form of a national progressive culture from which the college absorbed much (indeed, at times, perhaps too much). Other times these outside currents took the shape of conservative theological stances, fundamentalism, and later a less combative and more attractive evangelicalism, to which the college reacted in other ways.

In these and other cases, however, the metaphor of the dance remains appropriate because, despite the temptations, the college held back from full adoption of any of these currents. For a full century, the college did not follow the path towards secularization that many other institutions have taken; neither did it surrender its own particular sensibilities and ethics in exchange for complete absorption into the evangelical world. It borrowed from outside forces in a delicate exchange and, if lives of its graduates are an indication, has also given much in return.

Today, in a tree-shaded brick plaza on the campus of Bluffton College, there can be seen a small stone statue, pyramidal in shape. It is the greatest legacy of the artist John Peter Klassen. The figure is of a Russian Kobzar. It sits in front of a building named for a sixteenth-century leader of Swiss Anabaptism, just uphill from a flowing creek named for a nineteenth-century American pioneer. This minstrel is a rumpled but intense-looking fellow. His enormous coat drags on the ground. A misshapen hat points to the sky. A great bushy walrus mustache flows down over his instrument, a lute-like *bandura*. And his fingers lie poised across its strings, ready to continue the dance.

List of Abbreviations

AMC: Archives of the Mennonite Church, Goshen College, Goshen, Indiana
BC: Bluffton College
BCA: Bluffton College Archives
BN: *Bluffton News*
BCB: *Bluffton College Bulletin*
EDC: Eastern District Conference
GC: General Conference
GCMC: General Conference Mennonite Church
LN: *Lima News*
MC: Mennonite Church
MDC: Middle District Conference
MHL: Mennonite Historical Library, Bluffton College
ML *Mennonite Life*
MQR: *Mennonite Quarterly Review*
NCA: North Central Association
SCA: Student Christian Association
WIT: *The Witmarsum*

Notes

Introduction

1. Nancy Herman, "General Directives, Swinging Bridge Nature Preserve," January 1978, p. 4, Faculty Papers Collection, I-E-m, "Rural Life Center," BCA; Milton Trautman, *The Ohio Country from 1750 to 1977—A Naturalist's View* (Columbus: Ohio State University, 1977), 1-3, 8-9, 20.

2. George Marsden, *The Soul of the American University* (New York: Oxford University Press, 1994); Marsden and Bradley J. Longfield, eds., *The Secularization of the Academy* (New York: Oxford University Press, 1992); James Tunstead Burtchaell, *The Dying of the Light: The Disengagement of Colleges and Universities from their Christian Churches* (Grand Rapids: Eerdmans, 1998).

3. Sydney Ahlstrom, *A Religious History of the American People*, Vol. 2 (Garden City, N.Y.: Doubleday, 1975), 453-57; Winthrop S. Hudson, *Religion in America*, 3d ed. (New York: Scribners, 1981), 283-87; George Marsden, *Reforming Fundamentalism: Fuller Seminary and the New Evangelicalism* (Grand Rapids: Eerdmans, 1987), 6-8.

4. Thomas Askew, "The Shaping of Evangelical Higher Education Since World War II," in *Making Higher Education Christian,* ed. Joel A. Carpenter and Kenneth W. Shipps (St. Paul: Christian College Consortium, 1987), 141-48; Burtchaell, *The Dying of the Light*, 743.

5. Donald Kraybill, unpublished paper, "Passing on the Faith: A Tale of Three Colleges," June 1992; Burtchaell, *The Dying of the Light*, 746-810.

6. On the college's minimal initial constituency base, see *The Story of Bluffton College,* ed. C. Henry Smith and Edmund J. Hirschler (Bluffton College, 1925), 26.

7. On the separation of doctrine from ethics as part of the price of admission for full participation in segments of the American evangelical world, see John Howard Yoder, "The Contemporary Evangelical Revival and the Peace Churches," in *Mission and the Peace Witness,* ed. Robert Ramseyer (Scottdale, Pa.: Herald Press, 1979), 72-79, 84-85, 96-103.

8. President's Report to the Board of Trustees, November 17, 1944, p. 5; board meeting minutes and papers, I-B-a, no box number, "1936-1945," BCA.

Chapter One

1. Noah C. Hirschy, "Opening Address," in Bluffton College Histories Collection, I-L-0, Box 3, "N. C. Hirschy Opening Address," 1; Members of the Faculty, *Bluffton College: An Adventure in Faith, 1900-1950* (Bluffton College, 1950), 31-4. The account that follows is shaped by a number of key intellectual conceptualizations evident in recent Mennonite historiography. First, I am indebted to historian James Juhnke's depiction of creative Mennonite adaptation to change. "The story of American Mennonites," he writes, "is not simply one of how Mennonites in general became Americanized or modernized. Instead, it is a complex account of how groups related to each other and to the outside world as they made widely differing choices . . . about where to draw the lines of accepting and rejecting change." Like Juhnke, Paul Toews describes divergent Mennonite responses to the onrushing new urban/industrial order of the

nineteenth and twentieth centuries which he characterizes as "modernity." Whereas Mennonite traditionalists (like the Old Order groups) responded with disciplined resistance to acculturation, Mennonite progressives instead assumed "that Mennonite faith need not be encapsulated in cultural forms" and that "Mennonite faith and peoplehood could exist more near the center of society." In what I portray as an eager embrace of mainstream culture by some of Bluffton's thoroughly progressive leaders, and the emergence of a variant of progressive Bluffton Anabaptism, I draw heavily from these historiographical inheritances, including James Juhnke, *Vision, Doctrine, War: Mennonite Identity and Organization in America, 1890-1930* (Scottdale, Pa.: Herald Press, 1989), in general and specifically, as cited above, 31; and Paul Toews, *Mennonites in American Society, 1930-1970: Modernity and the Persistence of Religious Community* (Scottdale, Pa.: Herald Press, 1996), in general and 33, as cited.

2. Hirschy, "Opening Address," 1.

3. Ibid.

4. Ibid., 1, 3.

5. Juhnke, *Vision, Doctrine, War,* 28-29, 49-50, 164; Samuel Floyd Pannabecker, *Open Doors: A History of the General Conference Mennonite Church* (Newton, Kans.: Faith & Life Press, 1975), 16-120.

6. Samuel Floyd Pannabecker, *Faith in Ferment: A History of the Central District Conference* (Newton, Kans.: Faith & Life Press), 122-6; Juhnke, *Vision, Doctrine, War,* 133.

7. Juhnke, *Vision, Doctrine, War,* 46-7, 122; Pannabecker, *Faith in Ferment,* 139-160.

8. Delbert L. Gratz, *Bernese Anabaptists* (Goshen, Ind.: The Mennonite Historical Society, 1953), 128-185.

9. Pannabecker, *Faith in Ferment,* 44-52; Naomi Lehman, *Pilgrimage of a Congregation: First Mennonite Church, Berne, Indiana,* (Berne, Ind.: First Mennonite Church, 1982), 35-57; Juhnke, *Vision, Doctrine, War,* 97-8.

10. Delbert Gratz, "The Swiss Settlement of Bluffton-Pandora, Ohio," *Mennonite Life* 43 (December 1988): 4-9; Pannabecker, *Faith in Ferment,* 54-5.

11. Pannabecker, *Faith in Ferment,* 54-55; Howard Raid, *The First Seventy-Five Years: First Mennonite Church, Bluffton, Ohio* (Freeman, S.Dak.: Pine Hill Press, 1986), 23-4, 28.

12. Pannabecker, *Faith in Ferment,* 57-8; Gratz, "The Swiss Settlement of Bluffton-Pandora," 8-9.

13. Juhnke, *Vision, Doctrine, War,* 96; Pannabecker, *Faith in Ferment,* 120-24; "German Correspondent" quoted in *Grace Mennonite Church–An Overview of the First Twenty-Five Years* (Pandora, Ohio: Grace Mennonite Church, 1979), 2, Mennonite Historical Library (hereafter abbreviated MHL), Bluffton College.

14. Anna Kreider, "The Wadsworth School," *Mennonite Life* 19 (April 1959): 66-7.

15. Ibid.

16. Ibid., 68.

17. James O. Lehman, *Sonnenberg: A Haven and a Heritage* (Kidron, Ohio: Kidron Community Council, 1969), 98-9, 106-10, 112-116; Pannabecker, *Faith in Ferment,* 53-4.

18. Kreider, "The Wadsworth School," 69.

19. C. Henry Smith and E. J. Hirschler, eds., *The Story of Bluffton College* (Bluffton College, 1925), 23.

20. David L. Habegger, *The Hirschy Genealogy: The Descendants of Philip Hirschy (1787-1831) and Julianna Frey (1795-1839)* (copyright 1994 by David

Habegger), 43-4, MHL; Edmund G. Kaufman, *General Conference Mennonite Pioneers* (North Newton, Kans.: Bethel College Press, 1973), 173.

21. Habegger, *The Hirschy Genealogy*, 44; Kaufman, *General Conference Mennonite Pioneers*, 173-4; Letter of recommendation from L. M. Sniff, May 26, 1891, Hirschy Papers, I-A-a, Box 2, "NC Hirschy materials from daughter: recommendations," BCA.

22. Habegger, *The Hirschy Genealogy*, 45-6.

23. Ibid.; Kaufman, *General Conference Mennonite Pioneers*, 174.

24. Habegger, *The Hirschy Genealogy*, 46; Kaufman, *General Conference Mennonite Pioneers*, 174.

25. Pannabecker, *Faith in Ferment*, 97.

26. Smith and Hirschler, *The Story of Bluffton College*, 24-5; Pannabecker, *Faith in Ferment*, 98.

27. Hirschy to J. H. Tschantz, September 6, 1897, Hirschy Papers, I-A-a, Box 1, file titled "Early minutes, resolutions and trustees letters," BCA; J. H. Tschantz, "The School Question," *The Mennonite* 12 (January 1898).

28. Editorial, *The Mennonite* 11 (January 1898): 53.

29. "Report of the Educational Committee of the Middle District Conference," *The Mennonite* 12 (April 1897).

30. Smith and Hirschler, eds., *The Story of Bluffton College*, 28-9; Hirschy diary entry dated October 8, 1897, I-A-a, Hirschy Papers, Box 2, BCA.

31. N. C. Hirschy, "Wadsworth, Ohio"; C. D. Amstutz, "To the Ministers and Members of the Mennonite Church of the Central District Conference"; J. F. Lehman, "Berne, Indiana"; all in Hirschy Papers, Box 1, "Location of New School (College)," BCA.

32. George Lint to J. C. Mehl, September 17, 1898, Hirschy Papers, I-A-a, Box 1, "Location of new school (college)," BCA.

33. Smith and Hirschler, eds., *The Story of Bluffton College*, 26-7; Susan Fisher Miller, *Culture for Service: A History of Goshen College, 1894-1994* (Goshen, Ind.: Goshen College, 1994), 31-4.

34. "Minutes of the Educational Committee of the Middle District Conference, 1894-1899," minutes dated January 26, 27, and September 30, 1898, with Bluffton College Board of Trustees Minutes, 1899-1912, n.p., private collection of Elmer Neufeld, BCA; Smith and Hirschler, eds., *The Story of Bluffton College*, 28-9.

35. H. P. Krehbiel, answer to questionnaire, dated Nov 29, 1897, Hirschy Papers, I-A-a, Box 1, "Location of Bluffton (CMC), 1890-1910," BCA.

36. "H. J. Krehbiel to "Dear Brother," October 31, 1899, Hirschy Papers, I-A-a, Box 1, file titled "Central Mennonite College, H. J. Krehbiel letters, 1901-1913," BCA; "Mennonite College will be built at Bluffton," *Bluffton News*, October 6, 1898, quoted in *Life in the Bluffton and Pandora, Ohio, Community, 1877-1910: Excerpts from The Bluffton News*, ed. Edgar Schumacher (Bluffton, Ohio: Swiss Community Historical Society, 1977), 50; also see article from the *Berne Witness*, December 14, 1899, in Schumacher, 63.

37. "Minutes of the Educational Committee of the Middle District Conference, 1894-1899," minutes dated January 10-11, 1899, with Bluffton College Board of Trustees Minutes, 1899-1912, n.p., private collection of Elmer Neufeld, BCA.

38. Smith and Hirschler, eds., *The Story of Bluffton College*, 29-30, 275-6; Von Hardesty, *A Narrative of Bluffton College* (Bluffton College, 1974), 4; "Resolutions passed at Bluffton, Ohio, Dec. 12, 1899," in Hirschy Papers, I-A-a, Box 1, "Central Mennonite College, 1899-1900, minutes, constitution," BCA.

39. "The Cornerstone Laying of Central Mennonite College a Grand Success," *Tri-County Weekly* 2 (June 20, 1900), 1.

40. Address of Rev. N. C. Hirschy, *Tri-County Weekly*, June 27, 1900, Hirschy Papers, I-A-a, Box 1, file titled "Beginning of CMC," BCA. Here Central Mennonite College founders shared a task with creators of other Mennonite schools. "The colleges took on a creative but difficult task," James Juhnke has written," to reconcile traditional, rural Mennonite values with American democratic society and its progressivism." See Juhnke, *Vision, Doctrine, War*, 164-5.

41. Kaufman, *General Conference Mennonite Pioneers*, 71-4; Hirschy to H. J. Krehbiel, March 28, 1900, Hirschy Papers, I-A-a, Box 2, file titled "Noah Hirschy Letters, 3/12/1900–1/24/24," BCA; Smith and Hirschler, *The Story of Bluffton College*, 34.

42. H. J. Krehbiel to "Dear Brother," July 14, 1900, Hirschy Papers, Box 1, "Location of Bluffton College (CMC)," BCA.

43. Hirschy to H. J. Krehbiel, March 28, 1900, Hirschy Papers, I-A-a, Box 2, "Noah Hirschy Letters, 3/12/1900–1/24/24," BCA; Hirschy to Krehbiel, May 28, 1900, Hirschy Papers, I-A-a, Box 2, "Central Mennonite College, N. C. Hirschy Letters," BCA.

44. Amstutz to Hirschy, July 16, 1900, Hirschy Papers, Box 1, "Central Mennonite College, N. C. Hirschy Letters," BCA.

45. Krehbiel to Hirschy, May 21, 1900; Mehl to Hirschy, June 2, 1900; Hirschy to Krehbiel, August 20, 1900; all in Hirschy Papers, Box 1, file titled "Central Mennonite College, N. C. Hirschy Letters," BCA.

46. Noah C. Hirschy, "Opening Address," in Bluffton College Histories Collection, I-L-0, Box 3, folder titled "N. C. Hirschy Opening Address," 2, BCA.

47. The Town at the Fork of the Rileys Revisited: Historical Sketches of Old Shannon and Bluffton, Ohio, copyright 1986, Bluffton News, 29-32, 35, 16-17; Bluffton News, August 23, 1900, and March 31, 1910, in Schumacher, *Life in the Bluffton and Pandora, Ohio, Community, 1877-1910* (Bluffton: Swiss Community Historical Society, 1997), 68, 164.

48. *BN* (September 25, 1986), 1, 20.

49. Ibid.; *The Town at the Fork of the Rileys revisited*," 21. Delbert Gratz estimated that 25 percent of the countryside was still forested in 1900; see Gratz, "The Swiss Settlement of Bluffton-Pandora, Ohio," 7.

50. "The President's Fifth Annual Report, 1904-1905," in Hirschy Papers, I-A-a, Box 1, "Location of New School (College)," BCA; Hardesty, *A Narrative of Bluffton College*, 6.

51. Members of the Faculty, *Adventures in Faith*, 30; "Minutes of the Educational Committee of the Middle District Conference, 1894-1899," minutes dated January 27, 1898, Board of Trustees Minutes, 1899-1912, n.p., Neufeld Collection, BCA; Faculty Meeting Minutes Sept. 26, 1904, Faculty Minutes Collection, I-E-a, Box 1, "Faculty Minutes, Nov 5, 1900—Feb 19, 1912," BCA.

52. Smith and Hirschler, *The Story of Bluffton College*, 45, 49, 55; "The President's Fourth Annual Report, 1903-1904," in Hirschy Papers, I-A-a, Box 1, "Location of New School (College)," BCA; Hardesty, *A Narrative of Bluffton College*, 6-7.

53. Smith and Hirschler, *The Story of Bluffton College*, 56-7.

54. Smith and Hirschler, *The Story of Bluffton College*, 82; Hirschy, "Opening Address," in Bluffton College Histories Collection, I-L-0, Box 3, "N. C. Hirschy Opening Address," 2, BCA.

55. Hardesty, *A Narrative of Bluffton College*, 6-7; Hirschy, "The President's Annual Report for 1900-1901," in Hirschy Papers, I-A-a, Box 1, "Location of

New School (College)," BCA; Central Mennonite College *Catalogue*, 1901-1902, 10, Bluffton College Publications Collection, I-L-a, Box 1, "College Record, 1901-1910," BCA; science equipment and courses noted in the *The College Record* 3 (June and July 1904): 44, 47, same box and collection as above.

56. Members of the Faculty, *An Adventure in Faith*, 110; Bertha Goetsch, "Teacher Excellence recalled by Alumna," *Scope* 70 (January 1983), 6; Hardesty, *A Narrative of Bluffton College*, 6-7, *The College Record* quote.

57. Central Mennonite College *Catalogue*, 1901-1902, p. 10, Bluffton College Publications Collection, I-L-a, Box 1, "College Record, 1901-1910," BCA.

58. Members of the Faculty, *An Adventure in Faith*, 140; Hardesty, *A Narrative of Bluffton College*, 6-7.

59. *The College Record* 5 (June 1906): 26, in Hirschy Papers, I-A-a, Box 1, BCA; Central Mennonite College *Catalogue*, 1901-1902, p. 10, Bluffton College Publications Collection, I-L-a, Box 1, "College Record, 1901-1910," BCA.

60. Members of the Faculty, *An Adventure in Faith*, 136.

61. *The College Record* 4 (October 1905): 76, and 4 (November, 1905): 84; Central Mennonite College *Catalogue*, 1901-1902, p. 10, Bluffton College Publications Collection, I-L-a, Box 1, "College Record, 1901-1910," BCA.

62. Faculty minutes dated June 3, 1904, and June 17, 1907, Faculty Minutes Collection, I-E-a, Box 1, "Faculty Minutes Nov. 5, 1900–Feb. 19, 1912," BCA.

63. Smith and Hirschler, *The Story of Bluffton College*, 191.

64. Members of the Faculty, *An Adventure in Faith*, 35-8; *BN*, Nov. 1, 1900, in Schumacher, *Life in the Bluffton and Pandora, Ohio, Community, 1877-1910*, 71.

65. Hirschy to Krehbiel, February 4, 1907, Hirschy Papers, I-A-a, Box 1, "Beginning of Bluffton College (CMC)," BCA; "Minutes of the Educational Committee of the Middle District Conference, 1894-1899," minutes passed by correspondence May 23, 1907, and meeting minutes dated Feb 12-13, 1908, with Board of Trustees Minutes, 1899-1912, n.p., Neufeld Collection, BCA.

66. Smith and Hirschler, *The Story of Bluffton College*, 55; E. J. Hirschler, "Education as a Preparation for Service," *The College Record* 2 (November 1903): 86.

67. *Scope* 68 (January 1981), 5; *Scope* 70 (January 1983), 6.

68. Hardesty, *A Narrative of Bluffton College*, 4, 6; "To the Board of Trustees, Central Mennonite College," April 18, 1904, Faculty Minutes Collection, I-E-a, Box 1, "Faculty Meeting Minutes, Nov. 5, 1900-Feb. 19, 1912," BCA.

69. Faculty minutes dated June 8, 1903, and May 15, 1905, Faculty Minutes Collection, I-E-a, Box 1, "Faculty Minutes Nov. 5, 1900-Feb. 19, 1912," BCA; Pannabecker, *Faith in Ferment*, 100; Hirschy diary dated January 25, 1904, Hirschy papers, I-A-a, Box 2, BCA; "Intercollegiate Peace Conference," *The College Record* 5 (April 1906): 1; Smith and Hirschler, *The Story of Bluffton College*, 63.

70. "Commencement Week at the College," *The College Record* 4 (August 1905): 58-9.

71. *The College Record* 4 (August 1905): 58-9.

72. Ibid.

73. *BN*, Nov. 1, 1900, in Schumacher, *Life in the Bluffton and Pandora, Ohio, Community, 1877-1910*, 72; Hirschy to Krehbiel, September 21, 1901, Hirschy Papers, I-A-a, Box 1, "Central Mennonite College, N.C. Hirschy letters," BCA; Smith and Hirschler, *The Story of Bluffton College*, 65, 77-8.

74. Pannabecker, *Faith in Ferment*, 100; Hardesty, *A Narrative of Bluffton College*, 9; Smith and Hirschler, *The Story of Bluffton College*, 63; Krehbiel to Tschantz, November 24, 1905, Hirschy Papers, I-A-a, Box 1, "Central Mennonite

College, H. J. Krehbiel Letters, 1901-1913," BCA.

75. Krehbiel to Tschantz, Nov. 24, 1905.

76. "The President's Fifth Annual Report, 1904-1905," p. 2, Hirschy Papers, I-A-a, Box 1, File titled "Location of New School (College)," BCA.

77. Fred Kniss, *Disquiet in the Land: Cultural Conflict in American Mennonite Communities* (New Brunswick: Rutgers University Press, 1997), 1-12, 21-35.

78. Kaufman, *General Conference Mennonite Pioneers,* 312-14. For the opinion of Bluffton old-timers, see handwritten note by Howard Raid, August 17, 1988, in Hirschy Papers, I-A-a, Box 1, "Business manager J.A. Amstutz, J. H. Tschantz treas., Central Mennonite College," BCA.

79. Amstutz to Tschantz, March 20 and June 18, 1901, Hirschy Papers, I-A-a, Box 1, "Business manager J.A. Amstutz, J. H. Tschantz treas., Central Mennonite College," BCA; Krehbiel quotes in Kaufman, *General Conference Mennonite Pioneers,* 313.

80. *BN,* March 5, 1903, in Schumacher, *Life in the Bluffton and Pandora, Ohio, Community, 1877-1910,* 102; Hirschy comments on women in newspaper clipping in his diary entry dated December 13, 1903, Hirschy Papers, I-A-a, Box 2, BCA.

81. Hirschy to E. I. Bosworth, June 15, 1907, Hirschy Papers, I-A-a, Box 2, "N. C. Hirschy Papers," BCA.

82. Raid, *The First Seventy-Five Years,* 43-6; also see newspaper clipping accompanying Hirschy diary entry dated Sunday, May 4, 1902, Hirschy Papers, I-A-a, Box 2, BCA.

83. Raid, *The First Seventy-Five Years,* 25, 40; Hirschy photo found in Hirschy Papers, I-A-a, Box 1, BCA.

84. Hirschy diary entries dated September 8, 1901, and August 30, 1902, Hirschy Papers, I-A-a, Box 2, BCA.

85. Noah to Augusta Hirschy, June 24, 1905, Hirschy Papers, Box 4, unfiled letters, BCA.

86. Noah to Augusta Hirschy, Sept. 3, 1908, Hirschy Papers, Box 4, unfiled letters, BCA.

87. See diary entries dated February 19, 1902; November 30, 1903; and June 24, 1904; Hirschy Papers, I-A-a, Box 2, BCA.

88. Hirschy to Krehbiel, February 10, 1903, Hirschy Papers, I-A-a, Box 1, "H. J. Krehbiel Letters, 1901-1913," BCA.

89. Hirschy diary entries dated October 13, 1902, and June 24, 1904, Hirschy Papers, I-A-a, Box 2, BCA; Noah to Augusta Hirschy, September 1, 1908, Hirschy Papers, I-A-a, Box 4, unfiled letters, BCA.

90. Raid, *The First Seventy-Five Years,* 16-7, 33-4.

91. Ibid.; *Grace Mennonite Church—An Overview,* 3-4.

92. *Grace Mennonite Church—An Overview,* 5.

93. *Grace Mennonite Church—An Overview,* 5-7.

94. Ibid.; St. John Mennonite Centennial Committee, *St. John Mennonite Church, 1888-1988* (Pandora, Ohio: St. John Mennonite Church, 1988).

95. *Grace Mennonite Church—An Overview,* 7-8; *Bluffton News,* January 4, March 24, April 28, May 5, May 12, December 1, 1904, in Schumacher, *Life in the Bluffton and Pandora, Ohio, Community, 1877-1910,* 112, 114-6, 119.

96. Hirschy diary entries dated Jan. 25, 1898, Aug. 8, 1898 ("some rubs"); Jan. 26, 1900, all in Hirschy Papers, I-A-a, Box 2, BCA.

97. Hirschy diary entries dated March 27, 1904 ("the beast is wrangling"); July 15, 1903; September 25, 1903; October 2, 1903; March 7, 1904; March 10, 1909, all in Hirschy Papers, I-A-a, Box 2, BCA.

98. Hirschy diary entry dated June 25, 1903, Hirschy Papers, I-A-a, Box 2, BCA.

99. Hirschy to the Trustees, January 4, 1901, Hirschy papers, I-A-a, Box 1, "Central Mennonite College N. C. Hirschy Letters," BCA; Lehman, Tschantz and Hirschy to "the directors of the Mennonite Church near Bluffton, Ohio," undated letter, Development Office Papers, I-D-e, Box 1, "The 1923 Modernism according to some . . . ," BCA.

100. Hirschy diary entries dated Oct. 22 and Nov. 4, 1901, Hirschy Papers, I-A-a, Box 2, BCA.

101. Hirschy diary entry dated Nov 4, 1901. Two years later H. J. Krehbiel recognized the damage this move had inflicted; see Krehbiel to "Brethren," August 15, 1903, Hirschy Papers, I-A-a, Box 1, "Central Mennonite College, secretary H. J. Krehbiel, 1902-1909," BCA.

102. Smith and Hirschler, *The Story of Bluffton College*, 49-50; Hirschy diary entry dated Oct. 13, 1902, Hirschy Papers, I-A-a, Box 2, BCA.

103. Raid, *The First Seventy-Five Years*, 18, 65-7; Hirschy diary entries dated July 20, Sept. 30, and Oct. 2, 1903; *BN*, Sept. 14, 1905, March 29, 1906, in Schumacher, *Life in the Bluffton and Pandora, Ohio, Community, 1877-1910*, 125-6, 130-1.

104. *Grace Mennonite Church—An Overview*, 11.

105. Amstutz to Hirschy, July 16, 1900, Hirschy Papers, Box 1, "Central Mennonite College, N. C. Hirschy Letters," BCA; Smith and Hirschler, *The Story of Bluffton College*, 50-1, 72-3.

106. Raid, *The First Seventy-Five Years*, 44; Smith and Hirschler, *The Story of Bluffton College*, 51.

107. "Resolutions passed during meeting at Bluffton, Jan 23-5-06"; Lehman to Hirschy, February 19 and 24, 1906; Hirschy to Lehman, February 28, 1906; all in Hirschy Papers, I-A-a, "Central Mennonite Letters, 1906," BCA; Hirschy to Lehman, "Washington's Birthday," 1906, Hirschy Papers, I-A-a, "The 1906 concerns about continuing Central Mennonite," BCA. These letters are unsigned, but it is clear from the context that the sender was Hirschy.

108. "The Future of the Central Mennonite College" and "College Stays in Bluffton," in the *Berne Witness*, March 6 and 15, 1906, Hirschy Papers, I-A-a, Box 1, file titled "The 1906 concern about the continuing of Central Mennonite College," BCA; Lehman to Hirschy, April 5, 1906, Hirschy Papers, I-A-a, Box 1, file titled "Central Mennonite College Situation, 1906-7," BCA;

109. J. W. Kliewer to Hirschy, April 21, 1906, Hirschy Papers, I-A-a, Box 1, "Central Mennonite Letters, 1906," BCA. Reminiscences and speech by H. J. Krehbiel in Smith and Hirschler, *The Story of Bluffton College*, 179-80. On the fact that these were Krehbiel's memories, see S. K. Mosiman to Krehbiel, October 4, 1924, Mosiman Papers, I-A-b, Box 3, "Krehbiel Letters," BCA.

110. Smith and Hirschler, *The Story of Bluffton College*, 70; Beeshy to Tschantz, May 28, 1907, Hirschy Papers, I-A-a, "Business Manager J. A. Amstutz, J. H. Tschantz, treas., Central Mennonite College," BCA.

111. Smith and Hirschler, *The Story of Bluffton College*, 70-1; Krehbiel to Hirschy, June 28, 1907, Hirschy Papers, I-A-a, Box 1, "Central Mennonite College letters, 1902-08," BCA.

112. Musselman to J. F. Lehman, June 11, 1907, Hirschy to Krehbiel, July 2, 1907, both in Hirschy Papers, I-A-a, Box 1, "Central Mennonite College letters, 1902-08," BCA; Hirschy to the Board of Trustees, June 1, 1907, Hirschy Papers, I-A-a, Box 2, "N. C. Hirschy Letters 6-1-1907," BCA.

113. On Hirschy's contempt for the board, especially Krehbiel, see Hirschy

diary entries dated July 7 and August 20, 1907, Hirschy Papers, I-A-a, Box 2, BCA. Noah to Augusta Hirschy, August 12 and 20, 1908, I-A-a, Hirschy Papers, Box 4, unfiled letters, BCA; Augusta to Noah Hirschy, August 18, 1908, Hirschy Papers, I-A-a, Box 2, "Summer/Fall 1908 Resignation Decision," BCA; "Resolutions passed at Wayland, Iowa, Aug. 29-31, 08," Hirschy Papers, I-A-a, Box 1, "Minutes and Board of Trustees Letters, Central Mennonite College," BCA. On Mosiman's salary, see "Minutes of the Educational Committee of the Middle District Conference, 1894-1899," minutes dated Feb. 12-13, 1908, with Board of Trustees Minutes, 1899-1912, n.p., Neufeld Collection, BCA.

114. Noah to Augusta Hirschy, Aug. 20 and Sept. 10, 1908, I-A-a, Hirschy Papers, Box 4, unfiled letters, BCA.

115. Augusta to Noah Hirschy, August 7, 1908, Hirschy Papers, I-A-a, Box 2, file titled "Summer/Fall 1908 Resignation Decision," BCA; Noah to Augusta Hirschy, Sept. 10, 1908, I-A-a, Hirschy Papers, Box 4, unfiled letters, BCA.

116. Kaufman, *General Conference Mennonite Pioneers*, 315-6; *Bluffton News*, March 11, 1909, in Schumacher, *Life in the Bluffton and Pandora, Ohio, Community, 1877-1910*, 150.

117. Habegger, *The Hirschy Genealogy*, 47-8.

118. Ibid.; Kaufman, *General Conference Mennonite Pioneers*, 179-80; Hirschy to Mosiman, July 10, 1923, Mosiman Papers, I-A-b, Box 1, "Mosiman's correspondence with Hirschy," BCA.

119. Mosiman to W. H. Egly, Feb. 5, 1919, Peace Papers and Reports, I-X-a, Box 1, "Corr to People in the Army," BCA; Mosiman to C. C. Sommers, December 6, 1923, Mosiman Papers, I-A-b, Box 12, "S. K. Mosiman misc.," BCA.

120. Quoted in Kaufman, *General Conference Mennonite Pioneers*, 179.

121. Numbers taken from Kaufman, ibid.

122. Noah to Augusta Hirschy, September 10, 1908, Hirschy Papers, I-A-a, Box 4, unfiled letters, BCA.

Chapter Two

1. "Bluffton Educational Advantages: Address delivered by N. E. Byers at Bluffton Home Coming and College Day, Aug. 5, 1913," *The College Record* 12 (September 1913): 86.

2. Kaufman, *General Conference Mennonite Pioneers*, 183.

3. Kaufman, *General Conference Mennonite Pioneers*, 182-3.

4. Ibid.

5. Kaufman, *General Conference Mennonite Pioneers*, 183; Hirschy diary entry dated November 20, 1905, Hirschy Papers, I-A-a, Box 2, BCA; Smith and Hirschler, eds., *The Story of Bluffton College*, 92-3.

6. David Rempel, "The First 'Russian Boys' at Bluffton College, 1924-1929," p. 5, Student Organizations, International Student Papers, I-K-b, Box 2, "The First Russian Boys at Bluffton College, 1924-28," BCA; Ruth Unrau, *Encircled: Stories of Mennonite Women* (Newton, Kans.: Faith and Life Press, 1986), 36; *Scope* 78 (May 1991), 4.

7. Unrau, *Encircled*, 33-8.

8. Ibid.; *Witmarsum* (hereafter abbreviated as WIT) 1 (Oct 13, 1913), 7.

9. Oral interview, Perry Bush with Donovan and Barbara Smucker, April 3, 1998, BCA; *Scope* 78 (May 1991), 4.

10. Beeshy to Tschantz, Dec. 10, 1908, and June 8, 1909, Hirschy Papers, I-A-a, Box 1, "J. H. Tschantz, treas., Central Menn. College," BCA; Pannabecker, *Faith in Ferment*, 101.

11. Ramseyer memory in Unrau, *Encircled*, 39, also see p. 40; Emilie to Samuel Mosiman, undated letter, in Alumni and Faculty Records, 4-MS-C, no. 9, "Personal papers Mrs Mosiman," BCA.

12. Smith and Hirschler, *The Story of Bluffton College*, 93-4; Kaufman, *General Conference Mennonite Pioneers*, 185-6.

13. Smith and Hirschler, *The Story of Bluffton College*, 96, 98-9, 136.

14. Ibid., 100-03; student numbers obtained by tallying enrollment in *The College Record* for the following months and years: July 1908, pp. 46-7; July 1911, p. 51; April 1914, pp. 126-31; April 1916, pp. 134-146; April 1917, pp. 143-155; April 1918, pp. 149-161; April 1919, pp. 147-154; April 1922, pp. 117-131; April 1923, p. 135; April 1924, p. 135; April 1925, p. 140; April 1926, p. 143; April 1927, p. 140. Also *WIT* 3, Sept 1915: 14; *WIT* 12 (Sept 20, 1924), 3.

15. Byers to Mosiman, June 3, 1909, Hirschy Papers, I-A-a, Box 1, "Letters, Resolutions leading to the merger of Central Men. College into Bluffton College," BCA; Smith and Hirschler, *The Story of Bluffton College*, 215-6.

16. Smith and Hirschler, *The Story of Bluffton College*, 117-119; C. Henry Smith, "Report of a Meeting held at Warsaw, Indiana, May 29, 1913," n.p., pp. b-c, MHL; Mosiman to J. F. Lehman and also to Shelly, both on March 14, 1913, Byers to Mosiman, Feb. 2, 1913, and Byers to Mosiman, May 9, 1913, all in Hirschy Papers, I-A-a, Box 1, "Letters, resolutions . . . ," BCA.

17. Mosiman to Kliewer, March 14, 1913, Byers to Mosiman, Feb. 2 and May 15, 1913, both in Hirschy Papers, I-A-a, Box 1, "Letters, resolutions . . . ," BCA.

18. Mosiman to Kliewer, March 14, 1913, Byers to Mosiman, May 15, July 16, June 19, and May 9, 1913, all in Hirschy Papers, I-A-a, Box 1, "Letters, reso- lutions . . . ," BCA.

19. Byers to Mosiman, Aug 11 and April 10, 1913; on the name of "Bluffton College," see Hirschy to Mosiman, Aug. 6, 1913, all in Hirschy Papers, I-A-a, Box 1, "Letters, resolutions . . . ," BCA, and "Who should attend Bluffton College?" *The College Bulletin* 8 (August 1909): 48. For Mosiman's suggestion of "Witmarsum College," see Mosiman to Frank Diller, Feb. 7, 1933, Mosiman Papers, I-A-b, Box 6, "Correspondence, 1933," BCA.

20. Smith and Hirschler, *The Story of Bluffton College*, 119-25; Smith, "Report of a Meeting . . . ," pp. b-c, 1-14.

21. Smith, "Report of a Meeting . . . ," pp. b-c; Pannabecker, *Faith in Ferment*, 159-60, 171-73.

22. N. E. Byers, "The Times in Which I Lived," *Mennonite Life* 7 (January 1952): 45-7, (April 1952): 79-80; Byers to Mosiman, July 16, 1913, Hirschy Papers, I-A-a, Box 1, "Letters, resolutions . . . ," BCA.

23. Willard H. Smith, "C. Henry Smith: A Brief Biography," in Smith, *Mennonite Country Boy* (Newton, Kans.: Faith and Life Press, 1962), 233-247.

24. Danielle Horvath, "C. Henry Smith: A Product of Two Divergent Cultures," Bluffton College Student Paper, 1997, MHL; Robert Kreider, "C. Henry Smith: A Tribute"; Lloyd L. Ramseyer, "Obituary for Dr. C. Henry Smith," and "C. Henry Smith: A Tribute"; all in Smith Papers, 4-MS-C 17, Box 1, BCA.

25. Quotes from Juhnke, *Vision, Doctrine, War*, 164; and from Smith, *Mennonite Country Boy*, 202, 211.

26. Kratz to C. J. Claassen, June 18, 1919, Mosiman Papers, I-A-b, Box 1, "Claassen correspondence," BCA.

27. Byers, "The times . . . ," 46.

28. Smith, "The Forces that Make for Peace," *Christian Monitor* 2

(March/April/May 1910): 468-469, 502-503, 532-533, quoted p. 532; Peter Jansen to Mosiman, July 27, and Mosiman to Jansen, Oct. 25, 1920, Mosiman Papers, I-A-b, Box 1, "Jansen letters," BCA; "The Governor of Ohio," *The College Record* 12 (September 1913): 87-8.

29. *WIT* 7 (Jan. 10, 1920), 1, 3; *WIT* 7 (March 6, 1920), 3; *WIT* 12 (May 2, 1925), 1; *WIT* 13 (Dec. 12, 1925), 1, 4; *WIT* 8 (Oct. 9 and 16, 1920), 1; *WIT* 12 (Oct. 25, 1924), 1; *WIT* 16 (Nov. 3, 1928), 1.

30. Smith, "The Hand of God in American History," *Christian Evangel* 4 (May/June/July 1914): 186-188, 225-227, 262-263; Mosiman to Eddison Mosiman, Aug. 13, 1921, Mosiman Papers, I-A-b, Box 3, "Letters seeking funds," and to W. O. Thompson, March 29, 1921, Box 3, "W. O. Thompson . . . letters," BCA.

31. For examples, see *WIT* 3 (December 1915), 10; *WIT* 13 (March 13, 1926), 4; *WIT* 16 (Feb. 9, 1929), 1.

32. For Wilson's endorsement of *Birth of a Nation*, see Joel Williamson, *A Rage for Order*, (New York: Oxford University Press, 1986), 115; Smith, "The Hand of God," 226; Smith, "Conservation of Childhood," *The Christian Evangel* 3 (May 1913): 195-96.

33. WIT 4 (March 1917), 11; *WIT* 5 (April 27, 1918), 3.

34. *WIT* 2 (January 1915), 13; *WIT* 2 (February 1915), 10; *WIT* 13 (Dec. 5, 1925), 3; *WIT* 14 (Nov. 26, 1926), 1; 1918 *Ista*, 176-77.

35. N. E. Byers, "College Ideals," *The College Record* 12 (October 1913): 92.
36. Ibid.

37. H. W. Berky, "The Legend of the Birth of a Soul," *Bluffton College Bulletin* 54 (July 1967), 1; BN (Nov 20, 1958), 1.

38. Berky, "The Legend," 1-3.

39. *Scope* 58 (March 1980), 4.

40. Smith and Hirschler, *The Story of Bluffton College*, 129-30, 201-06; *WIT* 2 (December 1914), 7.

41. Smith and Hirschler, *The Story of Bluffton College*, 138; Mosiman to Kratz, Oct. 11, 1922, Mosiman Papers, 1-A-B, Box 9, "Kratz corresp., 1913-28," BCA; Mosiman to the Board of Trustees, Sept. 22, 1922, Mosiman Papers, I-A-B, Box 9, "Executive Committee meeting, Sept 9, 1922," BCA; *WIT* 2 (Jan. 4, 1924), 1.

42. "Dedication of New Science Hall," BCB 2 (June-July 1915), 1.

43. Mosiman to Kratz, Nov. 27, 1922, Mosiman Papers, 1-A-B, Box 9, "Kratz corresp., 1913-28," BCA; Hardesty, *A Narrative of Bluffton College*, 17-18.

44. Hardesty, *A Narrative of Bluffton College*, 17-18.

45. Smith and Hirschler, *The Story of Bluffton College*, 132; BCB Catalogue (April 1914), 46-7; *WIT* 4 (April 1917), 22; "Report of the Dean of the College of Liberal Arts," 1915-16 and 1916-17, both in Mosiman Papers, I-A-b, Box 7, "minutes Bd of Trustees," BCA; *WIT* 5 (March 23, 1918), 1, 3.

46. *BCB* 9 (April 1922), 49-50; Hardesty, *A Narrative of Bluffton College*, 14-15.

47. Mosiman to Howe, March 7, 1922, Brenneman to Mosiman, June 14, 1918, and Mosiman to Brenneman, June 19, 1918; all in Mosiman Papers, I-A-b, Box 2, "Faculty members corresp."

48. Berky to Mosiman, Feb. 24, July 13, and June 18, 1913, Hirschy Papers, I-A-a, Box 1, "Letters, resolutions . . . ," BCA.

49. Unrau, *Encircled*, 118-121.

50. "Prof. Otto Holtkamp Retires," BCB 47 (June 1960), 1; Smith and Hirschler, *The Story of Bluffton College*, 105; "A Citation," BCB 52 (June 1965), 2; Faculty Members, *An Adventure in Faith*, 191.

51. Larry Kehler, "John Klassen—BC's Dedicated Teacher, Artist, Citizen," *BCB*, 55 (October 1968), 1-4; Mosiman to John J. Davis, undated but with other letters of July 19, 1924, Peace Arts Center Papers, I-E-n, "John Peter Klassen— Artist as Peacemaker," BCA.

52. Kehler, "John Klassen," 1-4.

53. Moyer to Mosiman, April 24, 1928, I-A-b, Box 13, Mosiman Papers, "Mosiman Personal Letters," BCA; *BCB* 17 (February 1930), 16; Lloyd Ramseyer, "Citation: J. S. Schultz, Ph.D.," June 7, 1954, Ramseyer Papers, I-A-d, Box 15, "Sa-Se, 1951-5," BCA.

54. Samuel Pannabecker, *Ventures of Faith: The Story of Mennonite Biblical Seminary* (Elkhart: Mennonite Biblical Seminary, 1975), 14-17; Stephen C. Ainlay, "The 1920 Seminary Movement: A Failed Attempt at Formal Theological Education in the Mennonite Church," *MQR* 64 (October 1990): 325-51.

55. Pannabecker, *Ventures of Faith*, 18-21; Mosiman to Kratz, Oct. 6, and Kratz to Mosiman, Oct. 9, 1920, Mosiman Papers, I-A-b, Box 9, "Kratz corr.," BCA.

56. Ainlay, "The 1920 Seminary Movement," 340, 344-5; Hartzler to Whitmer, April 24, 1920, and Whitmer to Hartzler, Feb. 20, 1926, Paul Whitmer Correspondence in Faculty Papers, 4-MS-C, Box 1, "Some Letters about Starting Seminary," BCA.

57. Faculty Members, *An Adventure in Faith*, 141, 148, 151; *WIT* 12 (Jan. 10, 1925), 1; Smith and Hirschler, *The Story of Bluffton College*, 255-6, 267; *WIT* 2 (October 1914), 6.

58. Hardesty, *A Narrative of Bluffton College*, 15-16.

59. Ibid., 9; Lehman to Mosiman, July 7, 1922, Mosiman Papers, I-A-b, Box 12, "Glee Club," BCA; *Scope* 77 (January 1990), 4.

60. For Mosiman's correspondence with the Bible lecturers, see various files in Mosiman Papers, I-A-b, Box 3, BCA.

61. Smith and Hirschler, *The Story of Bluffton College*, 232-4, 246-9; 1917 *Ista* 59, 61; McPeak to Mosiman, undated but describing the 1915-16 school year, Mosiman Papers, I-A-b, Box 7, "Bd Meetings—etc., 1916," BCA; Faculty Members, *An Adventure in Faith*, 95.

62. Andrew J. Neuenschwander, "Biography," Robert Kreider Papers, I-A-e, Box 1, "N Correspondence," BCA. For larger historical accounts of these movements, see Clifford Putney, "Character-Building in the YMCA, 1880-1930," *Mid-America* 73 (January 1991): 49-70; Michael Parker, "The Kingdom of Character: The Student Volunteer Movement for Foreign Missions," (Ph.D. diss.: University of Maryland, 1995).

63. *Scope* 79 (March 1992), 6-7; *Scope* 77 (January 1990), 4.

64. Student tribunal meeting minutes Nov. 14, 1925, Ramseyer Papers, I-A-d, Box 10, "Student tribunal mtngs, 1925-36," BCA. For examples of Mosiman's discipline, see Mosiman to L. K. Roth, June 11, 1918, Mosiman Papers, Box 2, "Misc: Ramseyer, Rickert," and to J. F. Conrad, Aug. 3, 1926, Box 8, "Students presenting disciplinary problems, 1918-26," BCA.

65. Stratton, "BC student life in the '20s," 7; *WIT* 3 (March 1916), 13; *WIT* 4 (March 1914), 9; *WIT* 12 (Nov. 15, 1924), 2.

66. *Scope* 79 (March 1992), 7; Mosiman to Elizabeth Boehr, Aug. 6, 1925, Mosiman Papers, I-A-b, Box 2, "Faculty Members corresp.," BCA.

67. Hardesty, *A Narrative of Bluffton College*, 16; *WIT* 14 (Sept. 25, 1926), 1; Mosiman to J. H. Hamilton, June 3, 1925, Mosiman Papers, I-A-b, Box 3, "Responses to the policies of BC," BCA; Mosiman to L. Benson, Nov. 29, 1929, Citizenship Committee Papers, I-F-e, "Honor Court, 1930," BCA.

68. 1918 *Ista*, 201-3.

69. See 1915 *Ista*, 20, for class consciousness; faculty minutes dated Dec. 1, 1913, in Faculty Minutes Papers, I-E-a, Box 1, "Fac minutes March 11, 1912–May 13, 1919," BCA; Hardesty, *Narrative of Bluffton College*, 15; *Scope* 79 (March 1992), 6-7.

70. Student senate minutes dated Sept. and Oct. 28, 1926, Student Senate Minutes, I-F-q, Box 1, "Student Senate, 1924-29," BCA; *WIT* 7 (Oct. 5, 1919), 1; *WIT* 4 (Sept. 29 and Oct. 6, 1928), 1.

71. Mosiman to J. W. Litwiller, Dec. 9, 1922, Mosiman Papers, I-A-b, Box 8, "Students presenting disciplinary problems, 1918-26," BCA; faculty meeting minutes dated May 4, 1920, I-E-a, Box 1, "Faculty mins Sept 15, 1919–June 3, 1926," BCA.

72. Bauman memories in "Dr. and Mrs. L. L. Ramseyer Appreciation Chapel," May 7, 1965, Ramseyer Papers, I-A-d, Box 6, "Ramseyer misc corr. and writings," BCA.

73. Faculty Members, *An Adventure in Faith*, 152-3; Honor Court to Russell Stratton, March 15, 1923; tribunal to Mosiman, Dec. 10, 1924, and to A. C. Burcky, Dec. 12, 1925; tribunal meeting minutes dated Oct. 31, Nov. 2, Nov. 14, 1925, Jan. 16, 1926, all in Citizenship Committee Papers, I-F-e, "Honor Court, 1930," BCA.

74. Tribunal meeting minutes dated Nov. 8 and 16, 1925, in Ramseyer Papers, I-A-d, Box 10, "Student tribunal mtngs, 1925-36," BCA.

75. Smith and Hirschler, 260-63.

76. Ibid., 263; Faculty Members, *An Adventure in Faith*, 138-9, 143-45; 1915 *Ista*, 73.

77. President's Report to the Board of Trustees, Feb. 2, 1923, p. 5, Mosiman Papers, I-A-b, Box 5, "Exec. committee meeting Sept. 12, 1923," BCA; *BCB* 11 (April 1924), 15; *Scope* 77 (March 1990), 8.

78. 1926 *Ista*, 128.

79. 1927 *Ista*, 114.

80. 1917 *Ista*, 80; 1921 *Ista*, 143.

81. 1926 *Ista*, 143; faculty meeting minutes dated Nov. 16, 1926, Faculty Minutes Collection I-E-a, Box 1, "Minutes Sept 13, 1926–June 9, 1935," BCA.

82. Smith and Hirschler, 259-60; Hardesty, 17.

83. Faculty Members, *An Adventure in Faith*, 146.

84. Paul Welty, Waldo Schumacher, and Edwin Stauffer to the Board of Trustees, undated but clearly fall 1916; several different undated petitions from students; Kratz to board members, Feb. 9, 1915; all in Mosiman Papers, I-A-b, Box 12, "Athletics, 1915-31," BCA; Faculty Members, *An Adventure in Faith*, 146. The story of the football's funeral has long reverberated on campus. The 1918 *Ista* (pp. 203-4) presented it as fictional, but photos exist of the actual event.

85. Board minutes dated June 1, 1920, p. 15, Mosiman Papers, I-A-b, Box 7, "Bd of trustees meeting 1920," BCA; 1922 *Ista*, 110; Ramseyer "Appreciation Chapel" transcript.

86. Neuenschwander to Mosiman, Feb. 9, 1922, Mosiman Papers Box 6, "Neuenschwander corr, 1915-28," BCA; Burcky to Mosiman, Feb. 13, 1922, Mosiman Papers, Box 2, "Faculty members corresp," BCA; Faculty Members, *An Adventure in Faith*, 146-7.

87. Ramseyer to Mosiman, April 10, 1926, Mosiman Papers, I-A-b, Box 9, "Alumni corresp., 1918-30," BCA; Mosiman to Neuenschwander, May 23, 1922, Mosiman Papers, Box 6, Neuenschwander corresp., 1915-28" BCA; A. H. Miller to Mosiman, April 18, 1923, Mosiman Papers, Box 12, "Athletics, 1915-31," BCA.

88. David Kennedy, *Over Here: The First World War and American Society* (New York: Oxford University Press, 1980), 45-92.

89. Juhnke, *Vision, Doctrine, War*, 208-224; Gerlof Homan, *American Mennonites and the Great War* (Scottdale, Pa.: Herald Press, 1994), 57-86.

90. Juhnke, *Vision, Doctrine, War*, 229-30, 234-40; Homan, *American Mennonites and the Great War*, 87-88, 99-128; James Juhnke, "Mennonites and Ambivalent Civil Religion in World War I," *MQR* 65 (April 1991): 162.

91. Hirschy to Thierstein, Sept. 9, 1917, Hirschy Papers, I-A-a, Box 2, "photocopies of N.C. Hirschy," BCA.

92. Langenwalter to Mosiman, April 20, 1918, Mosiman Papers, I-A-b, Box 8, "J. H. Langenwalter.." BCA.

93. Mosiman to Aaron Augsburger, May 14, 1918, Mosiman Papers, Box 7, "Rev. Aaron Augsburger," BCA; Homan, *American Mennonites and the Great War*, 71.

94. Mosiman to J. Bechtel, May 23, 1917, Mosiman Papers, I-A-b, Box 9, "Corresp., A. S. Bechtel, J. B. Bechtel," BCA; Mosiman to P. H. Richert, March 23, 1918, Mosiman Papers, Box 12, "War Committee on Exemptions, 1917-19"; Mosiman to V. Schlagel, Aug. 10, 1918, Mosiman Papers, Box 11, "Mosiman personal corresp., 1913-31"; Mosiman to C. J. Claassen, Sept. 13, 1918, Mosiman Papers, Box 1, "Claassen corresp.," BCA.

95. Mosiman to Claassen, June 22, 1918, Mosiman Correspondence, I-A-B, Box 1, "Claassen Corr.," BCA; Mosiman to Cox, April 11, 1917, Mosiman Papers, Box 4, "Mosiman letters to Governor," BCA.

96. Mosiman to William Clegg, Nov. 2, 1917, Mosiman Papers, Box 12, "War, 1917-19," BCA; Mosiman to V.C. Ramseyer, July 25, 1918, Mosiman Papers, Box 2, "Misc, Ramseyer, Rickert," BCA; Mosiman to F. P. Keppel, Aug. 13, 1918, Peace Papers Collection, I-X-a, Box 1, "Corr. to people in the Army," BCA.

97. Mosiman to J. W. Kliewer, April 15 and June 28, 1918, Mosiman to Mussleman, Oct. 22, 1917, all in Mosiman Papers, Box 12, "War Committee on Exemptions, 1917-19," BCA; Homan, *American Mennonites and the Great War*, 132-3, 87, 91-2.

98. Mosiman to General Education Board, April 29, 1919, Mosiman Papers, I-A-b, Box 2, "Gen. Ed. Board," BCA; Kratz to Mosiman, May 31, 1918, Byers to Mosiman, May 3, 1919, both in Mosiman Papers, Box 2, "Faculty corresp.," BCA; Berky to Mosiman, Jan. 7, 1919, and Lehman to Mosiman, no date, both in Peace Papers Collection, I-X-a, Box 1, "Corr. to people in the Army," BCA;

99. *WIT* 6 (March 1, 1919), 1; *WIT* 5 (Oct. 27, 1917), 3; *WIT* 5 (May 4, 1918), 1; *WIT* 6 (Oct. 12, 1918), 1, 3; *WIT* 6 (Nov. 30, 1918), 1, 3; *WIT* 6 (March 29, 1919), 3.

100. 1918 *Ista*, 183, 189; *WIT* 4 (May-June 1917), 24-5; *WIT* 5 (Dec. 8, 1917), 2; *WIT* 5 (Nov. 10 and 17, 1917), 4; *WIT* 5 (May 18, 1918), 2; *WIT* 6 (March 29, 1919), 3.

101. Mosiman to William Harvey, Oct. 30, 1924, Peace Papers Collection, I-X-a, Box 1, "Peace, misc. materials," BCA; Mosiman, "The Limitless Christ," *BCB* 9 (October 1922), 1-8; C. H. Smith to Wilbur Thomas, Jan. 18, 1925, Mosiman Papers, I-A-b, Box 8, "American Friends Service Committee," BCA; Mosiman to Richard Lehman, June 25, 1919, Mosiman Papers, Box 5, "Rev. F. Richard Lehman," BCA.

102. Augsburger to Mosiman, Feb. 5 and May 14, 1918; July 12, 1921; Dec. 5, 1922; Nov. 11, 1924; and Mosiman replies Nov. 14, 1922, and Jan. 17, 1925, all in Mosiman Papers, I-A-B, Box 7, "Rev. Aaron Augsburger," BCA.

103. Augsburger to Mosiman, Nov. 1, 1922, Mosiman Papers, I-A-B, Box 7, "Rev. Aaron Augsburger," BCA.

104. Lehman to Mosiman, July 17, 1920, and undated "Report of Trustee Members on Bluffton College Board," Mosiman Papers, I-A-b, Box 2, "Mennonite Brethren in Christ relations," BCA; A. B. Yoder to Mosiman, June 18, 1923, Mosiman Papers, Box 12, "Letters of Condemnation and Commendation," BCA.

105. On the *Gospel Herald*'s attack, see I. A. Sommer to Mosiman, Jan. 7, 1910, Mosiman Papers, I-A-b, Box 10, "Corresp., 1916-22," BCA; Lehman to Mosiman, July 29, 1913, Mosiman Papers, Box 5, "L. F. Lehman," BCA; board meeting minutes dated Jan. 28, 1921, Mosiman Papers, Box 7, "Minutes of Board of Trustees, 1921."

106. E. F. Grubb to Mosiman, Jan. 13, 1920, Mosiman Papers, Box 1, "River Station Mission," BCA.

107. Raid, *The First Seventy-Five Years*, 51, 68-74; Gottschall to Miller, Oct. 18, 1927, Papers of Development, Public Relations and Advancement, I-D-e, Box 1, "The 1923 Modernism," BCA. "[T]here has been more or less opposition" from St. Johns and Ebenezer "ever since the college started," wrote Elmer Basinger to Mosiman (March 19, 1923, Mosiman Papers, I-A-b, Box 9, "Executive Comm. Meeting, Sept. 12, 1923," BCA).

108. Paul Toews, *Mennonites in American Society, 1930-1970* (Scottdale: Herald Press, 1996), 77; Richert to Mosiman, Sept. 21, and Mosiman's reply, Oct, 13, 1922, both in Mosiman Papers, I-A-b, Box 12, "Correspondence, 1920," BCA.

109. Mosiman to Richert, Oct. 13, 1922, Mosiman Papers, I-A-b, Box 12, "Correspondence, 1920," BCA.

110. Mosiman to L. J. Lehman, June 28, 1919, Mosiman Papers, Box 5, "L. J. Lehman," BCA.

111. Miller, *Culture for Service*, 53-122.

112. V. C. Ramseyer to Mosiman, July 20, and Mosiman's reply, August 9, 1923, Mosiman Papers, I-A-b. Box 2, "Misc., Ramseyer," BCA; Mosiman to Hirschy, Aug. 11, 1923, Mosiman Papers, Box 1, "Corresp. with Hirschy," BCA; Hartzler to MDC Ministers, Aug. 20, 1923, Mosiman Papers, Box 1, "Mosiman Corresp. w/ J. E. Hartzler," BCA.

113. Byers to Mosiman, July 16, 1913, Hirschy Papers, I-A-a, Box 1, "Letters, resolutions . . . ," BCA; Mosiman to Horsch, June 28, 1917, Publications Papers, I-D-e, Box 1, "Mosiman and John Horsch on Orthodox and Higher Criticism," BCA.

114. James Juhnke, "Mennonite Church Theological and Social Boundaries, 1920-1930—Loyalists, Liberals and Laxitarians," *Mennonite Life* 38 (June 1983): 18-20; Toews, *Mennonites in Mennonite Society*, 94 (Horsch quote).

115. Juhnke, "Mennonite Church Theological and Social Boundaries," 19.

116. Gottschall to Horsch, Oct. 31 and Nov. 24, 1924, Horsch Papers, I-8-I, Box 2, "Corr. 1924, G-N," AMC; Schroeder to Horsch, March 30 and April 21, 1926, Horsch Papers, Box 3, "Corr. N-Z, 1926," AMC; Board of Deacons, First Mennonite Church, Berne, Indiana, "Evidences of Modernism at Bluffton College," n.p., 1929, MHL.

117. Smith and Hirschler, *The Story of Bluffton College*, 288.

118. Kaufman, *General Conference Mennonite Pioneers*, 200-205; board meeting minutes dated Feb.11, 1915, Mosiman Papers, I-A-b, Box 7, "Board Meetings, 1914-16," BCA.

119. Mosiman to J. A. Bewer, Feb. 23, 1925, Mosiman Papers, Box 9, "Faculty members corresp.," BCA; Mosiman to Basinger, March 21, 1923,

Mosiman Papers, Box 9, "Exec. Comm. Sept 12, 1923," BCA; Kaufman, *General Conference Mennonite Pioneers*, 210.

120. Kaufman, *General Conference Mennonite Pioneers*; Rempel, "The First 'Russian Boys' at Bluffton College," 3, 5-6.

121. Kaufman, *General Conference Mennonite Pioneers*, 205-6.

122. Mosiman to Elmer Basinger, Aug. 11, and Mosiman to T. H. Brenneman, Feb. 17, 1925, both in Mosiman Papers, I-A-b, Box 9, "Semi-Annual Board Meeting, Feb. 6, 1925," BCA.

123. "Evidences of Modernism at Bluffton College," 5-9; James Juhnke, *Creative Crusader: Edmund G. Kaufman and Mennonite Community* (N. Newton, Kans.: Bethel College, 1994), 142.

124. On this point, see Toews, *Mennonites in American Society*, 66.

125. See Paul Toews, "Fundamentalist Conflict in Mennonite Colleges: A Response to Cultural Transitions?" *MQR* 57 (July 1983): 241-56.

126. Bender quoted in Albert N. Keim, *Harold S. Bender, 1897-1962* (Scottdale, Pa.: Herald Press, 1998), 178, and in Juhnke, *Vision, Doctrine, War*, 176. "There is a danger in the General Conference group that the movement will go in a liberal direction," Bender wrote Horsch from Germany in 1930. "I think the real battle in this line is still to come, and I want to get ready to do my part in it." See Bender to Horsch, July 20, 1930, Horsch Papers, I-8-I, Box 5, "Corr. 1930 A-B," AMC.

127. Mosiman to J. R. Thierstein, Sept. 20, 1921, Mosiman Papers, I-A-b, Box 8, "J. R. Thierstein, 1913-26," BCA; *WIT* 16 (April 6, 1929), 1.

128. Hirschy to Mosiman, May 29, 1923, Hirschy Papers, I-A-a, Box 1, "Hirschy Corr," BCA.

129. Mosiman to Mrs. Alfred Moser, March 20, 1925, Mosiman Papers, I-A-b, Box 9, "Alumni Corresp.," BCA; Mosiman to Adam Jones, Oct. 27, 1922, Mosiman Papers, Box 4, "Corresp. between Mosiman and other college presidents," BCA; Mosiman to H. L. Sullivan, June 12, 1925, Box 2, "NCA application," BCA; Mosiman to Thierstein, Jan. 26, 1929, Mosiman Papers, Box 4, "Board of Education of General Conference," BCA.

130. Mosiman to Bayard Hedrick, Oct. 10, 1928, Development Office Papers, I-D-i, "Financial drives . . . Mosiman, 1916-33," BCA; *BCB* 15 (Sept./Oct./Nov. 1929), 1-2.

131. "A Last Call," Aug. 20, 1929, Development Office Papers, I-D-i, "Financial drives . . . Mosiman, 1916-33," BCA; *BCB* 15 (Sept./Oct./Nov. 1929), 1-2.

132. *BCB* 16 (August, 1929), 1-4.

133. Ibid.

134. Members of the Faculty, *An Adventure in Faith*, 66.

Chapter Three

1. *WIT* 17 (March 29, 1930), 1; *BCB* 17 (April 1930), 2; *WIT* 17 (May 3, 1930), 1.

2. *WIT* 17 (June 14, 1930), 1; *BCB* 17 (September 1930), 9.

3. Mosiman to A. M. Eash, May 13, 1930, Mosiman Papers, I-A-b, Box 10, "Student Letters and Reports," BCA; Peter Nafziger to Mosiman, July 28, 1934, Mosiman Papers, Box 6, "Statement of Faith, Retreat," BCA; Toews, *Mennonites in American Society*, 77; Pannabecker, *Faith in Ferment*, 225.

4. Grubb to Mosiman, undated but probably July, 1930, Mosiman Papers, Box 8, "Corr.," BCA.

5. President's Report to the Board of Trustees, Witmarsum Seminary, Jan. 28, 1928, and Feb. 4, 1930, Witmarsum Seminary Papers, I-T, Box 3, "President's and Dean's Reports," BCA; John Thiessen to Graduates and Friends of Witmarsum Seminary, Aug. 15, 1930, Seminary Papers, Box 3, "Witmarsum Theological Seminary Minutes, Constitution," BCA.

6. Pannabecker, *Ventures of Faith*, 19-20; Toews, *Mennonites in American Society*, 77-8; Mosiman to W. S. Shelly, Oct. 23, 1931, Mosiman Papers, I-A-b, Box 11, "Corr., 1929-31," BCA; Bender to Horsch, July 20, 1930, Horsch Papers, I-8-1, Box 5, "Corr., 1930, A-B," AMC.

7. Wilmer Shelly to Mosiman, March 27 and July 23, 1930, Mosiman Papers, I-A-b, Box 11, "Corr., 1929-31," BCA.

8. Mosiman to Quiring, March 29, 1930, Mosiman Papers, I-A-b, Box 11, "Corr., 1929-31," BCA; Friesen memories in "Bluffton College Letters, Class of 1932, 50th Reunion," Hist. Mss. I-616, Roy E. Wenger Collection, AMC.

9. Kaufman, *General Conference Mennonite Pioneers*, 200.

10. Kaufman, 206.

11. Kaufman, 208-10.

12. Toews, *Mennonites in American Society*, 77; Pannabecker, *Faith in Ferment*, 225-6.

13. Board meeting minutes June 4, 1934, Bluffton College Board of Trustees Minutes, BCA; faculty meeting minutes dated Oct. 16, 1934, Faculty Minutes Collection, I-E-a, Box 1, "Faculty Mins. Sept. 13, 1926–June 9, 1935," BCA.

14. "Statement of Faith of Bluffton College," Mosiman Papers, I-A-b, Box 10, "Retreat and Findings," BCA; Rosenberger to Mosiman, Oct. 16, 1934, Mosiman Papers, Box 11, "Mosiman—Rosenberger Letters, 1934-37," BCA.

15. Langenwalter to Mosiman, Oct. 4, 1930, Mosiman Papers, I-A-b, Box 4, "Board of Ed. Gen Conf members," BCA.

16. Schroeder to Mosiman, Dec. 8, 1939, Publications Papers, I-D-e, Box 1, "P. R. Schroeder letters . . . ," BCA.

17. D. J. Sprunger to Mosiman, May 23, 1929, Publications papers, I-D-e, Box 1, "Berne Church, Bd. of Deacons . . . ," BCA; Alderfer to Mosiman, Nov. 30, 1934, Mosiman papers, I-A-b, Box 10, "S. K. Mosiman Refinancing . . . ," BCA.

18. Edward Robb Ellis, "What the Depression Did to People," in *The Private Side of American History*, ed. Thomas Frazier and John Morton Blum (New York: Harcourt Brace Jovanovich, 1979), 207-12, 226; *The Town at the Fork of the Rileys*, 34-37.

19. *BCB* 17 (June and July 1931), 3, 5; Bluffton *Alumnus* 1 (May 1933): 147, 150.

20. Members of the Faculty, *An Adventure in Faith*, 66; board meeting minutes dated June 8, 1931, and July 5, 1932, Mosiman Papers, I-A-b, Box 7, "Minutes of the Bd. of Trustees," BCA; S. F. to Lloyd Pannabecker, Nov. 5, 1933, personal papers of Alice Ruth Pannabecker Ramseyer.

21. Basinger to Mosiman, Oct. 31, 1931, and V. Ringelman to Mosiman, Nov. 12, 1931, both in Development Office Papers, I-D-i, "Mosiman, 1916-33," BCA.

22. Smucker interview.

23. Members of the Faculty, *Adventure in Faith*, 66-7; Walter Traubel to the College, July 5, 1954, Ramseyer Papers, I-A-d, Box 15, "T-V, 1951-55," BCA.

24. Members of the Faculty, *An Adventure in Faith*, 73; *BCB* 18 (October 1931), 4; Mosiman to W. H. Mohr, Dec. 7, 1933, Mosiman Papers, I-A-b, Box 2, "W. H. Mohr . . . ," BCA;

25. Mosiman to D. J. Jantzen, Oct. 28, 1931, Development Office Papers, I-

D-i, "Financial Drives, Mosiman, 1916-1933," BCA; Mosiman to "Holders of Bluffton College Bonds," undated, probably late fall 1933, Mosiman Papers, I-A-b, Box 5, "Bond Information," BCA.

26. John Wilhelm to "Gentlemen," Jan. 5, 1934; Frank Cerny to Mosiman, Feb. 26 and Oct. 10, 1934; J. E. Westbrook to Mosiman, May 31, 1934; A. B. Ford to Mosiman, May 10, 1934; Mosiman to John Boddie, Feb. 7, 1934; Mosiman to Lizzie Rees, June 12, 1934; all in Mosiman Papers, I-A-b, Box 5, "Bond Information," BCA.

27. Mosiman to A. C. Alderfer, Aug. 11, 1934; Mosiman to J. F. Hanley, Aug. 28, 1934; Mosiman to Mohr, Oct. 24, 1934; all in Mosiman Papers, I-A-b, Box 5, "Bond Information," BCA; Rosenberger to Florence Collins, Jan. 15, 1936, Rosenberger Papers, I-A-c, Box 1, "C Corr., 1935-38," BCA; Mosiman to "the Holders of the First Mortgage 6 1/2% Serial Gold Bonds of Bluffton College," Mosiman Papers, Box 5, "Bonds, 1935," BCA.

28. Members of the Faculty, *An Adventure in Faith*, 48-9.

29. *BCB* 19 (October 1932), 4-5; Baumgartner to Mosiman, Feb. 12, 1935, Mosiman Papers, I-A-b, Box 1, "Resignation, Retirement," BCA.

30. Hardesty, *A Narrative of Bluffton College*, 19; *BCB*, 24 (October 1937), 1-2.

31. Juhnke, *Creative Crusader*, 140; Mosiman to Byers, March 6, 1931, Mosiman Papers, I-A-b, Box 2, "Faculty Members Corr," BCA.

32. "Annual Report of the Dean to the Board of Trustees," June 4, 1937, and Rosenberger's Semi-Annual Report to the Board, Nov. 19, 1937, both in Rosenberger Papers, I-A-c, Box 1, "Board of Trustees, 1936-38," BCA.

33. Members of the Faculty, *An Adventure in Faith*, 117-20

34. *Scope* 63 (March 1976), 2.

35. Elmer Neufeld, "Periodic Report to the Board of Trustees," Oct. 15, 1981, Trustees Papers, I-B-a, no box number, "1980-84," BCA; *WIT* 4 (Oct. 6, 1928), 1; 1932 *Ista*, 25; Edna Ramseyer to Rosenberger, August 29, 1935, Rosenberger Papers, I-A-c, Box 3, "1925-37 Corr.," BCA.

36. Rosenberger to Bohn, Feb. 13, and Bohn to Rosenberger, Feb. 2, 1937, both in Rosenberger Papers, I-A-c, Box 1, "B Corr., 1936-7," BCA; *BCB* 24 (June 1937), 3.

37. S. F. To Lloyd and Lelia Pannabecker, July 2, 1933, personal papers of Alice Ruth Ramseyer; *BCB* 19 (January 1932), 3; *BCB* 22 (February 1935), 2; "The Bluffton College Faculty and the Depression," Rosenberger Papers, I-A-c, Box 3, "Reports on the College," BCA; board meeting minutes, Feb. 8, 1935, Board of Trustees Papers, I-B-a, no box number, "Bd. Mins. 1935-38," BCA; Rosenberger to "Friend," May 24, 1935," Rosenberger Papers, Box 1, "Form Letters, 1934-35," BCA.

38. "Annual Report of the Dean, April 30, 1935, Mosiman Papers, I-A-b, Box 3, "Board of Trustees Meetings 1934-35," BCA; Esther Berky Reed to author, Feb. 25, 1998, letter in author's possession.

39. "Study of Bluffton College," pp. 38-41, 33, 13, 27-8, Faculty Papers Collection, I-E-k, Box 2, "North Central Study . . . ," BCA.

40. "Study of Bluffton College," 36-7.

41. Mosiman to Hanley, Jan. 19, 1932, Mosiman Papers, I-A-b, "Mosiman Corr., alphabetic," BCA.

42. Mosiman to Hanley, Jan. 19, 1932 (quotes); B. F. Thutt to Mosiman, Jan. 27, 1932, Mosiman Papers, Box 13, "Personal letters," BCA.

43. Board meeting minutes dated May 18, 1932, Mosiman Papers, I-A-b, Box 7, "Minutes Bd. of Trustees," BCA; Hanley to Mosiman, Sept. 7, 1932, Mosiman Papers, Box 13, "Mosiman Personal letters," BCA.

44. Sylvia Pannabecker to Lloyd and Lelia Pannabecker, July 2, 1933, personal papers of Alice Ruth Ramseyer; Maurice Troyer to Rosenberger, June 16, 1935, Rosenberger Papers, I-A-c, Box 3, "Corr., 1935," BCA.

45. Epp to Rosenberger, Dec. 27, 1935, Rosenberger Papers, I-A-c, Box 1, "Dr. Peter Epp, 1933-36," BCA.

46. Peter Epp, "Memorandum on the Endowment Fund of Bluffton College," read at board of trustees meeting, Jan. 26, 1934, Rosenberger Papers, I-A-c, Box 1, "Dr. Peter Epp, 1933-36," BCA; Epp to Mosiman, Sept 5, 1933, Mosiman Papers, I-A-b, Box 11, "Various letters, unclassified," BCA.

47. S. F. Pannabecker letter, July 13, 1933; Kaufman, *General Conference Mennonite Pioneers*, 188.

48. *WIT* 22 (Feb. 16, 1935), 1-2; board meeting minutes dated Feb. 8, April and 30, 1935, Board of Trustees Papers I-B-a, "Board Minutes 1935-38," BCA.

49. Mosiman to members of the faculty, Feb. 9, 1935, Samuel to Eddison Mosiman, May 27, 1936, both in Mosiman Papers, I-A-b, Box 1, "Resignation and Retirement," BCA; Mosiman to Alderfer, March 11, 1936, Mosiman Papers, Box 13, "Letters to Friends," BCA.

50. Paul Welty to Mosiman, May 12, 1935; Ruth Locher to "Fellow Alumnus," undated; telegram from F. Stettler, secretary of Cleveland Alumni Association, undated; all in Mosiman Papers, I-A-b, Box 1, "Resignation and Retirement," BCA.

51. Mosiman to Alderfer, March 11, 1936; Kaufman, *General Conference Mennonite Pioneers*, 188-9.

52. *BN* 64 (Feb. 1, 1940), 1-2; Unrau, *Encircled*, 41.

53. Kaufman, *General Conference Mennonite Pioneers*, 188-9; Fretz to Emilie Mosiman, May 4, 1948, Emilie Mosiman Papers, 4-MS-C-i, Box 1, in volume entitled "From Loving Friends," BCA.

54. 1921 *Ista*, 31; Mosiman to A. J. Neuenschwander, Sept. 20, 1921, Mosiman Papers, I-A-b, Box 6, "Neuenschwander Corr., 1915-28," BCA; Mosiman to H. J. Krehbiel, Sept. 22, 1928, Mosiman Papers, Box 7, "General Conference Executive Committee," BCA; *BCB* 55 (January 1968), 3-4.

55. Board meeting minutes dated April 30, 1935, Mosiman Papers, I-A-b, Box 3, "Board of Trustees Corr.," BCA.

56. Hardesty, *A Narrative of Bluffton College*, 20; Rosenberger to Gilliom, April 16, 1938, Rosenberger Papers, I-A-c, Box 1, "G Corr.," BCA.

57. Mosiman, "To the Members of the Faculty," Feb. 9, 1935.

58. *WIT* 20 (March 4, 1933), 1; "Study of Bluffton College," NCA visitation report, p. 24; S. F. to Lloyd and Lelia Pannabecker, Nov. 5, 1933, personal collection of Alice Ruth Ramseyer; *WIT* 21 (Feb. 10, 1934), 1.

59. *WIT* 23 (Sept. 21, 1935), 2; *WIT* 19 (Oct. 24, 1931), 2.

60. *BCB* 18 (March 1931), 130; *BCB* 19 (April 1932), 32; *BCB* 23 (April 1936), 48; *BCB* 24 (April 1937), 72; *BCB* 25 (April 1938), 71; *BCB* 26 (April 1939), 71.

61. *BCB* 27 (April 1930), 8 (occupational survey), 10. On student religious composition, see "Dean's Report, 1932-33," June 5, 1933, Mosiman Papers, I-A-b, Box 3, "BC Board of Trustees," BCA; faculty meeting minutes dated Dec. 17, 1935, Faculty Minutes Collection, I-E-a, Box 1, "Faculty mins Sept. 1935–May, 1944," BCA.

62. Hardesty, *A Narrative of Bluffton College*, 16; Harry Yoder to Roy Wenger, undated, with "Bluffton College Letters, Class of 1932," Hist. Mss I-616, Roy Wenger Papers, AMC.

63. Student senate meeting minutes dated Oct. 19, 1936, Ramseyer Papers, I-A-d, Box 10, no folder; *WIT* 20 (Sept. 24, 1932), 1.

64. "Rules of Conduct for Students of Bluffton College," Rosenberger Papers, I-A-c, Box 1, "College Student Rules, 1936-37," BCA; Mosiman to Anthony Deckert, June 9, 1931, Citizenship Committee Papers, I-F-e, "Honor Court, 1930," BCA; Honor Court meeting minutes dated Nov. 11, 18, and 23, 1935; Oct. 12, 1931; Sept. 6, 1931; Nov. 16, 1931; Citizenship Committee Papers, Box 1, "Student Welfare Committee," BCA.

65. "Rules for Use of Automobiles by Bluffton College Students," Mosiman Papers, I-A-b, Box 12, "1930 Student Auto Registration," BCA; Hardesty, *Narrative of Bluffton College*, 16.

66. Faculty meeting minutes dated Nov. 4, 1930, Faculty Minutes Collection, I-E-a, Box 1, "Faculty mins Sept. 13, 1926–June 9, 1935," BCA; 1936 *Ista*, 59; Smucker interview; Harry Yoder to Roy Wenger, undated, with "Bluffton College Letters, Class of 1932"; *BCB* 22 (December 1936), 3.

67. *WIT* 23 (March 27, 1936), 1; Schultz, "Semi-Annual Report," Feb. 8, 1935, Mosiman Papers, I-A-b, Box 7, "Bd of Trustees Meeting, 1935," BCA; Members of the faculty, *An Adventure in Faith*, 153-4.

68. "Annual Report of the Dean to the Board of Trustees," June 4, 1937, Rosenberger Papers, I-A-c, Box 1, "Board of Trustees, 1936-38," BCA; 1936 *Ista,* 28; *Scope* 67 (July 1980), 7, and (November 1980), 6.

69. Stauffer to Wenger, Feb. 15, 1982, in "Bluffton College Letters, Class of 1932"; Hardesty, *A Narrative of Bluffton College*, 21.

70. Diller quoted in Hardesty, *A Narrative of Bluffton College*, 21.

71. *WIT* 26 (May 26, 1939), 2; Phyllis Driver, "Application for Summer Work at Bluffton College," May 7, 1939, Diller Collection, 4-MS-C, Box 1, "Application for Summer work," BCA; *WIT* 26 (Nov. 17, 1939), 2.

72. *Scope* 60 (May 1993), 4.

73. *Scope* 77 (March 1990), 8; Hardesty, *A Narrative of Bluffton College*, 21-2.

74. Hardesty, *A Narrative of Bluffton College*, 22; 1936 *Ista*, 60-66; "Andrew C. Burcky, Bluffton College 1922-1968," in Burcky Papers, 4-MS-C-8, Box 1, no folder.

75. Galen Leatherman to "Dear Classmates," Feb. 10, 1982, in "Bluffton College Letters, Class of 1932"; "Andrew C. Burcky, Bluffton College 1922-1968," in Burcky Papers, 4-MS-C-8, Box 1, no folder.

76. Tetlow's memory in memo received March 29, 1993, in Burcky Papers, 4-MS-C-8, Box 2, "A. C. Stories," BCA.

77. Yoder to Wenger, undated, in "Bluffton College Letters, Class of 1932."

78. Pannabecker, *Faith in Ferment*, 231-2.

79. *WIT* 20 (April 29, 1933), 1; *WIT* 21 (Jan. 13, 1934), 1; *WIT* 22 (April 12, 1935), 1; *WIT* 23 (April 18, 1936), 1; *WIT* 23 (Feb. 22, 1936), 1; *WIT* 24 (Nov. 7, 1936), 1; Members of the Faculty, *An Adventure in Faith*, 187.

80. *WIT* 19 (Feb. 13, 1932), 1; *WIT* 22 (Nov. 3, 1934), 1; *WIT* 24 (Oct. 2, 1936), 1.

81. *WIT* 18 (Nov. 22, 1930), 1, 3; *WIT* 20 (Jan. 28, 1933), 1.

82. Smucker interview; Mosiman to Smucker, April 20, 1932, Mosiman Papers, I-A-b, Box 6,"Corr, 1932," BCA.

83. Smucker interview; Rosenberger to Joseph Little, Nov. 10, 1937, Rosenberger Papers, I-A-c, Box 1, "L Corr.," BCA; *WIT* 23 (Jan. 11, 1936), 2.

84. Wiens to Rosenberger, Jan. 18, 1936, Rosenberger Papers, I-A-c, Box 3, "W Corr, 1935-38"; Gilliom to Rosenberger, Jan. 17, 1936, Rosenberger Papers, Box 1, "G Corr,"; Rosenberger to Baumgartner, Jan. 29, 1936, Rosenberger Papers, Box 1, "B Corr," BCA.

85. Oral interview, Perry Bush with J. Winfield Fretz, June 8, 1994,

Mennonite Library and Archives, Bethel College, North Newton, Kans.

86. Fretz interview; oral interview, Perry Bush with John Keller, Feb. 3, 1999, BCA; *BCB* 17 (April, 1930), 9; *WIT* 18 (Feb. 14, 1931), 1; Smucker interview.

87. Smucker interview; *WIT* 18 (Nov. 22, 1930), 1; James Liu and Stephen Wang, *Christians True in China* (Newton, Kans.: Faith and Life Press, 1988), 38.

88. *WIT*, 18 (March 21, 1931), 4; *WIT* 18 (March 28, 1931), 2; *WIT* 18 (April 11, 1931), 3.

89. Unruh to Mosiman, May 31, 1934, and to "the President and Trustees of Bluffton College," May 31, 1934, Mosiman to Unruh, June 28, 1934, all in Mosiman Papers, I-A-b, Box 6, "Corr., 1934," BCA; (J. S. Schultz), "Annual Report to the Board of Trustees of Bluffton College," April 6, 1936, Rosenberger Papers, I-A-c, Box 1, 'Board of Trustees, 1936-38" BCA.

90. Whitmer to Rosenberger, June 11, 1936, Rosenberger Papers, I-A-c, Box 3, "W Corr., 1936-38," BCA; "To Dr. S. K. Mosiman, President of Bluffton College," from Carl Smucker, J. Millard Fretz et al., undated memo, Mosiman Papers, I-A-b, Box 8, "Student Petition to Board," BCA.

91. *WIT*, 28 (Jan. 31, 1931), 1; Student Welfare Committee minutes dated Dec. 8, 1930, and undated memo from Laura Conrad, Elizabeth Habegger et al., both in Citizenship Committee Papers, I-F-e, "Student Welfare Committee, 1930-38," BCA; *WIT* 22 (Oct. 20, 1934), 4; Citizenship Committee minutes Oct. 20 and Nov. 17, 1930, Student Committee Papers, I-F-e, Box 1, "Honor System," BCA.

92. Soldner to Rosenberger, Dec. 2, 1936, Rosenberger Papers, I-A-c, Box 2, "Corr., 1936," BCA; Rosenberger to Roscoe Slack, April 20, 1937, Rosenberger Papers, Box 2, "Corr, 1937," BCA.

93. Rosenberger to Donovan Smucker, May 5, 1938, Rosenberger Papers, Box 2, "Corr., 1938," BCA; board meeting minutes dated March 25, 1938, Rosenberger Papers, I-A-c, Box 1, "Board of Trustees, 1936-38," BCA.

94. Rosenberger to Schultz, June 27, 1936, Rosenberger Papers, Box 2, "Corr., 1936," BCA.

95. Rosenberger to the Board of Trustees, Sept. 26, 1938, Lloyd Ramseyer Papers, I-A-d, Box 6, "Triplett use of bldg," BCA; Lloyd Ramseyer, "A Tribute to Rev. A. S. Rosenberger," personal papers of Alice Ruth Ramseyer; *BCB* 55 (January 1968), 4.

96. Board Executive Committee meeting minutes dated September 26, 1938, Bluffton College Board Meeting Minutes, Vol. 3, BCA; H. F. Alderfer to Clifton Sprunger, Oct. 29, 1938, C. O. Lehman to Sprunger, Oct. 31, 1938, Mosiman to Roland Bixler, Oct. 20, 1938, all in Ramseyer Papers, I-A-d, Box 9, "Search for a College President," BCA.

Chapter Four

1. "Dr. and Mrs. L. L. Ramseyer APPRECIATION CHAPEL," May 7, 1965, pp. 1-4 (quotes), Ramseyer Papers I-A-d, Box 6, "Misc Corr. and Writings," BCA; oral interview, Perry Bush with William Ramseyer, May 23, 1998, BCA.

2. Ramseyer Appreciation Chapel; oral interview, Perry Bush with Edna Ramseyer Kaufman, Oct. 10, 1998, BCA.

3. Oral interview, Perry Bush with Robert Kreider, May 23, 1998, BCA.

4. Kreider interview; William Ramseyer interview; "Prexy Tribute," undated, Ramseyer Papers, I-A-d, Box 1, "Board of Trustees, 1966-67," BCA.

5. Oral interview, Perry Bush with William Keeney, Feb. 24, 1999, BCA; L. L. Ramseyer to Whitmer, Sept. 24, 1940, Ramseyer Papers, Box 6, "Corr., 1941-

48," BCA.

6. Ramseyer to Wilmer Shelly, Nov. 10, 1939, Ramseyer Papers, I-A-d, Box 11, "Shelly, Wilmer, 1938-46," BCA.

7. "Ramseyer Appreciation Chapel," 5.

8. *Scope* 61 (January-February 1974), 2; Mosiman to S. F. Pannabecker, Feb. 24, 1939, personal papers of Alice Ruth Ramseyer. So alienated were MC leaders from the Mennonite progressivism represented by Bluffton that Lehman's mere willingness to allow himself to be considered for the position appeared to Bender as "another unfortunate move"; quoted in Toews, *Mennonites in American Society*, 267.

9. *Scope* 61 (January-February 1974), 2; Shelly to Ramseyer, Oct. 8, 1938, Ramseyer Papers, I-A-d, Box 11, "Shelly, Wilmer, 1938-46,"BCA; C. H. Suckau, Jan. 24, 1939, Ramseyer Papers, Box 6, "Corr, 1943-47," BCA; A. B. Curran to Ramseyer, June 1, 1939, Ramseyer Papers, Box 1, "A. B. Curran Letters, 1938-39," BCA; Mohr to Slabaugh, Dec. 19, 1939, Ramseyer Papers, Box 6, "Slabaugh, J.S., Corr, 1939-47," BCA.

10. Ramseyer to Smucker, Feb. 11, 1944, Ramseyer Papers, I-A-d, Box 6, "Don Smucker," BCA; Report of the President to the Board of Trustees, Nov. 16, 1943, pp. 1-2, board meeting minutes, I-B-a, " "Minutes of the Board, 1936-49," BCA.

11. Ramseyer to Bixler, July 17, 1939, Ramseyer Papers, Box 4, "Letters, 1938-42," BCA; Keeney interview, BCA.

12. For an example of such contributions, see Ramseyer to H. H. Baum, April 15, 1940, Ramseyer Papers, I-A-d, Box 1, "Church Gifts, 1939-44"; this box contained hundred of thank-you notes like this one.

13. Cutshall to Ramseyer, June 12, 1939, Ramseyer Papers, Box 1, "Guy Cutshall letters, 1939-42," BCA; Members of the Faculty, *An Adventure in Faith*, 70-1.

14. Ramseyer to Baumgartner, Slabaugh, et al., July 25, 1952, Ramseyer Papers, I-A-d, Box 7, "Baumgartner, E. W., " BCA; Members of the Faculty, *An Adventure in Faith*, 73-4; "Prexy Tribute," 2.

15. Yoder to Ramseyer, Jan. 10, 1946, Ramseyer Papers, Box 6, "Harry Yoder Corr., 1941-46," BCA; Ramseyer to A. B. Schertz, June 25, 1951," Ramseyer Papers, Box 15, "Sa-Se, 1951-55," BCA.

16. Board meeting minutes dated Oct. 20, 1939, BC Report to the GCMC, 1940-41, "The College at General Conference," BCB 28 (September 1941), 5.

17. Members of the Faculty, *Adventure in Faith*, 177-79; *Scope* 77 (January 1990), 7; *WIT* 27 (March 30, 1940), 1; *WIT* 27 (Dec. 1, 1930), 1; *WIT* 28 (Oct. 18, 1940), 28. *WIT* 27 (May 10, 1940), 1.

18. *WIT* 28 (Feb. 15, 1941), 2; Kreider interview; Lloyd Ramseyer, "Looking Forward," baccalaureate sermon June 9, 1940, Ramseyer Baccalaureate Sermons, Ramseyer Papers, I-A-d, Box 13, BCA.

19. Ramseyer to Smucker, Oct. 3, 1940, Ramseyer Papers, I-A-d, Box 4, "Letters, 1939-41," BCA; *WIT* 77 (March 15, 1940), 3.

20. Smucker to Ramseyer, August 22, 1941, Ramseyer Papers, Box 4, "Letters, 1939-42," BCA.

21. Ramseyer to Adam Amstutz, Dec. 9, 1941, Ramseyer Papers, I-A-d, Box 1, "Letters to Old Friendship Group, 1940-41," BCA; "Special Faculty Meeting" dated Jan. 14, 1942, I-E-a, Faculty Meetings Collection, Box 1, "Faculty Minutes Sept. 1935–May 19, 1944," BCA.

22. "Report of the Dean to the President and Board of Trustees," April 10, 1942; March 24, 1944 (Schultz quote); May 2, 1945; October 24, 1947; all in Board

of Trustees Papers, I-B-a, no box number, "Minutes of the Board, 1936-49," BCA; 1943 *Ista*, 60.

23. Ramseyer to William Dick, Sept. 28, 1942, Ramseyer Papers, I-A-d, Box 1, "Ramseyer-William Dick Letters, 1939-44," BCA; President's Report to the Board of Trustees, Nov. 11, 1944," Board of Trustees Papers, I-B-a, no box number, "Minutes of the Board, 1936-49," BCA; "Report of the President to the Board of Trustees," Nov. 13, 1942, Ramseyer Papers, Box 9, "Reports to the Trustees by the President, 1941-46," BCA.

24. Ramseyer to "Dear Blufftonite," Dec. 18, 1944, Ramseyer Papers, Box 4, "Ramseyer Form Letters, 1938-42," BCA; Dean's Report to the Board, May 2, 1945, Board of Trustees Papers, I-B-a, no box number, "Minutes of the Board, 1936-49," BCA.

25. 1943 *Ista* 15, 23, 13; Ramseyer, "Appreciation Chapel," 11-12.

26. *WIT* 32 (Oct. 28, 1944), 2; Ramseyer to Lowell Risser, Aug. 23, 1944, Ramseyer Papers, I-A-d, Box 2, "R, 1948-50," BCA.

27. *WIT* 29 (Jan. 12, 1942), 2; *WIT* 29 (March 30, 1942), 3, and (Feb 23, 1942), 2.

28. Student senate minutes dated Nov. 16, 1942, Ramseyer Papers, I-A-d, Box 10, no folder; 1943 *Ista*, 50; *WIT* 30 (Jan. 16, 1943), 1, and (April 19, 1943), 1942 *Ista*, 68.

29. Ramseyer to John McSweeney, Oct. 28, 1941, Ramseyer Papers, I-A-d, Box 4, "General, 1940-41," BCA; Ramseyer to "Whom it may concern," May 9, 1942, and to Robert Wagner, Dec. 2, 1942, both in Ramseyer Papers, Box 9, "Letters, 1939-42," BCA; Ramseyer to M. Dillon, May 8, 1942, Ramseyer Papers, Box 4, "Letters, 1939-41," BCA; *BCB* 28 (Sept., 1941), 7.

30. Ramseyer to Henry Fast, Jan. 11, 1943, Ramseyer Papers, Box 6, "Corr., 1938-46," BCA.

31. On Japanese-American transfer students, see undated memo in Ramseyer Papers, Box 1, "Publicity, 1942-3," BCA; memo to *Bluffton News* October 6, 1942, Ramseyer Papers, Box 1, "Japanese Students, 1939-46," BCA; Ramseyer to William Ramseyer, Oct. 1, 1942, Ramseyer Papers, Box 9, "Letters, 1939-42," BCA. On the Triplett refusal, see Ramseyer to Norman Triplett, Jan. 26, 1945, Ramseyer Papers, Box 6, "Corr., 1939-45," BCA; Keeney interview, BCA. The rumor at the time, Keeney remembered, was that Ramseyer had threatened to resign if the board had said yes to Triplett's request.

32. Melvin Gingerich, *Service for Peace* (Akron, Pa.: Mennonite Central Committee, 1949), 141, 147; Ernest Miller to Schultz, Nov. 1, 1944, and Ramseyer to Elmer Ediger, Sept. 17, 1943, both in Ramseyer Papers, I-A-d, Box 12, "CPS Camps," BCA; Members of the Faculty, *An Adventure in Faith*, 190-91; Perry Bush, *Two Kingdoms, Two Loyalties: Mennonite Pacifism in Modern America* (Baltimore: Johns Hopkins University Press, 1998), 111-2; Ramseyer to Edmund Zehr, Ramseyer Papers, Box 6, "Corr., 1938-49," BCA.

33. Ramseyer to Ellwyn Hartzler, Jan. 24, 1945, Ramseyer Papers, Box 6, "Corr., 1944-47," BCA; Ramseyer, "Lift up Your Eyes," pp. 1-2, Baccalaureate Addresses, Ramseyer Papers, I-A-d, Box 13, "Ramseyer bacc. sermons," BCA.

34. Ramseyer to Robert Simcox, Oct. 20, 1944, Ramseyer Papers, I-A-d, Box 6, "Corr., 1939-45," BCA; 1944 *Ista*, 42; Pannabecker, *Faith in Ferment*, 234.

35. Ramseyer to Dale Francis, Sept. 21, 1941, Ramseyer Papers, I-A-d, Box 4, "Ramseyer Letters, 1929-42," BCA; see Ramseyer letters of recommendation for Mark Houshower, Ramseyer Papers, Box 11, "Kaufman, Edmund G," BCA; for Richard Backensto, Feb. 2, 1942, Box 4, "Letters, 1938-42"; Ramseyer to Myron Brown, Jan. 7, 1943, same file; Fellers to Ramseyer, June 28, 1944,

Ramseyer Papers, Box 6, "Corr., 1938-42," BCA.

36. Calvin Workman to Ramseyer, Jan. 20, 1944, Ramseyer Papers, I-A-d, Box 6, "Corr., 1938-42," BCA.

37. Ibid., Fellers to Ramseyer, June 28, 1944, Dale Francis to Ramseyer, May 3, 1944, all in Ramseyer Papers, Box 6, "Corr., 1938-42," BCA.

38. *BCB* 32 (August 1945), 3; *BCB* 30 (February 1945), 3; *BCB* 30 (April 1943), 3; Keeney interview; Ramseyer to Fellers, July 12, 1944, Ramseyer Papers, I-A-d, Box 6, "Cor., 1938-46," and Fellers's response, Oct. 24, 1944, same file.

39. *WIT* 33 (March 5, 1946), 1.

40. *BCB* 28 (July 1941), 1; *BCB* 45 (July 1962), 1.

41. *BCB* 35 (October 1948), 1; *BCB* 29 (November 1942), 1.

42. Hardesty, *A Narrative of Bluffton College*, 22.

43. Ramseyer to Smucker, May 29, 1944, Ramseyer Papers, I-A-d, Box 6, "Don Smucker," BCA.

44. Ramseyer to Smucker, June 6, 1944, Ramseyer Papers, I-A-d, Box 6, "Don Smucker," BCA; "Lift Up Your Eyes," Ramseyer baccalaureate sermon, May 14, 1944, pp. 4-5, Ramseyer Papers, Box 13, BCA.

45. Ramseyer to the Board of Trustees, Oct. 24, 1938, Ramseyer Papers, I-A-d, Box 6, "Misc. Writings and Corr.," BCA; Ramseyer to Alvin J. Beachy, March 9, 1943, Ramseyer Papers, Box 8, "Corr., 1939-48," BCA.

46. Lloyd L. Ramseyer, *The More Excellent Way* (Newton, Kans.: Faith and Life Press, 1965), 8.

47. Keeney interview.

48. Jacob Fretz to Ramseyer, Oct. 5, 1941; also see Ramseyer's response, Oct. 8, 1941, both in Ramseyer Papers, Box 6, "Corr., 1938-46," BCA.

49. Mohr to Ramseyer, June 22, 1942, and Ramseyer to Mohr, July 7 and July 8, 1942; Feb. 11, 1944; all in Ramseyer Papers, Box 11, "Corr., 1940-46," BCA; Ramseyer to Alvin J. Beachy, March 9, 1943, Ramseyer Papers, Box 8, "Corr., 1939-48," BCA.

50. Schultz to Slabaugh, Jan. 27, 1944, Development Office Papers, I-D-e, Box 1, "Bluffton College, BCA; Ramseyer to Mohr, March 9, Feb. 17 and 19, 1944, all in Ramseyer Papers, Box 11, "Corr., 1940-46," BCA.

51. Ramseyer to Baumgartner, March 15, 1944, Ramseyer Papers, Box 9, "Baumgartner Corr., 1938-48," BCA; Ramseyer to R. L. Hartzler, March 22, 1944, Ramseyer Papers, Box 6, "Corr., Hartzler, 1938-47," BCA.

52. President's Report to the Board of Trustees, March 24, 1944, pp. 1-4, Ramseyer Papers, I-A-d, Box 9, "Reports to Trustees . . . ," BCA.

53. Ramseyer's Report to the Trustees, March 24, 1944, 1-4.

54. Ibid., 5-8.

55. Maurice Troyer to Slabaugh, June 29, 1944, and to Ramseyer, June 8, 1944, both in Troyer Papers, 4-MS-C-W, Box 1, "Ramseyer Letters," BCA; Ramseyer to E. G. Kaufman, April 3, 1944, Ramseyer Papers, I-A-d, Box 11, "Kaufman, Ed. G., " BCA.

56. Ramseyer to Slabaugh, March 31, 1944, Ramseyer Papers, I-A-d, Box 6, "Corr., 1939-47," BCA; H. D. Burkholder to S. F. Pannabecker, April 28, 1944, personal papers of Alice Ruth Ramseyer; Ramseyer to Rev. and Mrs. Paul McElroy, May 18, 1944, Ramseyer Papers, Box 2, "M, 1948-50," BCA.

57. Ramseyer to Slabaugh, Feb. 1 and May 9, 1944, both in Ramseyer Papers, Box 6, "J. S. Slabaugh Corr.," BCA; Ramseyer to Troyer, March 30, 1944, Troyer Papers, 4-MS-C-W, Box 1, "Ramseyer Letters," BCA; Kreider to Ramseyer, April 25, 1944, Ramseyer Papers, Box 11, "Corr, 1943-48," BCA.

58. Ramseyer to Mohr, Feb. 19, 1944, Ramseyer Papers, Box 11, "Corr.,

1940-46," BCA; Ramseyer to Yoder, Feb. 22, 1944, Ramseyer Papers, Box 6, "Harry Yoder Corr, 1941-46," BCA.

59. Robert Kreider, "A Statement concerning Paul Shelly," undated, in Kreider Papers, I-A-e, Box 6, "Shelly, Paul," BCA.

60. Shelly to Ramseyer, June 25, 1944, Ramseyer Papers, Box 1, "Corr., 1943-47," BCA; *BCB* 30 (July 1944), 1; Robert Kreider, "A Statement concerning Paul Shelly."

61. Ramseyer to Howard Baumgartner, Aug. 26, 1958, Ramseyer Papers, I-A-d, Box 5, "Ramseyer B," BCA; Baumgartner to Ramseyer, Jan. 18, 1946, Ramseyer Papers, Box 9, "Baumgartner Corr., 1938-48," BCA; *WIT* 33 (March 19, 1946), 1; Keeney interview.

62. Board meeting minutes dated April 18, 1939, Bluffton College Board of Trustee Minutes, no box or folder, BCA; President's Report to the Board of Trustees, November 17, 1944, p. 5, Board Meeting Minutes and Letters, I-B-a, no box number, "1936-1945," BCA.

63. President's Report to the Board of Trustees, November 17, 1944, p. 5.

64. Ibid.

65. Members of the Faculty, *An Adventure in Faith*, 247-48; for corroboration of Ramseyer's authorship, see Delbert Gratz to Robert Kreider, June 18, 1965, Bluffton College Histories Collection, I-L-o, Box 1, "Brief History, Bluffton College," BCA.

66. Members of the Faculty, *An Adventure in Faith*, 261-2, 264.

67. For examples, see Ramseyer chapel talks dated Sept. 18, 1958; Nov. 26, 1958; Feb. 12, 1959; "Prexy's Weekly Chapel programs, 1958-1959," in Student Organizations Papers, I-K-a, Box 2, "Current Folder," BCA; and Ramseyer baccalaureate sermons dated May 14, 1944 (quoted p. 6); May 20, 1945; June 3, 1951; June 1, 1952; June 2, 1957; June 7, 1959 (quoted pp. 11-12); June 4, 1961; May 31, 1964; all in Ramseyer Baccalaureate Sermons, Box 13, BCA.

68. Ramseyer to Wilton Hartzler, Feb. 1, 1946, Ramseyer Papers, I-A-d, Box 8, "Ramseyer Letters, 1938-50," BCA; board meeting minutes dated March 23, 1945, Bluffton College Board of Trustees Minutes, Vol. 3, BCA; *BCB* 34 (September 1947), 1, and May 1947), 1; *BCB* 36 (May 1949), 1; board meeting minutes dated Nov. 8, 1946, Bluffton College Board of Trustees Minutes, no box or folder, BCA; Report of the Dean to the Board of Trustees, Oct. 24, 1947, p. 3, Board of Trustees Papers, I-B-a, no box number, "Reports to the Board of Trustees," BCA.

69. Members of the Faculty, *An Adventure in Faith*, 22; *WIT* 34 (Sept. 26, 1946), 3; 1947 *Ista*, 33-4; *WIT* 33 (Oct. 13, 1945), 1.

70. *BCB* 33 (November 1946), 206; Ramseyer to E. K. Roth, Oct. 4, 1946, Ramseyer Papers, I-A-d, Box 11, "Corr., 1943-47," BCA.

71. *BCB* 36 (November 1949), 1; *BCB* 39 (June 1952), 1; *WIT* 39 (Feb. 14, 1952), 1, 4.

72. *BCB* 45 (May 1958), 5.

73. *WIT* 36 (Oct. 25, 1948), 1; 1948 *Ista*, 94; 1949 *Ista*, 20-21; *WIT* 33 (March 5, 1946), 1; *WIT* 34 (Jan. 24, 1947), 2, and (May 23, 1947), 5.

74. Report of the Dean to the Board of Trustees, Nov. 13, 1951, Board of Trustees Papers, I-B-b, no box number, "Reports to the Board of Trustees," BCA; *WIT* 40 (Oct. 11, 1952), 5; *WIT* 42 (Sept. 18, 1954), 3; Administration Committee minutes dated April 8, 1952, Kreider Papers, I-A-e, Box 3, "Minutes of Administration Committee, 1938-53," BCA; A. R. Baker to Ramseyer, undated but probably summer, 1948, Ramseyer Papers, I-A-d, Box 5, "Ramseyer B," BCA.

75. Zelle Andrews Larson, "An Unbroken Witness: Conscientious Objection to War, 1949-1953," (Ph.D. diss., University of Hawaii, 1975): 91-4; Michael Styer, "Bluffton College: A Study of Conscientious Objection and the Case of Larry Gara," Bluffton College student paper, 1997, pp. 16-19, Student Papers Collection, I-E-kk, no box number, BCA.

76. Styer, "Bluffton College: A Study of Conscientious Objection," 16-19.

77. Ibid.

78. Larson, "An Unbroken Witness," 90-6; Styer, "Bluffton College: A Study of Conscientious Objection," 20-2, 25-6; *Toledo Blade*, March 10, 1949, p. 29; *WIT* 36 (March 15, 1949), 2.

79. Lloyd Ramseyer, "The U.S. Government Vs. Larry Gara," *The Mennonite* 63 (March 22, 1949): 3; Ramseyer to Edgar Dale, March 15, 1949, Ramseyer Papers, I-A-d, Box 3, "D, 1948-58," BCA; Ramseyer to Emmerson Halverstedt, Dec. 22, 1949, Ramseyer Papers, Box 8, "Letters, H, 1945-50," BCA.

80. Brenneman to Ramseyer, July 24 and August 10, 1946, Ramseyer's reply, July 30, 1946, all in Ramseyer Papers, I-A-d, Box 8, "Corr., 1938-47," BCA.

81. *BCB* 37 (January 1950), 1; Lapp to Ramseyer, Jan. 2, 1949, and Jan. 4, 1950, Ramseyer's response, Jan. 16, 1950, all in Ramseyer Papers, Box 12, "Letters, 1945-50," BCA.

82. Administration Committee minutes dated Oct. 17, 1944, Kreider Papers, I-A-e, Box 3, "Admin. Comm. Minutes, 1938-53," BCA; Donovan Smucker to Ramseyer, March 21, 1940, Ramseyer Papers, I-A-d, Box 4, "Ramseyer Letters, 1939-41," BCA; Ramseyer to D. Smucker, Feb. 19, 1941, Ramseyer Papers, Box 4, "Ramseyer Letters, 1939-42," BCA.

83. Donovan Smucker to Ramseyer, August 1, 1940, and Feb. 13, 1945, both in Ramseyer Papers, Box 6, "Don Smucker," BCA.

84. Ramseyer to Carl Smucker, Aug. 5, 1944, Box 6, "Slabaugh, J. S., Corr, 1939-47," BCA; "Evaluation of the Sociology and Social Work Department," Elmer Neufeld Papers, I-A-g, Box 2, "Sociology and Social Work Review, 1975," BCA; *WIT* 38 (Feb. 26, 1951), 1, 4.

85. Gratz to Ramseyer, Jan. 18, 1946, Ramseyer Papers, I-A-d, Box 2, "Gratz, Delbert, 1946-50," BCA; Kreider interview.

86. Ramseyer to Kreider, Dec. 12, 1951, Ramseyer Papers, Box 7, "K, 1951-55," BCA; Kreider interview.

87. Ramseyer to Kreider, March 13, 1950, and May 28, 1948; Oct. 20, 1948; all in Ramseyer Papers, I-A-d, Box 12, "Letters, 1943-50," BCA; Ramseyer to B. L. Stradley, Jan. 15, 1951, Ramseyer Papers, Box 15, "Sh-Sw, 1951-55," BCA.

88. Kreider to William Snyder, Sept. 10, 1952, MCC Correspondence, IX-6-3, "Bluffton College, 1952," AMC; *BCB* 36 (October 1949), 1; Gratz to Ramseyer, Oct. 19, 1949, Ramseyer Papers, Box 2, "Gratz, Delbert, 1946-50," BCA.

89. Oral interview, Perry Bush with Dale Dickey, Luther Shetler, and Lawrence Templin, Aug. 12, 1999, BCA; *Scope* 71 (July 1984), 13; oral interview, Perry Bush with Richard and Margaret Weaver, March 2, 1999, BCA; Ramseyer to Richard Weaver, Dec. 29, 1943, and Feb. 4, 1944, Weaver's response, Jan. 8, 1944, all in Ramseyer Papers, I-A-d, Box 6, "Corr., 1936-47," BCA.

90. *Scope* 75 (July 1988), 7; Ramseyer to Slotter, May 10, 1956, Ramseyer Papers, Box 5, "S, 1949-62," BCA; *BCB* 48 (July 1951), 1.

91. Raid to Schultz, undated, and April 8, 1947, both in Ramseyer Papers, I-A-d, Box 11, "Corr., 1938-48," BCA; *Scope* 66 (November 1979), 6.

92. *Scope* 74 (July 1987), 6.

93. *Scope* 71 (July 1984), 8; *Scope* 75 (July 1988), 8; *BCB* 29 (November 1952), 1; Dean's Report to the Board of Directors, April 4, 1956, p. 20, Board of Trustees

Papers, I-B-b, "Reports to the Board of Trustees, April 4, 1956," BCA; *Scope* 80 (November 1992), 4; Hardesty, *A Narrative of Bluffton College*, 27; Dickey/Shetler/Templin interview.

94. Fretz to Ramseyer, Nov. 3, 1944; May 21, 1945; Fretz Papers, 4-MS-C, Box 1, "Fretz, J. Winfield," BCA; Lehman to Ramseyer, Sept. 17, 1945, Ramseyer Papers, I-A-d, Box 11, "Corr., 1939-46," BCA.

95. Keeney interview.

96. President's Report to the Board of Trustees, April 9, 1946, Ramseyer Papers, I-A-d, Box 9, "Reports to the Board . . . 1941-46," BCA.

97. *Scope* 73 (May 1983), 9; H. W. Berky, "The Material Universe as a Witness for God," Ramseyer Papers, 1-A-d, Box 8, no folder.

98. Members of the Faculty, *An Adventure in Faith*, 128-30.

99. Ibid., 130.

100. "Institutional Study, 1947-48," Ramseyer Papers, I-A-d, Box 8, "NCA Study, 1953-54," BCA: faculty meeting minutes dated Sept. 25 and Oct. 16, 1945, Faculty Papers, I-E-a, Box 1, "Fac. minutes Sept. 11, 1944–May 5, 1954," BCA; "Bluffton College NCA Self-Study Report, 1946-1947," Faculty Papers, I-E-k, Box 2, "NCA Reports/Proposals etc," BCA; *BCB* 35 (July, 1948), 1-2.

101. Members of the Faculty, *An Adventure in Faith*, 130-31; Faculty Curriculum Committee minutes dated Feb. 20, 1945 and April 23, 1951, College Committee Papers, I-F-a, Box 1, "Curriculum Committee Minutes, 1935-60," BCA.

102. President's Report to the Board, April 9, 1946; H. M. Gage, "Bluffton College," Dec. 15, 1946, Ramseyer Papers, I-A-d, Box 6, "Harry M. Gage, 1946-47," BCA.

103. Ramseyer to Gage, Nov. 8 and March 28, 1950, both in Ramseyer Papers, Box 2, "'G' Letters, 1946-50," BCA; Ramseyer to Stradley, Jan. 15, 1951, Ramseyer Papers, Box 15, "Sh-Sw, 1951-55," BCA; "Bluffton College N.C.A. Study Report, 1952-1953," Ramseyer Papers, Box 8, "NCA Study, 1953-54," BCA.

104. A. L. Pugley and Theodore P. Stephens, "Report to the Board of Review," Ramseyer Papers, I-A-d, Box 14, "NCA Accreditation, 1950-52," BCA; Manning Patillo to Ramseyer, March 6, 1953, Board of Trustees Papers, I-B-h, Box 1, "Accreditation of Bluffton College, 27 March, 1953," BCA; Ramseyer to Gage, March 28, 1950, and Gage to Ramseyer, April 1, 1950, both in Ramseyer Papers, Box 2, "'G' Letters, 1946-50," BCA; Gage to Ramseyer, Jan. 10, 1953, Ramseyer Papers, Box 7, "G, 1951-55," BCA; Weaver interview.

105. Robert Kreider, "Excerpts from the Report to the Bluffton College Board of Trustees," April 14-15, 1967, Board of Trustees Papers, I-B-a, "Supplemental Material to the Board of Trustees, 1966-68," BCA; Hardesty, *A Narrative of Bluffton College*, 26; Report of the Dean to the President and Board of Trustees, April 10, 1953, Board of Trustees Papers, I-B-a, Box 6, "1950-59," BCA.

106. Undated memo, signed by the faculty, in Board of Trustees Papers, I-B-h, Box 1, "NCA Accreditation of BC, March '53, '67," BCA.

107. Kreider, "Excerpts from the Report to the Bluffton College Board of Trustees," Hardesty, *A Narrative of Bluffton College*, 26.

108. Byers to Ramseyer, March 31, 1953, Ramseyer Papers, I-A-d, Box 7, "'B,' 1951-55," BCA; Gage to Ramseyer, Jan. 10, 1953, Ramseyer Papers, Box 7, "G, 1951-55," BCA.

109. Ramseyer to Rollin Moser, Oct. 23, 1951, Ramseyer Papers, I-A-d, Box 7, "Mi-Mu, 1951-55," BCA; Lloyd Ramseyer to Ray Ramseyer, Dec. 13, 1955, Ramseyer Papers, Box 15, "R, 1951-55," BCA.

110. Reports of the Dean to the Board of Trustees, March 30, 1954; Oct. 19, 1956; Nov. 31, 1958; all in Board of Trustees Papers, I-B-b, Box 1, "Semi-Annual Reports," BCA.

111. Dean's Report to the Board of Trustees, Nov. 31, 1958, Board of Trustees Papers, I-B-b, Box 1, "Semi-Annual Reports," BCA.

112. *BCB* 43 (April 1956), 93-4; *BCB* 44 (April 1957), 97-8.

113. Hardesty, *A Narrative of Bluffton College*, 25; Richard Weaver interview.

114. Jacob quoted in "Dean's Newsletter" no. 22, March 6, 1957, Ramseyer Papers, I-A-d, Box 3, "Faculty, 1957-57," BCA.

115. Hardesty, *A Narrative of Bluffton College*, 25; 1953 *Ista*, 53; Kreider to William T. Snyder, Oct. 5, 1952, MCC Correspondence, IX-6-3, "Bluffton College, 1952," AMC; "Dean's Newsletter," Sept. 24. 1957, Ramseyer Papers, I-A-d, Box 3, "Faculty, 1957-58," BCA.

116. "Dean's Newsletter," Sept. 24. 1957; *WIT* 32 (Oct. 28, 1944), 1; *WIT* 40 (Oct. 24, 1952), 1.

117. "Peace Club Report, 1951-52," Student Organizations Papers, I-K-f, Box 1, "Peace Club, 1940-1983," BCA; "Dean's Newsletter," March 5, 1958, Ramseyer Papers, I-A-d, Box 3, "Faculty, 1957-58," BCA.

118. Ruth Anne Sprunger to Robert Kreider, March 15, 1970, Kreider Papers, I-A-e, Box 1, "F Corr.," BCA; Ramseyer to Mrs. August Edeler, March 1, 1949, Ramseyer Papers, I-A-d, Box 3, "Elmer Ediger, 1948-50," BCA; William Ramseyer interview.

119. Citizenship Committee minutes, Jan. 24, 1956, Faculty Papers Collection, I-E-a, Box 1, "Citizenship Committee, 1955-58," BCA.

120. Members of the Faculty, *An Adventure in Faith*, 100-101, 224-5, 155; Hardesty, *A Narrative of Bluffton College*, 25.

121. On SCA cabinet business, see, for example, minutes dated Oct. 17, 1956, among others, in Student Organizations Papers, I-K-a, Box 1, "Student Christian Association," BCA; see various Student Council minutes in 1957-58, Faculty/Student Committee Papers, I-F-g, Box 1, "Student Council Minutes, 1952-58," BCA.

122. 1949 *Ista*, 82.

123. Richard Weaver interview.

124. Ramseyer "Appreciation Chapel," 13; Citizenship Committee minutes dated Oct. 16 and Dec. 18, 1953, and Jan. 5, 1954, Faculty Papers, Collection, I-E-a, Box 1, "Citizenship Committee, 1954," BCA; Lloyd Ramseyer to William Ramseyer, Jan. 27, 1950, Ramseyer Papers, I-A-d, Box 2, "R, 1948-50," BCA.

125. "'These are the Rules of the Game," Kreider Papers, I-A-e, Box 4, "Robert Kreider," BCA; faculty meeting minutes dated Sept. 12, 1948, Faculty Collections Papers, I-A-e, Box 1, "Faculty minutes Sept. 11, 1944–May 5, 1954," BCA; "Dean's Newsletter," Sept. 5, 1957, Ramseyer Papers, I-A-d, Box 3, "Faculty, 1957-58," BCA.

126. "Special Meeting," Feb. 5, 1949, Ramseyer Papers, Box 3, "Faculty Meetings, 1948-49,"; Ramseyer to Ellis Graber, Feb. 5, 1949, Ramseyer Papers, Box 2, "G Letters, 1946-50," BCA; H. C. DuBois to Ramseyer, Feb. 12, 1949, Ramseyer Papers, Box 3, "D, 1948-50," BCA; Roland Bixler to Ramseyer, Feb. 13, 1949, Ramseyer Papers, Box 5, "Letters, 1949-50," BCA; *WIT* 36 (Feb. 15, 1949), 1, 4; Edna Ramseyer interview.

127. Hardesty, *A Narrative of Bluffton College*, 27-8.

128. Ramseyer to Homer Dunathan, Oct. 13, 1942, Ramseyer Papers, I-A-d, Box 4, "Letters, 1939-41," BCA.

129. 1954 *Ista*, 27; 1953 *Ista*, 72; *WIT* 45 (May 30, 1958), 4; *WIT* 40 (March 12,

1953), 4; 1952 *Ista*, 75.

130. BC News Release, May 10, 1967, Kreider Papers, I-A-e, Box 7, "Inauguration," BCA; *BN* (May 25, 1967), 6.

131. 1952 *Ista*, 64.

132. BC News Release, May 10, 1967, Kreider Papers, I-A-e, Box 7, "Inauguration," BCA; *BN* (May 25, 1967), 6.

133. *BN* (May 25, 1967), 6; Hardesty, *A Narrative of Bluffton College*, 28-9.

134. *WIT* 45 (Oct. 18, 1957), 1; *BCB* 45 (November 1958), 2; *WIT* 47 (Oct. 2, 1959), 1; *WIT* 47 (Jan. 15, 1960), 1.

135. Kreider interview.

Chapter Five

1. "Freedom and Order: The 1968 Bluffton College Interterm: An Evaluation," I-W, pp. iv, 3, 45-6, no box number, "Interterm," BCA; *TM* 83 (Feb. 6, 1968): 92-5.

2. Ibid.

3. *BCB* 55 (February 1968), 1-3.

4. Diane Ravitch, *The Troubled Crusade: American Education, 1945-1980* (New York: Basic Books, 1983), 183; David Chalmers, *And the Crooked Places Made Straight: The Struggle for Social Change in the 1960s* (Baltimore: Johns Hopkins University Press, 1991), 6.

5. J. Richard Weaver, "Tribute to Lloyd and Ferne Ramseyer," May 20, 1995, Ramseyer Papers, I-A-d, Box 14, no file number; Ramseyer, "Report to the Board of Trustees," Nov. 1, 1963, pp. p-3," Boards of Trustees Annual Reports, I-B-b, no folder number, BCA. For examples of earlier planning, see Ramseyer Reports to the Board, same notation as above, April, 1956, pp. 7-10, and April, 1958, pp. 7-8; and *BCB* 44 (February and July 1957).

6. Ramseyer, "Report to the Board of Trustees," Nov. 1, 1963, pp. p-3," Boards of Trustees Annual Reports, I-B-b, no folder number, BCA.

7. *BCB* 49 (September 1962), 1, and *BCB* 49 (October 1962), 1; Hardesty, *A Narrative of Bluffton College*, 33; *BCB* 56 (September 1969), 1.

8. *WIT* 60 (Oct. 13, 1967), 1.

9. Kreider to James Miller, Feb. 3, 1966, Kreider Papers, I-A-e, Box 4, "Kreider–Corr., 1965-66," BCA; *BCB* 53 (April 1966), 43; Kreider to Bassett, Oct. 1, 1965, Kreider Papers, Box 6, "Bassett, James," BCA.

10. *BCB* 54 (November 1967), 1; Administration Committee minutes dated Jan. 3, 1962, Kreider Papers, I-A-e, Box 3, "Minutes of Administration Committee, 1954-69," BCA; Brenneman to Ramseyer, Jan. 19, 1962, Kreider Papers, Box 6, "Brenneman, Naomi," BCA.

11. *BN* (Sept. 26, 1963), 1; *BCB* 54 (November 1967), 1-2; *BCB* 52 (August 1965), 1; *BCB* 55 (August 1968), 1; *WIT* 56 (May 29, 1969), 1.

12. *BN* (April 21, 1966), 1; *Scope* 84 (July 1997), 3; *Scope* 81 (July 1994), 7; *Scope* 57 (November 1970), 1-2.

13. "Notes on an Architectural Statement for Bluffton College," June 3, 1965, Neufeld Papers, I-A-g, Box 1, "Site Development," BCA.

14. *LN* (Sept. 29, 1966), 24.

15. Kreider to William Klassen, Sept. 16, 1966, Kreider Papers, I-A-e, Box 4, "Kreider Corr., 1965–66," BCA; *LN* (March 31, 1968), 24.

16. Kreider to James Bassett and Jack Hodell, June 12, 1965, Neufeld Papers, I-A-g, Box 1, "Site Development," BCA; *BN* (Jan. 26, 1967), 1.

17. *BCB* 68 (August 1961), 1; Ben Sprunger, "Bluffton College: A Time for

Appraisal and Action,"p. 8, Sprunger Papers, I-A-f, Box 2, "Time for Appraisal and Action," BCA; *Scope* 74 (July 1987), 7.

18. *Scope* 74 (July 1987), 7; Kreider to Hans de Jonge, March 4, 1963, Kreider Papers, I-A-e, Box 6, "de Jonge, Johannes," BCA; Kreider, "Dean's Report to the President and Board of Trustees," April 17, 1963, pp. D-4-5, Board of Trustees Annual Reports, I-B-b, no folder number, BCA.

19. Mark Houshower, "Departmental Honors, 1972-3," May 23, 1972, Faculty Papers, Collection, I-F-e, "Honors Committee," BCA; George Rable, Senior Honors paper, April 21, 1972, Faculty Papers Collection, I-E-kk, Box 1, "Honors Papers," BCA.

20. Sprunger, "A Time for Appraisal and Action," 8; Carl Lehman, "The Robert Kreider Administration, 1965-1972," personal papers of Michael Edmiston; Hardesty, *A Narrative of Bluffton College*, 33; Joseph Pryor to Mark Houshower, April 22, 1967, Faculty Papers Collection, I-E-k, Box 2, "NCA Corr.," BCA; *BCB* 47 (April 1960), 130-32.

21. Perry Bush, *Two Kingdoms, Two Loyalties: Mennonite Pacifism in Modern America* (Baltimore: Johns Hopkins University Press), 141-2; Kreider, Report of the President to the Board of Trustees, April 16, 1966, pp. p-12-13, Board of Trustees Papers, I-B-b, Box 1, BC Board of Trustees, April 15-16, 1966, BCA; Sprunger, "A Time for Appraisal and Action," 8; John Unruh to NCA Self-Study Committee, Nov. 15, 1962, Faculty Papers Collection, I-E-k, Box 1, NCA Study Comm, 1962-63, BCA; Carl Lehman, "The Robert Kreider Administration," 7.

22. Ramseyer to Snyder et al., March 17, 1962, MCC Correspondence, IX-6-3, Bluffton College, 1962, AMC.

23. *WIT* 51 (Dec. 13, 1964), 3; *WIT* 51 (Feb. 14, 1964), 3; *WIT* 52 (March 19, 1965), 1, 2.

24. *WIT* 48 (Nov. 14, 1960), 1; *BN* (Nov. 28, 1963), 1; *WIT* 52 (Oct. 23, 1964), 1.

25. *BN* (April 7, 1960), 1; Howard Raid to George Reed, May 12, 1962, Kreider Papers, I-A-e, Box 2, "Fisk University, 1962," BCA; Keith Kingsley et al. to Robert Kreider, undated, and Kreider's response, March 27, 1964, both in Ramseyer Papers, I-A-d, Box 13, "Corr., 1959-64," BCA; *WIT* 52 (Nov. 20, 1964), 1.

26. Judy Hilty to Keith Kingsley, summary of Peace Club programs for 1961-1962 school year, undated memo in Student Organizations Papers, I-K-f, Box 1, "Peace Club, 1940-1983," BCA; 1960 *Ista*, 36; *WIT* 49 (Dec. 15, 1961), 2-3.

27. 1961 *Ista*, 35; Lima *Citizen* (Nov. 16, 1961), 1; Findlay *Republican Courier* (Nov. 16, 1961), 18; Judy Hilty, "We Protest," *The Mennonite* 77 (Jan. 2, 1962): 13-14; Mrs. Robert Cully to Ramseyer, Nov. 24, 1961, Ramseyer Papers, I-A-d, Box 13, "Corr, 1955-65," BCA; Ramseyer to Robert Blough, Jan. 3, 1962, Ramseyer Papers, Box 13, "Corr., 1959-66," BCA; Administration Committee minutes dated Dec. 20, 1962, Kreider Papers, I-A-e, Box 3, "Minutes of Administration Committee, 1954-69," BCA.

28. *WIT* 49 (March 16, 1962), 2-3; *WIT* 50 (Jan. 18, 1963), 2; *WIT* 50 (April 26, 1963), 2; *WIT* 51 (Dec. 13, 1964), 3; *WIT* 51 (Jan. 17, 1964), 1.

29. "Emergency Meeting of the Bluffton College Student Council," Jan. 13, 1964, Student/Faculty Committee Papers, I-F-q, "Student Council Minutes 1963-64," BCA; *WIT* 51 (May 15, 1964), 3 (Kingsley quote).

30. 1966 *Ista*, 103; "1992 Sports Hall of Fame Nominees," Athletics Department Papers, I-J-c, Box 5, "Sports Hall of Fame," BCA; 1970 *Ista*, 108; "1983 Sports Hall of Fame Inductees," Neufeld Papers, I-A-g, Box 1, "Hall of Fame, 1973-89," BCA.

31. "Department of Health, Physical Education and Recreation, Self Study Report," March, 1975, p. 5, Faculty Papers Collection, I-E-tt, "Health and Physical Education Evaluation," BCA.

32. BC yearly sports records, papers in authors' possession; *WIT* 54 (Feb. 24, 1967), 4; *WIT* 54 (April 14, 1967), 4; *WIT* 55 (March 8, 1968), 4; *WIT* 56 (May 29, 1969), 4; "1980s Sports Hall of Fame Inductees," Neufeld Papers, I-A-g, Box 1, "Hall of Fame, 1973-1989," BCA; Rachel Tuttle, "History of the Bluffton College Volleyball Program," Bluffton College student paper, Feb. 20, 1998, paper in author's possession.

33. "1991 Sports Hall of Fame Inductees," Athletic Papers Collection, I-J-c, Box 5, "Sports Hall of Fame," BCA; Bluffton College Press Release, May 10, 1967, Kreider Papers, I-A-e, Box 7, "Kreider—Inauguration," BCA; BC yearly sports records, papers in authors' possession.

34. Toledo *Blade* (Aug. 2, 1971); 1970 *Ista*, 100.

35. Kreider to Henry Weaver, April 8, 1965, Kreider Papers, I-A-e, Box 4, "Weaver, Henry," BCA.

36. *WIT* 53 (May 6, 1966), 1; Schultz to Ramseyer, July 23, 1951, Ramseyer Papers, I-A-d, Box 15, "Sa-Se, 1951-55," BCA; *Scope* 75 (July 1988), 7; *Scope* 63 (April 1976), 5-6.

37. Kreider to Winfield Fretz, July 20, 1959, Kreider Papers, I-A-e, Box 4, "Robert Kreider," BCA; *Scope* 71 (July 1984), 13; Robert Kreider, "Report of the President to the Board of Trustees," Nov. 10, 1967, p. 50, Board of Trustees Papers, I-B-b, Box 1, "Board of Trustees, 1967," BCA.

38. Oral interview, Perry Bush with Don Pannabecker, June 7, 1999, BCA; *Scope* 80 (July 1993), 9.

39. *Scope* 66 (September 1966),4; *WIT* 53 (May 6, 1966), 1; *Scope* 75 (July 1998), 8; *Scope* 85 (May 1998), 4.

40. *Scope* 74 (January 1987), 9-10; *Scope* 72 (July 1985), 3; Findlay *Republican Courier* (Dec. 24, 1971).

41. Schirch to "Former Students," Jan. 27, 1971, Faculty Papers Collection, I-E-hh, Box 1, "Science Building Plans," BCA; *Scope* 80 (July 1993), 9; HPER Self Study Report, March, 1975, 5.

42. *Scope* 63 (March 1976), 2; "The Home Economics Department at Bluffton College," undated memo, Neufeld Papers, I-A-g, Box 2, "Corr., etc, Home Ec Program Approvals," BCA; Weaver, "Tribute to Lloyd and Ferne Ramseyer," 3.

43. Kreider to John Bauman, Aug. 17, 1964, Ramseyer Papers, I-A-d, Box 13, "Corr, 1965," BCA; *Scope* 65 (January 1978), 1; Kreider to Erland Waltner, Jan. 11, 1957, Kreider Papers, I-A-e, Box 1, "W Corr., 1954-66," BCA.

44. Neufeld to John Claude, Aug. 16, 1965, MCC Corr., IX-6-3, "Bluffton College, 1965," AMC.

45. "Report of the President to the Board of Trustees," March 31, 1964, Board of Trustees Papers, I-B-b, Box 1, "March 31, 1964," BCA.

46. *Scope* 64 (September 1977), 1

47. Bluffton College news release, Oct. 12, 1965, Kreider Papers, I-A-e, Box 7, "Inauguration—Robt. Kreider," BCA; *BN* (July 23, 1964), 4.

48. Arnold Nickel to Lloyd Ramseyer, Dec. 31, 1959, Kreider Papers, I-A-e, Box 4, "Corr., N, 1959-66," BCA; "Form, Faith and Scholarship," Kreider Inaugural Address, p. 9, Kreider Papers, Box 4, "Robert Kreider," BCA.

49. Keeney interview.

50. Dick Weaver interview; Dickey/Shetler/Templin interview; oral interview, Perry Bush with Mark Houshower, May 5, 1999, deposited with BCA;

Faculty Reorganization Committee minutes dated April 15 and Sept. 8, 1969; FROC to Faculty, April 20, 1970; all in Faculty Committee Papers, I-F-j, "FROC," BCA.

51. Robert Kreider, "Expectations for Bluffton College for the Next Decade," Dec. 27, 1963, Ramseyer Papers, I-A-d, Box 13, "Corr., 1959-64," BCA.

52. Keeney interview; Lehman, "The Robert Kreider Administration."

53. Kreider to Ollie Diller et al., Sept. 27, 1965.

54. Kreider, "A Preliminary Statement: Nature Center—Conference Center for the Bluffton College Farm," Oct. 3, 1966; both in Faculty Papers Collection, I-E-m, "Rural Life Center, 1972," BCA; Kreider to Arden Slotter, March 18, 1966, Kreider Papers, Box 6, "Slotter, Arden," BCA; *WIT* 50 (May 7, 1963), 2; *BN* (Feb. 7, 1963), 1; *BN* (March 14, 1963), 1; *WIT* 49 (Dec. 15, 1961), 3; *WIT* 52 (Nov. 20, 1964), 1; *BCB* 54 (April 1967), 1; *Scope* 82 (January 1995), 5.

55. "Form, Faith and Scholarship," Kreider Inaugural Address, p. 3; Kreider, "The Mennonite Vision For and in the World," *Christian Monitor* 39 (September 1947): 266-67.

56. *BCB* 53 (August 1966), 1; Kreider interview; *Scope* 77 (July 1990), 3-4; *WIT* 50 (May 7, 1963), 3; Houshower interview; Kreider, "Off-Campus Studies," Feb. 1, 1968, Kreider Papers, I-A-e, Box 5, "Curriculum," BCA; "Columbia Program—Summer, 1969," Kreider Papers, Box 2, "Columbia International Education, 1968-70," BCA.

57. Kreider to faculty, Jan. 5, 1966, Faculty Papers Collection, I-E-l, Box 2, "Fac Meeting Sept.1, 1965–Aug. 31, 1966," BCA; Kreider, "The 1967 Inter-Term at Bluffton College," March 3, 1967, Faculty Papers Collection, no box number, "Evaluation of Interterm: Progress Report/Findlay Talk, 1967," BCA; "National Attention still focused on inter-term," Jan. 12, 1967," Public Relations Office Papers, I-D-b, Box 3, "News, 1966-67," BCA.

58. "Convocation Speakers for 1970 Inter-term," Dec. 15, 1969, Kreider Papers, I-A-e, Box 5, "Schedules—rm assignments, 1970," BCA; *LN* (Jan 2, 1972), B13.

59. *LN* (Jan. 2, 1973), B13; undated memo on the "structure of the 1971 Inter-term," Kreider Papers, I-Ae, Box 7, "Seminars," BCA.

60. Keeney interview; "Grass-Roots Meetings on Standards of Campus Conduct," Faculty/Staff/Student Committees Papers, I-F-g, "Student Senate Business, 1967-68," BCA; "Report on NCA Self-Study Workshop, Souderton, Pennsylvania," Nov. 20, 1965, Faculty Papers Collection, I-E-l, Box 2, "Faculty, 1965-66," BCA.

61. Keeney interview; oral interview, Perry Bush with Elmer Neufeld, August 5, 1999, BCA; "The Bluffton College Chapel (A Tentative Proposal)," undated memo, Faculty Papers, I-E-k, Box 1, "NCA, 1964-65," BCA; "Reports on Faculty Discussions on Standards of Campus Conduct," Oct. 18, 1966, Faculty Papers Collection, Box 2, "Faculty Meeting Sept. 1, 1966–Aug. 31, 1967," BCA; Kreider to Daniel Chamberlain, May 6, 1969, Kreider Papers, I-A-e, Box 2, "Corr. on Dancing, 1967-69," BCA.

62. Community Life Committee minutes, Oct. 6, 1970, and Kreider to Rodabaugh, July 13, 1970, Faculty Papers Collection, I-E-a, Box 4, "Fac Minutes 8/31-70–10/14/70," BCA; "Convocation Attendance, First Semester, 1967-68," Sept. 12, 1967, Faculty/Student Committee Papers, I-F-q, "Student Senate Business, 1967-68," BCA.

63. Kreider to "Bluffton College Students," June 21, 1967, Faculty/Student Committee Papers, I-F-q, "Student Senate Business, 1967-68," BCA; *BCB* 53 (October 1966), 2; "Class Attendance," undated memo, Kreider Papers, I-A-e,

Box 4, "Robert Kreider," BCA; Glenn Snyder, "Report of Student Personnel Services" to the Board of Trustees, Nov. 10, 1967, Board of Trustees Papers, I-B-b, Box 1, "Board of Trustees, 1967," BCA.

64. Kreider, "Images and Realities—Reflections at Two-Thirds of a Century," April 19, 1967, p. 3, Kreider Papers, I-A-e, Box 6, "Shelly, Paul," BCA.

65. Neuenschwander to Kreider, Jan. 30, Jan. 31, and April 5, 1968, and Kreider response, Feb. 14, 1968, all in Kreider Papers, Box 2, "Corr on Dancing, 1967-69," BCA; Henry Detwiler to William T. Snyder, May 14, 1968, Kreider Papers, Box 6, "Detwiler, Harry, 1965-8," BCA.

66. A Campus Pastor," Faculty Papers Collection, I-E-a, Box 4, "Fac minutes 1/14-70–5/26-70," BCA; "The Issue of a Campus Pastor," same box, "Faculty mins 3/4/69–5/27/69," BCA; *Scope* 58 (January 1971), 1; Bluffton College News Release, June 15, 1970; April 19, 1967, p. 3, Kreider Papers, I-A-e, Box 6, "Shelly, Paul," BCA.

67. Student Council minutes dated Feb. 5, 1960, Student Committee Papers, I-F-q, Box 1, "Student Council Minutes, 1959-60," BCA; "SCA Cabinet Fall Retreat," Sept. 6-7, 1963, Student Organizations Papers, I-K-a, Box 3, "SCA Notes, 1963-64," BCA; Ramseyer Report to the Board of Trustees, March 31, 1964, p. 1, Board of Trustees Papers, I-B-b, Box 1, "March 31, 1964," BCA; Judy Palmer, "Evaluation Summary," Feb. 20, 1966, Student Organizations Papers, Box 3, "SCA, 1965-66," BCA.

68. Minutes of SCA Cabinet Retreat, Sept. 1, 1968, and "Seminars, First Semester, 1967-68," both in Student Organizations Papers, I-K-a, "SCA," no box or folder number, BCA;

69. *WIT* 52 (Sept. 25, 1964), 1; "Service Committee News Letter," Feb. 10, 1965, Minutes of SCA Cabinet Retreat, Sept. 1, 1968, both in Student Organizations Papers, I-K-a, "SCA," no box or folder number, BCA; "SCA Evaluation," Feb. 11, 1965, Faculty Papers Collection, I-E-k, Box 1, "NCA, 1964-65," BCA.

70. Toledo *Blade* (Jan. 28, 1970), 20; *WIT* 50 (May 7, 1963), 2; *WIT* 52 (April 22, 1966), 2; Student Council minutes, May 15, 1972, Student Committees Collection, I-F-q, Box 1, "Student Senate Minutes 1971-72," BCA. For conservative charges on the opinion board, see statements by Birdie Baker; "Bluffton Men and the Draft" by Steve Lehman and Michael Nolte, with other signatures; Bill Groomes, March 31, 1969; and David Blank, Nov. 11, 1969. For lamentations by activists, see letters by Sara Templin and Baldemar Velasquez, March 26, 1968; Mary Goings, May 3, 1968; and *WIT* 57 (May 11, 1970), 1.

71. Social Action Organization minutes, Oct. 4 and Nov. 17, 1967, William Keeney Papers, 4-MS-C, Box 3, "Social Action organization," BCA; Kreider, "Reflections on Two-Thirds of a Century," 5; 1967 *Ista*, 144-145; "The South Lima Project," undated memo, Kreider Papers, I-A-e, Box 6, "David Schmidt," BCA.

72. "Power and Poverty in Lima, Ohio," May 1969, Faculty Papers Collection, I-E-yy, Box 1, "Pre-Release," BCA.

73. *Scope* 86 (May 1999), 7.

74. *Scope* 79 (May 1992), 4.

75. *Scope* 76 (November 1989), 4-5; Dickey/Shetler/Templin interview.

76. *Scope* 76 (November 1989), 5.

77. *BN* (May 10, 1968); *WIT* 52 (Nov. 6, 1964), 2.

78. *WIT* 52 (April 16, 1965), 2; Opinion Board postings by Joe Sprunger et al., Nov. 22, 1966, and March 14, 1967, both in Committee Papers Collection, I-F-q, "Opinion Board, 1968-69," BCA; Nathan Habegger, Letter to the Editor, *The*

Mennonite 84 (Dec 16, 1969): 765; oral interview, Perry Bush with Elmer Neufeld, Feb. 26, 1995, and August 5, 1999, BCA.

79. *LN* (Nov. 11, 1971); *LN* (May 16, 1971), A-5; "BC students join McCarthy brigade," May 2, 1968, Publications Office Papers, I-D-b, Box 3, "Newspaper Clippings, 1967-73," BCA; *WIT* 55 (May 24, 1968), 1; oral interview, Perry Bush with Greg Luginbuhl, Aug. 29, 1995, BCA; Kreider Report to the Board, Nov. 15, 1968, pp. V-8-9, Board of Trustees Papers, I-B-b, Box 1, "Nov. 15-16, 1968," BCA.

80. Jacoby to Faculty, "Plans for October 15," Oct. 9, 1969, Peace Papers and Reports Collection, I-X-c, "1969 Nation-Wide Moratorium," BCA; *BN* (Nov. 20, 1969), 9.

81. *BN* (May 14, 1970), 12; Kreider to "Students and Faculty of Bluffton College," with accompanying faculty statement, May 12, 1970, Faculty Papers Collection, I-E-a, Box 4, "Fac minutes 1/14/70—5/26/70," BCA; *WIT* 57 (May 11, 1970), 2.

82. *BN* (April 23, 1970), 10.

83. *BN* (Jan. 29, 1970), 1; Jacoby to Atkinson, Feb. 13, 1970, Faculty Papers Collection, I-E-h, no box number, "Interterm Study, Atkinson, Ti-Grace, 1970," BCA; Elizabeth Yoder, *The Centaur* 4 (Jan. 29, 1970): 6-7; Sara Templin Velasquez, in *The Centaur* 4 (Jan. 20, 1970): 10, both in Interterm Papers, I-W, no box or file number, BCA.

84. Citizenship Committee minutes dated Jan. 17, 1966, Student Committee Papers, I-F-e, "Citizenship Committee," BCA; *Scope* 62 (November 1975), 2; Jacoby to Atkinson, Feb. 13, 1970.

85. *WIT* 57 (Oct 3, 1969), 3; *WIT* 57 (April 11, 1970), 1-2; *WIT* 57 (Oct. 31, 1969), 2.

86. Pam Neff and Priscilla Friesen Luginbuhl, "Concerning the Home Economics Department at Bluffton College," undated memo, and response by Leland Lehman to Elmer Neufeld, March 22, 1971, both in Neufeld Papers, I-A-g, Box 2, "Corresp. etc, Home Ec Program Approvals," BCA.

87. Oral interview, Perry Bush with Judy and Phil Kingsley, May 27, 1999, BCA: "Hoosier-Buckeye League Schools," plus other Ohio and Neighboring Colleges," undated but probably early 1970s, Presidential Office Papers, "Intercultural Center," President's Office files.

88. "To Everyone Concerned" from Nate Fields et al., undated but probably April 1968, posting by Burton Yost, Oct. 10, 1968, both in Student Committee Papers, I-F-q, "Opinion Board, 1968-69," BCA.

89. *BN* (May 9, 1968), 1; *LN* (May 29, 1969), 2; posting by Steve Swartley, April 29, 1968, Student Committee Papers, I-F-q, "Opinion Board, 1968-69," BCA; Houshower interview; memo from John Unruh and Elmer Neufeld, May 5, 1969, Faculty Papers Collection, I-K-i, Box 1, "Black Student Union," BCA; oral interview, Perry Bush with Elmer Neufeld, August 5, 1999, BCA.

90. Faculty meeting minutes dated Feb. 10, 1970; Student Council minutes dated Feb. 10, 1970; memo from Don Pannabecker, March 13, 1970; Pannabecker to Nate Fields, March 25, 1970; all in Student Organizations Collection, I-K-i, "Black Power, 1970," BCA.

91. Memo from Don Pannabecker, March 13, 1970, and Pannabecker to Nate Fields, March 25, 1970, both in Student Organizations Collection, I-K-i, "Black Power, 1970," BCA; Kreider to Fields, May 28, 1970, Presidential Office Files, "Fields, Nate," President's Office; BSU to Kreider, May 22, 1970, Presidential Office Files, "BSU," President's Office; posting from David Patterson, Feb. 12, 1970, Student Committee Papers, I-F-q, "Opinion Board, 1969-70," BCA.

92. Houshower to Kreider, undated, BSU to the faculty, undated, BSU to trustees, undated, BSU memo, May 19, 1971, all in Student Organizations Collection, I-K-i, Box 1, "Black Student Union," BCA; Kreider to faculty, April 20, 1971, Faculty Papers Collection, I-E-a, Box 4, "1971," BCA.

93. Sandy Johnson to Nate Fields, Sept. 26, 1971, Student Organizations Collection, I-K-i, Box 1, "Black Student Union," BCA; Kreider to Fields, May 28, 1971, BC President Office Files, "Fields, Nate,"; *LN* (April 29, 1971), 10.

94. Oral interview, Perry Bush with Bob and Lois Kreider, May 25, 1999, BCA; Kreider to Trustees, Nov. 15, 1966, Board of Trustees Papers, I-B-a, Box 6, "Aug-Dec., 1966," BCA.

95. Tom Lehman to faculty, May 13, 1968, Kreider Papers, I-A-e, Box 5, "Curriculum," BCA; BC press release, Jan. 28, 1970, Kreider Papers, I-A-e, Box 4, "Letters to the Board, 1970," BCA.

96. *Scope* 74 (July 1987), 7.

97. Steve Stucky, "Bluffton Observed," *The Remnant* newsletter, undated, and posting by Isaac Riak, Sept. 23, 1969, both in Student Committee Papers, I-F-g, "Opinion Board, 1969-70,"; faculty meeting minutes dated Sept. 23, 1969, Faculty Papers Collection, I-E-a, Box 4, "Fac. mins 9-1-69–12-18-69," BCA; oral interview, Perry Bush with Mitchell Kingsley, Gary and Lois Wetherill, June 9, 1999, BCA.

98. Hardesty, *A Narrative of Bluffton College*, 33-34; Student Council minutes, Sept 22, 1964, and March 2, 1965, Student Committees Collection, I-F-q, Box 1, "Student Council Minutes, 1964-65," BCA; Kreider, "Reflections of Two-Thirds of a Century," 6.

99. Community Life Committee minutes, Oct. 6, 1970, Faculty Papers Collection, I-E-a, Box 4, "Fac. Mins, 8/31-70–10/14/70," BCA.

100. See letters from "A Dissenter," Oct. 9, 1967, and from Mitchell Kingsley, Oct. 4, 1967, both in Student Committee Papers, I-F-q, "Opinion Board, 1968-9," BCA.

101. Lois Rodabaugh Report to the Board of Trustees, April 23-24, 1971, pp. II-14, and Kreider to Board, Nov. 10, 1967, both in Board of Trustees Papers, I-B-b, Box 1, "April 23-24, 1971" and "Nov. 10-11, 1967," BCA; see various minutes from Citizen Committee meetings, 1968-69, in Student Committee Papers, I-F-e, "Citizenship Committee," BCA.

102. Judy Kingsley interview; Mrs. Erwen Graber to Kreider, Oct. 13, 1967, Kreider Papers, I-A-e, Box 1, "G Corr.," BCA; Wetherill/Kingsley interview.

103. *WIT* 56 (May 29, 1969), 2; *WIT* 57 (Sept. 19, 1969), 2; *WIT* 57 (Oct. 17, 1969), 2; *WIT* 58 (Sept. 18, 1970: 1; oral interview, Rachael Chapman with Sara Kisseberth, June 14, 1999, BCA.

104. Keeney interview; Kreider, "Reflections of Two-Thirds of a Century," 3.

105. Kreider interview, May 25, 1999; Houshower interview.

106. 1974 *Ista*, 129, 138, 133; 1970 *Ista*, 11; 1975 *Ista*, 12.

107. Peter Lehman to Kreider, March 9, 1970, Kreider Papers, I-A-e, Box 1, "L Corr," BCA; Dale Lehe to "Dear Friend," November, 1971, Central District Conference Papers, 3-C-l, Box 1, "Corr., 1952-1981," BCA; Luginbuhl interview.

108. Kreider, "A Statement on the Events of the Night of April 8-9," and undated later memo, probably from Kreider, both in Committee Papers Collection, I-F-q, "The reported riot on campus, April 10, 1970," BCA.

109. Ibid.; also see collection of newspaper stories, same file.

110. *LN* (Dec. 30, 1968), 11; Ramseyer's Report to the Board, April 9, 1965, p. 5, Board of Trustees Papers, I-B-b, Box 1, "April 9, 1965," BCA.

111. Lehman, "The Robert Kreider Administration," 11; Sprunger, "A Time for Appraisal and Action," 7-10; *BN* (May 13, 1971), 1; Hardesty, *A Narrative of Bluffton College*, 35.

112. *Scope* 58 (August 1971), 1; Kreider to Board of Trustees, April 9, 1970, Kreider Papers, I-A-e, Box 4, "Letters to the Board, 1970," BCA; Kreider to *The Mennonite* 86 (April 20, 1971), 260; Kreider to "Editor, The *Blade*," Jan. 29, 1971, Kreider Papers, Box 1, "B Corr.," BCA. It remains unclear whether or not this letter was ever sent.

113. Bob Suter, "Response to Sprunger Position Paper," Sept. 2, 1976, Sprunger Papers, I-A-f, Box 2, "Trustee Committee Reports, 1976," BCA; Kreider Report to the Board, April 23, 1971, p. 5, in Board of Trustees Papers, I-B-b, Box 1, "April 23-24, 1971," BCA.

114. Executive Committee minutes Jan. 29, 1971, Board of Trustees Papers, I-B-b, Box 1, "April 23-24, 1971," BCA; *Scope* 58 (November 1971), 3; Kreider, "Re: The Science Center," May 10, 1971, and Hodell to Kreider, Aug. 21, 1972, both in Kreider Papers, I-A-e, Box 7, "Science Learning Center," BCA.

115. *Scope* 58 (October 1971), 1; Kreider interview, May 25, 1999; *Scope* 59 (September 1972), 1-2.

Chapter Seven

1. *WIT* 2 (Oct. 31, 1975), 1.

2. Report of the Provost and Dean to the President, April, 1981, p. B-1, Neufeld Papers, I-A-g, Box 3, no folder number, BCA.

3. Don Schweingruber, Report of the Dean of Student Affairs to the Board of Trustees, April 25, 1986, p. 18, Board of Trustees Papers, I-B-b, Box 2, "April 25-26, 1986," BCA; Ben Sprunger, "Bluffton College: A Time for Appraisal and Action," p. 8, Sprunger Papers, I-A-f, Box 2, "Time for Appraisal and Action," BCA; "Fiscal and Physical Resources Review Meeting," Aug 24 & 25, 1973, Sprunger Papers, I-A-f, Box 2, "Letter to Board and Others, July 1, 1973," BCA; *Scope* 64 (December 1977), 1.

4. "New Bluffton College Curriculum for September, 1972," with faculty minutes dated January 1, 1972, Faculty Papers Collection, I-E-a, Box 4, "Faculty mins Nov. 30, 1971–Feb. 22, 1972," BCA; Mark Houshower et al., "Danforth Summer Workshop, 1971: A Report," Faculty Papers Collection, I-E-u, Box 1, "Danforth lecture, 1963," BCA.

5. Houshower et al., "Danforth Summer Workshop, 1971: A Report," 2-5.

6. Ibid., 3-4.

7. *WIT* 36 (May 24, 1979), 3; "Guidelines for Human Explorations Program," adopted by faculty Jan. 31, 1972, Faculty Papers Collection, I-E-a, Box 4, "Fac mins Nov. 30, 1971–Feb. 22, 1972," BCA; "#3, Exploring the Cultural Environment," undated list, Faculty Papers Collection, I-E-ll, Box 1, "Human Explorations and Other Curriculum Proposals, 1971," BCA.

8. "Results of Student-Faculty Preference Poll (as of Friday, Nov. 12)" [1971], Faculty Papers Collection, I-E-a, Box 4, "Fac mins May 25, 1971–Nov. 17, 1971," BCA; Yost to Houshower, March 24, 1972, Faculty Papers Collection, I-E-ll, Box 1, "Human Explorations and Other Curriculum Proposals, 1971," BCA.

9. Notes of telephone interview, Perry Bush with Steve Jacoby, June 17, 1999, notes in author's possession.

10. See the critiques of HUEX by Neufeld, Passage, LaVerne Schirch, Linda Suter, Leland Lehman, and Eileen Ewing, all in *Cross-Discipline*, May 1976, College Publications Collection, I-L-m, Box 2, "Cross-Discipline, 1974-79," BCA,

Neufeld quoted p. 2.

11. Committee on Instruction, "General Education Objectives," Sept. 13, 1977, Faculty Papers Collection, I-E-a, Box 4, "Fac mins Jan. 16, 1977–Dec. 14, 1977," BCA.

12. NCA Self-Study Report, December 1978, pp. 60, 40, 41-2, Faculty Papers Collection, I-E-k, Box 2, "Self Study Report, Dec. 16, 1978," BCA; NCA Evaluation Team Report, March 20-22, 1989, p. 14, same box as above, "NCA visiting team report, March, 1989," BCA.

13. "Position Paper on the Issues of Expanded Program Offerings," Nov. 1, 1974, Faculty Papers Collection, I-E-a, Box 4, "Fac mins May 13, 1974–Dec. 11, 1974," BCA.

14. Bob Suter to Sprunger, Dec. 21, 1973, and Suter, "Statement of need for Alternative Science facilities for Bluffton College," Jan. 1, 1974, both in "Board of Trustees Report: Special Board Meeting," Jan. 25, 1974, Sprunger Papers, I-A-f, Box 2, "Letters to Board and Others, July 1, 1973–July 1, 1974," BCA; Sprunger, "President's Report on Reconsideration of Resolving Science Facility Needs," Jan. 15, 1974, Board of Trustees Papers, I-B-b, Box 1, "1974," BCA; *Scope* 64 (March 1977), 1; *WIT* 62 (Aug. 13, 1976), 1-2; *Scope* 65 (December 1978), 1.

15. Ken Spiert, "Report to the Board of Trustees" and "Proposal for a Campus Newspaper," Approved by Committee on Community Life, May 7, 1974, both in Sprunger Papers, I-A-f, Box 2, "1974 Business and Educational Affairs," BCA; see *Profile* for 1972 and 1973; *WIT* 13 (May 18, 1973), 1.

16. *WIT* 1 (Oct. 12, 1973), 2; *Bluffton College Campus Newspaper* (Sept. 4, 1974), 1; *WIT* 2 (Sept. 13, 1974), 1; Von Hardesty to Perry Bush, April 30, 1999, letter in author's possession.

17. Neufeld to Board of Trustees, Nov. 3, 1978, Neufeld Papers, I-A-g, Box 3, no folder, BCA; *WIT* 65 (Nov. 10, 1978), 1-4.

18. *LN* (Oct. 13, 1993), B-1.

19. Unruh to Neufeld, Oct. 28, 1974, Sprunger Papers, I-A-f, Box 2, "1974 Business and Educational Affairs," BCA; *LN* (Oct. 13, 1993), B-1.

20. *Scope* 63 (April, 1976), 5-6; *LN* (Oct. 13, 1993), B-1; *WIT* 62 (Jan. 23, 1976), 6; *Washington Post* (April 1, 1979), E1.

21. *Scope* 60 (February 1973), 1; memo from Becky Shinn, President, W.S.G.A., March 2, 1972, Faculty Papers Collection, I-E-a, Box 2, "fac mins March 23, 1972–May 23, 1972," BCA; Committee on Community Life minutes, March 6, 1975, Faculty Papers Collection, I-E-a, Box 4, "fac mins Jan. 21, 1975–May 21, 1975," BCA; *Scope* 59 (September 1972), 1.

22. Sprunger to Charles Warren, Oct. 11, 1973, Sprunger Papers, I-A-f, Box 1, "C Corr., 1972," BCA; 1974 *Ista*, 58; 1975 *Ista*, 91; *BN* (April 12, 1973), 16; Neufeld and Schweingruber to faculty and staff, with attached memo, Dec. 27, 1976, President's Office Files, folder titled "Multi-Cultural Center"; Sprunger, "Report of the President to the Board of Trustees," April 1, 1976, P-3, Board of Trustees Papers, I-B-b, Box 1, "1976," BCA.

23. Committee on Community Life minutes, Feb. 5, 1974, Mecartney to "Colleagues," Feb. 12, 1974, and faculty meeting minutes, same date, all in Faculty Papers Collection, I-E-a, Box 4, "fac mins Jan. 22, 1974–Feb. 12, 1974," BCA.

24. 1976 *Ista*, 74-76, 69-70; newspaper clippings dated Jan. 18, 1973, and June 7, 1973, both in Publications Office Collection, I-D-b, Box 4, "July, 1971–June, 1972," BCA; 1977 *Ista*, 26-27.

25. *WIT* 63 (Oct. 29, 1976), 6-7.

26. *BN* (Feb. 28, 1974), 1; oral interview, Rachael Chapman with Sally

Weaver Sommer, June 28, 1999, BCA.

27. *WIT* 63 (Oct. 29, 1976), 6; *Gospel Herald* 65 (April 11, 1972), 330; *The Mennonite* 88 (Jan. 9, 1973): 22-23; *WIT* 59 (Oct. 15, 1971), 1; *WIT* 60 (March 3, 1972), 4; *Scope* 59 (September 1972), 1.

28. *Scope* 59 (January 1972), 1.

29. Rex Fortney to Howard Baumgartner, April 24, 1972, Student Papers Collection, I-F-q, "Opinion Board, 1966-72," BCA; William T. Snyder to Neufeld and Yost, April 28, 1972, Burton Yost Papers, 4-MS-C-71, Box 1, "Presidential Search, 1972," BCA.

30. Board meeting minutes June 24, 1972, Board Meeting Minutes, Vol. 3, BCA; *Scope* 59 (October 1972), 1.

31. *Scope* 59 (July 1972), 1; Sprunger to Mr. and Mrs. Olin Krehbiel, June 15, 1977, Sprunger Papers, I-A-f, Box 1, "K Corr., 1972," BCA.

32. Ben Sprunger, "The College's Mission: A Reaffirmation at a Crucial Time," Sprunger Papers, I-A-f, Box 3, "Ben Sprunger, Compendium of Speeches, 1972-77," BCA; *Scope* 60 (October 1973), 2.

33. Oral interview, Perry Bush with Don Schweingruber and Don Pannabecker, June 23, 1999, BCA; *Scope* 65 (January 1978), 1.

34. Sprunger to Jack Duncan, April 12, 1973, Sprunger Papers, I-A-f, Box 1, "D Corr., 1972," BCA. For an overview of these "young" or "New" Evangelicals, see Richard Quebedeaux, *The Young Evangelicals: Revolution in Orthodoxy* (New York: Harper & Row, 1974).

35. Sprunger to Alan Beitler, Nov. 19, 1973, Sprunger Papers, Box 1, "B Corr., 1972," BCA; Sprunger to Myron Augsburger, Sept. 19, 1974, and Sprunger to Tom Skinner, June 18, 1975, both in Sprunger Papers, Box 1, "S Corr., 1972," BCA; Sprunger to John Alexander, Aug. 16, 1976, Sprunger Papers, Box 1, "A Corr., 1972," BCA.

36. Wenger to Sprunger, Nov. 3, 1973, Sprunger Papers, I-A-f, Box 1, 'W Corr., 1972," BCA; Sprunger, "Books that have Shaped my Life and Thought," same box, "M corr, 1972," BCA; Sprunger to David Sullivan, Feb. 18, 1975, same box, "S Corr, 1972," BCA.

37. Sprunger to Lee Travis, May 15, 1973, I-A-f, Box 1, "T Corr., 1972," BCA; Sprunger, "Report to the Board of Trustees," April 1, 1976, P-3, Board of Trustees Papers, I-B-b, Box 1, "1976," BCA.

38. Faculty meeting minutes May 27, 1970, and Jan. 10, 1972, Faculty Collections Papers I-E-a, Box 4, "Fac mins Jan. 14, 1970–May 26, 1970" and "Fac mins Nov. 30, 1971–Feb. 22, 1972," BCA; *WIT* 59 (Nov. 22, 1971), 4.

39. 1975 *Ista*, 29; *Scope* 64 (December 1977), 1; Sprunger to "All Pastors," Dec. 1, 1974, Sprunger Papers, I-A-f, Box 2, "Letters to Board and Others, 1975," BCA.

40. Sprunger to Jack Augustine, July 22, 1976, Sprunger Papers, I-A-f, Box 1, "A Corr., 1972," BCA.

41. Sprunger to "All Pastors," March 21, 1974, Sprunger Papers, Box 2, "Letters to Board and Others, July 1, 1973–July 1, 1974," BCA; Pearl Bartel to Sprunger, March 24, 1975, Sprunger Papers, Box 1, "B Corr, 1972," BCA.

42. Sprunger to "All Pastors," March 21, 1974, Sprunger Papers, Box 2, "Letters to Board and Others, July 1, 1973–July 1, 1974," BCA.

43. Schweingruber/Pannabecker interview.

44. "Resolution Approved by the Board of Trustees," May 8, 1974, Faculty Papers Collection, I-E-a, Box 4, "Fac Mins, March 3, 1974–April 9, 1974," BCA; Sprunger to Richard Rosenberger, Nov. 16, 1976, Sprunger Papers, I-A-f, Box 2, "Trustee Committee Reports 1976," BCA.

45. Sprunger, "A Time for Appraisal and Action," pp. 1-17, quoted p. 17.

46. Ibid., pp. 18-23, quoted p. 22.

47. Ibid., pp. 23-26, quoted p. 30.

48. Ibid.

49. Sprunger, "Time for Appraisal and Action," 30; oral interview, Perry Bush with J. Denny Weaver, July 8, 1999, BCA.

50. For Suter and Hardesty responses, see Sprunger Papers, I-A-f, Box 2, "Trustee Committee Reports, 1972," BCA; also see a similar critique by philosophy professor David Schmidt in Sprunger Papers, Box 3, "Sprunger Papers and Faculty Responses, 1976-77," BCA.

51. Robert Long to Sprunger, Feb. 24, 1977, Sprunger Papers, I-A-f, Box 1, "L Corr., 1972," BCA; "Special Meeting of Teaching Faculty on Developing the 'Evangelical' Market," May 27, 1976, Faculty Papers Collection, I-E-a, Box 4, "Fac Mins May 11, 1976–Dec. 14, 1976," BCA.

52. Sprunger to all faculty and administration, Nov. 23, 1976, Sprunger Papers, Box 2, "Trustee Committee Reports, 1976," BCA.

53. *Scope* 60 (October 1973), 2; Waltner to Sprunger, April 9, 1973, Sprunger Papers, I-A-f, Box 1, "W Corr, 1972," BCA.

54. Elmer Neufeld, "Academic Affairs Report to the President," Nov. 12, 1974, P-4, Board of Trustees Papers, I-B-b, Box 1, "1974," BCA; Schweingruber/Pannabecker interview; faculty meeting minutes Jan. 13, Feb. 17, and administration committee minutes Feb. 17, and March 4, 1976, all in Faculty Papers Collection I-E-a, Box 4, "Fac Mins Dec. 9, 1975–Aril 13, 1976," BCA.

55. Neufeld to faculty, Dec. 3, 1980, Neufeld Papers, I-A-g, Box 4, "Memo to Faculty on Tenure and Documents," BCA; "Self-Study Report of Bluffton College, 1987-1989," pp. 28-9, Faculty Papers Collection, I-E-k, Box 2, "Self-Study Report, 1987-89," BCA.

56. Board meeting minutes April 9-10, 1976, pp. 3-5, Board of Trustees Collection, I-B-b, Box 1, "1976," BCA. For an example of faculty critiques of Sprunger's perceived marketing emphasis, see Hardesty, "Whatever Happened to the Liberal Arts?" *Cross-Discipline* (December 1973): 1-5, Publications Office Collection, I-L-m, Box 2, "Cross-Discipline, 1971-1973," BCA.

57. "Evaluation Procedures for Tenured Faculty Members," Feb. 6, 1976, and faculty meeting minutes Jan. 31 and March 30, 1977, all in Faculty Papers Collection, I-A-e, Box 4, "Fac Mins Dec. 9, 1975–April 13, 1976," and "Fac Mins Jan. 31, 1977–April 20, 1977," BCA; Sprunger to Trustees, Feb. 28, 1977, Sprunger Papers, I-A-f, Box 2, "Committee Reports etc., 1977," BCA; Sprunger to trustees, Jan. 16, 1977, Sprunger Papers, Box 2, "Trustees, 1976-76," BCA.

58. Sprunger to Milton Sprunger, June 15, 1977, Sprunger Papers, Box 1, "S Corr., 1972," BCA; Sprunger to trustees, June 5, 1975, Sprunger Papers, Box 2, "Letters to Board and Others, July 1, 1974–July 1, 1975," BCA; Houshower interview.

59. Carl Lehman to Richard Rosenberger, June 16, 1975, and Lehman, "Remarks at Faculty Luncheon," May 25, 1975, private papers of Michael Edmiston, copies in author's possession; oral interview, Perry Bush with Elmer Neufeld, August 12, 1999, BCA.

60. Sprunger to J. E. Amstutz, Sept. 28, 1977, Sprunger Papers, I-A-f, Box 1, "A Corr., 1972," BCA; "The Crisis in Leadership," Sprunger Papers, Box 3, "Faculty Study on the Leadership of President Ben Sprunger, 1977," BCA; *WIT* 35 (May 25, 1977), 1; *Scope* 64 (June 1977), 1 .

61. *Scope* 64 (June 1977), 1.

62. Robert Reinhard to Trustees, Sept. 12, 1977, Hereford Mennonite Church Council to Trustees, Sept. 16, 1977, both in Springer Papers, I-A-f, Box 2, "Committee Reports etc, 1976-77," BCA; Eastern District Conference Pastors to Trustees, July 5, 1977, Sprunger Papers, Box 1, "Evaluation/Resignation," BCA.

63. *Scope* 65 (January 1978), 1; *Scope* 67 (January 1980), 10-11; *WIT* 66 (Feb. 13, 1980), 5; Schweingruber/Pannabecker interview; Neufeld interview, August 12, 1999.

64. *Scope* 67 (January 1980), 10-11; *WIT* 66 (Feb. 13, 1980), 5.

65. *Scope*, January 1980; Schweingruber/Pannabecker interview.

66. Bauman to Neufeld, July 25, 1978, Burton Yost Papers, 4-MS-C-71, Box 1, "Burton Yost, J. Denny Weaver," BCA.

67. Neufeld to Yost, Weaver, and Pannabecker, Feb. 14, 1983, Neufeld Papers, I-A-g, Box 2, "Religion Dept., 1965-1980," BCA.

68. Neufeld to Stephen Strunk, Sept. 4, 1984, Yost Papers, Box 1, "Personal Letters, Memos etc.," BCA; Weaver interview.

69. Neufeld, "Academic Affairs Report to the President," April 15, 1975, Board of Trustees Papers, I-B-b, Box 1, "1975," BCA.

70. Neufeld, "President's Report to the Board of Trustees," April 24-25, 1981, p. 1, Board of Trustees Papers, Box 2, "Spring Board Meeting, April 24-25, 1981," BCA.

71. Schweingruber/Pannabecker interview.

72. *Scope* 71 (July 1984), 2; Neufeld, "President's Report to the Board of Trustees," Nov. 19-20, 1982, p. 3, Board of Trustees Papers, I-B-b, Box 2, "Nov. 19-20, 1982," BCA; Neufeld to Trustees, Oct. 22, 1982, Neufeld Papers, I-A-g, Box 3, no folder, BCA.

73. Ibid.; Neufeld, "President's Report to the Board of Trustees," Nov. 11-12, 1988, p. 11, Board of Trustees Papers, I-B-b, Box 2, "Nov. 11-12, 1988," BCA.

74. Schweingruber/Pannabecker interview.

75. *LN* (Nov. 26, 1986), A1; on departmental recruiting plans, see various responses from the business, art, education, English/speech and religion departments, all in Neufeld Papers, I-A-g, Box 3, no folder, BCA; Neufeld, "President's Report to the Board of Trustees," April 25-6, 1986, p. 11, Board of Trustees Papers, I-B-b, Box 2, "April 25-26, 1986," BCA; *Scope* 65 (October 1978), 1.

76. 1989 Self-Study Report, 71-3; *Scope* 71 (November 1984), 4.

77. *WIT* 72 (Oct. 31, 1985), 5; *WIT* 71 (March 21, 1985), 1; *Scope* 72 (November 1985), 20.

78. *Scope* 80 (November 1992), 4; *Scope* 71 (July 1984), 8, 13; *Scope* 75 (July 1988), 7; *Scope* 74 (July 1987), 6-7; *Scope* 72 (July 1985), 3; *Scope* 66 (September 1979), 4, and (November 1979), 6.

79. *WIT* 71 (Sept. 24, 1984), 5; Bluffton College 1999-2000 *Catalog*, 191-195.

80. Bluffton College 1999-2000 *Catalog*, 191-195.

81. Ibid.; Wenger to Sprunger, Oct. 16, 1973, Sprunger Papers, I-A-f, Box 1, "W Corr.," BCA; J. Denny Weaver interview.

82. Rich to Neufeld, Jan. 21, 1980, Neufeld Papers, I-A-g, Box 3, no folder, BCA; faculty meeting minutes, May 11, 1987, and March 28, 1988, Faculty Papers Collection, I-E-a, Box 5, "Fac Mins 4-6-87–5-8-87" and "Fac Mins Jan. 11, 1988–March 14, 1988," BCA.

83. *LN* (May 17, 1987), B-7; President's Report to the Board of Trustees, Fall 1988, p. 10, Board of Trustees Papers, I-B-b, Box 2, "Fall Board Meetings, Nov. 11-12, 1988," BCA.

84. 1987-1989 Self-Study Report, 37-38.
85. Ibid.; *Scope* 77 (July 1990), 5.
86. *Scope* 70 (May 1983), 3; *Scope* 81 (July 1994), 4.
87. *BN* (March 14, 1985), 1; *Scope* 73 (March 1986), 2.
88. *WIT* 71 (April 4, 1985), 5; *WIT* 72 (Nov. 21, 1985), 1.
89. 1989 NCA Self-Study, 38-9; *Bluffton Close-Up* (the newsletter of the Admissions Office) 4 (November/December 1980), 1.
90. 1989 NCA Visitation Report, 10-11; *Scope* 60 (January 1973), 1; *Scope* 76 (March 1989), 3.
91. *WIT* 72 (Sept. 26, 1985), 1; 1989 NCA Self-Study Report, 10.
92. Elizabeth Hostetler, "General Conference Development Fund Project," Feb. 11, 1985, Faculty Papers Collection, I-E-n, Box 1, "Proposal for Peace Center," BCA.
93. "The Lion and Lamb Peace Art Center," approximate date 1989, Neufeld Papers, I-A-g, Box 1, "The Lion and Lamb Peace Arts Center," BCA; *Scope* 85 (May 1998), 5.
94. Denny Weaver interview; 1989 Self-Study Report, pp. 48a-d, 49-50.
95. 1989 Self-Study Report, pp. 48a-d, 49-50; President's Report to the Board of Trustees, Fall 1985, p. 10, Board of Trustees Papers, I-B-b, Box 2, "Fall Board Meeting, Nov. 22-23, 1985," BCA.
96. *Scope* 70 (July 1983), 2; *WIT* 73 (Feb. 5, 1987), 1.
97. *Scope* 70 (July 1983), 2; 1989 NCA Self-Study Report, 42.
98. Pannabecker interview, June 7, 1999.
99. Pannabecker/Schweingruber interview; President's Report to the Board of Trustees, Nov. 11-12, 1988, 12-13.
100. *BN* (April 22, 1982), 6; Findlay *Republican-Courier* (April 2, 1983), A-8;), *Review* (Sept. 4, 1986), 12; faculty meeting minutes Dec. 19, 1984, Faculty Papers Collection, I-E-a, Box 5, "Fac Mins Oct 3, 1984–Dec. 19, 1984," BCA.
101. "Peace Club Officers' Meeting," Nov. 30, 1978, and "Peace Club, 1980-1981," both in Student Organizations Collection, I-K-f, Box 1, "BC Peace Club, 1940-1983," BCA; *WIT* 67 (Jan. 23, 1981), 1; *WIT* 69 (Oct. 8, 1982), 2; *WIT* 64 (March 10, 1978), 2-3; *The Lily* 3 (May 7, 1979), 1; Student senate minutes March 31, 1980, Student Committee Paper Collection. I-F-q, "Student Senate Minutes 1979-1980," BCA.
102. *WIT* 69 (Jan. 28, 1983), 2; *WIT* 75 (Sept. 22, 1988), 1.
103. Oral interview, Rachael Chapman with Dan Parent, June 10, 1999, BCA.
104. 1988 *Ista*, 82; 1987 *Ista*, 77; *WIT* 71 (April 18, 1985), 1; 1988 *Ista*, 83; *WIT* 69 (Oct. 30, 1981), 1; Denny Weaver interview; *WIT* 71 (April 25, 1985), 1; *WIT* 72 (Feb. 13, 1986), 1.
105. *WIT* 66 (May 9, 1980), 7; *WIT* 66 (June 20, 1980), 2; *WIT* 67 (Oct. 24, 1980), 8.
106. *Scope* 72 (May 1985), 4; *LN* (Feb. 23, 1986), D-3; *WIT* 68 (Feb. 26, 1982), 7; *WIT* 69 (Sept. 22, 1982), 5; *Scope* 75 (November 1988), 11; *WIT* 69 (March 4, 1983), 1.
107. *BN* (June 6, 1991), 8.
108. Ibid.; "BC Volleyball Year-by-Year," 1968-1996, records in author's possession (available from the BC Athletic Department).
109. "Past Yearly Football Records," 1905-1996, records in author's possession (available from the BC Athletic Department); *WIT* 65 (Feb. 9, 1979), 4.
110. *BN* (Oct. 3, 1985), 14; *LN* (Oct. 15, 1985), C-1.
111. *BN* (Oct. 24, 1985), 14; *BN* (Nov. 21, 1985), 16.

112. *Scope* 74 (May 1987), 11; *Scope* 75 (January 1988), 6; *Scope* 76 (January 1989), 14.

113. "Report of the NCA Review Team," March 20-22, 1989, 3-5, 20.

114. Ibid., 23.

115. "Report of Marketing Subcommittee of the Recruitment and Admissions Committee," pp. 10-11, Neufeld Papers, I-A-g, Box 2, "Recruitment/Admissions Committee, 1976-1996," BCA; Denny Weaver interview.

116. "Report of the NCA Review Team," March 20-22, 1989, pp. 24-25.

Chapter Eight

1. *LN* (May 21, 1989), B-3; *Scope* 76 (September 1989), 12-13.

2. *New York Times* (June 20, 1990), B9; *Chronicle of Higher Education* (June 14, 1996): A15.

3. President's Report to the Board of Trustees, Spring 1989, pp. 6-7, Trustees Papers, I-B-b, Box 2, "Spring Board Meetings, April 21-22, 1989," BCA; faculty minutes March 25, 1991, Faculty Papers Collection, I-E-a, Box 5, "Fac Mins Sept. 17, 1990–May, 1991," BCA.

4. See President's Reports to the Board of Trustees dated Nov. 8-9, 1991; Nov. 12-13, 1993; Nov. 11-12, 1994; April 21-22, 1995; Nov. 10-11, 1995; Nov. 1, 1997; all in Board of Trustees Papers, I-B-b, Box 2, BCA; Bluffton College, NCA Self-Study Report, 1998-1999, pp. 38, 2, 13, 46.

5. President's Report to the Board of Trustees, Nov. 10-11, 1995; "Minutes of the Planning Group," Nov. 7, 1991, Board of Trustees Papers, I-B-b, Box 2, "Spring Board Meetings, April 24-25, 1992," BCA; Neufeld to Schweingruber, Sept. 19, 1991, Neufeld Papers, I-A-g, Box 1, "BC Planning Documents, 1991," BCA.

6. *Scope* 82 (November 1994), 6.

7. Neufeld to Trustees, Feb. 5, 1990, Neufeld Papers, I-A-g, Box 3, "Reports to Trustees," BCA; *Scope* 77 (May 1990), 3; *Scope* 79 (July 1992), 4-5.

8. *Scope* 82 (November 1994), 4-5; *Scope* 83 (July 1996), 8.

9. *Scope* 80 (September 1992), 3; *Scope* 81 (November 1993), 4.

10. *WIT* 72 (Jan. 16, 1986), 1; *WIT* 72 (May 15, 1986), 1; 1998 Self-Study Report, 84.

11. 1998 NCA Self-Study Report, 11; *WIT* 83 (Feb. 7, 1997), 1; *WIT* 84 (Sept. 19, 1997), 1.

12. *Scope* 83 (July 1996), 4; *Scope* 83 (January 1996), 4-6.

13. *Scope* 83 (January 1996), 4-6.

14. Lee Snyder inaugural address, October 6, 1996, BC President's Office, copy in author's possession.

15. Neufeld Reports to Trustees, Fall 1987, p. 3, Fall 1995, p. 7, Pannabecker's Report to Trustees, Spring 1995, all in Board of Trustees Papers, I-B-b, Box 2, "Nov. 13-14, 1987," "Nov. 10-11, 1995," and "April 21-22, 1995," BCA; board of trustees meeting minutes, Feb. 17, 1996, BCA; Kreider interview, May 25, 1999.

16. 1998 NCA Self-Study Report, 9, 55-57; *Scope* 78 (July 1991), 9; *Scope* 79 (September 1991), 7; *WIT* 78 (May 1, 1992), 2.

17. Personal correspondence from Gerald Beisecker-Mast to author, July 18, 1999, letter in author's possession.

18. 1998 NCA Self-Study Report, 58; Will Slater, "Assessment Report 7," author's possession; "Self-Study Report for Church-College Review," February,

1995, pp. 17-18, Faculty Committee Papers, I-F-r, Box 1, "College-Church Conference," BCA.

19. 1998 NCA Self-Study Report, 110-112.

20. "Report of the Cross Cultural Sub-Committee," April 1989, Faculty Committee Papers, I-F-a, Box 10, "Cross-Cultural Task Force, 1985-92," BCA; 1998 NCA Self-Study Report, 111-113.

21. *Scope* 82 (May 1995), 4-5; *Scope* 84 (March 1997), 6-7.

22. 1998 NCA Self-Study Report, 13, 119-120, 133-134, 165-166; 1997 *Ista,* 137; Registrar's Report to the Board of Trustees, Nov. 1, 1997, Board of Trustees Papers, I-B-b, Box 2, "1997 Fall Meetings," BCA.

23. Faculty meeting minutes Dec. 2, 1996, Faculty Papers Collection, I-E-a, Box 1, "Fac mins July 1996–June, 1997," BCA.

24. Trustees Recruitment and Admissions Committee minutes, April 21, 1995, Neufeld Papers, I-A-g, Box 2, "Recruitment/Admissions Committee," BCA; 1998 NCA Self-Study Report, 38-40.

25. 1998 NCA Self-Study Report, 38-40; Neufeld Report to Trustees, Nov. 10-11, 1995, p. 7; "Bluffton College Graduating Majors, 1989-1998," Board of Trustees Papers, I-B-b, Box 2, "Fall 1998," BCA; "Self-Study Report for Church-College Review," February, 1995, p. 21; Snyder's Report to the Board of Trustees, Fall 1997, Trustees Papers, I-B-b, Box 2, "1997 Fall Meetings," BCA.

26. *Scope* 85 (July 1998), 7; 1997 *Ista,* 86; 1992 *Ista,* 74-6; *Scope* 83 (January 1986), 8.

27. 1993 *Ista,* 122-3; *WIT* 84 (Sept. 19, 1997), 1; 1996 *Ista,* 124; 1995 *Ista,* 67, 69; 1997 *Ista,* 93; *Scope* 85 (November 1997), 8; 1992 *Ista,* 94; *Scope* 82 (May 1995), 13.

28. 1998 NCA Self-Study Report, 17-24; "Report of the Higher Education Council Review Team on Bluffton College," June 28, 1995, p. 1, President's Office Files, Bluffton College.

29. Neufeld's Report to the Board of Trustees, Fall 1991 and Fall 1992, Trustees Papers, I-B-b, "Nov. 8-9, 1991," and "Nov. 13-14, 1992," BCA; Albert Meyer, "Mennonite Colleges and the Changing Educational Environment," Neufeld Papers, I-A-G, Box 3, "GC Higher Education Symposium Draft, 1992," BCA.

30. Meyer, "Mennonite Colleges and the Changing Educational Environment," 27; 1998 NCA Self-Study Report, 19, 21-22, 140, 142.

31. Will Slater, "Assessment Report 7," in author's possession.

32. "Self-Study Report for Church-College Review," February, 1995, 25-26; "Report of the Higher Education Council Review Team," 5.

33. Weaver to Neufeld, March 14, 1990, President's Office Files, "Christian College Coalition"; *BN* (August 8, 1991), 4.

34. James Dunn, "Campus Visit Report," Feb. 25-28, 1980, p. 2, Neufeld Papers, I-A-g, Box 3, no folder, BCA; "Report of the Higher Education Council Review Team," 1, 6; *Scope* 83 (January 1986), 20. For a similar statement by Neufeld, see his response to Rodney Sawatsky in "Mennonite Higher Education: Experience and Vision Conference Papers," June 26-28, 1992, pp. 101-02, Faculty Papers File I-E-u, Box 2, "Experience and Vision" Conference Papers, 1992, BCA.

35. Neufeld's Report to Trustees, Spring 1987, p. 1, Trustees Papers, I-B-b, Box 2, "April 10-11, 1987," BCA.

36. This description is taken from my notes, jotted down later that day, as a participant in the event. Also see *WIT* 85 (Jan. 22, 1999), 1.

37. Kreider to author, May 29, 1999, letter in author's possession.

38. James C. Juhnke, "A Historical Look at the Development of Mennonite Higher Education in the U.S." pp. 1-9, in Neufeld Papers, I-A-G, Box 3, "GC Higher Education Symposium Draft, 1992," BCA; Thomas Askew, "The Shaping of Evangelical Higher Education Since World War II," in *Making Higher Education Christian*, ed. Joel A. Carpenter and Kenneth W. Shipps (St. Paul: Christian College Consortium, 1987): 137-150.

39. Leo Driedger, "Monastery or Marketplace? Changing Mennonite College/Seminary Enrollments," *Journal of Mennonite Studies* 15 (1997) 57-79.

40. For alumni surveys, see, for example, "Central Mennonite College Graduates," Hirschy Papers, I-A-a, Box 1, "Central Mennonite College Graduates," BCA; Members of the Faculty, *An Adventure in Faith*, 193-217. Fretz to Lee and Del Snyder, Nov. 21, 1997, copy in author's possession.

41. Rosenberger to Snyder, Aug. 31, 1935, Rosenberger Papers, I-A-c, Box 2, "Corr, 1935," BCA; "William T. Snyder Citation," May 24, 1981, BC President's Office Files, "Snyder, William T."

42. *Scope* 83 (January 1996), 9.

43. *BCB* 55 (October 1968), 3.

44. Ibid.

Select Bibliography

A note on sources: As the endnotes indicate, the vast bulk of relevant material on the history of Bluffton College is found in the Bluffton College Archives, Musselman Library. Especially helpful collections include the following: the presidential papers of Noah Hirschy, Samuel Mosiman, Arthur Rosenberger, Lloyd Ramseyer, Robert Kreider, Benjamin Sprunger, and Elmer Neufeld; Faculty Papers Collection; Faculty/Staff/Student Committee Papers; Student Organizations Papers; Bluffton College Alumni, and Faculty Records and Writings. The student newspaper *The Witmarsum*, the yearbook *The Ista*, and the alumni bulletin, the *Bluffton College Bulletin* (later called *Scope*) are also key. Significant and useful secondary sources follow.

Ahlstrom, Sydney. *A Religious History of the American People.* Vol. 2. Garden City, N.Y.: Doubleday, 1975.

Ainlay, Stephen C. "The 1920 Seminary Movement: A Failed Attempt at Formal Theological Education in the Mennonite Church." *Mennonite Quarterly Review* 64 (October 1990): 325-51.

Askew, Thomas. "The Shaping of Evangelical Higher Education Since World War II." In *Making Higher Education Christian*, edited by Joel A. Carpenter and Kenneth W. Shipps. St. Paul, Minn.: Christian College Consortium, 1987.

Byers, Noah E. "The Times in Which I Lived." *Mennonite Life* 7 (January-April 1952): 44-47, 138-141.

Burtchaell, James Tunstead. *The Dying of the Light: The Disengagement of Colleges and Universities from their Christian Churches.* Grand Rapids, Mich.: Eerdmans, 1998.

Bush, Perry. *Two Kingdoms, Two Loyalties: Mennonite Pacifism in Modern America.* Baltimore: Johns Hopkins University Press, 1998.

Chalmers, David. *And the Crooked Places Made Straight: The Struggle for Social Change in the 1960s.* Baltimore: Johns Hopkins University Press, 1991.

Driedger, Leo. "Monastery or Marketplace? Changing Mennonite College/Seminary Enrollments." *Journal of Mennonite Studies* 15 (1997): 56-79.

Grace Mennonite Church. *Grace Mennonite Church–An Overview of the First Twenty- Five Years.* Pandora, Ohio: Grace Mennonite Church, 1979.

Gratz, Delbert. L. *Bernese Anabaptists.* Goshen, Ind.: The Mennonite Historical Society, 1953.

———, et al. "The Swiss Settlement of Bluffton-Pandora, Ohio." *Mennonite Life* 43 (December 1988): 4-12.

Habegger, David L. *The Hirschy Genealogy: The Descendants of Philip Hirschy (1787- 1831) and Julianna Frey (1795-1839).* David Habegger, 1994.

Hardesty, Von. *A Narrative of Bluffton College.* Bluffton College, 1974.

Homan, Gerlof D. *American Mennonites and the Great War, 1914-1918.* Scottdale, Pa. : Herald Press, 1994.

Hudson, Winthrop S. *Religion in America.* 3d. ed. New York: Scribners, 1981.

Juhnke, James C. *Creative Crusader: Edmund G. Kaufman and Mennonite Community.* North Newton, Kans.: Bethel College, 1994.

———. "A Historical Look at the Development of Mennonite Higher Education in the U.S." Unpublished paper, 1992, 1-9.

———. "Mennonite and Ambivalent Civil Religion in World War I." *Mennonite Quarterly Review* 65 (April 1991): 160-168.

———. "Mennonite Church Theological and Social Boundaries, 1920-1930—Loyalists, Liberals, and Laxitarians." *Mennonite Life* 38 (June 1983): 18-24.

———. *Vision, Doctrine, War: Mennonite Identity and Organization in America.* Scottdale, Pa.: Herald Press, 1989.

Kaufman, Edmund G. *General Conference Mennonite Pioneers.* North Newton, Kans.: Bethel College Press, 1973.

Keim, Albert N. *Harold S. Bender, 1897-1962.* Scottdale, Pa. : Herald Press, 1998.

Kennedy, David. *Over Here: The First World War and American Society.* New York: Oxford University Press, 1980.

Kniss, Fred. *Disquiet in the Land: Cultural Conflict in American Mennonite Communities.* New Brunswick: Rutgers University Press, 1997.

Kraybill, Donald. "Passing on the Faith: A Tale of Three Colleges." Unpublished paper, June 1992.

Kreider, Anna. "The Wadsworth School." *Mennonite Life* 19 (April 1959): 66-7.

Lehman, James O. *Sonnenberg: A Haven and a Heritage.* Kidron, Ohio: Kidron Community Council, 1969.

Lehman, Naomi. *Pilgrimage of a Congregation: First Mennonite Church, Berne, Indiana.* Berne, Ind.: First Mennonite Church of Berne, 1982.

Marsden, George. *Reforming Fundamentalism: Fuller Seminary and the New Evangelicalism.* Grand Rapids: Eerdmans, 1987.

———. *The Soul of the American University.* New York: Oxford University Press, 1994.

Marsden, George, and Bradley J. Longfield, eds. *The Secularization of the Academy.* New York: Oxford University Press, 1992.

Members of the Faculty. *Bluffton College: An Adventure in Faith, 1900-1950*. Berne, Ind.: Berne Witness Press, 1950.

Miller, Susan Fisher. *Culture for Service: A History of Goshen College, 1894-1994*. Goshen, Ind.: Goshen College, 1994.

Pannabacker, Samuel. *Faith in Ferment: A History of the Central District Conference*. Newton, Kans.: Faith & Life Press, 1968.

———. *Open Doors: A History of the General Conference Mennonite Church*. Newton, Kans.: Faith & Life Press, 1975.

———. *Ventures of Faith: The Story of Mennonite Biblical Seminary*. Elkhart, Ind.: Mennonite Biblical Seminary, 1975.

Quebedeaux, Richard. *The Young Evangelicals: Revolution in Orthodoxy*. New York: Harper & Row, 1974.

Raid, Howard. *The First Seventy-Five Years: First Mennonite Church, Bluffton, Ohio*. Freeman, S.Dak.: Pine Hill Press, 1986.

Ravitch, Diane. *The Troubled Crusade: American Education, 1945-1980*. New York: Basic Books, 1983.

Schumacher, Edgar., ed. *Life in the Bluffton and Pandora, ohio, Community, 1877-1910: Excerpts from The Bluffton News*. Bluffton, Ohio: Swiss Community Historical Society, 1977.

Smith, C. Henry. *Mennonite Country Boy*. Newton, Kans.: Faith & Life Press, 1962

Smith, Henry C., and Edmund J. Hirschler, eds. *The Story of Bluffton College*. Bluffton College, 1925.

Toews, Paul. "Fundamentalist Conflict in Mennonite Colleges: A Response to Cultural Transitions?" *Mennonite Quarterly Review* 57 (July 1983): 241-256.

———. *Mennonites in American Society, 1930-1970*. Scottdale, Pa. : Herald Press, 1996.

The Town at the Fork of the Rileys revisited: Historical Sketches of Old Shannon and Bluffton, Ohio. Bluffton, Ohio: *Bluffton News*, 1986.

Trautman, Milton. *The Ohio Country from 1750 to 1977—A Naturalist's View*. Columbus: Ohio State University, 1977.

Unrau, Ruth. *Encircled: Stories of Mennonite Women*. Newton, Kans.: Faith & Life Press, 1986.

Yoder, John Howard. "The Contemporary Evangelical Revival and the Peace Churches." In *Mission and the Peace Witness*, edited by Robert Ramseyer. Scottdale, Pa.: Herald Press, 1979.

The Index

A

A Cappella Choir, 97, 115
"A Time for Appraisal and Action," 226
Academic Accreditation, 95-98, 107-108, 122, 150-153, 165, 176, 235, 244-245, 251, 255, 259
Academic Assessment, 255
Acculturation, 26-29, 32-33, 50-51, 66-67
Adams Bridge, 235
Adelphians, 75, 124
Afro-American Cultural Center, 186, 192
Alderfer, Harold, 102, 110, 123
Alethians, 75
Allen County, 22, 28, 50, 51
"Alma Mater," 76
Althaus, Cheryl, 242
Althaus, Ralph, 134
Alvarez, Bob, 242
Amstutz, Agnes, 130
Amstutz House, 54, 207, 257
Amstutz, Jonas, 35, 47, 50-54, 63
Amstutz, P. D., 37, 50-53
Arba, Hama, 199
Arn, Karen, 241
Art Department, 73-74, 149, 171
Askew, Thomas, 258-259
Assimilation. *See* acculturation
Athenians, 75
Athletics, 71, 73, 87, 168, 204
    at Central Mennonite College, 41-42
    in 1910-1930, 80-83
    in 1930s, 116-117
    in World War II, 130-133
    in postwar years, 157-159
    in 1960s, 168-169, 183, 187
    in 1980s, 242-244
Atkinson, Ti-Grace, 183
Augsburger, Aaron, 65, 87
Awad, Mubarak, 80, 239, 260

B

Baer, John B., 30, 33, 46-47, 50-56, 88

Baker, Don, 213
The Barn, 71, 79, 80, 107, 143, 194, 200, 207
Baseball Team, 41, 80, 117, 157, 168, 242, 260
Basinger, Elmer, 103
Basinger, S. D., 44
Bassett, Jim, 162, 174
Bauman, Irwin, 74, 79, 118, 120, 130, 132, 156, 162, 169
Bauman, Ken, 233
Baumgartner, David, 104
Baumgartner, Elizabeth, 80
Baumgartner, Elmer, 104-105, 140
Baumgartner, Howard, 104, 201
Beaverbug, 143, 194
Beaver Hut, 258
Beckenbach, Frances, 201
Beer, Bob, 201
Beeshy, Isaiah B., 42-43, 49, 53, 55, 62, 213
Bender, Harold, 91, 94, 99, 124, 129, 135, 141, 277(n)
Berea College, 57, 141
Berky, Herbert W., 69-73, 86, 107, 109, 148-151, 169, 183, 210
Berky, Margaret, 131
Berky, Richard, 144
Berky, Wilbur, 115
Berky (Science) Hall, 63, 70-71, 76, 108, 132, 157, 163-164, 194, 208, 237
Berne, Indiana, 27, 30-34, 51, 54, 65, 89, 91-93, 98, 101, 104, 126, 140, 149, 177, 223, 231-233
Berry, Spike, 158
Bertsche, Nancy, 241
Bethel College, 89, 96, 141, 146-147, 171-173, 222
Bible lectures, 155
Bible and Religion Department, 106, 149, 170, 233, 236, 250
Bixel, Jim, 170, 235, 246
Bixel, John, 42
Bixel, Ruby, 202
Bixler, D. W., 127
Bixler, Mareen, 121

Black Student Union, 185, 212, 220
Blodgett, Marcene, 201
Blough, Neil, 165
Bluffton (town of), 18, 28-29, 33-38,
    71, 131,147, 158, 241
Bluffton Beaver, 81, 205
Bluffton College Chorale, 215
Bluffton College Education
    Organization, 253
Bluffton College Studies Center, 236
Bluffton High School, 42
Bluffton Mennonite Church, 53
Bluffton News, 29, 35, 38, 45, 51
Bluffton Spirit, 43, 59, 71, 87-89, 122,
    135
Board of Trustees, 39, 55-56, 104-105,
    108-110, 122-123, 126, 135,
    137-139, 140, 161, 163-164, 192,
    215, 222-231, 244, 247-251, 254,
    257-258
Boehr, Elizabeth, 106, 213
Boehr, Jeff, 221
Bogart, Madeline, 80
Bohn, Ernest, 106
Bond Sales, 103-104
Boutwell, Barb, 168
Bren-Dell Hall, 69, 163, 167, 219
Brenneman, Naomi, 72-73, 78, 130,
    133-134, 146, 163, 169, 183
Brooks, Greg, 242
Brown, Gladstone, 222
Brubaker, Don, 237
Bumbaugh, Jaye, 170
Burcky, Andrew C., 80-82, 116-117,
    130, 143, 158, 163, 169, 198, 243
Burcky Gym, 164, 191
Burkhard, Christine, 131
Burtchaell, James, 18-19, 254
Byers, Edna Hanley, 163
Byers, Noah, 19, 86, 97, 105, 108-113,
    119, 126, 130, 134-135, 152
    academic dean, 59-60, 64, 69, 71-
    74-79, 84, 90-91, 97, 108-109,
    112-113
    background of, 65-67
    as Goshen president, 44, 59, 63-64

C
Cage, John, 160
Campus Pastor, 178
Carpenter, Carlin, 243-244, 254

Carter, Jimmy, 219-221
Casey, Ken, 169
Caskey, Gene, 171, 246
Casper, Jamie, 253
Cecelia Cornelius Charitable Fund,
    257
Cedarville College, 81, 226
Centennial Hall, 257
Central Conference of Mennonites,
    27, 54, 64-65, 83, 87-88, 102,
    140
Ceren, Peter, 182
C. Henry Smith Peace Oratorical
    Contest, 238
Chapel, 164, 176-177, 187
Christian College
    Coalition/Consortium, 19,
    225-227, 256
Church-College Conflict
    at Central Mennonite College,
    46-57
    from 1910-1929, 87-94
    in 1930s, 98-102, 126
    in 1940s, 137-140
    in 1960s, 177, 189
    from 1970-1999, 225, 233
Church of the Brethren, 118
Citizenship Committee, 79, 155-156,
    188-190
Civilian Public Service (CPS), 129-
    132, 147, 149, 171
Clark, Alex, 168
Clemens, Romaine, 156, 159
Clemens, Stan, 235
Clements, Ryan, 200
Clippinger, Robert, 134
Coffman, Joven S., 34
Cold War, 142-144
Coleman, Ed, 243
College Choral Society, 41, 44, 124
College Colors, 44
College Faith Statements, 100
College Farm, 174
College Hall, 25, 37, 41-45, 96, 108,
    152, 156, 187, 194, 200, 209,
    214, 257
College Landscape, 35, 69-70, 235
College Motto, 64-65
College of Liberal Arts, 74
College Traditions, 44, 64-65, 75-76,
    81, 114-116, 187-188, 198, 241
Collingwood, Joe, 157

Commerce Club, 154
Conrad, Ron, 167
Conscription, 144
Council of Church Leaders, 254
Cox, James, 67, 85
Creel, James, 115-117
Criblez, Harriet, 115
Criminal Justice Program, 237
Crooks, Larry, 183
Cross-Country Team, 168, 242
Cross-Cultural Education, 175, 221, 251-252
Crowe, Tonya, 242
Curriculum
    at Central Mennonite College, 40
    from 1910-1929, 71-72
    in 1930s, 105-106, 150
    in postwar years, 150-151
    in 1960s, 175
    in 1970s, 192, 215-218
    in 1980s, 236-237
    in 1990s, 251
    Cutshall, Guy, 127

D
Danforth Foundation, 216
Daugherty, Bob, 253
Davidson, Jo, 166
Deeds, Minard, 134
Defiance College, 159
Defenseless Mennonites, 65, 88, 106
Democratic Socialist Organizing Committee, 221
Departmental Honors, 72
Detweiler, Irvin, 106, 109
Diakonia, 256
Dickey, Dale, 149, 217, 235, 240
Diehl, Walt, 117
Diller, Ed, 257
Diller, Ernie, 182
Diller, Florence, 62
Diller, Milburne, 116
Diller, Oliver, 70
Diller, Phyllis, 116
Diller, Sherwood, 116
Dillinger, John, 102
Downs, Hugh, 164
Drama, 45, 149, 171
Driedeger, Leo, 259

Dubenion, Elbert, 153, 158-159, 169, 243
DuMonte, Pete, 242
Durand, Michelle, 242

E
Earth Day, 182
Eastern District Conference (EDC), 27-30, 65, 88, 102-104, 112, 137-140, 177, 231
Eastern Mennonite University, 249
Ebenezer Mennonite Church, 50, 54, 89, 137
Economics and Business Department, 148, 171, 235, 238
Ediger, Elmer, 144
Edmiston, Mike, 235
Education Department, 74, 146, 238
Elkhart Institute, 34
Emmert, Jan, 167
English Department, 72, 150, 170, 235
Epp, Peter, 109, 110
Ernst, Don, 183
Evangelicalism, 100-101, 136, 221-224, 228, 233, 243, 255-259, 261
    "Evangelicalization," 18-21
    "New" Evangelicals, 18-19, 22. *See also* Fundamentalism
Evans, Steve, 212
Ewert, Rev. H.H., 37
Ewing, Eileen, 218

F
Faculty, 203
    at Central Mennonite College, 42-43
    from 1910-1930, 72-75
    from 1970s-1980s, 226-231, 235-240, 244-245
in 1930s, 105-110
    in World War II, 130, 134-135
    in postwar years, 146-150
    in 1960s, 169-172
    in 1990s, 247, 250-251, 255
    Faculty Governance, 173
Farm Labor Organizing Committee (FLOC), 181
Family and Consumer Sciences Department, 144, 237

Fast, Aganetha, 75
Fast, Henry, 74
Fellers, Russell, 133-134
Fellowship of Christians Athletes
        (FCA), 222, 256
Fields, Nate, 186
Finances, 125-127
        at Central Mennonite College, 45,
        55, 58
        from 1910-1929, 62-63, 95-96
        from 1940-1959, 127-130, 143-144,
        153
        in 1930s, 101-105, 116, 122, 125-
        126
        in 1960s, 162, 173-174, 191
        in 1970s, 191-192, 215, 229-131
        in 1980s, 234-235, 244-245
        in 1990s, 247. *See also*
        Fundraising.
First Mennonite Church, Bluffton, 53,
        62, 100
Fischer, Kim, 205, 242-243, 253-254
Football, 59, 87, 94
        Central Mennonite College, 41-42
        cancellation of, 82
        from 1910-1930, 81-83
        in 1930s, 117
        in World WarII, 130-131
        in postwar years, 143, 158-
        159
        in 1960s, 169
        in 1980s, 242-243
        in 1990s, 254
        renewal of, 83
Ford, Henry, 87
Fosdick, Harry Emerson, 76
Founders Hall, 71, 143, 160, 163-165,
        194, 215, 219, 225
Francis, Dale, 134
Freshman Olympics, 188
Fretz, Mary Lou, 168
Fretz, Winfield, 111, 118-121, 136, 146,
        149, 259
Friendship Group, 127
Friesen, Arthur, 99
Friesen, Ron, 171
Frost, Hugh, 155
Fundamentalism, 88-91, 93-102, 106,
        136-140, 233, 261
Fundraising Campaigns, 45, 62-63,
        95-96, 102-103, 109, 127, 153,
        231, 234-247. *See also* Finances.

Funk, John, 34
Future Teachers of America, 154

G
Gage, Harry M., 151-153
Gara, Larry, 144-145
Garmatter, Leland, 158
Geiger, Louella, 76
General Conference Mennonite
        Church (GCMC), 27-29, 32,
        36, 64, 84, 92, 94, 98, 100, 141,
        224
Glee Club, 79, 87, 94, 115, 202
Gilcrease, Greg, 243
Gilliom, Oliver F., 104, 119
Gilyani, Roger, 243
Goetsch, Bertha, 43
Goff, Gina, 253
Goings, Mike, 169
Golf Team, 168
Goshen, Indiana, 34-35, 66- 67, 90
Goshen College, 34, 44, 59, 63- 66, 73,
        90, 94, 96, 109, 126, 135, 146-
        147
Gospel Herald, 88
Gottschall, William, 89-93
Graber, Martha, 118
Grace Mennonite Church, 51-55
Gratz, Delbert, 147-148, 165, 218
Gratz, Homer, 134-135
Great Depression, 97, 113, 125-127
Gregg, Richard, 118
Griffin, John Howard, 174
Grothouse, Theresa, 253
Grubb, Nathanial, 30
Grubb, Silas, 98
Gump, Kevin, 254
Gundy, Don, 131
Gundy, Jeff, 235, 250
Gutridge, Rosemary, 202

H
Habegger, Arman, 228
Habegger, Nathan, 181
Habitat for Humanity, 253
Hamman, Ray, 170, 188, 201
Hancher Organization, 95
Hanley, Edna, 97, 108-109, 134
Hanover College, 243
Hardesty, Larry Kay 237

Hardesty, Von, 152, 154, 170, 215, 219, 220, 228
Harding, Vincent, 155
Harding, Warren, 67
Harmon Field, 158, 204
Harrington, Michael, 221
Harshbarger, Emmet, 129
Hartzler, John E., 75, 90- 91, 99, 104
Hartzler, Phyllis, 201
Hartzler, Greg, 257
Hauenstein, Sidney, 41, 130
Hawk, William, 165, 247, 249
Hazen, Marji, 167
Hazing, 79-80
Health, Physical Education, and Recreation (HPER), 171
Heidelburg College, 80-82, 158
Heiks, Ray, 115
Hemmert, Cliff, 243
Henry, Lyle, 181
Hershberger, Guy, 135- 136
Hertzfeld, Tara, 253
Hiebert, Harvey, 163, 189, 201
Hill, Lavera, 169
Hilty, Hiram, 115
Hilty, Peter B., 51
Hirschler, Edmund, 43, 62, 76, 79, 134
Hirschy, Augusta Hunsberger, 31, 48- 49, 56-58
Hirschy Cottage, 143
Hirschy, Noah, 19, 20, 25-26, 33-34, 59, 61, 69, 75, 84, 88, 95, 103, 163, 177, 179, 183, 196, 250, 258
    background and childhood, 30-32
    death of, 57
    presidency of, 39-50
    presidential selection of, 36-37
    post-college career, 57
    resignation of, 56
    theology of, 37, 47-48
History Department 147-148, 150, 170, 235
Hodell, Jack, 174, 192
Holtkamp, Otto, 73, 148, 169
Home Economics Department, 106, 171, 183, 237
Honor Court, 114
Honor System, 72
Horsch, Elizabeth, 90
Horsch, John, 90-93

Hostetler, Libby, 238, 252
Houshower, Mark, 135, 175, 185, 189, 191, 218, 223, 230, 235
Howe, Wilbur, 72
Human Explorations Program (HUEX), 216-217, 225, 236, 251

I
In Loco Parentis, 187
Inflation, 191
Inter-Cultural Center, 221
Intercollegiate Peace Conference, 44
International students, 239
Internet, 249
Interterm, 160, 174-176, 186, 217
Investment Club, 154
Ista, 69, 78, 124, 130-131, 189, 219

J
Jacoby, Steve, 170, 183, 189, 201
Jantzen, Daniel, 41-44, 55, 56
Johns, Loren, 257
Jones, Adah, 185
Jones, James, 253
Judicial Board, 188
Juhnke, James, 258-259, 263(n)
Jump, Harry, 117
Junior College, 63, 151
Junior Oral Exams, 252

K
Kampen, John, 249
Kaufman Edmund G., 75, 92, 100, 105, 124, 147, 171, 232
Kaufman, Maurice, 171, 210
Keeler, Randy, 256
Keeney, Betty, 128
Keeney Peace Lecture, 240
Keeney, William, 135, 149, 173, 176, 189, 258
Keller, John, 120, 121
Kent State, 179, 182, 222
Kern, Kathleen, 240, 260
KIDS, 221
King Jr., Martin Luther, 181, 184
King, Paul, 234
Kingsley, Keith, 167
Kingsley, Judy Hilty, 167, 184, 189

Kingsley, Phil, 168
Kingsley, Mitch, 187
Kirtz, Jim, 242
Klassen, John P., 73-74, 107, 122, 132,
    149, 164, 195, 237, 246, 258,
    260-261
Klassen, Otto, 240
Klassen, Paul, 237
Kloeb, Frank, 145
Kniss, Fred, 46
Knox, James, 217
Kohli, Ed, 80
Kohli, Hiram, 80
Kobzar, 22, 195, 246, 260-261
Korean War, 144
Kratz, Maxwell, 67, 75, 82
Kratz, Oliver, 86
Kraybill, Donald, 254
Krehbiel, Amalia, 60
Krehbiel (Adams) Bridge, 116, 211,
    235
Krehbiel, Henry J., 55, 60, 97, 258
Krehbiel, Henry P., 34-37, 45-49
Krehbiel, Howard, 171, 210
Krehbiel, Olin, 140, 223
Kreider, Amos E., 74, 139, 147
Kreider, Robert, 21, 146, 151-154, 162,
    167, 170-172, 197, 222, 236, 258
    as dean, 125, 159, 170, 174
    background of, 147
    recruitment of, 147-148
    president, 163-164, 169, 173-178,
        181-182, 185-192, 240, 250
Kresge Foundation, 219
Kruse, Tim, 182
Kurtz, Jonathan, 64

L
Lane, Denny, 168
Landes, Carl, 118
Langenwalter, Jacob H., 64, 77, 84, 101
Lantz, Russel, 73, 76, 128, 131, 148,
    162, 169, 212
Lapp, Ada, 146
Latchaw, Guy, 41
Leathers, Johnnie, 131
Leatherman, Gale, 117
Lehman, Andy, 253
Lehman, Carl, 149, 174, 230
Lehman, Clarence O., 123
Lehman Cottage, 143

Lehman, Earl, 135, 149, 170, 235
Lehman, Gustavus A, 44, 71, 73, 86
Lehman, J.F., 33-35, 47, 54, 65, 105
Lehman, L.J., 88
Lehman, Leland, 135, 171, 184, 235,
    258
Lehman, M.C., 126
Lima News, 191
Lima, Ohio, 39, 78, 84, 120, 152, 178,
    180, 184, 218, 221
Lincoln Hall, 63, 68, 70-73, 79, 108,
    111, 114, 119, 121,143, 153, 156,
    159, 194, 209
Lion and Lamb Peace Arts Center,
    238
Little, Kate, 168
Little Riley Creek, 17-19, 22, 35, 69,
    78-79, 133, 156, 174, 183, 190,
    198, 208, 235, 241, 258
Locher, Ralph, 115
Longanbill, Jesse, 134, 258
Lora, Melvin, 117
Lora, Ron, 158
Lott, Thom, 185
Lowell Literary Society, 40, 75
Luginbihl, H. R., 44
Luginbuhl, Darvin, 135, 149, 202, 235
Luginbuhl, Greg, 149, 182, 189, 202
Luginbuhl, Priscilla Friesen, 183

M
Machen, Gresham J., 93
Malone College, 226
Mann, Pearl Bogart, 73, 148, 169
Maple Grove Cemetery, 100, 111
Mara-Alva House, 143
Marbeck Center, 164, 174, 181-182,
    186-187, 199-200, 210
Marbeck Center Board, 226
Marsden, George, 18, 254
Martin, Lynn, 168
Mast, Ken, 156, 158, 169, 242
Mast, Russell, 115
Masters of Education Program, 252
Mathematics Department, 148, 171,
    235
May Day, 75, 115, 198, 241
McDaniel, Rod, 199
McIver, Ed, 179
McPeak, Edith, 76
Mead, Douglas, 239

Mecartney, John, 180, 181, 221
Mehl, J.C., 37
The Mennonite, 32-33, 145, 191
Mennonite Brethren in Christ, 65, 88
Mennonite Central Committee
    (MCC), 129, 132, 144, 146, 159,
    172, 192, 232, 260
Mennonite Church, 65-66, 74, 90, 94,
    109, 126, 141, 249-250
Mennonite Community Movement,
    136
Mennonite Peace Society, 118, 128
Mennonite Voluntary Service, 144
Men's Basketball, 80, 117, 157, 168,
    205, 242, 254
Men's Glee Club, 76, 115
The Messiah, 41
Meyer, Albert, 254
Middle District Conference (MDC),
    27-28, 32-36, 45, 49, 51-56, 65,
    88, 90, 102, 133, 140
Miland, Larry, 185
Miller, Lenore, 211
Miller, Cloy, 219
Miller, Emerson, 235
Miller, Jim, 117
Miller, Orie, 144, 146, 260
"Modernism" Changes, 20, 88-93, 98-
    102, 119, 137-140
Mohr, William H., 104, 137, 139
Moman, Richard, 178
Moon, M'Della, 70, 73, 132, 148, 163,
    169, 183
Moody Bible Institute, 88, 92, 119
Moser, John, 28, 36-37, 50, 52
Moser, Mary Ann, 163
Mosiman, Emilie, 62, 75, 196
    background of, 61
    death, 111
Mosiman, Samuel K., 19-20, 112, 123,
    131,134-136, 159, 196, 200-201,
    228-229, 232-233, 257
    BC president, 61-110, 121
    background of, 60-61
    death, 111
    initial hiring of, 43, 56
    presidential selection of, 61
    resignation of, 110-111, 126
    theology of, 91-92
    World War I, 84-87
Moyer, Katherine, 74
Moyer, Phyllis, 168

Muir, Laura, 42
Music Conservatory, 74
Music Department, 40-41, 73, 76, 148-
    149, 170, 241
Music Hall, 159
Musselman, Charles H., 95
Musselman Library, 97, 115,152, 163,
    194, 209, 211
Musselman, S.M., 56
Musselman, Vivienne, 118
Muste, A.J., 131
Myers, Aaron, 211
Myers, David, 212
Myers, Lenore, 148

N
Nafziger, Scott, 253
Naffziger, Arthur, 134
National Association of Evangelicals,
    224
National Progressivism, 47, 67-69, 261
National Youth Administration, 113
Neal, Guy, 254
Neff, Pam, 183
Nester, Darryl, 241
Neuenschwander, A.J., 74, 77
Neuenschwander, Gordon, 177
Neufeld, Elmer, 21, 189, 197, 201, 218,
    223, 229, 238
    academic dean, 223, 232
    BC professor, 182, 184
    background of, 171-172
    presidency of, 231-235, 247-250,
    254, 256-257
    recruited to faculty, 172
    theology of, 232-233
Neufeld, Iris, 240
Neufeld, LaVera, 231
Niswander, Yvonne, 168
Noncombatant Service, 84-85
North Central Association (NCA), 95,
    97, 105, 113, 216, 235, 244-246,
    255
Northwestern University, 65
Northwestern Ohio League, 80
Nursing Program, 218
Nyangaro, Deonestina, 239
Nyangaro, Josephine, 239
Nyangaro, Phineas, 239

O

Oberlin College, 31, 47, 57, 153
Ohio College Association, 95, 97, 122
Ohio Northern University, 39, 143, 158, 248
Ohio's Department of Education, 95
Olds, Kevin, 242
Osborn, Julie, 221
Oxford Pledge, 118
Owens, J. P., 44

P

Page, Kirby, 76
Painter, Edith, 235, 250
Palmer, Judy, 178
Pandora, Ohio, 37, 45, 50-51, 55, 121, 180
Pannabecker, Don, 156, 159, 170, 189, 216, 232, 234, 244, 249, 250
Pannabecker, Richard, 135, 148-149, 210, 235
Pannabecker, Samuel F., 103, 113, 148
Pannabecker, Sylvia F., 103, 109
Pannabecker, Tim, 237
Parent, Dan, 241
Parent, Herman, 238
Passage, Peter, 218
Peace Club, 128-131, 155, 240, 253
Peace Corps, 166-167
Peer Awareness Leaders (PALS), 253
Perry, Archie, 184
Philomatheans, 75
Porter, Frank, 168
Pranks, 156
Preheim, Gayle, 179, 181
Prexy, 124
Profile, 219
Progressive Anabaptism, 19-22, 66-67, 125, 133, 135, 140-142, 161, 174-175, 179, 216, 233-234, 251, 254-261
Purdy, Dan, 219
Purves, Christine, 170
Purves, Jack, 175
Putnam County, 28, 50-51

Q

Quakers, 118-119
Quiring, Jacob, 64, 92, 99, 106

R

Rable, George, 165
Race Relations
in 1910-1930, 68-69, 142
in 1960s, 167, 184-186
in 1970s, 220-221
in postwar years, 155
Raid, Howard, 148, 151, 171, 213, 217, 235, 238, 258
Raid, Larry, 159
Ramseyer, Alice Ruth Pannabecker, 258
Ramseyer, Alvin C., 104, 106
Ramseyer, Bill, 155-158, 243
Ramseyer, Edna, 106, 124, 129, 132,143, 151,157, 171, 183
Ramseyer Hall, 248
Ramseyer, Lloyd, 20-21, 62, 161-162, 171-173, 179, 196, 214, 228-229, 232-234, 243, 258
as BC president, 124-159, 166, 178, 191
background and BC student career, 79, 82-83
leadership style, 124-125, 173
peace commitments of, 129-132, 142
presidential selection of, 126
resignation and death, 172
theology of, 135-136
Ramseyer, Robert, 258
Ramseyer, Richard, 234
Reagan, Ronald, 233-234, 237
Recker, Clair, 168, 242
Red Cross, 85-86
Redfield College, 56-57
Religion Department, 72, 150, 170, 235
Riak, Isaac, 187, 189
Rich, Ronald, 236
Richard, Wesley, 235
Richert, Peter H., 89
Rickert, Charles, 144-145
Riley Court, 163, 191
Riley, William Bell, 93
Ringelman, Maria, 81
The "Riot" of April 1970, 189-190
Rodabaugh, Lois, 175, 240
Roosevelt, Franklin, 113, 118, 119, 128, 155, 191
Ropp Hall, 63, 69, 76-79, 86, 94, 116, 133, 143-145, 153-154, 159, 163, 187, 190, 194, 199, 208, 235

Ropp, John, 65, 70
Rosenberger, Arthur S., 104, 106, 109, 110, 139, 196, 260
  as associate president, 101, 112
  background of, 111-112
  as president, 112, 119, 122
  resignation of, 122
Rosenberger, David, 201
Rosenberger, Richard, 230
Roth, Jim, 167
Rutt, A.B., 65

S

Salzman, Dwight & Harriet, 248
Salzman Stadium, 248
Satterwhite, Jim, 235
Sauder, Jerry, 104, 248
Sauder, Jim, 213
Sauder Visual Arts Center, 248
Schirch, LaVerne, 156, 159, 171, 210
Schmidt, Brian, 200
Schroeder, Peter R., 89-92, 101, 228
Schultz, Arnold C., 106, 137, 140, 228
Schultz, Jacob S., 62, 74, 107, 109, 115, 122-125, 130, 132, 137-139, 145-148, 15-152, 169-170
Schweingruber, Don, 223, 226, 233-234, 240
Science Club, 154
Science Center, 164, 192
Science Department, 72-73, 148, 171, 235
Sears Athletic Complex, 248
Secularization, 18-20, 201
Sedlinsky, Bohimur, 160
Selection of College Location, 33-35
Senior Oral Examinations, 218
Senior Sneaks, 187
Shapiro, Karl, 174
Sharian, Bedros, 212, 239
Sheldon, David, 254
Shelly, Andrew S., 30, 36
Shelly, Paul, 139-140, 151, 178, 240, 256
Shelly, Wilbur S., 74, 99, 170
Shenk, Jerry, 156
Shenk, Tim, 115
Shetler, Luther, 148, 151, 210, 235
Shoker, Gursaran (Frank), 219
Shoker Science Center, 219, 257
Shoup, Mandy Burden, 253

Sider, Ron, 240
Simcox, Adam, 200
Simcox, Jim, 183
Slabaugh, J.S., 104, 138, 139
Slater, Will, 255
Slaughter, Paula, 242
Sloan, John, 39, 41, 81
Slotter, Arden, 148, 149
Smith, C. Henry, 19, 64, 84, 90-91, 102, 104,110, 117, 19-120, 126-130, 221, 250
  background of, 66
  death,134,147
  progressivism of, 67-68
Smucker, Bertran, 119, 128
Smucker, Boyd, 63-64, 75, 103, 120
Smucker, Carl, 118-121, 147, 180-181, 217, 237, 240
Smucker, Donovan, 62, 103, 110, 115, 119-121, 127, 129, 135, 146-147, 155
Smucker, Orden, 119
Snyder, Glenn, 156, 159, 242
Snyder, Lee, 197, 249-250, 257, 258
Snyder, William T., 146, 166, 260
Soccer Team, 168
Social Work Department, 146-147, 237
Soldner, Grover T., 74, 103, 122
Sommer, Betty, 237
Sommer, Jim, 168
Sommer, Lois, 147
Sommer, Phil, 181
Sommer, Sally Weaver, 235
Sommer, Willis, 235
Spanish-American War, 44
Spencer, Charles "Choo-Choo," 144, 158
Spiert, Ken, 219
Sprunger, Benjamin, 197, 220, 232, 245, 255
  background of, 223
  BC president, 219, 223-231, 236, 240
  resignation of, 230-231
  theology of, 224
Sprunger, Joe, 181
Sprunger, Samuel F., 27-31, 34, 51
Stahl, Lou, 253
Stauffer, A. S., 88
Stauffer, Edwin, 86
Stauffer, Paul, 115, 130
Stauffer, William, 115

Steer, Donald, 212
Steiner, C.K., 158
Steiner, Steve, 235, 250
Steinmetz, Mark, 183
Stettler, Barb, 171
Stoneback, George, 118
Strayer, Martin, 156-159
Strubhar, Valentine, 65
Student Christian Association (SCA),
    177-179
Student Council, 115, 177, 186-187, 192
Student Dances, 140
Student Demographic Data, 113, 165,
    234, 238-239, 253
Student Denominational Data, 63,
    113, 142, 165-166, 216, 239, 253
Student Enrollment, 230
    at Central Mennonite College, 39
    1908-1929, 63, 94-95
    1930s, 113, 128
    in World War II years, 129-130
    in postwar years, 142-143
    in 1960s, 161-162, 191
    in 1970s, 215-216
    in 1980s, 234
    in 1990s, 246-248, 252-253
Student Initiations, 78, 106, 114, 156,
    188-189
Student Life
    at Central Mennonite College,
        39-45
    in 1910-1930 years, 75-86
    in 1930s, 113-116
    in World War II, 128-131
    in postwar years, 144, 154-157
    in 1960s, 164-168, 176-190
    in 1970s, 219-222
    in 1980s, 239-241
    in 1990s, 252, 253
    Student Peace Activism, 117-118,
        128-129, 155, 167, 179, 181-182,
        240-241, 253
Student Political Party Preferences,
    in 1920s, 67-68
    in 1930s, 118
    in postwar years, 154-155
    in 1960s, 166, 182
    in 1970s, 221
    in 1980s, 241
Student Protest, 167-168, 179-180
Student Rules & Discipline, 39, 77-79,
    114, 157, 176-177, 187, 225-226

Student Senate, 115, 192, 253
Student Tribunal, 114
Student Work Day, 115, 187
Students Army Training Corps, 85
Stutzman, Jim, 238
Stutzman, Morris, 165
Sullivan, Mary Ann, 235, 250
Suter, Robert, 171, 191, 201, 228
Suter, Linda Falk, 170, 201
Suter, Peter C., 50-51
Suter, Tim, 253
Sutter, John, 42
St. Johns Mennonite Church, 50
Strubhar, Valentine, 83
Student Christian Association (SCA)
    155-156, 241
Student Volunteer Band, 76
Swartley, Steve, 184
Swartz, Freeman, 137-138
Swiss Mennonite Congregation, 28-
    29, 45, 50-53, 62
Szabo, Jean, 170

T
Taylor, Willie, 158
Templin, Lawrence, 170, 235
Tetlow, Chet, 117
Thierstein, John, 84
Thomas, Norman, 120-121, 154-155
Title IX Amendments, 184
Tobias, Shelie, 183
Track Squad, 80, 157
College Traditions, 44, 64-65, 75-76,
    81, 114-116, 187-188, 198, 241
Treaty of Versailles, 67
Trenite, Jan, 239
Trimble, Lois Hirschy, 258
Triplett Corporation, 132, 144
Troyer, Maurice, 118
Tschantz, J.H., 32-35, 45
Twining, Harold, 134
Toews, Paul, 98, 263(n)
Tuition, 153-154, 162

U
"Union movement" in Mennonite
    colleges,20, 60, 63-65, 96, 140
United Farm Workers, 221
University of Chicago, 92, 106, 147,
    172, 232

University of Findlay, 80, 117, 157
University of Toledo, 80-82, 117
Universal Military Training, 144
Unruh, Daniel J., 119, 120
Unruh, John, 160, 170, 184, 189, 219-220, 236
Unruh, Peter, 89
Urich, Joe, 158

V

Van Meter, Larry, 181
Varvel, Todd, 254
Velasquez, Baldemar, 180, 182, 221, 260
Velasquez, Sara Templin, 183
Vesper Choir, 131
Vespers services, 41, 155
Vietnam, 159, 180-181
Vietnam Moratorium, 182
Volleyball, 168-169, 242-243, 253-254
Voth, H. R., 30

W

Wadsworth Institute, 27-34, 37, 45-48, 52, 55, 95-96
Waltner, Erland, 229
War bond sales, 86
War Relief Committee, 131
Ward, Harry F., 76
Washington, Booker T., 68
Weaver, J. Denny, 226, 233, 236, 238, 250, 256
Weaver, Paul, 240
Weaver, Richard, 135, 148-151, 156, 165, 187, 235
Weidner, Marilyn, 156, 159
Welty, Clayton, 86
Welty, Magdalena, 73
Wenger, J. C., 224, 236
Wenger, Roy, 132, 155, 182
Wetherill, Gary, 188
Wheaton College, 223-228, 255-256
Whitmer, Paul, 64, 74, 121, 125
Wiens, F. J., 119
Wilberforce University, 82
Wilmington College, 81, 243
Wilson, Woodrow, 67-68, 86
Windau, Jamie, 212
Wingard, Gerald, 179
Witmarsum, 68, 75, 84, 86, 97, 110-124, 131, 144-145, 166, 178-179, 182, 219, 222, 225, 230, 241

Witmarsum Seminary, 74-75, 112
  closing of, 99
  founding of, 65, 74
Wittenburg College, 60, 82
Women's Basketball, 81, 121, 157-158, 168, 204, 242, 253
Women's Intercollegiate Sports, 81, 183

W

Women's issues, 77-78, 121-122, 183-184, 220, 241
Workman, Calvin, 133-134
Work Day, 187
Works Progress Administration, 102
World War I, 28, 57, 94, 133
  and Bluffton College, 83-87, 94, 131
World War II, 43
  and Bluffton College, 128-135
Worthington, Eleanor, 115
Wrestling Team, 168

Y

YMCA, 76-77, 85, 115-124, 155, 178
YMCA's War Fund, 86
YWCA, 76-77, 115, 155
Yoder, Allen and Marie, 248
Yoder, Elizabeth, 183
Yoder, Ferne, 126
Yoder Recital Hall, 210, 248, 256
Yoder, Harry, 115-118, 127-128, 139, 149
Yoder, John Howard, 155
Yoder, Louisa, 113
Yoder, Perry, 217
Yost, Burton, 170, 217, 218, 258
Yost, Elnore, 258
Yount, Jamie, 254
Ypsilanti, Michigan, 132, 178

Z

Zepp, Elida, 43
Zerger, John, 242
Zerger, Suzanne, 241
Zuercher, Olin, 240

The Author

Perry Bush, Bluffton, Ohio, is Professor of History at Bluffton College. He was born and raised in Pasadena, California, the son of a Fuller Theological Seminary professor. He received his B.A. in political science from the University of California, Berkeley. Following 1981 graduation from college, he spent a year in voluntary service with Habitat for Humanity in Americus, Georgia, then worked several years in Christian anti-nuclear activism in the San Francisco Bay area.

He completed his M.A. and Ph.D. in history from Pittsburgh's Carnegie Mellon University in 1987 and 1990, respectively. In his doctoral work he explored the historical changes occurring in Mennonite pacifism against the backdrop of extensive Mennonite socio-economic change in twentieth century America. This dissertation research brought Bush into direct contact with the Historic Peace Churches for the first time and was a major factor in his decision to move to a Mennonite college when the opportunity arose.

After revisions, Bush's dissertation, *Two Kingdoms, Two Loyalties: Mennonite Pacifism in Modern America*, was published in 1998 by Johns Hopkins University Press. His many articles, both scholarly and popular, have appeared in such periodicals as the *Mennonite Quarterly Review*, *Fides et Historia* and *Sojourners*.

Bush taught history at Phillips University in Enid, Oklahoma from 1990 to 1994 before moving to Bluffton College in summer 1994. He is married to Elysia Caldwell Bush. They have three children: Kerry, Jackson and Cassidy Bush. He is a member of First Mennonite Church, Bluffton.